Privileging
POSitioNs

THE SITES OF
ASIAN AMERICAN STUDIES

Association for Asian American Studies Series

Privileging

Positions

THE SITES OF
ASIAN AMERICAN STUDIES

EDITED BY

GARY Y. OKIHIRO, MARILYN ALQUIZOLA,

DOROTHY FUJITA RONY, K. SCOTT WONG

WSU
PRESS

Washington State University Press
Pullman, WA 99164-5910
(800) 354-7360

Washington State University Press, Pullman, Washington 99164-5910

Library of Congress Cataloging-in-Publication Data
Privileging positions : the sites of Asian American studies / editors,
    Gary Y. Okihiro . . . [et al.].
        p.   cm.
    Collection of essays based on the 1993 Annual Meeting of the Association for the Asian American Studies held at Cornell University.
    Includes bibliographical references.
    ISBN 0-87422-124-2 (pbk.)
    1. Asian Americans—Study and teaching—Congresses.   2. Asian Americans—Congresses.   I. Okihiro, Gary Y., 1945-   .
E184.06P75   1995
973'.0495—dc20   95-31475
                                                            CIP

Contents

PART TWO—GENDER

PART THREE—SEXUALITY AND QUEER STUDIES

PART FOUR—RACE AND ETHNICITY

Acknowledgment

Anita Affeldt not only managed a superb conference (the 1993 Annual Meeting of the Association for Asian American Studies), but also typed and edited this entire manuscript. The editors and Cornell's Asian American Studies Program director gratefully acknowledge her labor of love.

Part One
THEORY, CLASS, AND PLACE

Introduction

Gary Y. Okihiro

Privileging Positions: The Sites of Asian American Studies is a collection of papers selected from among the presentations at the 1993 Annual Meeting of the Association for Asian American Studies held at Cornell University. The gathering will be remembered for several distinguishing features, mirrored in the chapters of this book, of some consequence to the development of the field of Asian American studies. The meeting was the first hosted by an Ivy League institution and only the second held on the East Coast. The significance of place, of context can not be overstated. Without a whiff of the odium of institutional hierarchies, permit me to suggest that the presence of an Asian American Studies Program at Cornell, an active Asian American studies component at Brown, the search for an Asian Americanist at Penn, the efforts by students to establish Asian American studies at Yale, Columbia, and Princeton and the growing recognition of the field's importance at other Ivies are notable events in the maturation of a field begun by students who struggled to institutionalize their demand "of colonized peoples for freedom and self-determination—for the right to control and develop their own economic, political, and social institutions."[1]

But beyond the symbolic significance of place, Asian American studies students and scholars east of California demand a re-visioning of the landscape of Asian America, this land we claim as ours. Have we not, to paraphrase the narrator of Shawn Wong's evocative novel *Homebase*, "memorized someone else's family history, taken someone else's name and suppressed everything that [we] have chronicled for [ourselves]"? they ask (89). And have we not swallowed a skewed version of our past by beginning with California's golden shore, and by sighting other landings on other shores as mere peripherals, as mere adjuncts to the core story? What if we began our history in Louisiana with the Filipino American communities of the 1760s, or in Boston and Philadelphia with the arrival of Asian Indian indentures and slaves of the 1790s? What implications would that have for the field's paradigms and hierarchies of place, ethnicity, migration? And what of our U.S.-centered parochialism, within Asian American studies, bounded by our own brand of exceptionalism self-designed, that binds us to the nation-state when the lands north and south and indeed the world-system wreaks havoc with our tidy categories of borders and space? The 1993 meeting's location at "the other" coast affords us another perspective on the field's subject matter, interpretations, and leanings.

The 1993 Annual Meeting will also be remembered for the field's engagement with histories, cultures, and paradigms beyond the racial and intellectual borders of Asian American studies. Asian Americanists dialogued with, among others, scholars of African, Asian, Chicana/o, Puerto Rican, and U.S. studies, including Martin Bernal, Edna Bonacich, Manning Marable, Patricia Nelson Limerick, Jeff Nunokawa, Vicki L. Ruiz, and Jesse M. Vázquez, most of whose papers appear within these pages. Assuredly the field's compass must account for and embrace the trajectories of allied fields of study, including Asian studies which had been relegated to the dustbin of Orientalism in our eagerness to fashion ourselves as Americans, as the real thing. Hopefully the engagement will continue and expand to the mutual benefit of our several fields of study. As Patty Limerick observed of Western American and Asian American studies: "I remain convinced that we have considerable common cause. . . . I hope that this conversation, launched in Ithaca in June of 1993, goes on for a long time."

Finally, I believe the 1993 gathering at Cornell will be remembered as a turning point in the coming of age of a new generation of scholars with fresh ideas garnered from years of tutelage under feminist studies, cultural studies, Queer studies, literary criticism, and more. This generation has arrived with new questions, new tools and ways of seeing, new expressions, that build upon the previous generation's concerns and work, but also that deconstruct the old order and hierachies, replacing them with other imperatives and designs. In a sense we have come full-circle. The key notions of Third World identity, relevance, and community of the 1960s generation, are revitalized in the contemporary ideas of positions and crossings, hegemony and interventions, and appropriation and voice of the 1990s generation. The Subaltern Studies Group, however salubrious their work on South Asia has been over the past decade, did not invent the engagement of theory with political commitment! Still new discoveries have been made and more await us, and the rise of this generation of Asian American scholars, evident in many of the studies contained herein, will shake our very foundations, create new verities, and transform the field of study.

This collection of essays offer a flavor of the 1993 Annual Meeting. By titling it *Privileging Positions*, the editors seek to convey a double meaning. We have, within this anthology, privileged certain sites—race, ethnicity, class, gender, sexuality, and place. To be sure, these are not exhaustive of the locations of Asian American studies. We know that. Further, within each of those sites, we have privileged Asians over Latinos, East Asians over South and Southeast Asians, race over class, and we have artificially privileged single sites when we know full-well that individuals occupy simultaneously multiple and complexly related sites. In addition, the groupings of papers within these covers appear to show us to have conflated women with gender and homosexuality with sexuality. We recognize those appearances, those clear deficiences and errors. But we have tried to remain faithful to the organizing thematic structure of the conference, and have had to work with the contents of the presented papers. We understand *Privileging Positions* to be a modest beginning.

The other meaning we wish to convey in our title is that privileges (and wants) are accorded by the positions of race, ethnicity, class, gender, sexuality, and place. We know that white men are affirmatively admitted by virtue of their raced and gendered position, and we recognize that within the binarism of heterosexual-homosexual, the former is assumed, centered, and rendered natural and universal. Certain sites, thus, confer privileges. But we also know that privilege is gained through subjugation and exploitation, creating the ranks of the subjugated, the exploited, the subaltern. Our work, our labor is to problematize those positionalities, those sites of privilege and want, by dismantling the social relations that were built to sustain the hegemonic discourses. Through a recognition of those subject positions and their relations to power, *Privileging Positions* aspires to de-hegemonize and reposition the colonizing discourse for the liberation of our bodies and minds.

The essays included within this first section of the anthology are a mixed bag of studies on theory, class, and place. Elaine Kim's presidential address urges the field to move "beyond railroads and internment," to cast off the "old jargon and schema," to focus upon the "complexities, layers, paradoxes, contradictions." Asian American studies, Kim argues, has reached a critical juncture where the orthodoxies of race, ethnicity, and gender as presently conceived are inadequate to explain our current and future circumstances and strivings. "Unless we can assume a position of leadership in the new thinking about race[,] [ethnicity, and gender] we will need for the twenty-first century," she warns, "we will be unable to fulfill our primary responsibility, which is to help Asian Americans forge the tools and weapons Asian Americans will need for our lives."

Keith Osajima, Dana Takagi, Colleen Lye, and Mary Lui consider the intersections and divergences of Asian American studies and postmodernism and feminism. Osajima surveys the main contours of postmodernism and assesses the relevance of postmodern theory to Asian American studies. He proposes the development of an "oppositional postmodern analysis" that employs discourse analysis to examine and expose the power of language, but also to move beyond texts to the development of a critical consciousness that intervenes in the hegemonic social relations and that informs "political action to eliminate oppressive conditions and practices." Besides deepening our understanding of the subtle yet powerful discourses that influence the Asian American experience, concludes Osajima, an "affirmative postmodernism" will enable us "to envision and work toward alternative futures."

Takagi points out that the rise of postmodern theory has had an integrative impact upon the disciplines across the academy. Under the postmodern assault, writes Takagi, "the sharp edges separating history, philosophy, literature, and social science are softening." That integration of disciplinary knowledge has resulted in the emergence of new academic units, new journals, new challenges and opportunities. Feminists generally agree with many of the tenets of postmodernism, but are critical of its apparent slighting of social criticism and its relegation of women as subjects to the sidelines of theory production. Still, feminism has engaged postmodernism, and has thereby made the category "woman" central to the debate. Yet Asian American studies, a field like women's studies, conceived of as interdisciplinary from its inception, has failed to engage postmodern theorists or move into the intellectual spaces created by the feminist and postmodernist debates. Postmodernism's "call," Takagi offers, opens possibilities for Asian American studies to "debate across disciplinary boundaries both in- and out-side Asian American studies."

Lye and Lui reveal how Asian American studies might respond to postmodernism's call. Lye's concern is not to show how Asian American studies might acquire and employ postmodernism's tools, but how the field might intervene in the larger theoretical project called "postmodern." Asian American studies, she contends, is uniquely situated "to make important interventions in hegemonic national discourses. . . ." The Asian woman worker, Lye reveals, occupies a central position in the decentering of capitalist production from the core to the periphery, and her labor enables the sustenance of postmodern life-styles at the center. And the figuration of "Asia," she continues, represents an exemplary subject of both capital and labor, and thereby serves to discipline production within the U.S. and offers proof of capitalism's universality (if not triumph). Because of the centrality of Asia and Asians, writes Lye, Asian Americanists "are in an excellent position to make powerful interventions in the dominant understanding of postmodernism and late capitalism."

Lui examines the intersection of "woman" and "the Orient" in her study of the selling of the L'eggs Products' line of pantyhose, "Sheer Elegance," during the early 1980s. Instead of employing Whites, the television and magazine commercials used Asian models to emphasize the "different" and "exotic" natures of this new, silky product ostensibly from Asia. The Asian woman model, Lui points out, represented the intersection of two distinct cultural others: "woman" and "the Orient." Both are mysterious, foreign, and yet familiar to white Americans, because "woman" and "Orient" are domesticated, feminized, assimilated. And insofar as women's bodies are signifiers of consumption, transforming the female subject into the product of men's labor and object of men's desires, the advertisements speak to men, despite the fact that women are the consumers of the product. "Nothing beats a great pair of L'eggs," are words emanating from the male gaze, and women who wear "Sheer Elegance" appropriate "the Orient's" mystique. The most disturbing aspect of those representations, writes Lui, is the way in which we, the receivers, participate in their formulation and transmission, and ultimately attest to capitalism's triumph.

Edna Bonacich and Peter Kwong foreground class as a category of analysis and point to the revolutionary potential of a class analysis of capitalism's alleged triumph. Bonacich decries the "lipservice" paid to the importance of class, when "in practice class appears to have fallen into the background as a topic of central concern." Within the identity politics of multiculturalism and feminism, class appears as simply another form of identity, another basis of commonality or difference. "If we really want to change the class-race system, as it is manifested in the university," Bonacich writes, "we must do much more than change the identity composition of its faculty and students." Racial, gender, and class diversity, however admirable, does not challenge "the class-character of the university, and the role it plays in perpetuating the class system. To revolutionize the university from a class perspective," she reasons, "would require that we fight to change the role that the university plays within the society."

Race has been the predominant category of analysis within Asian American studies, states Kwong. That salience is understandable because of the history of racial exclusion, and because of the struggle for racial equality of the 1960s that gave birth to the field of Asian American studies. But the continued neglect of class analysis, particularly the plight of the Asian American working class, smacks of elitism and points to a fundamental failure. Asian American studies, Kwong reminds us, began as an intellectual but also social movement aimed at serving the community. "That commitment," he laments, "has eroded." And perhaps that erosion is indicative of a basic flaw in the character and consciousness of the field's practitioners. "Asian American studies' loss of connection with the community," posits Kwong, "also has something to do with the fact that many of 'us,' who engage in the field, come from middle-class backgrounds. Our roots in the community are not very deep and have been difficult to maintain." In addition, multiculturalism has swept the field, but it ignores class, functions "to divide the power of the oppressed," and confers privileges upon mainly the middle class. The "soul" of Asian American studies, Kwong urges, must be recaptured and redirected toward the working class and service to the community.

The final five papers by Patricia Nelson Limerick, John Kuo Wei Tchen, Karen K. Kosasa, William Sakamoto White, and Roy Miki explore the site of place. Limerick, an historian who has fundamentally reshaped our understanding of the American West, asks whether Asian American and the "new" Western American history can make common cause. The inclusion of Asians, and indeed of all of the West's inhabitants, she argues, exposes the mythical quality of the mainstream, dominant discourse of the westward movement of white men. The eastward movement of Asians simultaneously reverses the direction of U.S. history and corrects the exclusive racial binarism of Black-White. Further, Whites were not the sole pivot; Asians interacted with American Indians, Chicanos, and Africans. And Asian American studies stretches the Western borders to Alaska and Hawaii.

Those complexities, both geographical and racial, introduced by Asian American history shows the American West to be a "layered landscape" with peoples who hold "a common heritage . . . of intertwined stories." In turn, the new Western history has sought to understand the differences and connections between rural and urban life, and the interaction of humans with their physical environment and its impact upon their sense of identity and place. Perhaps Asian American history can profit from those insights, Limerick suggests, even as it continues "to push and provoke Western historians into thinking harder about their subject."

Tchen, writing from within Asian American studies, sees the dominant discourse of Asians moving from the Pacific eastward across the American landscape as hegemonizing of Asian sensibilities and histories on the "right coast." The field's emphasis on Hawaii and the Pacific coast, argues Tchen, has resulted in an ignorance of other regions and has created a "skewed historical understanding." Chinese communities did not begin in California, and they were not simply transplanted intact wherever Chinese migrants settled in their journey eastward. Chinese, brought to America by international world trade, settled in lower Manhattan decades before the establishment of San Francisco's Chinatown, and they intermingled freely with non-Chinese, at least one-third of them took on Anglo names, and substantial numbers of them intermarried, helping to create an "ethnically creolized international port district." Indeed, proposes Tchen, New York's Chinese negotiated the "highly-racialized cross-cultural discourse" of America long before Chinese arrived on the West coast, and like the movement of Anglo-American Victorian culture from the Northeast to the West, the patterns of that negotiation, first traced on the East coast, might have formed the contours of the "left coast" experience.

Kosasa offers a critique of the University of Hawai'i's "formalist art" curriculum, wherein students are taught to reproduce a body of work that speaks in the visual language of Europe and the U.S. mainland. That effacing of the "local" vision of the university's students, 74 percent of whom are people of color, writes Kosasa, is indicative of a deep, colonial problem that elides the histories, cultures, and identities of those students. Contrary to the formalist assertion, Euro-American modernist aesthetics is not universal; rather, its assumed universality constitutes a colonizing, hegemonic project. "In order to counter the effacement of the 'local visions' of art students in Hawai'i by a visual narrative from somewhere else," concludes Kosasa, "a critical pedagogy must develop practices that actively attend to the differences of our students—their gender, class, ethnicity, and race. It must also emphasize how each person is differently situated and positioned in relation to a historical past and a lived present."

Sociologist White describes the rapidly growing Asian community in Atlanta, where Asians are transforming the Chamblee-Doraville area with businesses and community institutions. The developing community, he proposes, constitutes a site of ethnic affiliation, class struggle, and racial conflict, and offers a test of the hypotheses of the ethnic enclave economy. The establishment of this Asian community in the American South presents problems and opportunities for Asian American studies. White observes: "These are the next challenges within our own community: to not only identify how Asian immigrants can coexist without conflict when interacting with American society but, perhaps most important, to also identify how to be our own critics and urge an examination of the conditions within the enclave economy."

"The pervasive power of 'English-Canadian' centrality—white and Anglo-Saxon—has acted as such a weighty cultural pall that the process of overcoming imposed representations, misrepresentations, and erasures has been an almost insurmountable obstacle for Japanese Canadians and other communities of color in Canada until only recently," writes Miki. But writers, artists, and cultural workers of color, he reports, have begun to create oppositional theories, texts, and visual works that "foreground issues of representation, appropriation, race and ethnicity, and subjectivity." Those productions, Miki cautions, must be "one that can articulate difference in such a way that the very notion of 'otherness,' which western thought has used to centralize 'selfness' as source, as hierarchically prior, becomes obsolete as a way of defining people and cultures. What is important for a culture to thrive," he declares, "is a renewed belief in the viability of agency, so that writers from a diversity of subject-positions can develop the conditions in which social justice can be achieved through a language free from the tyranny of hegemonies of all kinds."

Note

1. From a 1969 statement from U.C. Berkeley's Third World Liberation Front, quoted in Murase (1976:208).

References

Murase, Mike. "Ethnic Studies and Higher Education for Asian Americans." In *Counterpoint: Perspectives on Asian America*, edited by Emma Gee. Los Angeles: UCLA Asian American Studies Center, 1976.
Wong, Shawn. *Homebase*. New York: Plume, 1991.

Beyond Railroads and Internment: Comments on the Past, Present, and Future of Asian American Studies[1]

Elaine H. Kim

In the United States, racism's "traveling eye" has created and cordoned off race-based communities, affixing meaning to them according to the degree of threat they are thought to pose to the dominant culture at particular points in time. Asian origin communities were called "Oriental," east of and peripheral to an unnamed center. Historically, Asian Americans, as we re-named ourselves, have had no place in the discourse on race and culture in the U.S. except as "model minorities" on the one hand or as unassimilable aliens on the other, as statements about the ultimate goodness of the dominant culture and the ultimate badness of those who refuse to go along with the program. Faced with sets of mutually exclusive binaries between "East" and "West," between Asia and America, and between suspect alien and patriot, those seeking a third space as "both/and" instead of "either/or" are usually considered racist, un-American, even anti-American. Within the context of these silencing systems of domination, Asian Americans are supposed to deny our cultural heritages, accept positions as sojourning "exotic aliens," or "go back" to Asia.

A generation ago, I attempted to define Asian American literature as work in English by writers of Chinese, Filipino, Japanese, and Korean descent about U.S. American experiences. I admitted at the time that this definition was arbitrary, prompted by my own inability to read Asian languages and my own lack of access to South and Southeast Asian communities. But for these shortcomings, I wrote, I would have included in my introductory study works written in Asian languages and works by writers from Vietnamese American, Asian Indian American, and other communities.

Nonetheless, it is true that I wanted to delineate and draw boundaries around whatever I thought of as Asian American identity and literature. Clearly, Asian American experiences and creative visions had been
excluded from or distorted in the established texts: although I had majored
in English and American literature in the 1960s at Ivy League universities
and at the University of California, Berkeley, I was never assigned the work
of a single writer of color, not even Ralph Ellison or Richard Wright, whose
books I had to read on my own, together with the work of many other
"Third World" and American writers of color. A century-and-a-half of
persistent and deeply rooted racist inscriptions in both official and mass
literary culture in the United States perpetuated grotesque representations
of Asian Americans as alien Others. Like many other Asian Americans, I
felt an urgent need to insist that these were not "our realities." Our strategy
was to assert a self-determined Asian American identity in direct opposition to these dehumanizing characterizations, even if it was limited by
being contained within the exclusive binary system that occasioned it.

For the most part, I read Asian American literature as a literature of
protest and exile, a literature about place and displacement, a literature
concerned with psychic and physical "home"—searching for and claiming
a "home" or longing for a final "homecoming." I looked for unifying thematic threads and tidy resolutions that might ease the pain of displacement and heal the exile, heedless of what might be missing from this
homogenizing approach and oblivious to the parallels between what I was
doing and dominant culture attempts to reduce Asian American experiences to developmental narratives about a movement from "primitive,"
"Eastern," and foreign immigrant to "civilized," Western, and
"Americanized" loyal citizen.

The cultural nationalist defenses we constructed were anti-assimila-
tionist. But while they opposed official nationalisms, the Asian American
identity they allowed for was fixed, closed, and narrowly defined, dividing
"Asian American" from "Asian" as sharply as possible, privileging race over
gender and class, accepting compulsory heterosexuality as "natural," and
constructing a hierarchy of authenticity to separate the "real" from the
"fake." According to this definition, there were not many ways of being
Asian American. The ideal was male, heterosexual, Chinese or Japanese
American, and English-speaking. The center of Chinese America was San
Francisco or New York Chinatown, and the heart of Japanese America was
in Hawaii or along Highway 99, which cut through the agricultural fields
the issei and nisei had lost during World War II. Asian American history

was about railroads, "bachelor societies," and internment. The sacred Asian American texts—such as Carlos Bulosan's *America Is in the Heart,* John Okada's *No-No Boy,* and Louis Chu's *Eat a Bowl of Tea*—were by "dead yellow men" instead of "dead white men." Asian American literary studies usually did not question the concept of canonization but simply posited an alternative canon. It seemed that every film, every article, and even many novels had to be a uni-dimensional documentary filled with literal and solemnly delivered history lessons. Given the enormity of general ignorance about Asian Americans, it was difficult to do anything but play a dead straight part. Dealing with subtleties, hybridities, paradoxes, and layers seemed almost out of the question when so much effort had to be expended simply justifying Asian Americans as discursive subjects in the first place.

Cultural nationalist agendas have the potential to contest and disrupt the logic of domination, its exploitation and exclusions. Certainly it was possible for me as a Korean American female to accept the fixed masculinist Asian American identity posited in Asian American cultural nationalism, even when it rendered invisible or at least muted women's oppression, anger, and ways of loving and interpreted Korean Americans as imperfect imitations of Chinese Americans, because I could see in everyday life that not all material and psychic violence to women of color comes from men, and because, as my friends used to say, "No Chinese [American] ever called me 'gook.'"

While I was preoccupied with defining Asian American identity and culture in the 1970s and with uncovering buried stories from "early" Asian America, changes in U.S. immigration quotas in 1965 were already resulting in massive and highly visible transformations in Asian American communities. Indeed, it might be said that until recent years, Asian American communities and cultures were shaped by legal exclusion and containment, while contemporary experiences are being shaped by the internationalization of the world's political economies and cultures. Yesterday's young Asian immigrant might have worked beside his parents on a pineapple plantation in Hawaii or in a fruit orchard on the Pacific Coast, segregated from the mainstream of American life. Today's Asian immigrant teenager might have only Asian friends, but she probably deals daily with a not necessarily anguishing confusion of divergent influences, a collision of elements she needs to negotiate in her search to define herself. In this regard, she is not unlike other Americans: as Trinh T. Minh-ha has pointed out, "There is a Third World in every First World and vice versa" (1989:98).

Her collisions, however, are probably tied to the particularities of her cultural background at a particular point in time. Thus, she might rent Korean language video melodramas from a shopping center in Southern California today, after having watched "McGyver" and "Entertainment Tonight" on television in Seoul as a child.

During the past two decades, some Asian and Pacific American populations have increased by 500 to 1,000 percent. New Asian American communities have taken root all over the country, as Vietnamese refugees settle in Westminster, California and Korean immigrants gather in Flushing, New York. Newcomers are diverse in terms of origin and ethnicity, language, social class, political positions, educational backgrounds, and patterns of settlement. They have moved to cities and towns where few Asian Americans had lived before and are doing things to earn their livelihoods that they could not have imagined when they were in their homelands: Cambodians are making doughnuts, Koreans are making burritos, South Asians are operating motels, Filipinos are driving airport shuttle buses. The lines between Asian and Asian American, so crucial to identity formations in the past, are increasingly blurred: transportation to and communication with Asia is no longer daunting, resulting in new crossovers and intersections and different kinds of material and cultural distances today.

Asian American identities are fluid and migratory: the Minnesota social worker who clings to the idea of Hmongs as limited-English-speaking refugees from a pre-literate society may be surprised to encounter a Hmong teenager who composes rap music, plays hockey, and dates Chicano boys or girls. Cultures, whether Asian origin cultures or the "majority culture," which is no more monolithic and unitary than "Asian" or "Asian American culture," have never been fixed, continuous, or discrete. The notion of an absolute American past, a single source for American people, a founding identity or wholeness in America, is rooted in the racist fiction of primordial white American universality, as is the fear that "American culture" is now being broken down by rowdy brown and yellow immigrants and other people of color who refuse to melt into the final identity of "just Americans."

I often hear people lament that things are getting worse all the time, that Americans are more divided, that there is less tolerance and more racial violence than ever before. But according to my own experience of the Wonder Bread days before the civil rights movement, there was much more racial violence and much less racial tolerance then than now. Maybe some people remember the "good old days" of the Ozzie and Harriet 1950s as peaceful and harmonious; I do not. The races were more divided in the past, when segregation was the rule and racial hierarchies were accepted as natural and permanent. In Maryland, where I grew up, interracial marriages were illegal, and job announcements routinely stipulated "Whites only" as well as "men only." It is true that hate crimes against Asian Americans are more and more frequently in the news. But if anyone thinks that racial violence is a 1990s phenomenon, maybe that is because racial violence in the "good old days" was not documented except in the lived experiences of Americans of color. In my view, the "good old days" were not so good for women and people of color.

The America that is ever "becoming" has always been a polyglot nation of immigrants, but this has never been all: it is also the site of Native America, of African slavery and resistances to it, of the war between the U.S. and Mexico and the yet to be fully honored Treaty of Guadalupe-Hidalgo. Knowing that there has never been a unified Mayflower-and-Plymouth Rock beginning to "return to" makes me feel hopeful about the future.

No matter what we wish for, things do not necessarily come to a harmonious resolution. Perhaps after all there is no "home," except for a place of contestation that negates as well as affirms. And identity, like "home," is ever in process, less a refuge than the site of contending, multiple meanings. Inevitably, the Asian American identity offered by cultural nationalism could not but produce conflicts that portended its own undoing: what was excluded and rendered invisible—the unruly, the transgressive, and the disruptive—begins to seep out from under the grids and appear from between the cracks. Eventually the seams burst and are exposed. In the case of Asian America, this unruliness has come from women who never stop being both Asian and female, as well as from others rendered marginal by the essentializing aspects of Asian American cultural nationalism.

Those of us who teach Asian American studies need to focus on three primary responsibilities. First, we can try to present students with an array of the best readings and educational materials we can possibly find through our own concentrated searches. Our job is to sift and sort, to give students a short-cut, at least from our own standpoints. Second, we can provide examples for students, not in the goody-goody moral sense, but in the sense of showing them how our knowledges are situated and how our own thinking has been moving, haltingly, in fits and starts, often stymied by terrible moments of self-doubt, through revision after revision so that they might profit from what we have been through. Third, we can try to provide students with opportunities to address in their writing questions they need to answer for their lives. We can tell them that they have to conceptualize, shape, and articulate their questions so that the materials in their classes can be used to address these questions. If they have tried their best and can find no connection between what they want to know and what is being offered in their courses, then, we need to tell them, something is wrong with their courses, and not with them. We can tell them to always look for what is missing and ask themselves why it is missing. They have to look for what has not been seen, for what has not been written. Our overall goal can be to do what we can to help students equip themselves with the weapons and tools they will need for their lives.

In these extraordinary times, it is extraordinarily challenging to fulfill our responsibilities as Asian Americanists—as people who teach, write, and care about Asian American studies. Asian American studies has historically provided a space from which dominant notions of history, identity, and culture could be critiqued, a site for recovery where, as Chandra Mohanty has suggested, new spaces could be opened for historically silenced people to construct knowledge and authorize marginalized experiences, to validate their personal experiences as systematic, self-conscious resistance (1989-90:179-208). By uncovering the banished stories of those lying prostrate before the winners of history, Asian American studies helps bring into view what David Lloyd has called "the history of the possible" (1991:88). But because our approach was in large part defensive and oppositional, the various national and racial groups often adopted benignly laissez faire attitudes toward each other, glossing over differences and paying little attention to internal contradictions among groups of color and the valences of gender, location, generation, and sometimes even social class. Our projected alternative knowledges in some ways homogenized the oppressed, rendering invisible specific experiences and consciousness. For example, during the years following the murder of Vincent Chin in 1982, the mostly Chinese and Japanese American-led and legalistically oriented Asian American movement's focus has been on anti-Asian violence as an issue around which to organize and unify diverse Asian and Pacific American communities. The victims of the violence against which we are encouraged to rally are always male and the perpetrators are always White. Our situations today call for a casting off of the old jargon and schema. We need to pay new attention to complexities, layers, paradoxes, contradictions. Unless we can assume a position of leadership in the new thinking about race we will need for the twenty-first century, we will be unable to fulfill our primary responsibility, which is to help Asian Americans forge the tools and weapons Asian Americans will need for our lives.

Asian America, and consequently the field of Asian American studies and its professional organ, the Association for Asian American Studies, are all on the threshold of important changes. It is an exciting new moment for us, because the possibilities are myriad. The tasks before us are by necessity many as well. I see some of these as the following:

(1) We must discuss thoroughly the definitions of our discipline at this juncture. What are the specific intellectual, social, and ethical charges to which we wish to commit ourselves? What is unique about Asian American studies? My colleague, Lane Hirabayashi, has raised the questions to the Association for Asian American Studies, what is an Asian American studies critique? How are Asian American studies faculty to be evaluated? How can we better network to encourage and stimulate inscriptions of Asian America in images and words? How can we nurture our relationships with Asian American communities? How can we make certain that our work does not simply trail the issues facing our community but is useful for analyzing and addressing real problems outside the academy?

(2) What should be the relationship between Asian American studies and other disciplines, such as not only African American, Chicano, Native American, and women's studies, but also American studies, Asian studies, and cultural studies? We plan to conduct our 1995 annual meeting at the same time with the National Association for Chicano Studies and the National Association for Black Studies. My colleague Sau-ling Wong points out that if the sensibilities are similar, bridges can be built. Another colleague, Michael Omi, warns that although many Asian Americans no longer feel the need for the clear distinction between themselves as Americans and their links with Asia, we cannot assume that the disciplines are ready to relinquish their old colonizing stance toward Asian American studies. And Ling-chi Wang notes that vis-a-vis Asian studies, Asian American studies scholars are better positioned to conduct diaspora studies because many Asian studies programs are trapped within the traditional narrow confines of area studies foci.

(3) As a Korean American, I have been disappointed that our field has not been better able to help Asian Americans understand the complexities of multi-racial race relations in the 1990s. I was appalled, for example, when some of my Chinese and Japanese American brothers and sisters headed for the hills screaming "I'm not Korean" after the Los Angeles civil disaster in the spring of 1992. Perhaps they wished to dissociate

themselves from us because our tragedy disrupted their narrow and risk-free focus on white violence against Asians. I cannot help feeling that these predominantly Chinese and Japanese American legal activists were mostly concerned that other communities of color see them as different from Du Soon Ja.

Can Asian American studies continue to exist under the old umbrella? Many of our South Asian and Filipino students encounter East Asian American chauvinism in our programs. At the University of California, Berkeley, South Asian students complained about the name of the Asian American student journal. It was called *Slant.* Although this name is finally being changed, the South Asian students have spearheaded their own publication, a rich anthology of many different writers that should be available this fall. Filipino American students have been chafing against what they perceive to be tokenism in Asian American studies programs. Filipinos are the fastest growing Asian Pacific American population. But who is reading the writings of Cecilia Brainard, Han Ong, Ninotchka Rosca, and Marianne Villanueva in Asian American studies classes, and who is looking at the work of visual artists like Ileana Lee, Eric Manabat, Paul Pfeiffer, and Rudjen Roldan? How can we shape our field so that our work is more responsive to Filipino, Korean, South Asian, and Southeast Asian communities and knowledge needs? Should we develop old fashioned "area studies" paradigms of the kind that are holding Asian studies scholars back, or can we imagine new conceptual frameworks that move beyond railroads and internment camps to speak to the experiences of new groups of various national origins, and not just on the West Coast?

(4) And finally, many Asian American women complain that they encounter racism in women's studies and sexism in ethnic studies. How can we make gender central to the study of Asian American experiences? How can we more quickly eliminate sexism from Asian American studies and the Association for Asian American Studies?

I am sure that everyone in this room has other issues and questions to add to this list. I know that you will all contribute to addressing these problems as we work together to create an Asian American studies for the future.

Note

1. Portions of this paper were published in the preface to *Charlie Chan Is Dead: An Anthology of Contemporary Asian American Fiction,* edited by Jessica Hagedorn. New York: Penguin Books, 1993.

References

Lloyd, David. "Race UnderRepresentation." *Oxford Literary Review* 13 (1991):62-94.

Mohanty, Chandra Talpade. "On Race and Voice: Challenges for Liberal Education in the 1990s." *Cultural Critique* 14 (Winter 1989-90):179-208.

Trinh, T. Minh-ha. *Woman, Native, Other: Writing Postcoloniality and Feminism.* Bloomington: Indiana University Press, 1989.

Postmodernism and Asian American Studies: A Critical Appropriation

Keith Hiroshi Osajima

This essay appears at the intersection of two developments: (1) in the past two decades there has been a tremendous upsurge of interest in postmodern perspectives in a range of cultural and intellectual spheres. Throughout academe in particular, postmodern debates have forced a critical rethinking of long-standing social theories and practices. The result has been a reshaping of intellectual life featuring an infusion of new voices and viewpoints (Best and Kellner 1991). (2) During the same period of time, Asian Americanists have been struggling to build a new field of inquiry, which not only generates new knowledge about the Asian American experience, but seeks to use that knowledge to transform pedagogical and political practices (Endo and Wei 1988). Central to the building of Asian American studies has been on-going efforts to develop theoretical tools to analyze the changing dynamics of Asian America (Tong 1971; Surh 1974; Liu 1976; Liu and Cheng 1986; Okihiro 1991; Omi 1988).

My organizing question is, in what ways can the developments and interests in postmodern theories contribute to the theoretical needs within Asian American studies? Exploring the potential and limits of postmodernism involves a number of considerations. To begin, the study outlines some of the main contours of postmodernism. This is necessarily a limited discussion given the range of perspectives and works that fall under the rubric of postmodern theory. The objective is simply to provide a foundation from which to move into the next section—an assessment of the relevance of postmodernism to Asian American studies. Here, I explore how the building of Asian American studies and the analysis of Asian American experiences, particularly from social scientific approaches, can benefit from developments in postmodernism.

The third section tempers the enthusiastic interest in postmodernism by examining some of the criticisms leveled against the new theoretical developments. It describes possible dangers that should be avoided in the appropriation of postmodern theories in Asian American studies. The study concludes with suggestions for developing an oppositional Asian American postmodernism. It explores how a mediated postmodern critique, which does not totally abandon the emancipatory and political aspects of the modernist project, can benefit Asian American studies.

Making sense of postmodernism is a difficult task. Its dizzying array of sometimes contradictory perspectives, its reach into a wide range of cultural, aesthetic, and philosophical spheres, and its tendency toward abstract and obtuse language present formidable obstacles to comprehension. As a step toward clarification, it is useful to think of postmodernism as a relational phenomenon, as perspectives situated in opposition to the power and practices associated with modernism. Understanding postmodernism, then, must begin with a brief overview of what many postmodernists are critical of—modernism.

Jurgen Habermas outlines some of the main contours of the modernist project in the following:

> The project of modernity formulated in the eighteenth century by philosophers of the Enlightenment consisted in their efforts to develop objective science, universal morality and law, and autonomous art according to their inner logic . . . . The Enlightenment philosophers wanted to utilize this accumulation of specialized culture for the enrichment of everyday life—that is to say, for the rational organization of everyday social life (Habermas 1993: 103).

In modernity, reason, rationality, and science were held high as emancipatory forces enabling free-thinking, autonomous individuals to master and control their environment. Modernism promised to free people from the irrationalities of myth, religion, superstition, and emotion, and to uncover "the universal, eternal, and the immutable qualities of all of humanity." Emancipated from traditional bounds, new forms of rational social organization could be developed to alleviate the fears of "scarcity, want and the arbitrariness of natural calamity" (Harvey 1989:12).

The emancipatory promise of modernity was accompanied by an optimistic belief in the idea of progress. History and human development was assumed to be inexorably forward moving, made possible by the immense capabilities of the free-willed, autonomous, rational human subject. In modernity, it was commonly believed that the present surpassed the past, and the future would inevitably bring further improvements.

In the mid-nineteenth century, the idea of progress, as a continuous, linear, evolutionary process came to represent what it meant to be "modern" and was held as a universal truth for all human societies (Smart 1992).

Modernism did have its share of critics. Observers noted that while modernism created new and positive change, it also destroyed much of the world before it. Nietzsche, Marx, Weber, and Durkheim were among those who described the contradictory and problematic by-products of modern development. The currents of criticism, however, did not shatter the strong faith in reason and the ideal of progress. Modernist sensibilities have dominated twentieth-century thinking, and have been affirmed by the advancements in science, transportation, and communication. The modern, bourgeois ideals of democracy, equality, and liberty continue to inspire dramatic political transformations in the world. Modernism, it seems, has enabled "mankind to do what the Bible said only God could do: to 'make all things new'" (Berman 1992: 33).

In the past two decades, the critical questioning of modernism's promise has been renewed and has accelerated greatly. Dramatic shifts in economic and cultural arenas have led some observers to suggest that we have moved beyond modernism into a distinctly different postmodern condition. David Harvey (1989) argues that modernist economic arrangements, predicated on Fordist assembly line production, large-scale fixed capital investments, and steady growth in consumer markets have been superseded by processes of "flexible accumulation," where production is organized around the flexible use of part-time, non-union labor, extensive subcontracting, expansion of service sector businesses, and the internationalization of low cost labor. The shifts in production are accompanied by a changing cultural aesthetic featuring a volatile and fleeting consumer market, with rapidly changing consumer fads, fashions and tastes (Jameson 1991). Harvey writes:

> The relatively stable aesthetic of Fordist modernism has given way to all the ferment, instability, and fleeting qualities of a postmodernist aesthetic that celebrates difference, ephemerality, spectacle, fashion, and the commodification of cultural forms (1989:156).

The modern, linear sense of time and bounded space has also been altered in the postmodern condition. Telecommunications and transportation advances have "shrunk" the world, allowing transnational corporations to conduct business and coordinate production instantaneously around the globe. This has not only internationalized production, but has globalized a popular style and culture which transcends national boundaries, compressing space and linking people around the world.

These postmodern changes have disorienting and destructive effects on individual and social life. Kenneth Gergen, a social psychologist, argues that the explosion in communication and technology has so accelerated and intensified social relations that people have become oversaturated with information and stimulation. This "saturated self" is increasingly unstable and volatile, unable to find a grounding in identity and community (Gergen 1991). Anthony Giddens, writing about "high modernity" rather than postmodernity, notes that the separation of time and space, the disembedding of social institutions, and the dialectic of the local and global has disrupted people's "ontological security and trust" (1991).

In the midst of these changes, questions arise not only about modernity as a term to describe contemporary conditions, but also about the applicability of modern sensibilities and perspectives in the postmodern condition. The strongholds of modernism—reason and science, progress and universal truth—have come under increasing scrutiny in the last two decades. The resulting shifts in thinking constitute postmodern theories.

Postmodern theories share a deep suspicion and criticism of modernism. Pauline Rosenau describes this critical posture:

> Post-modernists criticize all that modernity has engendered: the accumulated experience of Western civilization, industrialization, urbanization, advanced technology, the nation state, life in the "fast lane." . . . They argue that modernity is no longer a force for liberation; it is rather a source of subjugation, oppression and repression (1992:5-6).

A central feature of the postmodern critique is to question modernist claims to universal truth. Postmodern theorists argue that these claims, such as the unequivocal value of science and reason, the ideal of the autonomous subject, and the notion of progressive development, are not universal truths, but represent a narrow worldview emanating from a western European experience. An organizing question for many postmodernists, then, is how have the narrow western European perspectives come to represent normative and universal positions?

The key to answering this question lies in analyzing how language and discourse have power to construct, constrain, and shape social life. Michel Foucault makes important contributions in this area. He argues that discourses can "induce regular power effects" by defining a "regime of truth." This regime of truth establishes standards by which true and false statements are determined; it sanctions techniques and procedures for acquiring truth; and it accords status upon those who are charged with saying what is true (Foucault 1980:131). Postmodern theorists argue that certain modern claims, such as the value of reason and science, constitute "metanarratives" which are powerful precisely because they have come to be commonly accepted as true, and can define the normative standards by which the truth of other claims can be made. They constitute closed systems of knowledge by anticipating questions and then providing fixed, predetermined answers (Rosenau 1992:6). Fraser and Nicholson write that a metanarrative: "purports to be a privileged discourse capable of situating, characterizing, and evaluating all other discourses but not itself to be infected by the historicity and contingency which render first-order discourses potentially distorted and in need of legitimation" (1990: 22).

Postmodern critics note how metanarratives subsume difference and diversity by imposing singular, homogenizing models of explanation or development. Metanarratives are exclusionary for they narrowly define what is acceptable, legitimate, and present, while excluding, silencing, and rendering invisible other views. They are also criticized for being misleading and misrepresentative. In the name of a universal truth, they provide seemingly incontrovertible support for narrow, hierarchical thinking and judgments.

Little of modernism has been spared the postmodern critique of metanarratives. The Enlightenment metanarrative which privileges science, reason, and rationality has been a common target of postmodern criticism. The implication that human reason as applied through objective science is the only or best avenue to knowledge has been harshly criticized as exclusionary and hierarchical.

The ideal of progress, with its emphasis on linear, evolutionary development is another metanarrative challenged by postmodernists. Marx's vision of emancipation through the inevitable triumph of the proletariat, and social Darwinist views of the evolution of species and societies have been criticized for imposing universal models of linear development which denies the specificity of local conditions (Docherty 1993:11; Laclau 1993:337).

In literature, the conventional wisdom that the author is the "final arbiter of meaning," and that the text accurately represents the author's intentions, motives, and meanings has been critiqued by postmodernists (Rosenau 1992:27). They argue that a reading of the text may uncover a multitude of meanings, and that efforts to find the one true meaning intended by the author are misguided. Similarly, postmodern theorists are critical of modern positions arguing that the human subject is a coherent, unified, free-willed, autonomous, rational being. This too constitutes a normative definition of the subject, based on a western European, bourgeois, heterosexual male model, which excludes and marginalizes those who have not been assigned or given access to those qualities (e.g. women, gays and lesbians, workers, people of color). Through the critical analysis of texts and narratives, postmodern theories seek to unveil the constructed nature of truths, thereby defusing their power and opening up new areas of inquiry and understanding. Postmodern theorists focus on "all that the modern age has never cared to understand in any particular detail, with any sort of specificity" (Rosenau 1992:8). This implies an inquiry and analysis that is plural, heterogeneous, and local; an approach that is inclusive, seeking to refocus on histories, peoples, experiences not deemed valuable and central in modern discourses.

In what ways can Asian American studies benefit from the developments in postmodernism? There are two areas of potential benefit. The first involves drawing on the interests in postmodernism to help build Asian American studies in academe. The second employs postmodern theories in helping Asian American studies address challenging theoretical issues related to the study of the Asian experience in the United States.

In the first area, Asian American studies has long recognized the obstacles to establishing a place in academe (Loo 1988). Often located on the margins of the college or university, Asian American studies has always been vulnerable to criticism and cuts. The periodic attacks have been commonly fueled by questions of academic credibility. The challenge of building Asian American studies requires that proponents develop a new field of inquiry in a context of institutional norms, values, and practices that are counter to and hostile toward those efforts. Asian American scholars, seeking to stabilize programs through their own advancement in the institution, often have had little choice but to accommodate to the standards set forth by academe. This has meant adhering to an ideal of scholarship defined by traditional disciplinary values, which includes an emphasis on publishing in "prestigious" academic journals, and a priority on positivist research models. As Omi (1988) and Mar (1988) note, these forces have led Asian American studies further away from its original orientation toward social change and serving the community.

The inroads postmodern theory and theorists have made into many academic fields can contribute to a more supportive intellectual and political climate for Asian American studies. The general critique of metanarratives, for example, has inspired considerable rethinking and debate about existing arrangements in academe. Postmodernists see the organization of the university into rigid disciplines as a remnant of modernism—an effort to define and privilege Enlightenment principles of reason and science (Rosenau 1992:8). They offer compelling arguments for crossing boundaries, and for developing institutional support for interdisciplinary theoretical and methodological approaches to knowledge. Even though postmodern voices are still in the minority and are often found on the margins of academe, their presence can break some of the isolation Asian Americanists have experienced in their longstanding efforts to develop multidisciplinary work. Those scholars on campuses, who seek to develop postmodern critiques of metanarratives and a more inclusive cross-disciplinary approach to inquiry, may be potential allies of Asian American studies or sympathetic to the work that Asian Americans are attempting to do.

The postmodern critique of modernism's exclusionary tendencies can also help to legitimate Asian American studies' longstanding effort to bring neglected histories, experiences, and struggles to light. Asian Americans have, from the beginning of the field, been acutely aware of the dangerous consequences of invisibility. Lowell Chun-Hoon, in his analysis of racism in textbooks writes: "the omission of Asian Americans or a neglect for their sensibilities in these books can only inform the reader that this group of people is marginal and irrelevant, if not absolutely expendable" (1975:41).

Postmodern theories provide an important justification for the importance of bringing Asian American histories, experiences, and voices into view. As Harvey writes: "The idea that all groups have a right to speak for themselves, in their own voice, and have that voice accepted as authentic and legitimate is essential to the pluralistic stance of postmodernism" (1989:48).

Moreover, postmodern critiques of metanarratives can deepen our understanding of the forces that have rendered Asians invisible. For example, the analysis of modernist discourses reveals its Eurocentric bias, which places Europe and later the United States at the pinnacle of developmental hierarchies. Asian nations and peoples, their significant contributions to culture and science notwithstanding, are marginalized in this discourse, defined as merely exotic "Orientals" (Said 1979). This analysis can be extended to the treatment of Asian American history, where often the contributions and struggles of Asian immigrants are left unmentioned in modern histories which primarily focus on white, male heroes as the force of progress.

In the second area, postmodern theories can be used to address theoretical concerns facing Asian American studies. Gary Okihiro observes that one of the failures of Asian American studies has been an inability to critically challenge and break free of the theoretical paradigms inherited from traditional disciplines. He writes: "Despite the radical origins of the field, very few Asian American scholars have truly challenged the 'tyranny of received paradigms'" (Okihiro 1991:23).

He argues that theoretical developments in Asian American studies have been hindered by a tendency to rely on cultural explanations of phenomena and to emphasize descriptive rather than analytic studies. He also notes that Asian American studies has been too heavily influenced by European American ideology and European ethnic studies. People like "Marcus Hansen, Robert Park, Oscar Handlin, and Milton Gordon have exerted a greater influence over Asian American Studies than have W. E. B. Du Bois, Carter G. Woodson, and E. Franklin Frazier" (Okihiro 1991:20).

The general thrust of postmodern theory offers guidance in thinking about the theoretical concerns that Okihiro raises. The strength of postmodern theory is its insistence on analyzing the construction of powerful discourses and the ways they limit and define social life. The critical posture toward metanarratives can be used to examine some of the central theoretical constructs that have governed analyses of Asian Americans, particularly in the areas of social science.

A postmodern critique of modernism, for example, can help us to unravel and understand the continuing influence of Robert Park's (1950) work. His race relations cycle formulated in the 1910s and 1920s drew heavily from the evolutionary discourse which held a powerful explanatory force in many scientific fields. The cycle of contact, competition, accommodation, and assimilation, gained power and popularity, in part, because it was presented as a "truthful," scientifically verified process—a purportedly inevitable, irreversible, universal outcome of intergroup relations.

The appropriation of Park's race relations thinking into popular, common sense discourses and policies on race, further infused his views with power. In the 1920s, concerns about the massive influx of immigrants triggered nativist hysteria. Building on Park, nativists argued that the assimilation of immigrants was the only viable solution to potential intergroup strife. Moreover, assimilation was taken to mean Anglo-conformity, where the immigrant and racial minority groups should give up their own cultural heritages and adopt the values and customs of Anglo-America. This view has since become institutionalized and reappears in many policy debates, from the educational efforts to "Americanize" immigrants in the 1920s, to the anti-bilingual education arguments for English Only in the 1980s.

Second, Park's assumptions underscore the "immigrant analogy" perspective that continues to inform common sense and academic analyses of race relations. This view holds that the experiences of ethnic and racial groups follow essentially the same trajectory in American society. Differences between groups would eventually disappear, in an evolutionary manner, as they work their way up the meritocratic ladder of American society. The immigrant analogy has been at the heart of explanations of Asian American success. Asian Americans are simply the latest example of an upwardly mobile ethnic group, making it through hard work and perseverance. The immigrant analogy simultaneously offers a common sense explanation for minority group failure and inequality. The failure of African Americans, for example, is attributed to their inability to take advantage of meritocratic opportunities, generally due to cultural deficits.

Like other metanarratives, the race relations cycle and the immigrant analogy impose an ideal of progress and evolution that glosses over important differences in experience. Assessing the continuing impact of these constructs on popular and academic analyses of race is an important component in efforts to break from received paradigms.

A postmodern analysis can address another limitation of the received paradigms of contemporary race relations work—a tendency to conceptualize racial issues in binary terms, as matters of Black and White (Cho 1993). Dualist constructs have informed thinking since antiquity, but became dominant in modernity as oppositional, either/or thinking played an important role in clarifying and solidifying the primacy of reason over superstition, mind over matter, rationality over emotion, White over Black (Hodge 1990:95). The influence of dualism in contemporary analyses of race relations was evident in the media coverage of the 1992 Los Angeles uprising, where the situation was framed in terms of Black rage. Media pundits and academics were hard pressed to understand the multi-racial dynamics of Los Angeles. As a result, the impact of the events on the Korean and Latino community was initially ignored. The postmodern appreciation for inclusiveness, plurality, heterogeneity, and locality may offer direction out of binary conceptions of race relations, enabling analysts to incorporate the complex and contradictory experience of Asian Americans into the study of race in the United States.

As a final example, postmodernism can stimulate a rethinking of received psychological paradigms used to analyze the Asian American experience. Existing psychological theories are steeped in modernist dis-courses. They privilege reason and rationality, and the possibility of realiz-ing a coherent, unified identity. Any departure from this model is viewed as an individual failing, abnormality, or psychopathology in need of a cure. Kenneth Gergen (1991) argues that the psychological, mental health dis-course places a heavy burden of blame on the individual, and adheres to a standard of a unified self that runs counter to life in the postmodern context.

Psychologists, for too long, have uncritically applied modernist psy-chological theories and methods to the study of Asian Americans. Draw-ing credibility from a scientific "regime of truth" featuring "validated scales," "controlled experimental designs," and "statistically significant" findings, psychological studies have unfortunately developed a pathological inter-pretation of Asian Americans, attaching labels such as unassertive or mal-adjusted to their experience. This unwittingly reinforces a tendency of Asian Americans to blame themselves for experiencing dislocations in American society, and diverts attention away from the historical and structural im-pact of racism. A postmodern analysis can critically examine, not the indi-vidual who is deemed abnormal or pathological, but the practice and discourse of psychology that relies so heavily on positivistic models that locate blame on the individual.

The foregoing discussion identified a number of ways that the postmodern turn can benefit Asian American studies. Does this mean that we should rush uncritically toward postmodernism for theoretical guid-ance? The answer, as will be developed in this section, is no. Postmodernism is far from a seamless, coherent perspective. The term refers to a wide range of theoretical views and practices, which carry sometimes contradictory and problematic implications for analysis. It is important to proceed with caution, and to note how some postmodern positions may present dangers and limits to Asian American studies.

First, both Rosenau (1992) and Best and Kellner (1991) warn us from falling into an extreme postmodern position. Best and Kellner describe an extreme wing that "declares a radical break with modernity and modern theory" (1991:256). The postmodern theories of Jean Baudrillard, Deleuze and Guattari, parts of Lyotard and Foucault are so thoroughly critical of modernism that they leave little room to maneuver. The extreme critique of all metanarratives celebrates and privileges uncertainty, ephemerality, and fragmentation to the point of making it difficult to find any ground to formulate alternative conceptualizations. Best and Kellner write: "For extreme postmodernists, social reality is therefore indeterminate and unmappable, and the best we can do is live within the fragments of a disintegrating social order" (Best and Kellner 1991:258).

Rosenau adds that for skeptical postmodernists, life in a disintegrating social order is pessimistic, gloomy, and meaningless. These positions fuel a sense of hopelessness, malaise, and paralysis (Rosenau 1992:15). The radical critique of the free-willed, autonomous subject, for instance, leads some postmodern theorists to abandon any notions of human agency. Moreover, as Bryan Palmer (1990) observes, the extreme postmodern emphasis on discourse can reify language, resulting in a privileging of textual analysis and the removal of materialist economic, social, and political forces from the scene. The primacy of discourse results in the disappearance of the subject, as all human thinking and action is seen as constituted within the power of discourses. From this position, the possibility of change through political action is virtually eliminated. Postmodern theories, in the extreme, can be apolitical and nihilistic.

Such positions are antithetical to a fundamental position of Asian American studies—the importance of developing knowledge to inform political action. We should be wary of the political paralysis that may arise from skeptical postmodernism, and guard against reifying discourse at the expense of human agency. Nancy Hartsock (1987) correctly suggests that we should be suspicious of postmodern theories that abolish the subject at the very moment that women and other marginal groups are constituting themselves as empowered subjects.

Aside from the problematic implications arising from the substantive content of some postmodern theory, Asian American studies should also guard against the dangers emanating from the convoluted form of many postmodern presentations. Postmodern works are often written in abstract, confusing, and difficult language, reflecting its strong philosophical lineage, and its location in academe. The specialized jargon of postmodernism is partially justified, for the development of new theoretical formulations requires new vocabulary and constructs. Also some postmodern writers intentionally break from familiar narrative and linear forms as part of their efforts to move away from modernism. Still, the difficulty of the language can render these works inaccessible and incomprehensible. Ironically, the effort to critique modernists discourses as exclusionary and hierarchical has generated a postmodern discourse and language that can be equally exclusionary and hierarchical. Asian American studies, which currently faces accusations that it is increasingly academic, depoliticized, and distant from the community, must be careful not to exacerbate matters by uncritically adopting the language of postmodernism.

In a related vein, we must not let the explosive interest in postmodernism act as a divisive element within Asian American studies. Rosenau notes that interest in postmodernism often constitutes a generational divide, with graduate students and young scholars gravitating toward postmodernism, while older scholars remain skeptically distant (1992:11). An assortment of problematic tensions can arise from such a division.

On the one hand, the enthusiasm and excitement surrounding postmodernism can lead advocates into a distinctly modernist trap—hailing the "new" theory as naturally better than the outdated "older" works. Asian American scholars who suggest that postmodern theories are a "new and improved" approach to understanding the experiences of Asian Americans run the risk of underestimating and unappreciating the historical development of Asian American scholarship. Long before postmodernism cried out for inclusion, new histories, and recovered voices, Asian American scholars were working to bring to light the invisible history of Asian Americans; to focus attention on the ignored resistance of Asian laborers; and to reclaim the silenced voices of Asian women and writers. Asian American studies was part of the international movement in the late 1960s that politically challenged modernism, and laid the groundwork for postmodern work. That history must be acknowledged to locate the current postmodern analyses as coterminous, not opposed to, the existing body of Asian American work.

On the other hand, the challenge of postmodern theories may be greeted by a disabling, rigid criticism, defensiveness, and/or resistance on the part of more established Asian Americanists. Defensiveness arises when the criticisms of modern theoretical paradigms and metanarratives are taken as personalized attacks, rather than important calls to critically rethink analytic perspectives. The difficult language of postmodernism is often grounds for a quick dismissal of all the works, without consideration of their analytic potential. Older scholars may simply find it difficult to accept that younger scholars working with postmodern theories have anything important to offer. Such positions will make it difficult to fully discuss the potential and limits of postmodern theories.

In recent years, theorists have attempted to chart a course away from the extremes of postmodern theory (e.g. Giroux 1991; Best and Kellner

1991; Rosenau 1992). Refusing to succumb to the nihilist tendencies of some postmodern work, theorists have developed positions that draw from postmodern critiques, and hold on to a progressive, emancipatory vision of modernism. These syntheses, what Rosenau calls affirmative postmodernism and Smart refers to an oppositional postmodernism (Smart 1992:178), offer some direction for Asian American studies.

Developing oppositional postmodernism involves utilizing the critical impulses of postmodernism to reveal oppressive constraints and problems of modernism, while avoiding the extreme positions of total repudiation, where it is impossible to fashion alternative visions of the future. It means, for example, that it is important to criticize the modernist emphasis on reason for its repressive effect of narrowly defining a concept of knowledge that excludes and minimizes the experiences of women and people of color (Fraser and Nicholson 1988:101). This critique, however, does not require that we abandon reason entirely. Rather it leaves open the possibility that a critical use of reason to interrogate oppressive facets of modernism can inform the development of a politics of change (Smart 1992:181).

An affirmative postmodernism would look to develop the plural, local analyses that have been ignored or homogenized through the imposition of modernist metanarratives. It would bring in the voices and specific experiences of those who have been marginalized by universalizing discourses. But it would not so privilege the locally specific as to ignore the important analytic insights to be gained by seeing how the local is affected by larger societal macrostructures (Fraser and Nicholson 1988:101).

An oppositional postmodern analysis would use discourse analysis to examine and reveal the power of language to construct limited and biased views of the subject. It can reveal, for example, how our conceptions of ourselves are restricted by modernist discourses on rationality and reasoned judgment. In Asian American studies, it can show how the model minority discourse, or the discourse on assimilation problematically restricts many people's views of and actions toward Asians. The emphasis on discourse analyses, however, should not restrict our inquiry to texts, nor should the analysis of Asian American experiences be portrayed as simply overdetermined outcomes of discursive power. Such positions run the risk of denying the possibility for Asian Americans to develop a critical consciousness and to engage in political action.

In sum, postmodern theories can be useful in Asian American studies so long as their application contributes to one of the fundamental objectives of the field—to develop critical analyses of the Asian American experience, which can inform political action to eliminate oppressive conditions and practices. An affirmative postmodernism can deepen our understanding of the subtle but powerful ways that discourses influence the Asian American experience. These understandings can loosen the power of common sense, simplistic, homogenizing discourses which often restrict our views and limit our analyses. Moving beyond problematic modernist boundaries, Asian Americans may find it easier to envision and work toward alternative futures.

References

Berman, Marshall. "Why Modernism Still Matters." In *Modernity and Identity*, edited by Scott Lash and Jonathan Friedman. Oxford: Blackwell, 1992.

Best, Steven and Douglas Kellner. *Postmodern Theory—Critical Interrogations*. New York: Guilford Press, 1991.

Cho, Sumi K. "Korean Americans vs. African Americans: Conflict and Construction." In *Reading Rodney King - Reading Urban Uprising*, edited by Robert Gooding-Williams. New York: Routledge, 1993.

Chun-Hoon, Lowell. "Teaching the Asian American Experience: Alternatives to the Neglect and Racism in Textbooks." *Amerasia Journal* 3 (Summer 1975): 40-58.

Docherty, Thomas, ed. *Postmodernism: A Reader*. New York: Columbia University Press, 1993.

Endo, Russell and William Wei. "On the Development of Asian American Studies Programs." In *Reflections on Shattered Windows: Promises and Prospects for Asian American Studies,* edited by Gary Y. Okihiro, Shirley Hune, Arthur A. Hansen, and John M. Liu. Pullman: Washington State University Press, 1988.

Foucault, Michel. *Power/Knowledge*. Edited by Colin Gordon. New York: Pantheon, 1980.

Fraser, Nancy and Linda J. Nicholson. "Social Criticism without Philosophy: An Encounter between Feminism and Postmodernism." In *Feminism/Postmodernism*, edited by Linda J. Nicholson. New York: Routledge, 1990.

Gergen, Kenneth J. *The Saturated Self.* New York: Basic Books, 1991.

Giddens, Anthony. *Modernity and Self-identity*. Stanford: Stanford University Press, 1991.

Giroux, Henry A. "Modernism, Postmodernism and Feminism: Rethinking the Boundaries of Educational Discourse." In *Postmodernism, Feminism, and Cultural Politics*, edited by Henry A. Giroux. Albany: State University of New York Press, 1991.

Habermas, Jurgen. "Modernity - an Incomplete Project." In *Postmodernism: A Reader*, edited by Thomas Docherty. New York: Columbia University Press, 1993.

Hartsock, Nancy. "Rethinking Modernism: Minority vs. Majority Theories." *Cultural Critique* 7 (Fall 1987): 187-206.

Harvey, David. *The Condition of Postmodernity*. Cambridge: Basil Blackwell, 1989.

Hodge, John L. "Equality: Beyond Dualism and Oppression." In *Anatomy of Racism*, edited by David T. Goldberg. Minneapolis: University of Minneapolis Press, 1990.

Jameson, Fredric. *Postmodernism or, the Cultural Logic of Late Capitalism*. Durham: Duke University Press, 1991.

Laclau, Ernesto. "Politics and the Limits of Modernity." In *Postmodernism: A Reader,* edited by Thomas Docherty. New York: Columbia University Press, 1993.

Liu, John. "Towards an Understanding of the Internal Colonial Model." In *Counterpoint: Perspectives on Asian America,* edited by Emma Gee. Los Angeles: UCLA Asian American Studies Center, 1976.

Liu, John, and Lucie Cheng. "A Dialogue on Race and Class: Asian American Studies and Marxism." In *The Left Academy: Marxist Scholarship on American Campuses,* edited by Bertell Ollman and Edward Vernoff. New York: Praeger, 1986.

Loo, Chalsa. "The 'Middle-aging' of Asian American Studies." In *Reflections on Shattered Windows: Promises and Prospects for Asian American Studies,* edited by Gary Y. Okihiro, Shirley Hune, Arthur A. Hansen, and John M. Liu. Pullman: Washington State University Press, 1988.

Mar, Don. "The Lost Second Generation of Asian American Scholars." In *Reflections on Shattered Windows: Promises and Prospects for Asian American Studies,* edited by Gary Y. Okihiro, Shirley Hune, Arthur A. Hansen, and John M. Liu. Pullman: Washington State University Press, 1988.

Okihiro, Gary Y. "African and Asian American Studies: A Comparative Analysis and Commentary." In *Asian Americans: Comparative and Global Perspectives,* edited by Shirley Hune, Hyung-chan Kim, Stephen S. Fugita, and Amy Ling. Pullman: Washington State University Press, 1991.

Omi, Michael. "It Just Ain't the Sixties No More: The Contemporary Dilemmas of Asian American Studies." In *Reflections on Shattered Windows: Promises and Prospects for Asian American Studies,* edited by Gary Y. Okihiro, Shirley Hune, Arthur A. Hansen, and John M. Liu. Pullman: Washington State University Press, 1988.

Palmer, Bryan D. *Descent into Discourse.* Philadelphia: Temple University Press, 1990.

Park, Robert. *Race and Culture.* New York: The Free Press, 1950.

Rosenau, Pauline M. *Post-modernism and the Social Sciences.* Princeton: Princeton University Press, 1992.

Said, Edward. *Orientalism.* New York: Pantheon, 1979.

Smart, Barry. *Modern Conditions, Postmodern Controversies.* London: Routledge, 1992.

Surh, Jerry. "Asian American Identity and Politics." *Amerasia Journal* 2: 2 (1974): 158-72.

Tong, Ben. "The Ghetto of the Mind." *Amerasia Journal* 1: 3 (1971): 1-31.

Postmodernism from the Edge: Asian American Identities

Dana Y. Takagi

It seems that these days everyone is talking about postmodernity and postmodernism.[1] The luminaries, Jameson, Derrida, Lacan, Lyotard, Habermas, and even Hegel (who has risen from the ashes of Marxism) are at the center of theoretical discussions of postmodernity—its meanings, implications, and icons. In turn, the work of these individuals has spawned a wide-ranging and often free-wheeling set of debates *across* the disciplines—from political science to sociology, literature to music, and art to philosophy. It is not that consideration of postmodernity has produced a singular cross-disciplinary perspective, but rather, that the questions raised by postmodernity have had an integrative function in the academy. The sharp edges separating history, philosophy, literature, and social science are softening. Postmodernism and its related theoretical movements—post-structuralism, existential feminism, semiotics, and deconstructionism—have tended to link rather than separate the disciplinary knowledge.

In the past several years, it has often been noted that virtually *every* corner of the academy has been touched by the discussion of postmodernity.[2] Even we, in Asian American studies, appear to have at least partly signed on to take part in this discussion. "Site(s)," the theme of the 1993 Annual Meeting of the Association for Asian American Studies, and "Crossing Boundaries," the theme for 1994, both signal an important shift in thematic orientation of Asian American studies. "Site(s)" in postmodernist lingo expands the modernist conception of place as geography to place as cognitive cartography.[3] Thus, a "site" is no longer simply the geographic place where it happens but is an arena of cognition that reveals to us the dialectical codes, representations, and subversions of space (and our understanding of space) of global capitalism.

Naturally, there are those who rejoice and those who lament the arrival of poststructuralist theory to Asian American studies. A chief and frequently heard complaint, that "they (postmodernists) have a language all their own," carries an ironic dose of anti-"immigrant" and assimilationist bias. Postmodernism, like the so-called recalcitrant new "immigrants," (read Asian or Latino) who are accused of clinging stubbornly to their own language—a language that we do not all have—has occasioned a "nationalist" backlash over language. The plea for a common language seems at first glance a reasonable request. But that we in Asian American studies, an *a priori* interdisciplinary project, are able to speak across the jargons of the disciplines, suggests that there is something more at stake than simply language. In what follows, I want to outline several issues that, when the obfuscating charges over language are abandoned, remain as urgent areas of theoretical debate for Asian American studies.

It is difficult, if not impossible, to say *exactly* what postmodernity *is*. But our inability to point to a clear consensus among critics and theorists on what constitutes the postmodern condition is a sign of healthy debate and uncertainty rather than intellectual incompetence.[4] At best, in summary, we can say there are certain basic themes common to postmodernist theories even though there is considerable difference amongst theorists on what exactly constitutes the postmodern (e.g. aesthetic v. cultural and political realities).[5] For example, a central feature of the debates about the postmodern is that *everything* we know of is in crisis—starting with Enlightenment ideals followed by the ever after—forms of reason, the construction of knowledge, notions of subjectivity, objectivity, assumptions about time and space, the relationship between rational thought or apprehension of the material world, and perhaps most important of all, theory itself. In short, not only is everything we know about in crisis, but the way that we think we "know" is a central part of the crisis.[6]

Readers will note that up to this moment, I have said nothing of feminism and feminist theory. In this discussion, I have segregated feminism from postmodernism because of the very important differences and debates between these two fields. Feminist theory, like postmodernist theory, is not a singular body of theory or knowledge, and moreover, should not be confused or equated with postmodernism. While there exists a substantial and growing core of feminists (which include of course, male writers) who say they have made the postmodern "turn," there remains a vocal and articulate group who have not.[7] More importantly, the relationship between feminism and postmodernism is, I think, best characterized as an uneasy one marked by conflict and regular trading of criticisms.[8] A number of feminists, while generally welcoming of postmodernism are wary of what postmodernism *seems* to demand of feminist theory.

Two areas of criticism central to the divide between feminism and postmodernism are the relation between politics and postmodernist theory, and the status of the category "women" and its relationship to theory. For example, a core element of feminism for many writers has been the expressly *political* nature of a feminist research agenda. That postmodernist theories tend to challenge foundationalism of any sort, particularly of politics, has been of great concern to many feminist, including those who are sympathetic to post-structuralism. For example, Fraser and Nicholson (1993) adopt an anti-metanarrative stance simultaneous with their lament that postmodernism (especially Lyotard) reflects an uncomfortably weak expression of social criticism.[9] In a different vein of criticism, Morris (1993) updates the "old" complaint that theory work tends to exclude women's experiences. She notes that in the "new" theory, women are relegated to the all too familiar sidelines of theory construction. If women are not producers of theory, then they do not occupy a central place as constitutive subjects either, says Morris (1993). In a revealing passage, Morris (1993) critically analyzes what she views as a tendency in the postmodernist literature to see feminism "*as* postmodernist but not as 'engaging' in debate." In other words, while feminism may have been an enabling aspect of postmodernist theory, women as subjects, continue to be baffling, absent, and silent.[10]

Despite these criticisms, there has been a concerted move by American feminists toward postmodernist theories since the late 1980s. The engagement with postmodernist theory, most explicitly seen in the works of Alice Jardine, Donna Haraway, Joan Scott, Janet Wolff, and Judith Butler to list some of the better known names on the marquee, has set off debates within feminist circles over the relationship of feminism to postmodernism.

The relationship between feminism and postmodernism is significant for us to consider because it is highly suggestive of a parallel set of comparisons between Asian American studies (and ethnic studies) and postmodernism. Afterall, women's studies programs, the institutional location for much of American feminist theory, shares with Asian American studies a common organizational experience. Although women's studies and ethnic studies differ in substantive focus, both are attempting to gain greater institutional security, are increasingly concerned with attempts to appropriate "our" subject matter, and are clamoring for intellectual respectability at the university. By invoking a comparison between feminism, women's studies, and ethnic studies, am I saying that WE should be postmodernist because THEY are? Certainly not. But I am suggesting that we should be thinking about why, if we are organizationally/institutionally situated in similar ways to many feminists, we are so much less concerned with the impact of the debates in postmodernism theory on Asian American studies?

As I noted earlier, it is not that postmodernism and post-structuralist theory have gone unnoticed in Asian American and ethnic studies. Rather, I am suggesting that we look more closely at the way in which we in ethnic studies have appropriated postmodernist terms and concepts to service our study of Asian America. Even though the themes of the 1993 and 1994 annual meetings of the Association for Asian American Studies suggest that we are not too far out of sync with theoretical currents in other disciplines, we are, in my opinion, more likely to APPLY the terms associated with postmodernist discourse to an Asian American experience than we are to invoke Asian America to discuss the context in which debates about postmodernism might be further considered, developed, changed, or even forsworn. In other words, we *borrow from* rather than *invest in* debates about the postmodern. I want to be very clear here in saying that while I might take a partisan position on postmodernism and ethnic studies, I am not arguing for a particular position. Rather, I am arguing for US having more theoretical arguments.

Of course, there is the potential for a response of the type described by Morris (1993), who notes that many feminists have turned a deaf ear, waiting patiently for the postmodernist wave to pass. There is that tendency among many of us in Asian American studies, that is, to seek refuge from postmodernism because "those" debates are not about "us"; Foucault never even acknowledged an Asian diaspora, the Lacanian subject is never Bruce Lee, Daniel Inouye, or even Connie Chung, and, postmodern aesthetics is as Asian American as *Blade Runner*, which is to say, hardly. Another tendency among us is the feeling that there might be something there (in postmodernism) but that the language is burdensome and pretentious—indeed, that postmodernism is a better argument for "English only" than are ethnic enclaves like Monterey Park. All those slashes, diacriticals, parentheses, and brackets—what exactly is being disrupted except language which is precisely the point.

I suggest below two reasons why we in Asian American (and by extension, ethnic) studies might listen up, read up, and decipher the hieroglyphics of postmodernism. One is that the issues which are the grist for postmodernist and feminist mills are very much about ethnic and racial minorities, in particular, the way that we write about them. A second reason for enlarging the domains of our theoretical imaginations is that an increasing number of identity politics theorists who draw their life-force from post-structuralist thinkers, seem to be turning their sights toward racism, race relations, and racial identities. Of course, ethnic studies is not the exclusive domain of identity politics, nor should it be, but clearly the issues of identity formation which occupy those who write mainly about gender or class now overlap with Asian Americanists who write explicitly about race.

While we are not too late to enter the theoretical fray of postmodernist debates, we cannot afford to enter such debates in the ways we have entered theory discussions in the past. In the past, we have, I think, taken the liberty of borrowing concepts from other disciplines that seem useful to US—terms like "segmented labor markets," "psychoanalytic" models, the concept of "strangers," and so on. But the weakness of our borrowing habit is that we deploy these concepts decontexualized of their original meanings.

But the debates about feminism and postmodernity have altered the very terms on which we "think" about and "use" theory. As a discipline, we do not, I think, tend to enroll Asian American experiences in interdisciplinary debates; rather, we tend to *deploy* theory, often in an *ad hoc* fashion, to service our descriptions of Asian America. The result is that we stand at the edge of theoretical debates rather than sit in their midst. Hence, I use the phrase, "postmodernism from the edge," to describe how we in Asian American studies may be unwittingly setting ourselves up to sit on the outer fringes of postmodernist theory.[11]

There are, I think, three major areas of discussion in postmodernism and feminism that are especially crucial for us in Asian American and ethnic studies—theorizing the subject, the role of experience in narratives, and politics in postmodern society. While these topics are not expressly about Asian Americans, the terms and consequences of the debates hold important intellectual and institutional consequences for Asian American studies.

One issue concerns the broad question of identity formation of the Subject. A commonplace reading of postmodernist theory is that subjects, once thought to be *centered* in rationalist thought and coherent/integrated knowledge are now *decentered*, that is, multiply determined by competing and conflicting identit*ies*. However, I think the gist of claims about decenteredness challenge us to theory rather than to describe Asian American identities. In particular, for example, a question such as, "how should we theorize the relationship of the individual to society?" a basic question guiding early twentieth century American sociology, can now be re-phrased at the end of the decade, "what is the Subject?" or in the case of Asian American studies, "what is an Asian American Subject?"[12]

A second issue, one which has been at the core of feminist research and ethnic studies as well, is "experience." We rely heavily on life histories, oral histories, depth interviews, and in general, the "telling" of Asian American experiences, to fill in the gaps where the disciplines, history/sociology/political science/economics/literature, have marginalized or excluded Asian Americans. But postmodernists and feminists are increasingly suspicious of such accounts and ask whether such accounts are profitable for research. The major critics, and feminists have I think taken the lead on this matter, have suggested that experience represents a new "foundationalism"—by swearing out a "truth" that avoids challenges by consumers of the account. The real question, according to Scott (1990) who has most sharply posed this debate, is not experience itself but why the discursive telling of experience became possible at any given historical moment.

Third, neighboring the topics of the subject and experience, is the issue of politics. Ethnic studies shares with women's studies and feminism, an expressly political stance. Postmodernism's challenge to conceptions of rationalized subjects extends to how subjects apprehend the world in which they live. Politics, of course, is a central piece of apprehending the external world. But politics is based on our ability to make ethical, fair, and normative judgments when it is precisely those bases for making judgments that has slipped away (or never really existed) with totalizing narratives. Has postmodernism tossed out politics with totalizing narratives? As Docherty notes in his introduction to *Postmodernism: A Reader*, "It is here that the real political burden and trajectory of the postmodern is to be found: the search for a just politics, or the search for just a politics" (1993:27).

Historically, there has been a tacit embrace of a civil rights agenda in Asian American studies. But is that agenda still tenable, particularly in the wake of waning enthusiasm following various political struggles that have strained the terms of coalition?[13] The question may be weighty in theoretical terms but also has enormous pragmatic consequences for contemporary Asian American communities.

I mention the above areas in an effort to sketch some concerns that affect US because they are at the core of assumptions about how we approach the study of Asian America. But my larger point is not that we should be thinking about how to approach or re-envision Asian American studies in light of postmodernist and feminist theoretical intervention. My point is that discussion and debate about Asian America can no longer afford to move apart, particularly in an intellectual sense, from postmodernism and feminism.

The above mentioned topics and questions have cut a wide swath through the traditional disciplines—literature, history, anthropology, sociology, geography, and so on. In effect, there has been a blurring of disciplinary boundaries that manifests itself both in institutional arenas and in intellectual life. For example, institutionally, the emergence of programs or academic units that are interdisciplinary, like cultural studies programs that link film, art, music, literature, social sciences, and history in an organizational unit, goes beyond singular disciplinary knowledges. And in the arena of intellectual life, the emergence of journals such as *Cultural Studies* and *Critical Inquiry* appeal to a variety of disciplinary interests.

That disciplinary lines weaken under the weight of postmodernist queries raises an interesting question for Asian American and ethnic studies, fields which are already, by definition, interdisciplinary projects. If one of the effects of post-structuralism has been to produce an interdisciplinary public intellectual life, then why has ethnic studies, a program conceptualized as interdisciplinary research, not been central to the organizational and intellectual center of such debates? The broader question here concerns our relationship to disciplinary debate and asks, what is the impact of feminist and postmodernist debates on the intellectual and research practices of Asian American and ethnic studies and vice versa?

I do not pretend to have more than a sketchy answer to this question. But let me suggest, if only as a means for stimulating further discussion of the matter, that as we turn toward the intellectual spaces created by postmodernist and feminist debate, we might take a hard look at our relationship to disciplines and inter-disciplines. That look will reveal a central paradox about Asian American and ethnic studies—which is that while we are *organizationally* interdisciplinary, we are not, for the most part, *intellectually* interdisciplinary. What I mean by this is that while Asian American studies programs are staffed by individuals who have disciplinary specialties, we do not, in general, debate across the disciplines, that is, argue over similar or separate methods, theories, approaches to our common subject matter, the historical experiences of Asian America. Indeed, we have, I think, been less than vigilant at pushing ourselves toward interdisciplinary debate.[14] Thus postmodernism's call to us is an opening of possibilities— debate across disciplinary boundaries both in and outside Asian American studies.

Notes

1. The appearance of several anthologies about postmodernism is but one sign of its importance in academic debates. See for example, Docherty (1993); and Nicholson (1990).
2. Interestingly enough, there is an integrative quality to the sweeping discussions of postmodernism. A range of topics related to the status of knowledge in different disciplines became recognizable as epistemological questions across the disciplines.
3. This point is made by Jameson (1991).
4. See for contrasting examples of interpretation of the postmodern Habermas (1993) and Lyotard (1993) on the possibility of consensus through discursive politics.
5. The most oft-cited themes include: (a) challenging the universality of meta-narratives; (b) fragmentation and pluralism of voice and subjects; and (c) radical shift and understanding of discursive practices.
6. In sociology for example, the subfields sociology of knowledge, sociology of culture, and social problems theory became invested in postmodernist debates relatively early compared with other parts of the discipline precisely because of postmodernist discussions about HOW we know.
7. See for example, Hartsock (1990) and Bordo (1990).
8. See for example, Morris (1993), Fraser and Nicholson (1990), and especially Brown (1991).
9. Fraser and Nicholson (1993) argue for an intermediate position between postmodernist thinking and feminist theory to serve as a basis for a postmodern feminism.
10. Morris's discussion is a compelling one: the relationship of women and feminism to postmodernism is to be either, "situated" in postmodernism as topics of commentary but not as postmodernist theorists, or assume the familiar stance of the "excluded" and hence silent women who continue as they have done so historically, to baffle men.
11. Sitting at the edges of theoretical debates bears, in my opinion, a heavy disciplinary cost, namely, that studies of the Asian diaspora become ever more marginalized from public intellectual discussions outside Asian American and ethnic studies.
12. There are numerous questions animated by postmodernist claims that might be examined in the context of Asian American communities. For example, how should we translate the theoretical significance of postmodernist claims about the disappearance of the subject, to racialized experiences in Asian American communities? Do the claims about loss of personal style and an orientation toward pastiche function similarly in different ethnic communities?
13. In particular, I am thinking of the controversy over admissions and inter-racial conflict most recently dramatized in Los Angeles in 1992, as examples of fissures in political coalitions.

14. The "new" wave of social theory demands that we go beyond our disciplinary moorings—reading across fields as well as within fields.

References

Bordo, Susan. "Feminism, Postmodernism, and Gender-Scepticism." In *Feminism/Postmodernism,* edited by Linda J. Nicholson. New York: Routledge, 1990.

Brown, Wendy. "Postmodern Exposures, Feminist Hesitations." *Difference* 3 (1991):63-84.

Docherty, Thomas, ed. *Postmodernism: A Reader.* New York: Columbia University Press, 1993.

Fraser, Nancy and Linda Nicholson. "Social Criticism without Philosophy: An Encounter between Feminism and Postmodernism." In *Postmodernism: A Reader,* edited by Thomas Docherty. New York: Columbia University Press, 1993.

Habermas, Jürgen. "The Entry into Postmodernity: Nietzsche as a Turning Point." In *Postmoderism: A Reader,* edited by Thomas Docherty. New York: Columbia University Press, 1993.

Hartsock, Nancy. "Foucault on Power: A Theory for Women?" In *Feminism/Postmodernism,* edited by Linda J. Nicholson. New York: Routledge, 1990.

Harvey, David. *The Condition of Postmodernity.* Cambridge: Basil Blackwell, 1989.

Jameson, Frederic. "Postmodernism, or the Cultural Logic of Late Capitalism." *New Left Review* 146 (1984):53-92.

Lyotard, Francois. "Answering the Question: What Is Postmodernism." In *Postmodernism: A Reader,* edited by Thomas Docherty. New York: Columbia University Press, 1993.

Morris, Meaghan. "Feminism, Reading, Postmodernism." In *Postmodernism: A Reader,* edited by Thomas Docherty. New York: Columbia University Press, 1993.

Nicholson, Linda J., ed. *Feminism/Postmodernism.* New York: Routledge, 1990.

Scott, Joan. "Experience." In *Feminists Theorize the Political,* edited by Judith Butler and Joan W. Scott. New York: Routledge, 1993.

Toward an Asian (American) Cultural Studies: Postmodernism and the "Peril of Yellow Capital and Labor"

Colleen Lye

In responding to the charge of investigating the "limitations and possibilities of postmodernism and feminism for Asian American studies," I do not presume to be able to settle such long-debated and unresolved questions as: What is postmodernism?[1] What kind of feminism are we talking about? What is the relationship between postmodernism and feminism? I will take as a necessary starting point, however, the presumption of making a categorical distinction between postmodernism and feminism, despite their status as mutually conditioning and implicated discourses. To paraphrase Margaret Ferguson and Jennifer Wicke, postmodernism can be thought of as the name for the way we live now, while feminism is a form of contestation (Ferguson and Wicke 1992:1-2). I see Asian American studies too as a contestatory project, and in that sense, feminism and Asian American studies are the parallel terms; where their political agendas intersect may be suggested by what I will have to say about post-Fordism as an intrinsic component of postmodernism. My interest in this discussion lies in the question not of how Asian American studies might "acquire" theory conceived as commodity tool, but of how it may intervene in a larger theoretical and social formation which we take the liberty of calling "postmodern." My present concerns are therefore to try to locate subjects of relevance to Asian Americanists within a prevailing formation that extends far beyond this still discursively marginal discipline. My belief is that Asian American studies is uniquely placed to make important interventions in hegemonic national discourses, but this also requires a radical rethinking of its project.

To attempt to locate Asian American studies within a prevailing theoretical framework is to immediately remark on its relative absence. Meaghan

Morris seems to be one of few cultural critics, for example, to have noticed that the Pacific Rim was missing from the cultural studies map drawn up by the mega-conference at Champagne-Urbana (Grossberg, Nelson, and Treichler 1992:476). But the neglect of the subject of "Asia" by broad cultural studies discussions is not to be redressed by putting "Asia" back in, nor is it simply a question of extending theory's reach to subjects which have until now been left standing on the margins. Instead, it may be more useful to read "Asia's" absence within cultural discussions as a symptomatic occlusion, one connected to "Asia's" importance to contemporary reformulations of the economic, on which the notion of postmodernism's universality depends. In this sense, without being a subject of postmodernist discourse, "Asia" has already been figured by it.

Insofar as they envision no outside to the postmodern condition, Marxist formulations of postmodernism have participated in the production of an apocalyptic narrative in which no possibilities of social change can any longer be imagined. Warren Montag, for example, critiques Fredric Jameson's proclamation of an End to Art as a confusion of the disintegration of the object with a crisis of Marxism's own method. According to Montag, Jameson's attempt at a "cognitive mapping" of postmodernism as the cultural dominant of late capitalism ironically opens the way to postmodern apostles Lyotard and Baudrillard, who simply add Marxism to the list of radical losses (Montag 1988:99; Lyotard 1984; Baudrillard 1981, 1983). Meaghan Morris even goes so far as to call postmodernism itself a "phantasmagoria" of Marxism meditating upon its own death.[2] This is not to underestimate the degree to which Marxist theories of postmodernism of postmodernity are outflanked by influential and widespread theoretical developments identified as "post-Marxist." The point is that simply positing a link between postmodernism and the domination processes of late capitalism can differ from a celebratory view only in its evaluation of postmodernism. As a description of the cultural object, it agrees with a Fukuyamian view of the "end of history" in which liberal democracy no longer faces any systemic challenge on the level of universal ideas (Fukuyama 1992). In part, this problem of the "postmodern totality" derives from the way capitalism is itself often represented within Marxist theory as, what Marxist-feminist critic J. K. Gibson-Graham calls, "an impossible object of transformation" (1992:5).

Yet the very totality of postmodernism itself has depended upon a certain spatial imaginary of inside and outside. Against the universality of postmodernism presumed by theorists such as Baudrillard and Lyotard,

Jennifer Wicke follows Gayatri Spivak in pointing out how postmodernism inscribes a pre-modern in a different sense (Spivak 1988:171; Wicke 1988:156). Both Spivak and Wicke underscore the spatial specificity of postmodern subject-production by turning our attention toward the Sri Lankan woman who has to work 2,287 minutes to buy a T-shirt, and the female microchip assembly worker in the Philippines. As a symbol of the information technologies that characterize postmodernism, the particular product assembled by the Filipina worker helps expose how a belief in the consumer character of the postmodern condition depends upon rendering invisible the processes of production which have shifted to distant sites. In another widely read essay, Donna Haraway also turns to the Asian female microchip worker as a representative cyborg who may "guide effective oppositional strategies" for a renewed socialist feminism in the United States (Haraway 1989:178). Whether as a subject of super-exploitation at the periphery who helps sustain postmodern lifestyles at the center, or as a subject experiencing the encroachment of capitalist practices who exemplifies a postmodern politics of resistance, the Asian woman worker is invoked by materialist critics either to mark an outside to postmodernism, or to show that postmodernism has no outside.

The significance of the Asian woman worker to either position, of course, lies in the decentering of capitalist production processes from Euro-America which have marked a historical shift in the primary role of the periphery from the extraction of raw materials to the extraction of surplus-value from labor, a labor which has shown itself capable of producing *increasingly* value-added commodities. The most striking consequence of this has been actual capital accumulation outside the "West," throwing into question any notion of capitalism based upon the model of a single center radially expanding upon multiple peripheries. "Asia" is the primary site of that shift and therefore, in the discourses of postmodernism, the most oft-invoked sign of capitalism's decentering. Not so long ago the subject of anxieties about a domino theory of communist revolution, "Asia" is now identified with the notion of the "economic miracle." The very possibility of linking the terms "Japan" and "postmodernism" however tentatively, as the book *Postmodernism and Japan* has illustrated, is enabled as Masao Miyoshi and H. D. Harootunian note, by the fundamental success of Japan's economy (1989:x).

The hegemonic construction of Asia as economic subject has been critical to, on the one hand, problematizing monochronic ideas of capitalist development, and on the other, helping seal the triumph of capitalist ideology. Francis Fukuyama's use of the Newly Industrializing Countries (NICs) to debunk theories of dependency and underdevelopment is a case in point. Regardless of the heterogeneity of positions occupied by various Asian countries within the new international division of labor from mainland China (with the lowest labor costs, soon to be outdone by Vietnam) to South Korea (with the highest labor costs), Asia is important because it represents the "smart choice" of the capitalist path of development. That the spectacle of Asia is being directed at Marxist or neo-Marxist viewership is made amply clear when Fukuyama writes: "The East Asian economic miracle was carefully observed around the world, nowhere more than in the communist bloc" (1992: 41).

The figuration of "Asia" within theoretical debates about our "postmodern" condition is thus indicative of a material economic development that can authorize a range of politically heterogeneous constructions. Asia can represent either an exemplary subject of labor (hardworking, non-confrontational) or an exemplary subject of capital (organized, surplus). This dual representation may enter into contradiction, or be mobilized to help doubly regulate and discipline production forces in the United States. "Economic Asia" has the effect of sapping the power of Eurocentric discourses—hence those who admire Japanese business techniques are often the most ardent critics of racist forms of Japan-bashing—but it does function to consolidate "proof" of the universality of capitalism. Thus, we must pay attention to representations of Asia not because "dominant narrative conventions" fail to grasp our multiplicity, but because they form a keystone in the architecture of contemporary discourses of capitalist hegemony against which Marxist thinkers are having trouble formulating a defense. Asian American critics, precisely because of the centrality of constructions of the subject of Asia and of Asians to these discourses, are in an excellent position to make powerful interventions in the dominant understanding of postmodernism and late capitalism.

What does the subject of Asia have to do with Asian American positionality? Here we must turn to the other way in which the critique of Jameson has been launched. If some critics have pointed to the inscription of the "pre-modern" in a different scene, others have shown that space to be "closer to home." The invisibility of super-exploitation in Asia is matched by the invisible economy that now sustains so many First World nations. Mike Davis points out how L.A.'s Bonaventure Hotel, implicitly celebrated in Jameson's politically inattentive analysis, actually signals the polarization of the city into radically antagonistic spaces. As such, Davis argues that postmodernism needs to be redefined as a logic of social control whose "popular" texture consists of a deeply anti-urban impulse in the face of Third World immigrant arrival (1988:86-87). Architecturally, a postmodernist aesthetic marks the transformation of the metropolis into the image of the colonial city that once stood at the periphery. Davis' reading of L.A. is in line with other theorists of post-Fordism and flexible accumulation such as Swasti Mitter, who shows how a homework economy subcontracts for multinationals not just in the periphery but at the heart of the metropolitan center (1986). The gendering and ethnicization of labor suggested by the exemplary figure of the Asian woman worker is thus carried to a spatially universal completion. In this account, postmodernism is understood not as an aesthetic that erases historical knowledge of its material dependence upon exploitation elsewhere, but as an aesthetic which itself reflects a response to the Third Worldization of labor at home. Thus, if one critique of postmodernism turns our gaze upon the export-processing zone, the other material dimension thought to be constitutive of the postmodern imaginary is transnational migrancy.

The extent to which this phenomenon is *not* associated with Asians as with other migrant groups in the U.S.—particularly Chicanos—reflects how hegemonic U.S. discourses of race and class have effectively positioned Asian Americans among other racialized identities. The inclusion of Asian Americans within the coalitional construct articulated by the 1968-69 Third World strike at San Francisco State and U.C. Berkeley has over the last two or so decades been increasingly difficult to sustain. In the period of reaction to the civil rights challenge to the myths of racial equality, Asian Americans have come to function as the exemplary figure of otherness crucial to the recuperation of equal opportunity. Within the hegemonic nationalist discourse of immigration, the *migrant* subaltern is reconstituted as the *immigrant* citizen-subject and absorbed into a narrative of upward mobility, released from the iron cage of race and into ethnicity. There are striking parallels between the way in which "Asia" functions within a global frame to debunk dependency theory and the way in which "Asian Americans" are used to shore up a national ideology of "equal opportunity." The extent to which Ethnic Studies as a counter-hegemonic project has not succeeded in demolishing the dominant, and popular, perception of the "Black-Asian conflict" may tell us something about the problems of its own entrapment within a discourse of racial exclusion that cannot make visible the deeply-vested stakes of that construction. The 1992 L.A. riots, as well as the Korean-Black grocery store conflicts in New York City, are the most sensational examples of the construction of the economic subject of Asia—the "Peril of Yellow Capital and Labor," whose oppression of non-productive brown and black bodies introduces the necessity of mediation by a magnanimous white law.

I would like to end by reading the story of the "smuggling" of Chinese into the United States which has recently so captured public attention and whose spectacularity has served to provide the moral justification for wholesale reevaluation and stiffening of this nation's immigration and asylum laws.[3] This is how the story goes. The number of Chinese entering illegally is estimated to triple the number immigrating legally. In order to pay off the passage price of U.S. $30,000 to the smugglers, the illegal alien is effectively "indentured" to hard labor at exploitative wages for many years after arrival. One of the major consequences of this illegal inflow has been the expansion of Asian mafia operations which have discovered the profitability of human cargo. The elements of which this story is composed tap an abundance of issues, but I will restrict myself to making three points, based on coverage by Pamela Burdman in the *San Francisco Chronicle*, the first major daily to run a special investigative series on the topic in April 1992.

(1) The news story's use of visual analogies to slave cargoes as well as narrative conventions of the American dream reveal the difficulty of presenting the case of transmigration as a form of labor that is either fully coerced or fully willed. Within the ideology of capitalism as a liberal democracy, the news narrative must overlook the necessary contradiction between law and capital. Thus, Burdman remarks, "if it were legal, the traffic in humans would be one of the success stories of contemporary capitalism," a hypothetical proposition that covers over the fact that the generation of such extraordinary surplus value derives precisely from the illegalization of a large sector of this country's labor demand.

(2) As against an underground economy represented as primitively exploitative (like slavery), twentieth century law is represented as "humanitarian." A U.S. assistant attorney is cited as saying "the main reason to eradicate this sort of crime is the abuse of the individuals who are being trafficked." On the one hand, we are presented with a transnational Asian criminal network in the illicit pursuit of profit through the "primitive trade" in human flesh—on the other hand, a humane and nationally confined, and therefore helpless, U.S. law. The illegal Chinese aliens themselves are victims in this narrative, as they are guilty of nothing other than the desire foundational to and ideologically legitimated by U.S. national identity.

However, the underground passage by which they enter, and the underground economy and criminal networks within which they are enmeshed, means that their innocent desire financially supports, and often itself shades into criminal activity. Thus, in the case of both the smugglers and the smuggled, the transnational Asian pursuit of capital, even when it involves the lauded commitment to hard labor, lies outside the law.

(3) The Asian American critic is having difficulty gaining critical purchase on the dilemma of exploitation on the one hand, and border policing on the other. Given the foundationalist critique of Asian exclusion within Asian American studies, it may strike us as ironic that some Asian American critics are responding by endorsing the government's efforts to stem the migrant tide. What seems to be a reversal of an Asian American political position on "immigration" discloses the inevitable inconsistencies of a position based solely upon the principle of racial exclusion, a critical perspective whose confinement to a national frame can all too easily devolve into a *nationalist* position. The very basis of appeal to U.S. law to stop the exploitative peddling of the American dream which it is simultaneously represented as helpless to stop depends upon investing it with a humanitarianism that is counterposed to the negative example of other nations' laws—Chinese law which is faulty and corrupt (because complicitous in illegal emigration) or Japanese law which is efficient and ruthless (because uncompromising toward illegal immigration). Yet whether this "late capitalist" form of American indentured labor is so different from its nineteenth century form under which most Asians entered this country after all needs to be seriously considered, but in terms that incorporate an understanding of the impact of global capital and labor flow upon each particular national negotiation of race and citizenship.

I will conclude by insisting that the connection between the Third World inside and the Third World outside can simply no longer be made at the analogical level. A critique based upon the founding logic of Asian exclusion—to which Asian liberation struggles were not confined—has shown itself to be insufficiently resistant to hegemonic immigration discourses of inclusion. Indeed, a politics of resistance based upon exclusion may well be a function of the logic of inclusion, insofar as it only knows how to read the phenomenon of transmigration as a desire for national belonging. The reality of transmigration gives us a material basis for linking up Asian communities within and beyond U.S. borders, as well as the interests of Asian communities with those of other minority groups, but this means expanding our object of analysis beyond the nation-state and our analytical frame beyond the governance of nationalist history. Indeed, it is precisely the contradiction between global capital and national law in the instance of illegal immigration that needs to be examined, so as to open up the arena of analysis to those arriving in upwards of 100,000 a year who are presently occluded by a liberal citizen-subject based politics.

Otherwise, the *intellectual* left may well be the last of all to attend to the persuasive logic of capital. In virtually every news story about the South Central post-1992 L.A. riots, we are being told that political-legal confrontation is a thing of the past and that starting black businesses is now at the head of the civil rights agenda. Unless we are willing to admit that Francis Fukuyama is right, that we can no longer think of any better alternative to "free-market economics," our politics must re-engage the terrain that may ironically provide the lever for a renewed interracial solidarity. Post-Fordism's particular preference for the doubly invisible and flexible labor of migrant women may also provide the basis for reopening a theory of materialist feminism that has vanished with the onset of what Teresa Ebert calls a "ludic postmodern feminism" (1993). And, at the other end of the scale of values-production, as subjects to whom the "glass ceiling" is famously peculiar, the Asian American minority and women may have further reason for common ground. For it is perhaps from the position of identities most heterogeneous in their relation to capital, including the most privileged and empowered of us, that we are forced to complicate and question our essentializing politics of identity on which Asian American studies, feminism, and so much else is founded.

Notes

1. I would like to thank Michael Berkowitz for his clips from the *San Francisco Chronicle*, and Timothy Watson and Nikhil Pal Singh for reading drafts of this paper.
2. Based on a conversation with Joe Cleary, Qadri Ismail, Rebecca McLennan, Meaghan Morris, Nikhil Pal Singh, and Alys Weinbaum.
3. The spectacularity of the "smuggled Chinese" can at once be grasped when we compare the 3,250 illegal Chinese apprehended in the period October 1992-August 1993 to the same number of illegal Mexicans apprehended and deported *daily*. Prior to the major press story concerning the "smuggled Chinese," numerous anti-immigrant bills were already on the agenda in California. Public alarm surrounding this story's headlines, however, has legitimated a deeply reactionary set of articulations on citizenship by government officials in the form of proposals ranging from the informal to the legislative. Most noticeably, those recognized as "liberal" Democrats have been among the foremost of those eager to "crack down" on immigration. Among the government responses are: (1) an August 9, 1993 letter by the California Republican Governor

Pete Wilson in the West Coast edition proposing, among other things, that public education be denied children who are illegal aliens, and that citizenship no longer be granted to the children of illegal aliens born on U.S. soil; (2) the Expedited Exclusion and Alien Smuggling Enhanced Penalties Act (S13333) proposed by Senator Edward Kennedy, and backed by the Clinton administration, which allows for the summary dismissal of people with no or false documents at the port of entry unless "credible fear" can be proved. As against the current United Nations convention that a refugee applicant be given consideration as long as the refugee has not already been "safely resettled" in another country, this bill insists that the U.S. be the first port-of-call for a person to be able to apply for refugee status; a mere stop-over in any other country considered "safe" prior to U.S. arrival in the U.S. warrants deportation to that country. The bill also greatly enhances the investigatory and surveillance powers of the Immigration and Naturalization Service, including wiretapping, etc. The enhanced penalties provision raises the penalty for smuggling from five to ten years per alien, and moreover, does not distinguish between smuggling for profit or not for profit— thus subjecting sanctuary movement activists to the same penalties; (3) a Mazzoli bill under consideration in the House that limits the period of time in which a person must file a notice of an intent to file an asylum application to thirty days after entry in the U.S., and the actual application to sixty days; and (4) California Democratic Senators Diane Feinstein and Barbara Boxer's Senate proposals that the National Guard be used for increased border patrols and that a $1 toll be charged for border crossing.

References

Baudrillard, Jean. *For a Critique of the Political Economy of the Sign*. St. Louis: Telos Press, 1981.

____. *In the Shadow of the Silent Majorities*. New York: Semiotexte(e) Foreign Agent Series, 1983.

Burdman, Pamela. "Business of Human Smuggling Tests U.S. Immigration Policies." *San Francisco Chronicle*, 30 April 1993.

____. "Grim Life for Smuggled Chinese—American Dream Sours in NY." *San Francisco Chronicle*, 29 April 1993.

____. "How Gangsters Cash in on Human Smuggling." *San Francisco Chronicle*, 28 April 1993.

____. "Huge Boom in Human Smuggling—Inside Story of Flight from China." *San Francisco Chronicle*, 27 April 1993.

Davis, Mike. "Urban Renaissance and the Spirit of Postmodernism." In *Postmodernism and Its Discontents*, edited by E. Ann Kaplan. London: Verso, 1988.

Ebert, Teresa. "Ludic Feminism, the Body, Performance and Labor: Bringing Materialism Back in Feminist Cultural Studies." *Cultural Critique* (Winter 1993): 5-50.

Ferguson, Margaret and Jennifer Wicke. "Introduction: Feminism and Postmodernism; or The Way We Live Now." *Boundary 2* 19 (Summer 1992): 1-9.

Fukuyama, Francis. *The End of History and the Last Man*. New York: Avon Books, 1992.

Gibson-Graham, J. K. "Waiting for the Revolution or How to Smash Capitalism while Working at Home in Your Spare Time." Paper presented at plenary session of the "Marxism in the New World Order: Crises and Possibilities" conference, University of Massachusetts, Amherst, 12-14 November 1992.

Grossberg, Lawrence, Cary Nelson, and Paula A. Treichler, eds. *Cultural Studies*. New York: Routledge, 1992.

Haraway, Donna. "A Manifesto for Cyborgs." In *Coming to Terms*, edited by Elizabeth Weed. New York: Routledge, 1989.

Jameson, Fredric. "Postmodernism and the Logic of Late Capitalism—Postmodernism and Consumer Society." In *Postmodernism and Its Discontents*, edited by E. Ann Kaplan. London: Verso, 1988.

Lyotard, Jean-Francois. *The Postmodern Condition*. Minneapolis: University of Minnesota Press, 1984.

Mitter, Swasti. *Common Fate, Common Bond*. London: Pluto Press, 1986.

Miyoshi, Masao and H. D. Harootunian, eds. *Postmodernism and Japan*. Durham: Duke University Press, 1989.

Montag, Warren. "What Is at Stake in the Debate on Postmodernism?" In *Postmodernism and Its Discontents*, edited by E. Ann Kaplan. London: Verso, 1988.

Spivak, Gayatri. "Scattered Speculations on the Question of Value." In *In Other Worlds*, New York: Routledge, 1988.

Wicke, Jennifer. "Postmodernism: The Perfume of Information." *Yale Journal of Criticism* 1 (Spring 1988): 145-60.

"Sheer Elegance": The Intersection of Woman and "the Orient"[1]

Mary Ting Yi Lui

An "exotic" Asian woman stands in front of the window of a penthouse apartment overlooking a night time scene somewhere in "the Orient." Her straight long shiny black hair in a "China doll" haircut lightly brushes the shoulders of her bright scarlet silk dress. She begins describing to the television viewing audience the elegance and sensuousness of silk and its worth. Lounging across a plush pink satin chaise, with her legs fully extended and showing off the smoothness and sheerness of her pantyhose, she finishes her discussion of silk by introducing the L'eggs new "Sheer Elegance" pantyhose line—the pantyhose "that looks and feels like real silk."

In the early 1980s, L'eggs Products began an advertising campaign to introduce a new line of pantyhose—"Sheer Elegance." Unlike the ordinary nylons worn by women working in nine-to-five jobs, they were meant for occasions calling for "sheer elegance." These television and magazine advertisements, instead of employing Caucasian models, usually portrayed Asian women wearing sheer silk stockings while discussing the mysteries of "the Orient," enticing the audience into buying these exotic wares from Asia. The advertisements were instantly memorable because their use of Asian models was enough to make audiences note that these pantyhose were "different."

"The Orient" as depicted in these advertisements is distinctly linked with "the feminine" and constitutes a mysterious "Other" which is both familiar yet foreign to the audience. The Asian woman model represents the intersection of these two distinct cultural others: Woman and "the Orient." In this essay, I will explore the link between the use of Asian women in advertising and the exoticizing and feminizing of Asia as "the Orient." In particular, I will examine the evolution of L'eggs' "Sheer Elegance" pantyhose advertisements from the early to late 1980s. How do

these L'eggs "Sheer Elegance" advertisements construct or reinforce existing stereotypes of the passive and exotic Asian woman? Whose construct is
she and how is she employed to appeal to predominantly non-Asian female audiences?

I will pose some theoretical questions to understand the interplay
between race and gender in constructions of the "Other" when reading
advertisements. If, as Luce Irigaray (1985) suggests, the exchange of women
sustains a society of "hom(m)o-sexuality," what does this imply for Asian
women who can easily belong to different marginalized groups in American society? How does this exchange of ethnic minorities—Asian women—
sustain a dominant Western patriarchal discourse through those who belong
in that culturally constructed category known as "Other"? Judith
Williamson discusses in her article, "Woman Is an Island," that Western
capitalist societies are culturally and economically dependent on the
"Other," but at the same time "our culture deeply rooted in imperialism,
needs to destroy genuine difference, to capture what is beyond its reach; at
the same time, it needs constructs of difference in order to signify itself at
all" (1986:101). How do the L'eggs "Sheer Elegance" advertisements reflect Williamson's argument?

Luce Irigaray suggests that in a patriarchal society, the display of
women's bodies in the media as objects or signifiers of consumption transforms the female subject into an object bearing the desires and needs of
men. Such a body becomes a text, one which can be read to understand
the masculine values of a particular society. Irigaray writes that "woman
has value on the market by virtue of one single quality: that of being a
product of man's 'labor' " (1985:175). It is in their reproduced form, encompassing male desires, that women are able to be consumed, defining
their particular value in the society. This is an important statement for
understanding who is the subject of these L'eggs advertisements. While
these advertisements are meant to sell American women on a new line of
silky sheer pantyhose, the advertisements' subject does not appear to be
female.

Irigaray argues that "[t]he work force is thus always assumed to be
masculine, and 'products' are objects to be used, objects of transaction
among men alone" (1985:171). While the pantyhose may be meant to be
used by women, men, not women, are the ones who state that "nothing
beats a great pair of L'eggs." This is voiced by someone who is doing the
watching—a masculine subject. Thus women, by wearing "Sheer Elegance"
become products of masculine labor or emulate the masculine subject's

notion of elegance and beauty. The visible absence of this male subject makes this statement appear to be a universal truth, one commonly recognizable by a Western audience. Yet, the appearance of this slogan in both advertisements suggests to the audience that the appreciation of a great pair of legs cuts across racial boundaries and is universal.

The presence of the white male subject is detectable in a 1981 L'eggs advertisement printed in *Vogue,* where the Asian woman appears as a manifestation of a Western sexual fantasy. E. Ann Kaplan discusses in her article, "Is the Gaze Male?" the power men have in their gaze which women lack in theirs. The male gaze, Kaplan argues, "is designed to annihilate the threat that woman (as castrated, and possessing a sinister genital organ) poses" (1984:323). Because of this threat, men attempt to turn women into a phallus-like object so as to mitigate woman's threat. Men, that is, turn "the represented figure itself into a fetish so that it becomes reassuring rather than dangerous (hence overvaluation, the cult of the female star)" (Kaplan 1984:323). The woman in a seductive pose is constructed as an object of the male gaze in this particular advertisement. The model is alluring in her submissiveness as she offers herself: "The look . . . the feel . . . of silk from the Orient. Now yours in a pantyhose."[2] She suggests that she is available because she speaks to the white male subject in saying that I/Orient/silk am "now yours [while I am] in a pantyhose." She is exemplary of the familiar Western stereotypes of Asian woman: submissive, mysterious, and seductive. Thus, the Asian woman and "the Orient," as the invisible male subject's fantasy, are rendered harmless because in her exoticized form she is familiar. She comes packaged in the Western form of L'eggs pantyhose.

The absence of an Asian model in a 1980 L'eggs advertisement is also accompanied by the lack of references to "the Orient." The white female model in this picture strikes a pose which is distinctly different from the Asian model in the 1981 advertisement. She is photographed in a sitting rather than semi-reclining position. While the Caucasian model's haircut and dress are representative of the styles in the early 1980s, the Asian woman's "China-doll" cut is distinctly meant to give her a more ethnic and exotic appearance. Thus, the contrast between these two different advertisements serve to make the Asian woman in the 1981 version appear to be "authentically Oriental."

The 1980 advertisement which employs a white model to sell "Sheer Elegance" pantyhose states that "She's got sheer elegance!" References to Asia are omitted and replaced by a discussion of silk as a sign of "elegance" and the almost natural quality of L'eggs pantyhose: "soft as silk, smooth as silk, with a fit that's pure L'eggs."[3]The model strikes a pose which appears casual because of the comfort which the pantyhose is supposed to provide as well as projects the look of "Sheer Elegance." Unlike the Asian model in the later advertisement, the white woman only wears the product; she herself is not for sale. We are told that "she's got sheer elegance," not that she is "sheer elegance." The audience in the 1981 advertisement is told that the Asian model in the photograph is part of the product. Her exotic qualities, which appear to be authentic, are able to be consumed in the form of L'eggs "Sheer Elegance" pantyhose.

Trinh T. Minh-ha states that the West uses the notion of authenticity as a way of domesticating the "Other" by creating standards of what is real by how much it is not the West. The authentic as a desired object can be "a product that one can buy, arrange to one's liking, and/or preserve" (1986-87:23). Thus, the Western fascination with the authentic reflects capitalism's simultaneous exploitation and celebration of difference.

The images of the East are not "authentic" in the sense that they are recognizable by Asians as true, but are constructed representations of the East by Western society. Edward Said in *Orientalism* (1979) argues that such images are not merely harmless misunderstandings between groups of people, but is indicative of "a corporate institution for dealing with the Orient—dealing with it by making statements about it, authorizing views of it, describing it, by teaching it, settling it, ruling over it: in short, Orientalism as a Western style for dominating, restructuring, and having authority over the Orient" (2). Advertisements through its employment of symbolism is by no means innocent of this kind of power.

The success of using such images of Asia are contingent on the West's need to make the East its cultural "Other." Thus Said states that Orientalism

> is, rather than expresses, a certain will or intention to understand, in some cases to control, manipulate, even to incorporate, what is a manifestly different (or alternative and novel) world; it is, above all, a discourse that is by no means in direct, corresponding relationship with political power in the raw, but rather is produced and exists in an uneven exchange with various kinds of power. . . (1979:12).

While he argues that Orientalism is not "some nefarious 'Western' imperialist plot to hold down the 'Oriental' world" (1979:12), Said writes that it "is, rather than expresses, a certain will" to construct the East in such a way as to deny it real power when in contact with the West. The L'eggs "Sheer Elegance" pantyhose advertisements use "the Orient" as a sign of something which is "foreign" to the West yet desired because of its forbidden nature. Thus, these advertisements depend on the audience to understand Asia and Asians as such and by doing so, the product takes on these qualities of the mystical and forbidden "Other."

Judith Williamson in *Decoding Advertisements* (1978) states that advertisements operate on a symbolic level by employing signs established by what she calls "referent systems." "The systems which provide ads with this basic 'meaning' material. . . . They are clearly ideological systems and draw their significance from areas outside advertising" (19). The advertisement sends us messages through these signs which we, as active receivers, must recognize as true. There is not a moment of hesitation for us to deliberate whether these signs inherently possess such meanings. Thus, when we see the Asian woman in the 1981 advertisement, we automatically assume it is about the East. The lack of Asian images in the media heightens the audience's awareness of the "Other" when such images are actually present. In order for these signs to have meaning for us, however, we must first become "subjects" capable of decoding what may otherwise be considered as meaningless in a different cultural or historical context.

Ideology, as discussed by Althusser, makes what is actually culturally constructed appear to be universal or true. Ideology does not work on a conscious level and we cannot see it working because we are its chief agents. We become good subjects when we do not question these false assumptions and readily understand the meanings of these images. Because we constantly reproduce it when trying to understand the meaning of advertisements, we are vital in perpetuating the existence of ideology. Thus, advertisements make the assumption that we, as receivers, will be able to decode its messages because we operate within the same referent systems.

The L'eggs advertisements work to form their own referent system. The use of the Asian model in the 1981 version, allows the product—"Sheer Elegance" pantyhose—to become part of what is signified by the sign—the mysterious and alluring "Orient." Thus "Sheer Elegance" pantyhose with "the look . . . the feel . . . of silk from the Orient" comes to be what is signified by an "exotic" looking Asian woman from "the Orient." The use of the word "Orient" as silk's place of origin further invokes mystical images of Asia. However, as other pantyhose advertisements show, "silk" does not in itself mean Asia. Rather, the use of the Asian model in the 1981 advertisement causes the audience to think that the connection between silk and the Orient is absolute.

After the Asian woman and the "Orient" come to mean silk and "Sheer Elegance" pantyhose, the product will then come to signify "the Orient." The female consumer who wears "Sheer Elegance" pantyhose will bear the mystique of "the Orient." Because the advertisement states that "Sheer Elegance" pantyhose "looks and feels like real silk," L'eggs products have made "the Orient" marketable and able to be consumed in the form of its pantyhose. Even the average white American female consumer can have "the look . . . from the Orient." The movement is "circular" in that the sign—"the Orient"— comes to incorporate the product as part of its meaning; the product, "Sheer Elegance" pantyhose, comes to signify what the Asian woman in the 1981 advertisement does. Once the product is able to signify the same as the "exotic" Asian woman, the advertisement is no longer necessary for linking L'eggs "Sheer Elegance" pantyhose to "the Orient."

By the late 1980s, L'eggs Products had expanded its line of "silk like" pantyhose to include products like "Silky Support" and "Sheer Elegance Control Top." These L'eggs products were promoted through the use of Asian female models. As noted earlier, however, these models appeared very differently from the original versions in the early 1980s. Most of these models no longer strike the same sleek, seductive poses as those seen in the original 1980s advertisements. They do not have the "China-doll" haircut and are not located in "the Orient," but appear to be completely at ease in the West.

A 1989 "Sheer Elegance Silky Support" advertisement refers back to the earlier 1980s "Sheer Elegance" renditions using the exotic Asian woman.[4] In this version, the female Asian model with her hair up and dressed in glamorous Western-style evening wear, only has a "whisper" of "the Orient" about her. On one level, this statement suggests to the audience that to be elegant one must remain subtle. Despite the fact that the model is not as exotic looking, the audience still cannot overlook the fact that she is Asian. The statement, "Dressy support that looks and feels like real silk from the Orient," appears at the bottom, telling the audience that this is yet another L'eggs "Sheer Elegance" advertisement. As discussed earlier, the 1980s advertisement allowed for the sign (the Asian model) and the product (L'eggs "Sheer Elegance" pantyhose) to signify the same thing— the "exotic Orient." Once this occurs, L'eggs "Sheer Elegance" in itself becomes a sign which continues to signify the mystic Orient. Hence, in this 1989 advertisement, "Sheer Elegance" gives meaning to the statement "a whisper of support." The "whisper" comes to mean the silencing of

Asian women in both their own culture and in American society. Thus, as long as Asian women "whisper," they will be accepted in the most privileged areas available to Western women. With only a "whisper" of "the Orient" in their look, they are even more culturally accepted because they are familiar and not too different.

In 1988, L'eggs Products began marketing "Silken Mist" pantyhose by running a series of advertisements depicting a young and Westernized looking Asian model interacting with different male representatives of Western culture. The familiar slogan of "She's got L'eggs" is attached to all of these advertisements. This woman, however, does not just have L'eggs like the other models shown in the "Sheer Energy" and "Silky Support" campaigns, but she has "theater," "dinner," and "opera" L'eggs.[5] In these versions, she poses with Mistoffelees from *Cats*; Andre Soltner, owner/chef of Lutece; and Sherril Milnes respectively.

The audience sees that "Silken Mist" pantyhose is a new product, one which was "inspired by Sheer Elegance." "Silken Mist" is not "Sheer Elegance" and the model with "opera legs" is not an "Oriental" woman. These "Silken Mist" advertisements also do not have the old slogan "looks and feels like real silk from the Orient." Thus, the absence of this message tells us that "Silken Mist," unlike "Sheer Elegance," is not interested in simulating "the Orient." The model in these advertisements does not even have a "whisper" of "the Orient" about her. She not only looks Western, but she can also function in all of the cultural settings of the West: the opera, dinner at Lutece, Broadway, and nightclubs.

The only reason we even notice the absence of "the Orient" in this advertisement is because of the referent system established by the previous L'eggs "Sheer Elegance" pantyhose advertisements. As discussed earlier, the early 1980s "Sheer Elegance" versions allowed the audience to connect the mystique of "the Orient" with this particular brand of silk-like hosiery. The "Silken Mist" advertisements no doubt assume that the audience recognizes "Sheer Elegance" as a sign of "the Orient." Thus, we receive the message that "Silken Mist" pantyhose gives us something which "the exotic, erotic Orient" does not offer: glamour and social acceptance in Western culture.

The advertisement no longer makes a pretense of celebrating difference in that the model looks Asian but cannot be called "Oriental." She is exemplary of the familiar stereotype of Asian Americans as the "model minority," one which has managed to assimilate fully into American society. The changes in the look of the Asian models in L'eggs advertisements in the 1980s reflect the gradual incorporation of the "Other" into the Western world. While the early 1980s renderings are undeniably linked to images of "the Orient," the "Silken Mist" advertisements attempt to eliminate the foreign. In each of these advertisements, the culturally assimilated Asian American woman is portrayed as mimicking the actions of these male guardians of Western culture. In a series of 1989 advertisements, she is placed with cross over African American jazz saxophonist Najee, another domesticated Other.[6] In another version, she stands next to Kevin McKenzie, the principal dancer of the American Ballet Theatre.[7] She is also pictured singing along with Sherrill Milnes as Don Giovanni.[8] But whose voice are we supposed to hear? Because he stands behind her and sings past her, the advertisement suggests that she only serves to function as a receiver—a mouthpiece. She is devoid of a language of her own and mimics or projects what is fed to her from the West.

The series of L'eggs "Sheer Elegance" advertisements in the 1980s show the gradual incorporation of the "Other" into the West. The "Oriental" model in the 1981 advertisement goes through a slow transformation of de-exoticization. By the late 1980s, the American audience is introduced to the latest product—"Silken Mist"—a completely Westernized Asian woman. The audience may even ask if the model is Eurasian. The L'eggs "Sheer Elegance" campaigns not only attempted to capture that authentic mystique of "the Orient" but they also domesticated it. Thus, "Silken Mist" shows the triumph of American capitalism and cultural imperialism.

Perhaps what is most disturbing about advertisements like the L'eggs "Sheer Elegance" pantyhose is the fact that we, as active receivers, become part of the mechanism which perpetuates the existence of these images. Because advertisements are in themselves full of signs which are not naturally connected to one another, we must work to link these images together. When we actively participate in giving meaning to them, we are "unleashing" these highly troubling messages of Asian women's sexuality. Because the stereotypes float through popular culture, they are familiar to us and effective for the purposes of advertising. This is not to say that we cannot be sensitive to these uses in advertising. Rather, the lack of non-white models in fashion and advertising would suggest the purposeful repression of difference by these industries and society at large. The advertisements which do employ Asian women make the pretense of celebrating difference by reconstituting it in terms which are made acceptable to Western audiences. The "Other" must look authentic without being culturally or sexually threatening.

Notes

1. I wish to thank Diana Fuss and Gary Okihiro for their comments and encouragement on this essay.
2. "Sheer Elegance" advertisement in *Vogue*, September 1981, p. 300.
3. "Sheer Elegance" advertisement in *Vogue,* December 1980, p. 89.
4. "Sheer Elegance Silky Support" advertisement in *Vogue*, January 1989, p. 241.
5. This series of three advertisements for "Sheer Elegance Silken Mist" appear in the September 1988 issue of *Vogue*. The "opera L'eggs" advertisement appears on p. 445, "dinner L'eggs," on p. 447, and "theater L'eggs," on p. 449.
6. "Silken Mist" advertisement in *Vogue*, September 1989, p. 521.
7. "Silken Mist" advertisement in *Vogue*, February 1990, p. 217.
8. "Silken Mist" advertisement in *Vogue,* February 1989.

References

Irigaray, Luce. *This Sex which Is Not One.* Ithaca: Cornell University Press, 1985.

Kaplan, E. Ann. "Is the Gaze Male?" In *Desire: The Politics of Sexuality,* edited by Ann Snitow, Christine Stansell, and Sharon Thompson. London: Virago Press, 1984.

Said, Edward. *Orientalism.* New York: Vintage Books, 1979.

Trinh, T. Minh-ha. "Difference: 'A Special Third World Women Issue.' " *Discourse* 8 (Fall-Winter 1986-87):11-37.

Williamson, Judith. *Decoding Advertisements: Ideology and Meaning in Advertising.* London: Marion Boyars Publishers, 1978.

_____. "Woman Is an Island." In *Studies in Entertainment*, edited by Tania Modleski. Bloomington: Indiana University Press, 1986.

The Site of Class

Edna Bonacich

Although lip service is often paid to the importance of class, for example, in university classes entitled "Race, Class and Gender," in practice class appears to have fallen into the background as a topic of central concern. Both feminism and multiculturalism have placed great emphasis on the politics of "identity." They focus upon "difference" based on race, ethnicity, and gender. Within this framework, class gets treated as another form of identity, another basis of difference. Class comes to refer to class background: does a person have a working class or a middle class background as part of their identity? Each individual can then be categorized in terms of their race, their gender, and their class: for example, one is a working class, African American woman, or one is a middle class, white man. These clusters of difference then determine identity, which in turn affects both experience and consciousness. Multiculturalism urges that institutions take account of all these varied identities, and make sure that they are represented both in the people who participate in the institution, and in the ideas and concerns with which the institution deals. For example, the university should include a more diverse faculty and student body, in terms of race, class, and gender, and the curriculum should reflect this diversity.

In my view, this approach to class strips it of its most important features. Class is not an identity, but a system of economic power and domination. Class relations are not relations of identity, but relations of dominance and resistance.

To show the contrast, consider the meaning of the idea that the university should be composed of people with class-based diversity. This is a contradiction in terms. The university occupies a position within the class system. It is an institution that is closely linked to the ruling, capitalist class in this society, and to the state. One of its important missions is to train the professional and managerial stratum. All the faculty are already a part of the professional elite, and students are in the process of preparing to enter that elite.

To speak of class diversity in the university is thus to speak of diversity solely in terms of sources of recruitment. Students may originate from working class families, but their sojourn in the university is aimed at transforming them from working class to middle class individuals. Unlike race and gender, their "class" is not a fixed identity, but a changing one.

Now certainly a case can be made that class background affects one's consciousness. Students who come from working class backgrounds are much more likely to be conscious of social inequality and injustice. And they are possibly more likely to use their professional and managerial training to try to work on behalf of social change (though there is no guarantee that they will). Furthermore, recruiting university students from diverse class backgrounds is obviously a good thing in itself. The university should not be the private property of the wealthy and powerful. But we should avoid confusing the class from which one has come with the class into which one is moving. The university obviously does employ working class people — as secretaries, custodians, and groundskeepers — but its students and faculty share a certain current and potential class homogeneity. The faculty and students are middle class now and in the near future. While one may strive to make the institution more diverse in terms of racial and gender composition and orientation, the requirement that it change in class composition and orientation has much more revolutionary implications. In practice, our claims that multiculturalism increases the class diversity of the university are false. When the university recruits more women and people of color, it may not recruit only FROM the middle class, but it certainly recruits only TO the middle class.

I use this illustration to show how the concept of class has been distorted within "multiculturalism." As a background characteristic, or element of identity, the concept of class has had its teeth pulled. It becomes a relatively non-threatening idea. After all, who in mainstream U.S. society can object to the recruitment of people from diverse backgrounds into the middle class? This is exactly what is meant by "equality of opportunity" within the dominant ideology. Everyone, regardless of class background, should have an equal opportunity for upward mobility within the system. If the university, and other institutions, are able successfully to incorporate people from working class backgrounds is this not a clear sign that the system is working as it is supposed to?

The basic issue, as I see it, is how capitalism works to produce economic and political inequality, and how we can fight against these tendencies. I do not believe we can talk about class in the United States without talking about race, since the class system of the U.S. is highly racialized. By this I mean that the exploitation of labor, upon which the capitalist system rests, depends upon racial disability and a racial division of labor. Thus we have a race-class or a class-race system, neither of which can be discussed separately.

I do recognize that gender also plays a part in the class-race system, but it does not operate on the same level. While women, as a category, do share some common disabilities, women in each race-class group face very different circumstances, and their race-class position is more determinative of their overall position in the social system than is their gender. Thus white, upper class women participate in, and benefit from, the social order that extracts surplus from people of color even if they have lower status in relation to their husbands. Efforts to homogenize race, class, and gender as equivalent types of oppression are, I believe, misplaced.

The fundamental class issue in capitalism is the issue of private property. Private property allows for the expropriation by a small elite of the socially generated surplus. Put another way, everyone in the society participates in the generation of the wealth of our society, but only a few people are able to lay claim to the bulk of it. This they do, not on the basis of how hard they have worked, but on the basis of having made investments, or by taking a risk with their capital. The returns to property have absolutely nothing to do with work. They only have to do with gambling, and only those with a big stake can play.

One can, of course, raise the question of how they got the big stake in the first place. Did they not work hard for it? Sometimes they did, but all too often the origins of the major fortunes of this country are rooted in some form of theft. There was, of course, the initial theft of land from the American Indian and Mexican population that enabled some people to amass huge estates. Then there was the theft of African people from their homeland and the creation of a class of workers who received no returns for their labor. The labor of slaves allowed the illegitimate accumulation of fortunes by their owners, through a form of daily theft, in which the products of their labor were expropriated simply on the basis of ownership. Similarly, waged workers, too, were robbed by the fact that owners did not pay workers the value of what they produced, but only paid them sufficient to cover their subsistence. This kind of theft continues to this day. In other words, property owners are able to steal the social surplus from the rest of the society because the latter lack the power to claim it.

Not only does the capitalist class expropriate most of the wealth that is generated, by taking out profits, interest, and rent, but they also make all of the major decisions of the society. Formal democracy is very limited in what it actually can control. In fact, most of the important decisions that affect our daily lives and livelihoods are made by a group of people whose sole criterion for making them is whether or not they, or the property holders they represent, will make money. They decide what the society will build, what goods it will produce, and who will produce them under what conditions. They also spend billions of dollars trying to shape and manipulate the demand for products. They control most of the communications media, thereby exercising a kind of stranglehold over ideology. And they control state institutions.

Capitalism has developed an ideology that says that the owners of property deserve this kind of power and these kinds of rewards, that the social allocation we have is just. The system is rationalized by the argument that owners are the creators of wealth, and that everyone else is dependent upon them. This ideology, of course, turns reality on its head. People are only dependent on capitalists for their livelihood because they have been robbed of any property themselves and have no means of survival other than to sell themselves, their time, and their ability to work to those who control all the property. In reality, workers do not need owners who take out profits. They may need a management team and they may need to have a group that makes investment decisions, but there is no social need for a group of property owners who simply take out profits.

However, the ideology of the system argues that capitalists, rather than workers, are the great creators of wealth. They are great benefactors who create jobs for the rest of us, and we should be eternally grateful for the gift they provide us. This mythical rendering of the way the system works masks the fact that these relationships are purely a social-political construction. The system does not permit public entities to engage in productive enterprise; only private production is permitted, and therefore only private entities can create wealth. This is not inherent in production, but in a particular legal-political set of institutions.

Because private production is the only legitimate form, both workers and communities are placed in a dependent relationship on the owners of private property. Cities, for example, must bend over backwards to woo businesses to come to their area, and provide jobs for their residents and a tax base for their social services. Property owners have all the power in this relationship and can threaten to leave if they are not given what they want: a cheap, controllable labor supply, the absence of intrusive regulations, and low taxes. Because they control production, they control wealth, so everyone else is at their mercy.

In late capitalism another important class has emerged, namely the managerial and professional stratum. This group also expropriates the so-cially-generated surplus, but in the form of bloated salaries as opposed to profits. The huge size and growth of U.S. CEO salaries, for example, has recently received some negative publicity, as the gap between the earnings of production workers and executives has sky-rocketed. These high earnings are usually justified by the claim that managers and professionals have scarce human capital; their salaries are bid up by companies competing in the market for their much-needed skills. In fact, at least to a certain extent they act more like a club that has the power to reward its own members exorbitantly.

Both the owners of capital and the managerial-professional stratum tend to be heavily White. They have the real power in this society, and they often collude and overlap. For example, high level managers are often granted stock options that bring them into the ownership class, while many higher level professionals are able to use their large salaries for investment purposes. Moreover, managers and professionals play a critical role in providing institutional support of all kinds for private property. They are the implementers of capital's rule.

Another important class in U.S. capitalism is the petite bourgeoisie, or small business sector, a class of special relevance to Asian Americans. Like managers and professionals, small business owners serve as an intermediary class that also can perform a controlling role. While there are obviously small business people of all ethnicities, there is a tendency for Asian immigrants to be over represented in this class.

I would like to illustrate how the class system works by briefly describing my current work, namely a study of the garment industry in Los Angeles. The garment industry is hierarchically, as well as racially organized. Manufacturers, who design and market clothing, and who are mainly White, contract out the sewing, mainly to Asian contractors, especially Koreans. The contractors, in turn, employ workers, who are mainly immigrant Latinos, although Asian immigrants also comprise a significant minority of the working population. The contracting shops often violate labor and safety standards, and workers are poor, abused, and live under harsh conditions.

Despite the poverty of workers, considerable wealth is generated by this industry. I have tried to figure out where this "surplus" goes. My tentative conclusion is that it goes to two broad categories of people: owners of property, and high-paid managers and professionals. Let us consider the owners first. Three types of owners are relevant:

(1) Owners of businesses. These include the contractors, the manufacturers, and also the retailers of apparel, who exercise considerable power over the manufacturers. These people, who are sometimes stockholders, make profits..

(2) Owners of financial institutions. Apparel manufacturing uses standard banking, but also has a special form of financing, namely factoring. Factors are intermediaries between manufacturers and retailers, who pay the former what the retailers owe them before it is due, thereby providing the manufacturers with operating capital. They later collect these debts from the retailers themselves. Financial agents make money in the form of interest. Some make it indirectly, particularly through interest owed on leveraged buyouts, which were prominent in the apparel retailing sector.

(3) Owners of real estate. This group takes out surplus in the form of rent. They include the owners of the downtown buildings where sweatshops are located, the owners of the California Mart, where manufacturers rent showrooms, and the owners of malls where retailers are located. To give one example, Jack Needleman, owner of several downtown buildings where garment contracting shops are located, is estimated to be worth $250 million.

Apart from owners, upper-end managers and professionals take a chunk of the surplus in the form of bloated salaries. This is especially clear with the top executives of manufacturing and retailing firms. These executives sometimes overlap with owners when they take advantage of stock options. For example, an article in the *Los Angeles Times* reported the earnings of the 100 California CEOs with the highest earnings in 1992. Topping the list was the president of The Gap, a garment specialty store. He made $41.9 million in that year, $40 million of which was in stock awards, and most of the remaining $1.9 million in salary.

Professionals include garment lawyers, CPAs, designers, advertisers, teachers in industry related schools, and journalists. While their earnings are variable, the higher end usually makes six-digit salaries, and can work in relatively luxurious surroundings.

There is a widening divide in Los Angeles between rich and poor, which is heavily correlated with race. The garment industry illustrates the dynamics of capitalism that produce this effect. The extraction of surplus is sanctioned by the state in its endorsement of these property relations. In addition, in this case (as in many Los Angeles industries), workers are frequently undocumented, a product of immigration law that creates, in practice if not in overt intention, a group of especially rightless, disenfranchised workers. These workers are not racially defined according to the law, as in the old Jim Crow South, but in reality they suffer from a combination of racial and class oppression. They are typically indigenous Americans, though not from the United States, who are still being ripped off by the conquering Europeans.

The implication of a class-race analysis is that there is a need to struggle against the fundamental economic and political institutions of our society. In order to achieve justice and equality, and an end to racism, it is necessary for us to fight against the existing property relations of this society. This would require a massive redistribution of all the ill-gotten gains that have depended on the theft from, and exploitation of others. And it would require the construction of a new social order, based on principles of nonexploitation, of sharing the socially generated surplus, and providing for the well-being of every society member.

Needless to say, our society is a million miles from such a vision, let alone program. The discussion of such issues is completely drowned out from the public discourse, since the owners of capital and wealthy managers and professionals control the government and virtually all means of communication. They control the media and the schools. They control the military and police. As an aside, police relations are an especially vivid instance of class relations in that one of the main purposes of the police is to protect private property from the typically racially defined dispossessed, whose anger at their dispossession might be expected to arouse efforts to effect their own low-level efforts at redistribution. A non-capitalist police force might aim its efforts at punishing the theft inherent in private property. A capitalist police force does not recognize this theft and only punishes the victims' efforts to regain what has been stolen.

The task of those who want to engage in class struggle against the system of domination under which we live must keep in mind this larger picture, and must try to have their political work move towards the goal of revolutionizing property relations, however remote that goal might seem. There are numerous struggles to pursue along these lines, including working with the labor movement, working in communities to gain more control of capital, experimenting with alternative organizations of production, fighting for greater political representation for the disenfranchised, creating alternative media, working against police abuse, fighting for changes in numerous state regulations, and on and on.

I started with the university and want to end there. Part of my purpose has been to show the limitations of treating class as an identity. If we really want to change the class-race system, as it is manifested in the university, we must do much more than change the identity composition of its faculty and students. We must also go beyond changing the curriculum to reflect the diverse histories and cultures of the various class-race-gender groups in the United States (and in the world). These are admirable goals, and I do not want to minimize their importance in themselves, but they do not really challenge the class-character of the university, and the role it plays in perpetuating the class system.

To revolutionize the university from a class perspective would require that we fight to change the role that the university plays within the society. This includes research that is done primarily on behalf of the propertied classes and the state. (Even critical research often has a reformist cast, aimed at finding ways to ameliorate the worst aspects of the system and getting it to function more smoothly.) It includes fighting against the creation and propagation of ideology in support of dominant property relations. And it involves fighting against the teaching role played by the university in constructing the next generation of managers and professionals. We need to develop a concept of the university that moves our society beyond its current exploitative class-race relations.

I do not by any means expect the easy achievement of these goals. What I am calling for is greater clarity about what we mean by the class struggle, and what its political implications are. Somewhere along the line, our concerns over gender and race have led us to lose sight of property relations, or to treat them as an old issue, whose time has passed. Marxist ideas are denounced as male and Eurocentric. While there are certainly some shortcomings along these lines in Marx's original writings, I believe that he started a school of thought that is still of vital relevance to understanding our society today, and to understanding both what needs to be changed and how to struggle to change it.

Asian American Studies
Needs Class Analysis

Peter Kwong

Racial oppression being the dominant experience of Asians in America, the lack of class analysis in Asian American literature is understandable. Asians have long been the targets of intense racial discrimination. They were excluded from immigration, isolated into ghettos, and suppressed economically. Asians were initially recruited by capital as cheap labor, and doubled as instruments to undermine white workers' wages and conditions. In response, white workers refused to work alongside them and championed for their exclusion. Employers conveniently abandoned them, once the anti-Asian sentiment began to agitate. In effect, Asians were locked out of the labor market. They could not be a part of the working class and certainly could not develop strong American class consciousness.

Economic isolation has contributed to the distortion of capital formation within Asian American communities. As a result, conflicts between Asian labor and Asian capital were tempered and often muted by kinship and regional affiliation. Many Asian immigrants had already witnessed colonial oppression in their homelands. Once here, their sense of nationalism strengthened as they had to group together with their countrymen for mutual aid and self-protection, giving shape to their nationalistic identity as Chinese, Japanese, or Filipinos. Asian Americans thus acquired strong racial and national but not class consciousness.

By the 1960s, with the advent of the civil rights movement, Asians emulated African Americans in the struggle for racial equality. "Asian American" consciousness began to form, in response to the need for broader solidarity beyond individual Asian national groupings. This "Asian" consciousness is a reactive one. While Asians share common interests as victims of white racism, their union is merely a pragmatic alliance of different nationalities, languages, cultures, and religions. Proponents of Asian panethnicity, understandably, want to stress the collective attributes to reinforce this unity and avoid issues, such as class, that might be divisive.

American society, certainly, promotes the value of individual achievement and shuns class analysis. Asians and particularly new immigrants are susceptible to this kind of ideology. They come to this "land of opportunity" aspiring to make it into America's middle and property class. The professionals, many of whom were members of the elite in their native country, come for political stability and better utilization of their skills. Initially thrown into America's average middle class, they aspire to move upward into positions of comparable social status that they enjoyed at home. Those Asians who are not optimistic about their own upward mobility try to create favorable conditions for their offspring. Hence, most Asian Americans consider their present class position transitional, to be broken and overcome. In fact, some Asians appreciate America precisely because of its "open" class structure.

It is difficult for most Asians to find their bearings within America's racial structure, which is deeply marked by its historical black versus white biracial conflicts. They tend to reckon race in its crude formulation, i.e. an identity along skin color and physical features. We are "Asians"! We look different! Therefore, we are being discriminated against! The remedy is to work harder and to show the Whites that we are just as good if not better! This simplistic formula misunderstands racism which is much more sophisticated. The exclusion of Chinese labor at the end of the nineteenth century came about not just because European Americans did not like the way Chinese looked, but because the Chinese were *recruited* as cheap and docile labor to undermine white workers.

White reaction against the Chinese (and all other colored minorities) only weakened the workers ability to confront capital. Historically, American labor's impotence in uniting workers across racial lines deprived it of an independent power base, such as workers in other advanced democratic countries have in their Labor or Socialist parties. To this day, American labor still relies on the diffusive Democratic party to represent it.

By focusing exclusively on race, we underestimate the power of class. For instance, when we discuss the conflicts of Asian American small business operators in African American communities, the contradiction is not just an issue of race. Much more important is that Asian immigrant entrepreneurs are situated in a hostile class position—property ownership in the midst of *massive* poverty. Hence Asian businesses are seen as surrogates of white corporate power. Those Asians who insist on looking at this as an intra-minority conflict are only isolating the Asian community from national realities with ominous consequences.

It is my contention that if we do not understand the class aspect of our experience, we do not understand the power of racism. Still, in the field of Asian American studies, merely a handful of scholars have adopted explicit class analyses. Only Alexander Saxton, Carlos Bulosan, Edna Bonacich, [and writers in Bonacich and Lucie Cheng's collection *Labor Immigration under Capitalism* (1984)], and others like Michael Omi, Yuji Ichioka, and myself come to mind.

While few works in Asian American literature focus primarily on class, class formation within the Asian American community is very much a reality. Because of the selection process in the immigration law, many Asian American groups have been bipolarized. One group—what I called the "Uptown Asians"—is the professional middle class, whose members are well educated and financially secure though they experience the "glass ceiling." They tend to live in the suburbs and invest heavily in their children's education. The young Asians getting scholastic awards and attending Ivy League universities tend to be the offspring of this first group.

And then there is the other group, the working-class Asians, who live in concentrated ethnic ghettos, are paid low wages, have been neglected by American authorities, and suffer from all types of social problems. I called them the "Downtown Asians." The two groups have very different experiences and aspirations. For instance, the "Uptown Asians" tend to be interested in combating the glass ceiling and quotas in Ivy League universities. They want to see more Asian executive appointments and more representation on commissions. The working-class "Downtown" Asian Americans are interested in minimum-wage enforcement, police protection against organized crime, effective action against racial violence in ghetto schools, affordable housing, and reasonable medical costs.

In addition, we are seeing more and more Asian workers being exploited by their co-ethnics. Class conflicts within Asian American communities are increasingly regular. Immediately after the 1965 Immigration Act, a significant proportion of Asian immigrants were middle-class professionals. Now, the influx is disproportionally working class. They are working as low-wage laborers in restaurants, and in the construction, agricultural, retail, and transportation industries. Some of the most exploited are Asian women engaged in garment, domestic, nursing, electronic, and sex industries. The rank of working-class Asians are further swelled by the increased arrival of the undocumented. A flood of undocumented, un-skilled rural mainland Chinese, for instance, is pouring in to work as sweat-shop laborers in America's underground economy.

Asian American scholars prefer to ignore this class development within the Asian community for fear of introducing division that could affect ethnic unity. One clear indication of this is that there are very few contem-porary community studies. Take the studies on Chinatown. Most of them are historical, and they avoid internal class analysis. They stress instead the strength of community organizations and the virtue of ethnic enclaves. If poverty is mentioned, it is only used to refute the Asian "model minority" image.

By ignoring the class issue, Asian American studies is depriving an important segment of the Asian community of its voice. The field also remains blind to a tremendous international and national transformation in which Asian immigrants have played a significant role—as the critical cornerstone in the restructuring of the American economy. Since the 1960s, American corporate interests have been trying to maintain high profit margins by exporting manufacturing jobs to the Third World. Domesti-cally, they try to decentralize the large assembly-line production into a small subcontracting system located in areas where workers are least orga-nized or better yet, subcontracting jobs in new immigrant communities. The benefits are that corporate capital no longer has to worry about pro-duction or labor management issues and can still expect high profits from "docile and motivated" immigrant labor.

In Chinatown, American garment manufacturers parcel out jobs to Chinese contractors, who in turn retain Chinese female immigrants to labor in highly exploitative conditions. The manufacturers do not have to face class confrontations, which have been shifted to within the Chinese community between contractors and workers. And yet, this exploitation is primarily caused by the manufacturers, who do not offer sufficient prices to the Chinese contractors to pay decent wages to the workers in the first place.

In the meantime, contractors are able to get away with hiring Asians at extremely low wages in part because the immigrants have been aban-doned by American organized labor, and in part because the American government fails to enforce labor laws. In addition, Asians are dominated by their communities' informal political structure, which protects the in-terests of the propertied class.

Since the publication of my book *The New Chinatown* (1987), the conditions in New York's Chinatown have grown worse. As the number of undocumented immigrants increased, the wage level in the community has dropped even further. One or two dollars pay per hour is now a common wage. The deterioration goes beyond low wages. Homework and withholding of back wages are rampant. The issue is no longer simply the violation of the minimum-wage law; it is an attack on the most basic right of all workers—getting paid for their work. Worse, many of the undocumented are controlled by organized crime, forcing them to work under conditions reminiscent of nineteenth-century indentured servitude. That such horror still exists in 1993 is a national disgrace!

Yet few voices of indignation have been heard from the field of Asian American studies. It is silent at a time when we realize from the public statements of most Asian American leaders that they are only concerned about how incidents like the *Golden Venture*, the immigrant freighter that grounded near Queens on June 6, 1993, give Asians a negative image. Some leaders are even yielding to the national anti-foreign sentiment to call for immigration restrictions.

Asian immigrants are not the issue; American employers' unending desire to exploit the vulnerable undocumented is. The way to counter the anti-Asian sentiment is not to single out Asians and Latinos for exclusion. Asian and Latino immigrants, including those undocumented, are part of the American working class. They are victims who should be protected. It is our responsibility to see to it that all working people in this country, be they native or foreign, enjoy decent wages and respectable conditions. Only then can we be sure that the present crisis will not spread into a massive inter- and intra-racial hostility. Those Asians who take a defensive position are effectively encouraging the replay of the 1882 Exclusion Act against the Chinese, the 1907 Gentlemen's Agreement against the Japanese, and all the exclusion acts against Asians. Except this time, Asians participate in their own execution! That is why a clear class analysis is essential in stopping this vicious cycle of racial hatred.

The interplay between race and class is complex and dynamic. Again, Asian American studies rarely engages it as an issue, because the field has lost the connection with its own community. Ironically, Asian American studies owes its very existence to the support of the Asian American community in the late 1960s and early 70s—particularly the working-class community. At the very outset, one of the main objectives of Asian American studies was to serve the community. That commitment has eroded. There are many reasons for this. In order for Asian American studies to survive in the academic community as a field, it has had to conform to established standards. Community research, particularly the kind lacking in sophisticated quantitative data analysis, is not considered scholarly.

Asian American studies' loss of connection with the community also has something to do with the fact that many of "us," who engage in the field, come from middle-class backgrounds. Our roots in the community are not very deep and have been difficult to maintain. Another reason for not engaging in class analysis is that Asian American studies has been seduced by the ideology of multiculturalism, which stresses diversity. I have nothing against multiculturalism, which has given minorities the opportunity to be a part of America's cultural discourse. But diversity, according to the established convention, perceives American society as made up of many independent and autonomous parts, including different racial, ethnic, gender, sexual orientation, religious, and nationality groups. Class is not visibly considered an element in this assemblage. Diversity as a concept is being used to divide the power of the oppressed.

The politics of diversity absorb a few individuals from the upper crust, and leave the rest out in the cold. The beneficiaries of almost all the civil rights and affirmative action programs have been the middle-class members of minority communities. Their representation assumes that the system has addressed the problem of the whole. Those fighting for minority inclusion (with very good original purpose) end up serving their own interests and bring no improvements to others. While the successful election of Mayor David Dinkins as the first African American mayor of New York City seemed a victory for all minorities, we can not ignore the fact that during his administration the African American working-class community suffered from even more unemployment, more social services cuts, worse education, less police protection, and poorer health care services. When we look at the Clinton administration's program of inclusive appointments, we must question how African American interests are being served by the appointment of someone like Ron Brown to the Cabinet. Many Asians, too, are into this "eye on the prize and not necessarily the people" kind of politics. They are interested in being appointed leaders, who devise policies, without a serious attempt to contact, consult, and understand their Asian American community.

I believe that Asian American studies as a field should redirect its commitment to its own community. The application of class analysis is vital to understanding our community. We have come to a critical juncture—fighting to reclaim the soul of Asian American studies. Are we, Asian Americans, simply interested in identity issues, so we could feel good about ourselves? Is Asian American studies, as some have accused, a field that serves mainly the middle-class constituency? Or is it a field trying to serve its community by utilizing all the available resources and tools to try to understand the full scope of our oppression across class boundaries?

Common Cause?
Asian American History and Western American History

Patricia Nelson Limerick

Like many children growing up in the small towns of the American West, I spent years under the impression that I had gotten stuck in a pretty dull place. On the edge of the desert, my hometown Banning, California seemed to have been as dull in the past as it was in the present. Then, in my early twenties, I met the California writer and activist Carey McWilliams, and mentioned that I was from Banning. "What an interesting town," he said, which was news to me. "Banning was where Sadakichi Hartmann lived."

Sadakichi Hartmann? With a German father and a Japanese mother, Hartmann had been a writer and art critic, a figure in Greenwich Village intellectual society, later a member of John Barrymore's circle of friends in Hollywood and the person cast by Douglas Fairbanks as the court magician in *The Thief of Baghdad*. Hardly a household name now, Hartmann was a magnet for memorable characterizations in his time. "I have more hopes of him, more faith in [Hartmann]," Walt Whitman said, "than any of the boys." "If one had not been oneself," Ezra Pound said, "it would have been worthwhile being Sadakichi." "Sadakichi," Gertrude Stein said, in a typically memorable and impenetrable observation, "is singular, never plural" (Hartman 1971:vi).

After his daughter married an Indian man on the Morongo Reservation, Hartmann spent the years before his death in 1944 on the reservation outside my hometown where, from time to time, celebrity-freighted limousines from Hollywood pulled up at gas stations and asked for directions to the Hartmann home.

My "discovery" of Sadakichi Hartmann was one big step in the process of realizing that I had done my home region a disservice. The version of Western American history that I had learned in school had been the familiar old story: white pioneers had moved westward into unclaimed wilderness, bringing Christianity, civilization, and railroads with them; then, somewhere around 1890, the pioneers finished up their job of mastering the continent, and the West settled down and became dull.

That old story had no place for Sadakichi Hartmann—a man of German and Japanese ancestry, living on an Indian reservation after a life at the edges of avant-garde society. It did not take a great deal of time or thought to reach this conclusion: a version of Western American history *with* Sadakichi Hartmann was a lot more interesting than a version without him.

In this case and many hundreds of others, attention to the presence of people of Asian origin has played a key role in revitalizing Western American history, setting the region free of the stale old story of Manifest Destiny, and making it clear that the West is a much more interesting region than it could be while under the captivity of the old "frontier" school of history. But what exactly is the relationship between regional studies and ethnic studies, between Western American history and Asian American history? How much common cause do these two areas of inquiry really share? I want to explore, first, the areas of overlap, the territory where Asian American scholars and Western American scholars share the same issues, questions, and agenda. Then, second, I want to examine the areas where the two fields seem to take different directions—though I believe that these differences would be reciprocally productive and stimulating, if scholars in the two fields stayed more in touch, exchanged notes, and compared conclusions.

For me and for a number of other historians of the West, the presence, activities, and ideas of Asian Americans played a central part in the process of rethinking how we tell the story of Western America. Trying to do justice to Asian American history proved to be one of the best, most effective, and most direct ways to revitalize and reconceive the history of the American West.

If you want to show, quickly and efficiently, what was wrong with the old, Turnerian variety of Western history, and why this field badly needed reconceptualization, there is no better way to go than to look at the way the Old Western Historians handled the topic of Asian American history.

The very titles of these books put their point of view on record; one does not have to puzzle over the plot-line likely to be followed in a book called *Westward Expansion* or *America Moves West*.

In the fifth edition of *America Moves West*, by Robert E. Riegel and Robert G. Athearn, the index entry reads: "Chinese population, p. 533." The Chinese make their only appearance, in this six-hundred-page book, in two sentences, and even those two sentences are devoted to the Workingmen's Party of California, Denis Kearney, and their campaign to exclude the Chinese (1971:533). In Ray Allen Billington's and Martin Ridge's *Westward Expansion*, fifth edition, when you look up Chinese Americans in the index, this is what you find: "Chinese, build the railroad, p. 583." When you turn to page 583, you find a page devoted to the Central Pacific Railroad, and in the middle of the page are these two sentences:

> The construction gangs were in the mountains then, battering their way over steep grades and around precipices of living rock, but the promoters had solved their worst problem—how to obtain labor in a frontier community— by importing gangs of Chinese coolies. Seven thousand pig-tailed workers hacked out the right-of-way, their broad straw hats and flapping trousers forming a picturesque sight as they trundled wheelbarrows of dirt or scampered away from charges of blasting powder (583).

That is it for Asian Americans: two sentences—and two peculiar sentences, at that—in an eight-hundred-and-ninety-two-page book. Books called *America Moves West* or *Westward Expansion* intrinsically canceled out the significance of an eastward population movement. Moreover, by the terms of the Old Western History, the frontier ended in 1890, and Western history ended with it. Japanese, Filipino, Korean, and Asian Indian immigrants, and even more so, Vietnamese, Cambodian, and Laotian immigrants had missed the deadline. Since one of the main things wrong with the Old Western History was its treatment of Asian Americans, then one of the principal ways to get Western history onto firmer ground was to pay closer attention to the Asian American presence in the West.

In a similar way, the treatment of race relations in American history textbooks makes a clear statement about what American historians lost when they left out the American West, the American West taken seriously and viewed realistically. Three years ago, I spent a couple of weeks reading most of the college-level American history textbooks, page by page, in order to write a review of their treatment of the West. Reading fifteen textbooks, one after the other, is an experience I would not recommend, though the relief, when one is finished, is immense. Still, having done it gives me the authority to say that American history textbooks, down to 1991 publications, are still constructed on a model of American race relations which casts African American/Anglo American relations as the essential core of the story. Over and over again, after lengthy sections on black/white relations, come the trailer paragraphs on Mexican Americans and Indians and, somewhat less regularly, Asian Americans (Limerick 1992a).

The textbook discussion of civil rights is particularly revealing: repeatedly, at the end of the lengthy section on the African American civil rights movement, you will find some variation on this sentence: "The black movement inspired other minority groups to mobilize and aggressively press their claims"; or "black protest . . . encouraged other minorities to assert themselves and demand redress of their grievances." I do not mean to take anything away from the importance of the black civil rights movement of the 1950s and 1960s, but this conventional periodization of the civil rights movement obscures—more concretely—ignores much pre-1950s activism and protest, on the part of African Americans as well as everyone else. Members of Mexican American *mutualistas* protested discrimination at the turn of the century; Japanese plantation workers in Hawaii fought planter domination; Chinese individuals and groups eagerly took to the courts in pursuit of their civil liberties in the mid-nineteenth century; and the Indian wars were, in their own way, a kind of civil rights and land rights protest movement. And yet, in the textbooks, all these movements disappear, flattened by a model in which, to quote one book, "the example of the [black] civil rights movement inspired other groups to press for equal opportunity," as if this idea had never occurred to these other groups (or, for that matter, to African Americans) before 1954.[1] My impression is that the textbook authors are particularly addled when it came to Asian American activism: the textbooks' list of groups "also-inspired-by-the-civil-rights-movement" regularly includes American Indians, Mexican Americans, and women, but only occasionally includes Asian Americans. My sense is that, here, the textbook writers encounter their own version of the model minority myth, and simply assume that Asian Americans did not have much to protest.

It is not a very inspiring experience, reading these textbooks, but the reader cannot miss the fact that she is in the presence of a "Capital P" Paradigm: to most American historians, American race relations occurred along a black/white axis. Consider these quotations from a couple of textbooks:

The black exodus [during and after World War II] from the South made civil rights a national, not a sectional, issue.

[S]ome 1.6 million blacks left the land of their ancient enslavement to seek jobs in the war plants of the West and North. Forever after, race relations constituted a national, not a regional, issue.

Until you have a significant presence of African American people in other regions than the South, these passages say, explicitly and implicitly, then race relations and civil rights are localized, Southern regional issues, not national issues (Henretta et al. 1987:923; Bailey and Kennedy 1991:844).

Or consider this passage, perhaps the most explicit: "Through most of the nation's history, Americans had been accustomed to thinking of themselves as essentially a society of two races: whites and blacks (Brinkley et al. 1991:976). This proposition makes absolutely no sense for Asian American history, but I am pleased to say that it makes equally little sense for Western American history. This is where I see the common cause of Western American historians and Asian American historians in the clearest terms. If we could get these textbook writers to take the Western half of the country seriously, then they would give up making these goofy remarks about a simple, two-sided pattern of American race relations. If we could get them to take Western America seriously, then, in that same step, they would take the presence and the significance of Asian Americans seriously, and what is presently a very much truncated and excerpted version of American history would become a great deal more whole, and a great deal more useful in guiding us through our present, puzzling times.

So why on earth do the textbook writers cling to an inaccurate and over-simplified model of the American population? Is there any hope in asking for a more complex treatment of American race relations? Can a paradigm this well-rooted ever yield ground? I actually have a fairly optimistic response to those questions, and my optimism rests on my knowledge of how fast my own field changed in the last ten years. As recently as the mid-1980s, Western American history was a very stale field, with old ideas, and ethnically exclusive ideas, very much in control. And then, just in the space of a few years, everything changed. New voices came into the conversation; fresh air began to circulate; and the field generally came to life.

I want to tell here a story that is the best I have found for sympathetically explaining why people fall into patterns of thought, and then have a hard time breaking free from those habits. I borrow this story from Larry

McMurtry, one of my critics and rivals in the interpreting of the American West, though I am putting it to a use that McMurtry did not intend (1968:9-11).

McMurtry was writing about the weird process of watching his book, *Horseman Pass By*, being filmed into the movie *Hud*. He arrived in the Texas Panhandle a week or two after they had started filming, and he was particularly anxious to learn how the filming of the buzzard scene had gone. In the buzzard scene, Paul Newman was supposed to ride up and discover a dead cow, and in his distress over the loss of the cow, he was to look up at a dead tree branch lined with buzzards and fire his gun at one of the buzzards. When he did that, all the other buzzards were supposed to fly away into the blue Panhandle sky.

But when McMurtry asked people how the buzzard scene had gone, all he got, he said, were stricken looks.

The first problem, it turned out, had to do with the quality of the local, available buzzards—buzzards that apparently had responded to a curious High Plains-style casting call of dead meat left out for their discovery. The local buzzards who responded to this casting call proved to be an unappealing and excessively scruffy group, and so more appealing, more photogenic buzzards had to be flown in from some distance and at some considerable expense.

But then came the second problem: how to keep the buzzards sitting on the dead tree branch, until it was time for their cue to fly?

That seemed, at first, easy. How to get them to stay on the branch? You wire their feet to the branch, and then, after Paul Newman fires his shot, then you pull the wire, release their feet, and they all take off.

But, as McMurtry said in an important and memorable phrase, the filmmakers had not reckoned with "the mentality of buzzards."

With their feet wired, the buzzards did not have enough mobility to fly. But they did have enough mobility to pitch forward.

So that is what they did: with their feet wired, they tried to fly, and pitched forward, and hung upside down from the dead branch, with their wings flapping.

I had the good fortune a couple of years ago to meet a woman who had been an extra for this movie, and she added a detail that McMurtry left out in his essay: namely, the buzzard circulatory system does not work upside down, and so, after a moment or two of flapping, the buzzards passed out.

Twelve buzzards hanging upside down from a dead tree branch: this is not what Hollywood wanted from the West, but this is what Hollywood had produced.

But then we get to the second stage of buzzard psychology. After six or seven episodes of pitching forward, passing out, being revived, being replaced on the branch, and pitching forward again, the buzzards gave up . . . . Now, when you pulled the wire and released their feet, they sat there, saying in essence, "We *tried* that before; it did not work; we are not going to try it again." The filmmakers had to fly in high-powered animal trainers to restore buzzard self-confidence, and it was all a big mess, and Larry McMurtry got a wonderful story out of it.

Now what bearing does all this have on the problem of the textbooks and their failure to pay proper attention to the American West and to Asian Americans? In most fields, you go to graduate school to get your feet wired to the branch. There is some real value in this; it is important to have some common ground, some common knowledge with other scholars in your area. But in the process of getting your feet wired, you do have some awkward moments, and the intellectual equivalent of pitching forward, and hanging upside down, if you do it in a public place like a graduate seminar, is no pleasure. And so scholars fall into habits of thought, and hold onto those habits of thought. American historians get themselves tied to a vision of American race relations as organized along a black/white axis, and it is not an easy matter to persuade them to untie themselves from that model. But, as I know from Western history, things can change very fast. There is really no very good reason for remaining on dead tree branches, and as McMurtry's story shows, even the most negatively conditioned birds can be persuaded to fly again.

Let me return, then, to the common cause of Western American history and Asian American history. In the mainstream textbooks and apparently in the minds of most American historians, the history of the American West and the history of America's westward movement are the same thing. In the index in many of the books, the West and the westward movement appear as synonyms. But letting the westward movement of white Americans set the terms of the story of the American West sacrifices most of the interest and reality of a complicated and instructive region. Put the westward movement at the center of your study, and unless you take constant precautions, you merge your point of view with white, English-speaking pioneers, and lose much of your independent judgment.

I do not think there is any better solution to this problem than to take seriously the *eastward* movement of Asians, across the Pacific and into the American West. Reversing the geographical directionality is itself close to a cure: taking Asian immigration seriously, you are ejected out of a paradigm that puts white Americans and their assumptions at the center of attention, and you are, in that same step, invited into the study of a wider, more interesting region, where the eastward movement of Asians, the northward movement of Spanish-speaking people, and the prior presence of Indian people can be as consequential as the westward movement of Anglos (Limerick 1992b).

A student of mine once used the memorable phrase: "When shifting paradigms, it is important to remember to put in the clutch." This recognition of an eastward movement across the Pacific and into North America seems to me to be one of the best ways of putting in the clutch, of recognizing that the old paradigm of the westward movement and the closed frontier cannot address the richer, more complex reality of the American West. Let New York Harbor and Ellis Island share the historical spotlight with San Francisco Bay, and Angel Island, and the Ports of Los Angeles and Seattle, and Western history, as well as American history in general, comes to rest on much firmer ground.

The thematic overlap between Asian American history and regional history remained strong, long past the point of arrival of immigrants in West Coast port cities. The conditions of the California Gold Rush, and subsequent rushes, shaped the early years of Chinese American history. The presence in California of a population of white men, carrying with great and typically Western expectations of rewards and bonanzas, and facing an also typically Western reality of uncertain wage work, created the conditions most conducive to racial scapegoating. Writing the history of the white American response to Asian immigration requires close attention to that unsettled context.

There is, in other words, more than an accident of geography at work here, more than a coincidence of which coast happened to border on which ocean. In 1850, the American West was the part of the nation still in the midst of the process of invasion and conquest. The Mexican American War was barely over, and the land claims of Mexican Californians were still unsettled. Miners in the California Gold Rush were all trespassers on Indian land and on the public domain; in 1849, no treaties had secured a right of access to the streams and foothills of the Sierras. If there is any more remarkable event—remarkable in its astonishing speed and presumption—than the creation of the Foreign Miners' Taxes, imposed on Chinese miners in the 1850s in California, it is hard to think of what that event might be. Two or three years earlier, the members of the California legislature would have been, themselves, *foreigners* in Mexican California. The recentness of the acquisition of the territory—and the instant adjustment in definitions of who was a foreigner and an outsider and who was a citizen and an insider—offers a telling example of this whole curious struggle over legitimacy in a society so recently under construction.

As a society resting on such a recent and unstable foundation of conquest, the American West was and is a place of constantly contested legitimacy. The miners who had been in California in 1848, right after the discovery, resented the miners who crowded the area in 1849; the miners who came in 1849 resented the ones who had been there for the greater and easier opportunities of 1848. This was, in other words, a place where white Americans felt precarious, and where the line between legitimate resident and illegitimate invader, between proper settler and improper late arrival, between rightful user of the West's natural resources and usurpers of those resources, was constantly a source of friction and contest. That Western condition of contested legitimacy hardly reached a resolution in 1900. With the enormous population movements during and after World War II, states like California were, in the twentieth century, once again populated by a majority of people who were not native to the West, and who thus had to fight, once more, over who was a real and legitimate Westerner, and who was not. That unsettled and precarious sense of identity helps to explain some things that are otherwise inexplicable, like, for instance, the adoption of English as the official language in California in the 1980s .

Asian immigrants who came to the American West arrived in the part of the nation where white Americans were at their peak of prickliness, defensiveness, and jumpiness in meetings with others, in part because of the recentness of their own arrival in the area and in part because of the greater diversity of the Western population. White Southerners might have been able to concentrate their energies on the subordination of African Americans, but white Westerners took on a multi-front campaign for supremacy, simultaneously working to subordinate Indians, Hispanics, Asians, and African Americans. Say the word "segregation" and nearly everyone's first thought is of the South, but Western America has a serious, parallel history of segregation in public facilities, and Asian Americans were often its targets.

This context—of the complexity of Western American race relations—provides another case where the history of Asian Americans and the history of the Western United States best work to illuminate each other. The diversity of Asian Americans alone would make this point: Chinese, Japanese, Korean, Filipino, Asian Indian, Vietnamese, Cambodian, and Hmong—along with every variable of class and gender within each group, and with complicated interactions between and among all of those groups: the diversity of Asian Americans is itself a reminder of how we flatten the world when we see American history in bi-polar terms, cast as a relationship between white Americans and "the others."

In the same spirit, attention to Asian American history puts a spotlight on the complexity of relations between different groups of people of color. In his reminiscence of the California Gold Rush, Granville Stuart remembered an attack by California Indians on Chinese miners; since, again, miners of all backgrounds and origins were equally trespassers on unceded Indian territory, an Indian attack on the Chinese had its own logic, even as it gave Stuart the chance to provide a pretty odd picture of white miners rushing, this time, to help the Chinese by searching after and killing Indians who might or might not have been responsible for that particular attack (1977:79-80). One of the worst occasions of violence against Asian men occurred in 1866, when Paiute Indians in Nevada attacked a party of Chinese miners (Stratton 1983:113). The Paiutes, by 1866, had been pressed about as far as an invaded people can be pressed, and there was, again, considerable logic in their acts of violence against invaders. These events embody the moral complexity of Western American history, in which participants in the invasion of Indian territory often were, in their own view, engaged in a simple and justified pursuit of resources and opportunity. In a similar spirit, we have to reckon with the events in 1933, when Mexican agricultural workers went on strike against Japanese berry growers in El Monte, California, who were themselves working hard against the unjust disadvantages of the California Alien Land Law (Daniel 1981:146-49). When we look at the El Monte berry strike, the true complexity of Western labor history goes on record, making it clear that we will never again have a completely clear, John Wayne-like casting of consistent good guys and consistent bad guys to structure our understanding of the region's past. This whole cause will receive a great increase in momentum with the publication of Quintard Taylor's work; his book on African Americans, Japanese Americans, and Anglo Americans in Seattle will be out soon. His synthesis of Western African American history will be along in a few more years.[2]

In his recent novel, *River Song* (1989), the writer Craig Lesley creates an Indian character, Danny Kachiah, who is haunted by dreams and visions of a massacre that occurred in Nez Perce territory, though without Nez Perce participation—an attack along the Snake River in which Whites killed thirty-seven Chinese miners. A compelling novel on every count, *River Song* is also a valuable reminder of two crucial lessons about the American West: first, how much it has become a layered landscape, with remembered tragedy now an important feature of many places; and second, how much Westerners have come to hold a common heritage—if also often an unrecognized heritage—of intertwined stories, an interweaving in which a Nez Perce man wrestles with the terror and tragedy of an event involving people with origins very different from his own.

Geographical location is absolutely crucial in this matter of layered and intertwined memory, crucial in ways that are clear and concrete and visible. Asian American labor and entrepreneurship remade the agricultural landscape of the West Coast, just as much as Asian American labor and entrepreneurship have remade and are still remaking the urban and commercial landscape of a number of West Coast cities and towns. In the history of the physical environment and the history of the landscape, environmental historians have offered us a way of making history whole again. Anyone, for instance, who wrote the history of the agricultural development of the Sacramento/San Joaquin Delta, without significant attention to Asian labor, would offer a terribly incomplete story. To use another example, in his environmental history of the California fishing industry, *The Fisherman's Problem* (1986), Arthur McEvoy logically includes all the players: Indians, Italians, Chinese, Japanese, Anglo. Leave out any one human group from an environmental history, and the historian commits an error as clearly as chemists would make a mistake if they left out one element from the analysis of a complicated chemical reaction.

McEvoy's study of California fishing also offers an important lesson on the history of environmentalism in the West. In the late nineteenth century, McEvoy observes, white Californians used conservationist rhetoric to cloak a campaign to drive the Chinese out of the fishing trade. Statements about the need to protect and preserve a fish population gave a thin veneer to a movement to deny opportunity to a particular human population. As environmentalism, in our times, remains far too true to its origins as a white middle-class crusade, without much empathy for working-class people and with few ties between mainstream environmental groups and people of color, the lessons of McEvoy's environmental history remain far too relevant.

Environmental history has another dimension, of course, beyond contested resource use, and that is the matter of the tie of sentiment and emotion between people and places. With the exception of Indian people, the history of the American West has been a history of immigrants and outsiders adjusting to new environments. With a preoccupation with the West as an exotic place on the edge of Anglo American imaginings, Western historians have spent too little time investigating how people arriving in the West have made that shift in perception from exotic to familiar, from disorientation to orientation, from new location to home.

The ways in which new arrivals become old-timers, the ways in which families from far-off places take root and become local, the ways in which immigrants become residents have received far too little attention from Western historians. The historian Elliott West is one of the exceptions; in his book *Growing Up with the Country* (1989), West looked at children, brought to the West or born there, who had every reason to take the exotic open spaces of the West as normal, as, indeed, the conditions of home. This is a book, as West acknowledges, entirely focused on the children of white pioneers, but it is a book that asks for comparison with the children of Asian immigrants, and with the development of their sense of the West as home. It was one thing, to come to feel at home in a new place when the society around you was welcoming and helpful; and it was a much more remarkable thing—to develop a sense of home and of roots when the surrounding society had set itself the task of making sure that Asian immigrants and their children would never feel at home. We will not really understand the full dimensions of the process of shifting from new arrival to resident, from immigrant into the West to Westerner, until we pay equal attention to the Westerners who crossed the Pacific, as well as those who crossed the Plains. The focus on generations, in much of Asian American studies, would make a very helpful combination with a focus on adaptation to particular places.

That very term "Westerner" goes to the center of the problem of regional identity. Say "Westerner," and an image of a handsome white man on a handsome horse is the first thing brought to mind. Handsome white men on horseback are, and have long been, a very tiny minority in the West, and yet we have handed the whole region's identity over to this narrow and brittle stereotype. If we can expand the word "Westerner," past its strict, stern, and thoroughly unrealistic white-cowboy limits, if we can stretch the term to include the full diversity of the region's residents, then the movement called the New Western History will fulfill its principal purpose. We will have finally broken free of the Marlboro Man when the word "Westerners" can as easily evoke images of Asian American workers and business people, most likely not on horseback. My own highest hope is for the occasion when the phrase "Western Hero" brings to mind Gordon Hirabayashi, and not John Wayne.

But what has the word "Westerner" got to do with all this? What relevance could, or should, regional boundaries have for the history of Asian Americans? Or, to put the question more personally, why do I behave in such a peculiar way when I stand in a bookstore and look at a book like Peter Kwong's *The New Chinatown* (1987)?

This is what happens: I see the title and reach for the book, and then I notice the words "New York." New York, or to put it another way, the wrong side of the Mississippi river. I start, then, to put the book back on the shelf. But half-way to the shelf, my hand stops, and I think, "This is not sensible. If you are interested in Asian American history, you cannot take the stand that people go off the edge of the earth when they go to the Eastern United States. New York's Chinatown is the biggest Chinese American settlement, and this looks like a pretty interesting book."

I bought the book; my decisions at least make some sense, even if my process of reaching those decisions is questionable. I found the book interesting and stimulating, and, predictably, I ended up wondering how much the patterns Kwong describes in New York's Chinatown differ from the patterns in San Francisco's Chinatown, and what might be the origin of those differences.

But I want to look for a moment more at this curious pattern of response in libraries and bookstores when I see an interesting book on Asian American studies and then hesitate if it proves to be set on the other side of the Mississippi. In literature, for instance, I am a big fan of the stories of Fae Myenne Ng and Hisaye Yamamoto and Frank Chin and Amy Tan and Maxine Hong Kingston. Their work provides some of the best evidence to support the now common claim, in the late twentieth century, that Western America is enjoying its greatest and finest era of literature ever. But I have not read Gish Jen, or David Mura, or David Wong Louie, and as far as I can tell, the only reason for that choice is my curious sense of regional loyalty.

As I examine this behavior, this is my assessment of what happens in my mind. I had so much assumed that Western American studies and Asian American studies shared a common cause in rebalancing American history. Thus, without any very conscious reflection, the sight of an important and well-written book about people of Asian background in the Eastern United States can make me feel as if a coalition, on which I have come to rely quite heavily, was breaking down.

I am admitting this, and putting the full peculiarity of my thinking on record, not to defend it, but to suggest the pleasant relief that comes with the next stage of thought here: namely, the recognition that Western American history was never supposed to be a study in uniqueness and incomparability. On the contrary, the reason for doing local history, history based in particular places, is to give grounding to large issues and themes, to find both the similarities and the differences of people from diverse origins, to follow historical meaning through local, regional, national, and international levels. On that count, the moment when I hesitate while reaching for Peter Kwong's book, is a moment when I deny the promise of Western American history and refuse the rich and important opportunities for comparing the Asian American experience in different regions and locales of the United States.

I am more and more of the opinion that this fork in the road—the place where Asian American history and Western American history appear to part ways—is actually a fine opportunity for provoking Western historians to move beyond provincialism, into a larger world of national and international meaning. And it is important that that invitation comes in a form that reverses the usual east-to-west directionality of American history.

Asian American studies invites the Western American historians to expand the range of their thinking in another direction as well, toward the non-contiguous United States, both Alaska and Hawaii. Asian labor was central to the salmon canning business of the Pacific coast, including, of course, Alaska. Think about that for a moment, and one very-much-taken-for-granted pattern in the writing of Western American history suddenly calls for rethinking: that is, we have hundreds and hundreds of books on the Western American industries of mining, farming, cattle-raising, oil-drilling, and logging, and yet we have somehow or other steered our attention away from the Pacific coast fishing industry. Cowboys and farmers and miners and loggers populate our Western American history surveys, and fishermen and cannery workers fall off the edge of our attention. Alaska is a state still a bit drunk on its own pioneer mythology, celebrating the image of rugged white prospectors in the frozen Alaska bush. "The Last Frontier," every license plate in Alaska proclaims, and yet a glance at a book like Tooru J. Kanazawa's *Sushi and Sourdough* (1989) is a quick way to remember how diverse the participants in that "final frontier" really were.

Like American historians in general, Western historians have also been hesitant and halting in reckoning with Hawaii. Serious attention to Asian American history forces the reckoning: an understanding of Pacific coast Asian immigration simply has to rest on an understanding of immigration to Hawaii. Moreover, Western historians are forever wrestling with the powers to mislead, built into the many myths of the West. In those terms, Gary Okihiro's (1991) appraisal of the Hawaiian "aloha myth" of friendly race relations, for instance, provides a necessary comparison and contrast to those other Western dreams.

Asian American studies productively stretches the thinking of Western American historians. I would hope that there is some service to be performed in the opposite direction as well. I think, for instance, of the current concerns of Western historians in reckoning with the differences and connections between rural life and urban life. The American West has become the most urbanized region of the country, and yet the image brought to mind by the word "West" rests almost entirely on the image of wide open spaces and rural enterprises. We are still very much under the influence of Jeffersonian images of rural virtue in opposition to urban vice, or, sometimes with the values reversed, rural ignorance and bumpkinness in opposition to urban sophistication and grace. The rural and urban parts of the West can seem very different and very separate, just as Asian American populations in Chinatowns and Koreatowns and Little Saigons can seem very different and very separate from the rural residents of places like Cortez, California, in the Japanese American farm community studied by Valerie Matsumoto (1994). Has there been a set of customs and practices and understandings, called the "rural way of life" that cuts across other cultural boundaries? Or, on the other side, has an adaptation to city-living added up to its own kind of subculture, again cutting across boundaries of ethnicity? In the enterprise of figuring out how to think about the relations between the rural West and the urban West, studies of Asian American Westerners would be of particular value.

My hope, then, is that studies in Asian American life, whether they are set on the western or eastern side of the Mississippi river, will continue to push and provoke Western historians into thinking harder about their subject. My hope, as well, is that place-centered history—local history and regional history—will provide one of several routes for the writing of Asian American history. Asian Americans were founding participants in Western American society; their actions transformed, and indeed, are now transforming, many parts of the Western natural, urban, and social landscapes; Idaho in the 1870s was close to 30 percent Chinese; Monterey Park, California has an Asian and Asian American majority, and the Central Valley of California has the greatest concentration of Hmong Americans today; the majority of Asian Americans still live in the Western states; crucially important cases of litigation—*Wong Kim Ark, Ozawa, Lau,* to name a few— grew out of Western American settings. As Sucheng Chan has said, the political, social, and economic climate of the American West played a crucial role in setting the Anglo American response to Asian immigration (1991:xiv). Often disheartening and tragic, but crucial nonetheless, the ties between Asian American studies and Western American studies cannot be dissolved, but they can, I think, be creatively put to use. I remain convinced that we have considerable common cause when it comes to asking that the mainstream American historians rethink their premises and take off from their dead tree branch.

But I still ask for help with the big question here: how much do place and region matter? In collections of interviews with Southeast Asian immigrants, books like James Freeman's *Hearts of Sorrow* (1989) and John Tenhula's *Voices from Southeast Asia* (1991), the editors do not always bother to identify the location, in the United States, of the person they are interviewing. Maybe I am the only reader concerned by this, pausing and asking an unresponsive text, "*Where* is this person?" How much is location a variable in these narratives, and how much attention does it deserve from interpreters of Asian American experiences? Or perhaps more important, is region—and this unit, "the American West"—a necessary category in taking place and setting seriously? Is it a data-and-idea-organizing category that works at all for Asian American studies? I am not entirely sure of the answer to these questions, but I hope that this conversation, launched in Ithaca in June of 1993, goes on for a long time.

Notes

1. Quotations are from Boyer et al. (1990:1066), Brinkley et al. (1991:923), and Martin et al. (1989:983).

2. His overview of Western African American history will be published by W. W. Norton.

References

Bailey, Thomas A. and David M. Kennedy. *The American Pageant: A History of the Republic.* Lexington: Heath, 1991.

Billington, Ray Allen and Martin Ridge. *Westward Expansion: A History of the American Frontier.* New York: Macmillan, 1982.

Boyer, Paul S., Clifford E. Clark, Jr., Joseph F. Kett, Thomas L. Purvis, Harvard Sitkoff, and Nancy Woloch. *The Enduring Vision: A History of the American People.* Lexington: Heath, 1990.

Brinkley, Alan, Richard N. Current, Frank Freidel, and T. Harry Williams. *American History: A Survey.* New York: McGraw-Hill, 1991.

Chan, Sucheng. *Asian Americans: An Interpretive History.* Boston: Twayne, 1991.

Daniel, Cletus E. *Bitter Harvest: A History of California Farmworkers, 1870-1941.* Berkeley: University of California Press, 1981.

Freeman, James A. *Hearts of Sorrow: Vietnamese-American Lives.* Stanford: Stanford University Press, 1989.

Hartman, Sadakichi. *White Chrysanthemums,* edited by George Knox and Harry W. Lawton. New York: Herder and Herder, 1971.

Henretta, James A., W. Elliott Brownlee, David Brody, and Susan Ware. *America's History.* Chicago: Dorsey, 1987.

Kanazawa, Tooru J. *Sushi and Sourdough.* Seattle: University of Washington Press, 1989.

Kwong, Peter. *The New Chinatown.* New York: Hill and Wang, 1987.

Lesley, Craig. *River Song.* Boston: Houghton-Mifflin, 1989.

Limerick, Patricia Nelson. "The Case of the Premature Departure: The Trans-Mississippi West and American History Textbooks." *Journal of American History* 78 (March 1992a): 1380-94.

_____. "Disorientation and Reorientation: The American Landscape Discovered from the West." *Journal of American History* 79 (December 1992b):1021-49.

Martin, James, Kirby Randy Roberts, Steven Mintz, Linda O. McMurry, and James H. Jones. *America and Its People.* Glenview: Scott, Foresman, 1989.

Matsumoto, Valerie. *Farming the Home Place.* Ithaca: Cornell University Press, 1994.

McEvoy, Arthur F. *The Fisherman's Problem: Ecology and Law in the California Fisheries, 1850-1980.* New York: Cambridge University Press, 1986.

McMurtry, Larry. *In a Narrow Grave: Essays on Texas.* New York: Simon & Schuster, 1968.

Okihiro, Gary Y. *Cane Fires: The Anti-Japanese Movement in Hawaii, 1865-1945.* Philadelphia: Temple University Press, 1991.

Riegel, Robert E. and Robert G. Athearn. *America Moves West.* Hinsdale, Illinois: Dryden Press, 1971.

Stratton, David H. "The Snake River Massacre of Chinese Miners, 1887." In *A Taste of the West: Essays in Honor of Robert G. Athearn,* edited by Duane A. Smith. Boulder: Pruett Publishing, 1983.

Stuart, Granville. *Prospecting for Gold: From Dogtown to Virginia City, 1852-1864.* Lincoln: University of Nebraska Press, 1977.

Taylor, Quintard. *The Forging of a Black Community: A History of Seattle's Central District, 1870-1970.* Seattle: University of Washington Press, 1994.

Tenhula, John. *Voices from Southeast Asia: The Refugee Experience in the United States.* New York: Holmes & Meier, 1991.

West, Elliott. *Growing Up with the Country: Childhood on the Far Western Frontier.* Albuquerque: University of New Mexico Press, 1989.

Conjuring Ghosts in a Journey East

John Kuo Wei Tchen

When I first considered speaking at this "Site(s)" mega-session, I was feeling a bit undecided. As some of you know, there is a small but growing cabal of us east of the Pacific coast who are fomenting dissent within Asian/Pacific American studies. Yes, the work that has been pioneered at Berkeley, in San Francisco, at UCLA, in Seattle, of course Hawaii, and elsewhere has been critically important—BUT—it has been Pacific rim-centric. The mantra that has been repeated since the inception of Asian American studies was that Chinese from Guangdong and then other Asian Pacific groups arrived in California, thus beginning the Asian/Pacific experience in the United States; and as anti-Chinese riots escalated and as the Japanese Americans relocated after the camps, Asian/Pacific peoples started spreading to the rest of the United States.

In many respects, it is an obvious and sound argument framed within a nationalist history, after all, if we look at the demographic statistics who could argue? The great majority of Asians and Pacific Islanders in the United States, up until quite recently, have been located on the left coast. But, with a series of "East of California" conferences and the increase of new local and regional studies, our loose confederation was making a valiant effort at making Pacific coasters a bit insecure. Then along comes the likes of Patricia Nelson Limerick and her cohort of smart revisionist historians who argue that the American West has never received its full due! Of course they are right, but what does that mean for Asian/Pacific American studies?!? Well, all of you doing left coast studies must feel further empowered that you knew all along and will now continue to work in California-centric and Hawaiian-centric ways. But, you'all are not getting away so easily.

Yes, American social, cultural, intellectual, and even labor histories have been terribly skewed towards the patrician, Protestant Northeast, but this has *not* been true for Asian/Pacific American studies. In fact, I would argue that the emphasis on the Pacific coast and Hawaii and lack of understanding of other regions has created a likewise skewed historical understanding. Clearly the issue of an Asian/Pacific American place is central to this argument.

My argument is not with Limerick and the other revisionist scholar/activists of the West. In fact, having read some of Limerick's work, I have found two aspects of her perspective that immediately endeared her to me and that is what I wish to address—both I believe help us get at the notion of place, as well as reclaiming a fuller history of Asians in the Americas. First, she ends her provocative article in *The Journal of American History* (1992) "Disorientation and Reorientation" with one of my favorite passages about ghosts from the work of Fei Xiaotung, the pioneering Chinese sociologist and anthropologist. And secondly, she begins that same article with a discussion of her personal journey driving from southern California to New Haven, Connecticut where she "discovered" the East for the first time (Limerick 1992). This is a journey that I have also been taking in my life and my work, but with superficially different results. I believe these two seemingly incidental coincidences actually reveal some shared theoretical and practical political concerns that provide a basis for some dialogue about the centrality of "place" in Asian/Pacific American studies.

Parenthetically, I also very much appreciate Limerick's style of writing and speaking because she is, as many feminist scholars are, very willing and effective at integrating her personal voice and political perspective while not presuming to speak in such universalistic terms. In that spirit, I would like to add some thoughts to her already rich conversation.

Fei Xiaotung acutely observed that America was "a land without ghosts." He observed the constant dislocation of Americans, the impersonal quality of everyday work, the cold uniformity of institutional spaces, and the preoccupation with the future did not make everyday life hospitable to contemplation of "the lingering past." "I cannot get used to people today who know only the present moment," Fei wrote. "Our every act contains within it all the accumulated history from the beginning of the universe right down to the present, and this every act will determine the destiny of endless future generations." Yet, in the United States memories tied to place and coming to terms with the past are constantly subverted by a blind faith in progress and the pursuit of material comfort (Fei 1989:177-80). Therefore, when the past unexpectedly erupts onto the present scene, impulses of fear, hatred, and escape ensue.

Surely, if Fei was right, it is not because Americans are not obsessed with ghosts and demons. In modern and postmodern America, astral spirits pervade our electronic airwaves. Ghosts are not only creaking around in our old Victorian mansions and not-so-old attics, but invading the rest of the national landscape. Filmmaker George Romero's vastly popular "living dead" are emerging from graves, attacking cities and suburbia, and even taking over our modern day shrines of consumption—shopping malls. Grandpa Harry's memory should be repressed at all costs. No, no! We cannot let him emerge from the grave! Beat him back! Fascination is mixed with morbid fear. Inevitably the panic about astral spirits revolves around the inconvenience they impose; they disrupt the smooth flow of contemporary life and progress.

In this sense, the founding fathers' fear of reproducing European class hatreds and Federick Jackson Turner's faith in the safety valve of the western frontier (or a chain of exurbias) both framed the frenetic, escapist modernism that is American culture and politics. Living with the past in this cultural practice, especially a past which has been laced with racial injustice, represents anti-modernism and being mired in traditionalism. It is not that ghosts do not inhabit the American landscape: it is that the culture's ahistoricity makes Americans terrified of ghosts and prompts them to want to exterminate all phantom spirits representing people's memories of the past, especially those memories which relate to injustices and social problems.

Hence the act of reclaiming, remembering, and reconstructing specific Asian/Pacific American histories in specific sites across the country is, in effect, conjuring those feared ghosts of this nation's wrongs. If it is done privately, well okay, everyone is entitled to their memories, nostalgic or bitter. But if done publicly within the context of a social movement, and not ensnared within the controlled zones of tourism or acceptable bounds of elite cultural orthodoxy, then it is declared a dangerous, fractious, subversive activity. But, if a people needs to relink with its past to find its voice, then so be it. These conjured ghosts revivify life as lived and threaten only the sterility of established law and order.

Surely the public humanities and academic debates of recent years around multiculturalism, canons, and the "wholes versus the parts" can be understood within these distinctions of what is sacred versus profane, normative versus taboo. "Organic intellectuals" grounded in collective hopes and aspirations of non-elites, as Gramsci has posed them, simply do not honor academic disciplinary boundary guards. The most prestigious research universities in the United States are premised on a German academic model. That model's emphasis on pure unfettered specialist research as the primary source of knowledge, its emphasis on filtering out the best and the brightest from living communities, and its prevailing insistence on the fragmentation of knowledge into micro-specializations have to this date made academic life inhospitable for engaged, activist intellectuals. If such scholars are able to help relink living communities with their pasts, it is done so despite the pressures of the prevailing standards of our publish or perish universities (Canino 1993:5; Boyer 1990:10).

In contrast, Limerick's work on the North American West has managed to evoke some powerful and much feared ghosts. Her research and writing has already had a major impact on how land use and conservation issues are now debated and thought about. The *New York Times* series on the "Forsaken Frontier" paid her the ultimate of back-handed compliments when they first made her out as an "extreme" revisionist who pushes "feminist and environmentalist" interpretations of the West too far. Yet they fully acknowledge such challenges have dramatically altered the whole way the West is talked about on a grass roots level. And in traditional academic circles, Limerick has been identified as part of a Yale American studies conspiracy against the West (Egan 1993). Who would think we were in the presence of such a powerful demon! What are they afraid of?!? Such is one of the consequences of making the past come alive in the public's present.

For those of you familiar with older Chinatowns, you know there are ghosts everywhere. At the Chinatown History Museum (CHM) in New York City, we have tried to help resuscitate some otherwise lost spirits by asking the basic question: how do everyday people use and think about history? Reunions, for example, are one very meaning-rich way we all reconnect with fragmented parts of our past lives, and such events have been highly successful in bringing back seventy years of students and teachers in the old public school building in which our museum is located. Over 500 Italian and Chinese alumni have been engaged in identifying individuals in photographs, having their decade "class" photographs taken, and reuniting with past flames. From the vantage of the post-civil rights era, they have been able to reflect upon and debate how well ethnicities and genders got along in the classroom. The work of the CHM continues to ask how we can jointly collaborate with the bearers and interpreters of our living communities' collective memories in a shared exploration of the meaning of the past from the vantage of the present (Tchen 1987:242-50; 1990a:285-326; 1990b:186-92).

Such grassroots reimagining of the present with the fragmented past, I believe, is at the heart of what those of us who think of ourselves as community-oriented intellectuals should be doing much more of. Academic historians tend to dismiss reunion gatherings as simply nostalgic because they are not fit for scholarly scrutiny. Yet, such activities, which give expression to the voices and sensibilities of those who have been otherwised silenced from public discourse and/or the canonical texts and textbooks, are the very means by which everyday folks naturally link up with the past. In our society evoking memories of past injustice loosens feelings and values that neither the commercial marketplace nor the two-party system can so easily contain. The forces of possessive individualist-driven modernity fear such living memories and want to repress their activation (Tchen 1992). This is precisely the reason for us to conjure, and then to embrace, such ghosts. We cannot be afraid of them.

This coming to awareness process (of how the present must be interrogated by the past) is part of a personal and political life's journey. I believe every person of Asian heritage in the United States necessarily makes a symbolic, if not real, journey to the East—a sort of Monkey's journey in reverse. Like the sixteenth-century fictionalized epic novel of the Chinese monk Hsuan Tsang *Xiyouji (A Journey to the West)*, it is a metaphoric and actual encounter with cross-cultural "otherness" in its various manifestations. I believe Asian/Pacific American individuals and scholars ultimately have to go eastward because the Atlantic Northeast has historically been the hub of power from which this nation developed socio-economically and culturally. Please allow me to illustrate how I have come to this conclusion by quickly sketching my research that has led me to this analysis.

In 1978, while working at Basement Workshop, this Midwestern boy who grew up in a ticky-tacky twenty-something-year-old suburb, found original glass plate negatives of San Francisco's old Chinatown from 1895 to 1906 at the Library of Congress. To me this was a historical treasure trove, a sacred connection with real people who were a part of Chinese American history. I sought to undo their anonymity with oral histories and other historical methods of recovery and the results were *Genthe's Photographs of San Francisco's Old Chinatown*. For me San Francisco seemed to be the spiritual home and original pilgrimage site. With the generous help of the scholar that has been properly called the dean of Chinese American history, Him Mark Lai, and others, I found fragments of stories which could be reconstructed and reclaimed into one small study (Tchen 1984).

I soon discovered that what began as an oral history and community documentation project, necessarily led to an exploration of issues of representation and otherness. We now know that Genthe's mental image of Chinatown defined and proscribed what photographs he took, when he took them, what he did to them in the darkroom, and what he said about them. Besides being a gifted photographer, the German émigré subscribed to a European American faith in orientalism. He wanted to make that community a pure, exotic imaginary, what he called a "Canton of the West" (Tchen 1984:14).

I felt at this time, my main theme would be Genthe's "tampering" with these powerful representational images. Certainly, it demonstrated how structured and structuring cultural attitudes had been. What would a pre-racially proscribed Chinese settlement be like when the formation of Chinatown itself was a response to the delimited race relations of the time? With these photographs I could not get to some purer, pre-racist site and began to question whether such a quest was even desirable.

What surprised me was my growing interest in the creolization of the visible street cultures that Genthe was a part of, yet tried to obscure. I slowly began to realize my search for a pre-racist Chinese American home only paralleled Genthe's own futile and misguided imaginings. As with many such life's journeys, I did not find the initial object of my quest— some uncomplicated, cultural nationalist spiritual home I could call my own.

In 1983, I then had the good fortune to go to Guangdong Province with Judy Yung, Wei Chi Poon, among others. Although my family came from Jianxi, another part of southern China, I had come to feel that this area was part of my roots as a Chinese and Asian American. The strong feelings and politics of anti-imperialism that many of us who were a part of the Asian American student movement led me to want to visit the sites of local resistance to British and Western colonialisms.

Yet, traveling through the various counties outside of Guangzhou, I more fully realized what I was just beginning to understand about the Genthe images of San Francisco. For some unexplained reason at the time, I was most interested in the cross-cultural mixing and zones of contact between Chinese and non-Chinese. The places that drew my imagination were: Sanyuanli, that small rural village in which peasants first rebelled against the British during the opium wars, the international zone in Canton City which bordered the foreign concessions with that mix of native

Cantonese and Western architecture, avant-garde painter Yun Gee's family home which had beveled glass from America integrated into a stained glass window, and filmmaker Steve Ning's classic family portrait from Hoisaan (Taishan) in which everyone is stiffly posed in a black and white print wearing traditional dress except for those high top sneakers from America. Like the Chinese in Genthe's images, these Chinese were part of a diasporic and creolized sensibility of overseas Chinese in Europe and the Americas.

In founding the New York Chinatown History Project, Charlie Lai and I decided to begin with documenting the history of Chinese hand laundries. It became clear in our research that laundries began in San Francisco and other locations in the West as a response to the systematic occupational eviction of Chinese workers by anti-Chinese European American ethnics. With little start up monies, some source of water, and a good location a hand laundry could be set up without much hostility. Chinese traveled eastward, finding niches across the North American landscape to make a living this way—among the Yuma Indians in Arizona, in mining towns, and most certainly in the urban areas of the Midwest and Northeast. In New York City, among other cities, laundering became the primary occupation and these modest operations helped build Chinese communities.

This work on laundries led me to examine Paul C. P. Siu's 1952 Ph.D. dissertation on microfilm. Siu rightly asserted that each laundry was a sort of frontier outpost—a gathering place for the otherwise isolated Chinese in the area to share a meal, exchange news about their home villages, and help each other out. Siu was the original investigator of Georg Simmel's notion of "the stranger" and its relevance to the American immigrant and racialized social relations. He sought to explore the complex dynamics of isolated hand laundries to home villages and nationalism on one hand, and to racist laws and culture in mixed cultural neighborhoods on the other (Siu 1987). Without being fully aware of what laundries meant to me, I now know that I identified with much of the experience of those friends who grew up in the back of laundries. The feelings of being a subjugated "other" is particularly intense where there are few Chinese in the many non-Asian frontier zones of the United States.

How do we understand these isolated individual's relationships to Chinese American settlements when they cannot or do not want to return to their "home" in China? As has become clear with the oral history interviews we conducted, home villages were often increasingly mythologized the longer these "sojourners" were away. Indeed, many returnees to China did not feel they fit into village life anymore and moved to a nearby city. Lots of basic questions follow: Does a Chinese American consciousness begin with saying that America is my home? Or could what Tu Wei Ming calls a consciousness of being culturally Chinese, not tied to a specific place, emerge? (Tu 1991) Or is there a diasporic consciousness? (Hall 1990:222-37) Or a creolized consciousness? (Goldman and Ybarra-Frausto 1991)

Surely Chinese American consciousness does not develop in a vacuum. It is necessarily projected spatially and parallels cultural geographic questions about the formation of Chinese communities, especially those east of the Rockies. How and why did Chinese communities and Chinatowns begin? For New York City the answer is very different than for Chicago, which is very different than San Francisco. For awhile I believed New York followed the Chicago pattern proposed by Siu and others. As anti-Chinese attitudes and actions increased on the Pacific coast, Chinese primarily taking up the occupation of hand laundries migrated eastward, creating little pockets of settlements across the country. After obtaining a sufficient threshold number of laundries, then stores, services, and organizations were formed in a given locality where immigrants generally settled, thus creating a Chinese commercial hub and homebase.

From 1870 onward, this pattern seemed to have been largely true in New York City, thus substantiating the Pacific coast origins of Chinese in the United States. These laundry and other types of workers were linked in associations and in memory with far more established Pacific coast and Hawaiian communities, which were linked to home villages and cities in Hong Kong, Macao, and southern China. And, as evident by the San Francisco photographs of Genthe, these settlements were not simply "Cantons in the West" or Midwest or East with no interaction with their specific regional and local surroundings. In fact, I will state the obvious that each laundry or commercial district was affected by and interrelated with the specific mix of people and part of the city they were located in. Not all Chinese settlements have been, nor are presently, the same.

Yet, even such elaborations to this theory of the West Coast origins of Chinese Americans is not fully satisfactory against the empirical research of northeastern Chinese communities, research which is just beginning to develop. In the past, the occasional reference to traveling Chinese acrobats or touring Chinese women put on display in the Northeast have been treated as isolated anecdotes that had little to do with the social history of Chinese Americans. However, a closer examination of the New York City census records, for example, reveal that those individuals were not the only

Chinese in Gotham. Indeed, small pockets of Chinese lived in lower Manhattan decades before the discovery of gold at Sutter's Mill and well before San Francisco. There were two interesting qualities to these individuals: first, they were largely mariners who had traveled the seas as part of the European and European American trade with various parts of Asia and the Pacific, and second, contrary to assumptions of Chinese clannishness, they freely intermingled and intermarried with non-Chinese in lower Manhattan. Fully one-third of these men took on Anglo names such as John Thompson. And among the Chinese found in the 1850s were Cuban-Chinese cigar makers and escaped Chinese-Peruvian guano harvesters. These individuals and performers were part of another migration pattern that was independent of the Pacific coast (Tchen 1990c:157-92).

These insights about the importance of particular locales ironically led my research to explore more fully the larger contexts of American history and world-systems analysis. Within these frameworks, I believe we can better understand the initial port settlements of Chinese in the Americas, north, central, south, and the Carribbean, as part of interlinked movements of people, ideas, and goods. The nineteenth-century Hawaiian and Pacific coast settlements, and the earlier migrations of Chinese and Filipinos to the Americas with Spanish colonizations, were in fact extensions of the Atlantic-centered world of European and Euro-American empire building and nationalisms. As "occidental" routes to Asian trading ports proliferated, Chinese could be found traveling from Hong Kong to Lima to Jamaica to New York to Liverpool to Cape Town and back to Asia (Tchen forthcoming a). Hence the appearance of Chinese in Anglo-America followed the nation's territorial expansionism, from the Northeast ports to the Pacific coast, and then with the building of transcontinental routes from west to east. This approach challenges the conceptual narrowness of much of U.S. immigration history and encourages us to adopt a more diasporic approach to Chinese American history.

But people were not the only part of this globalizing system. The fabled luxury goods of the "Orient" were the motive force for much of East-West interactions. In studying the journey of the *Empress of China* which left New York harbor in 1784, the first ship of the new nation to trade with China, I was able to find linkages with Native Americans in the Appalachian foothills digging ginseng root in exchange for tea and porcelain teacups which were brought to the port of New York. American specie and goods were traded in Canton for the prized luxury items made by the tens of thousands of craftspeople working in southern China (Tchen

1992:6-35). Hence, translocal, transregional, and transnational relationships were established among very diverse peoples and economies. Indeed, we understand from the indentured workers of Panama, Peru, and Cuba, and the contract workers of Louisiana, North Arlington, New Jersey, and the railways that "coolies" were only valued for their labor. And that with the rise of reaction against radical Reconstruction after the Civil War, Chinese were thought to be easily expendable and not part of "We the People."

In this sense, the transplantation of Anglo-American ideas westward from the northeastern, Atlantic world structured the experiences of Chinese in the United States, first and foremost. The American variant of a Protestant, Victorian capitalist culture created the various urban contexts within which Chinese found themselves trying to make a life and earn a living.

The formation of tourist-driven and ghettoized Chinatowns of the 1880s, layered on top of the commercial districts created to serve the needs of the residents themselves, operated within the Victorian cities of sunshine and shadows. If the Victorian-American ideal was possessive individualism, male rationality, and "white" Protestants who could "freely" operate in the global marketplace, then "others" had to be created to help reinforce such an idealized self-conception. To be cultured then was to be encultured with the proper values and behavioral norms and to distance civilized behaviors from those of designated inferiors. The ethnically creolized international port district of lower Manhattan, and especially Chinatown, became the embodiment of all that was antithetical to proper and racially-defined Americanism. Within this sensibility we do not need Freud to understand that such sites of repression also became sites of fascination and obsession.

Hence, an increasingly exoticized and segregated Chinese settlement became a touristic, downtown Chinatown. With the rise of Protestant reformers, the Chinese settlement became criminalized as a site for gambling, rat-eaters, fetid opium dens, and miscegenous race-mixing. This place became a Victorian symbol for all that was to be feared and hated, while simultaneously serving as a source of endless allurement and popular media attention. The entire notion of the Anglo-American self, and its various modifications to the present, constructed norms of what it meant to be an American and created the need for non-normative, or bizarre others to act as a carnivalesque safety valve and to help keep the norms in line. In this sense, Victorian orientalism has defined Asians as forever alien and non-American (Tchen 1992:432-75).

The elite Victorian home, figurative and literally, then—as it has been defined in the dominant culture—has not been a home for Asian/Pacific peoples. For Asian/Pacific peoples unacculturated in proper behavioral norms, their lives in the United States were necessarily marginalized resulting in low self-esteem and social dislocation. "Orientals" have had to be terribly self-conscious about how "normal" people look upon them as aliens. In this cultural system of polar dualisms, Dr. Jekyll created Mr. Hyde and could not live without him.

Orientalism appears to be fastened into the basic architecture of U.S. cultural identity. Just when we feel we have made progress in striking down stereotypes or stemming anti-Asian violence, these obsessive orientalist fears pop up somewhere. It is hydra-headed and can only be effectively eradicated by striking repeatedly at its core. The American-way-of-life (that has enculturated and habituated most European Americans as normal, healthy, caring people) automatically keeps the socially embedded discourses of orientalism, primitivism, and other forms of dominance alive and powerful (Tchen forthcoming b; 1993).

My research has taken me on a journey from trying to conjure ancestral ghosts and reclaim community histories to increasingly look at the complexities of how our efforts to find homes, places of comfort, and affability are necessarily elusive, frustrated, and ephemeral. If I have learned anything from laundry workers, it's that I realize there are no safe places waiting for us out there. We have had to aggressively create nurturing spaces for ourselves. Where is home???—that basic question of my personal search. It is not in New York City at large, nor is it in tourist-driven old Chinatown. For me it is in that seldom acknowledged international district of lower Manhattan in which many cultures past and present have coincided and often intermixed. It has taken me many years to finally realize that the intercultural zone is where I feel most comfortable.

I have taken you hostage on a journey from the Pacific rim to the Atlantic world. In order to discover the origins of the Chinese American experience, we have necessarily gone from the West to the Northeast. Anglo-American Victorian culture dominated San Francisco and that urban culture was derivative of New York's, and other northeastern cities, patrician urban culture. So, in a sense, those acrobats and other performers who traveled throughout the Northeast in the early history of this new nation first encountered and negotiated what the San Francisco Chinese, Toishan Chinese, and Chinese launderers were to later have to deal with. They had to negotiate the peculiarities of a highly-racialized cross-cultural discourse in order to survive. Some found refuge in and helped to create creolized, international pockets of settlements, while others were marginalized and targets of immense intolerance. I firmly believe Chinese American studies has to come to terms with the contours of this dominant Anglo-American culture in order to fully reconcile our relationship to American studies and American history.

Asians in America have had to negotiate two historical, cultural mega-systems coming into clashing contact with one another (Tchen 1994).[1] Each system embodies deeply embedded relations between at least three sets of temporal and spatial relations: first, the living linkages and disjunctions expressed between past-present-future; second, the connections that are understood between specific locales to other locales regionally and internationally; and finally, how concepts of a normative self are interlinked to spatialized notions of otherness.

I end with a series of questions directed at activist scholars. How can we create spaces in which we can help conjure ghosts in places in which we live and work in order to help reconnect the present to the past to the future??? And, how can we help our beloved communities to continue to explore the meaning and value of our life's journeys??? And finally, how can we all gain some sense of how our different attachments to particular places are all interrelated and shared in a number of different ways???

I hope my indulgent reflections are a useful illustration of the central role played by reconceptualizing place in our pursuit of reclaiming an Asian/Pacific American chronology and giving voice to Asian/Pacific American peoples. The explicit use of cultural geography and comparative spatial relations can help us interlink the many disparate and diverse localized community experiences with the rather impersonal "invisible hands" of national and international political economic forces. This not only makes sense intellectually, but can help us formulate more effective political strategies to build deeply-rooted movements for justice and equality across the myriad sites in which we work and live.

Note

1. Whether we can actually consider Asia as one cultural system is the subject of much important debate and research. Sucheta Mazumdar's book (1994), Janet Abu-Lugoud's work on the world before European empire on the world before European empire hegemony (1989), and K. N. Chaudhuri's Annales-type study of the Indian subcontinent (1990) are helpful in this regard.

References

Abu-Lughod, Janet. *Before European Hegemony: The World System, A.D. 1250-1350.* New York: Oxford University Press, 1989.

Boyer, Ernest. *Scholarship Revisited: Priorities of the Professorate.* Princeton: Princeton University Press, 1990.

Canino, Maria Josefa. Keynote Address, Centro de Estudios Puertorriquenos 20th Anniversary Event, 29 October 1993, Hunter College, City University of New York.

Chaudhuri, K. N. *Asia before Europe: Economy and Civilization of the Indian Ocean from the Rise of Islam to 1750.* Cambridge: Cambridge University Press, 1990.

Egan, Timothy. "Offspring of Indians and Settlers Edit Histories of the Oregon Trail." *New York Times,* 31 May 1993.

Fei, Xiaotung. "The Shallowness of Cultural Tradition." In *Land without Ghosts,* edited by R. David Arkush and Leo O. Lee. Berkeley: University of California Press, 1989.

Goldman, Shifra M. and Tomás Ybarra-Frausto. "The Political and Social Contexts of Chicano Art." In *Chicano Art: Resistance and Affirmation,* edited by Richard Griswold del Castillo, Teresa McKenna, and Yvonne Yarbro-Bejarano. Los Angeles: UCLA Wight Art Gallery, 1991.

Hall, Stuart. "Cultural Identity and Diaspora." In *Identity: Community, Culture, Difference,* edited by Jonathan Rutherford. London: Lawrence & Wishart, 1990.

Limerick, Patricia Nelson. "Disorientation and Reorientation: The American Landscape Discovered from the West." *Journal of American History* 79 (December 1992):1021-49.

Mazumdar, Sucheta. *Sugar and Society in China: Peasants, Technology and the World Market.* Cambridge, Mass.: Harvard University Press, 1994.

Siu, Paul C. P. *The Chinese Laundryman: A Study of Social Isolation,* edited by John Kuo Wei Tchen. New York: New York University Press, 1987.

Tchen, John Kuo Wei. "Ancestor Worship, Sacred Pizzerias & The Other: A Few Conceits of Anglo-American Modernism." In *Different Voices: A Social, Cultural, and Historical Framework for Change in the American Art Museum,* edited by Marsha Tucker. New York: Association of Art Museum Directors, 1992.

_____. "Towards a Dialogic Museum." In *Museums and Communities,* edited by Ivan Karp and Steven Lavine, Washington, D.C.: Smithsonian Institution Press, 1990a.

_____. "The Chinatown-Harlem Initiative." In *Building Bridges,* edited by Jeremy Brecher and Tim Costello. New York: Monthly Review Press, 1990b.

_____. "Historical Amnesia & Collective Reclamation: Building Identity with Chinese Laundry Workers in the United States." In *Vers des Societes Pluriculturelles: Etude Comparatives et Situation en France.* Paris: L'Orstom, 1987.

_____. *Genthe's Photographs of San Francisco's Old Chinatown, 1895-1906.* New York: Dover Publications, 1984.

_____. "New York Chinese: The Nineteenth-Century Pre-Chinatown Settlement." *Chinese American History and Perspectives* (1990c):157-92.

_____. "Quimbo Appo's Fear of Fenians: Anglo-Irish-Chinese Relations in New York City." In *The New York Irish, 1625-1990*, edited by Ronald H. Bayor and Timothy Meagher. Baltimore: Johns Hopkins University Press, forthcoming a.

_____. "New York before Chinatown: Orientalism, Identity Formation, and Political Culture in the American Metropolis, 1784-1882." Ph.D. diss., New York University, 1992.

_____. "The Politics of Pluralism: The 'Chinese Question,' 'Whiz Kids,' and Racial Hierarchy in New York City." In *Beyond Pluralism: Essays on the Definition of Groups and Group Identities in American History*, edited by Wendy Katkin and Ned Landsman. Urbana: University of Illinois Press, forthcoming b.

_____. "Rethinking Who 'We' Are: A Basic Discussion of Basic Terms." In *Voices from the Battlefront, Achieving Cultural Equity*, edited by Marta Moreno Vega and Cheryll Y. Greene. Trenton: Africa World Press, 1993.

_____. "Believing Is Seeing: Transforming Orientalism & the Occidental Gaze." In *Asia/America: Identities in Contemporary Art*. New York: New Press, 1994.

Tu, Wei-ming. "Cultural China: The Periphery as the Center." *Daedalus* 120 (Spring 1991): 1-32.

Effacing Specific Visions: Viewing "Here" from "Elsewhere"

Karen K. Kosasa

A prominent feature of the "formalist art" curriculum, widely utilized by universities in the United States, is its tendency to decontextualize its knowledge. Without contextualizing the visual language a student is given to work with by addressing its historical formation and cultural bias, art students are vulnerable to having the particularities of their "local" vision obscured behind and within a visual language developed in another place that has something else to say.

My overall critique of the visual arts curriculum in this presentation will be informed by the recent work in postcolonial theory, especially as it intersects with the problems of identity and race. I will be using my experience as a studio art instructor at the University of Hawaiʻi where I taught for eight years, to locate specific concerns. More importantly, I will utilize a postcolonial analysis to describe how the current art curriculum enacts the colonial legacy in Hawaiʻi, the domination of one culture over others and the disavowal of the history of that subjugation.

I will also follow a cultural studies approach to examine how a formalist art program, informed by Euro-American modernist aesthetics, is able to speak to the complicated needs of students of color, who comprise seventy-four percent of the student body at the University of Hawaiʻi.[1] The present curriculum, I will argue, enables students to use visual languages to "express" themselves but at the expense of an elision of their own identity. How a student is configured by an intersection of race, class, gender, and ethnicity, seems of little interest to a program that represents itself as democratically and benevolently engaged in providing *everyone* with visual languages developed in the Western world. Eliding a student's identity leads to a dismissal of differences and precludes the possibility of using those differences to interrogate the limitations and deficiencies of the curriculum and the visual languages it promotes as universal.

My overarching interest in this essay is to sketch out the complexities of how a vision from a specific "here," meaning Hawai'i, may be co-opted by a visual language from another place, a generalized "over there." While I am not prepared to deny the agency and creative ability of students to manipulate "ready-made" visual schemas (I am not advocating a strict visual/media determinism), I am more concerned with how the subtlety of their "local" narratives may be obscured by the languages used to tell their stories.

I speak from the position of a teacher of the formalist art curriculum as well as a product of it. In more ways than one, my academic work is a way of reflecting upon and working my way out of a "colonial" education that encouraged me to forget that I was of Asian ancestry, that I was not White. Only recently have I begun, like so many of us, a process of "remembering to remember" who I am and how my identity is connected to a past that reaches beyond the memory and history of my immediate family.

Despite the recent interest by many contemporary artists in "anti-aesthetic" issues—political, environmental, racial, gender, and historical problems—most art schools and university art departments remain committed to a formalist art program in which the skillful manipulation of materials is given priority over an examination of visual content and subject matter. This focus, explains art historian and educator, Howard Risatti, is largely due to the influence of the National Association of Schools of Art and Design (NASAD) which drew up national guidelines for university-level art curricula in the mid-1940s (1989:24). NASAD was established to ensure that artists and designers were educated as professionals according to the aesthetic ideals of the day, which were heavily informed by "late modernist" practices (like Abstract Expressionism, Color Field Painting, Minimalism) and the writings of the art historian Clement Greenberg. Risatti notes the irony of current programs which consider themselves to be at the forefront of art education, but still pattern themselves after NASAD guidelines (1989:24).

B.F.A. students are often required to take sixty percent of their total credit hours in the art department whereas other degree programs in the humanities require that their students take only thirty percent of the credit hour total in their major area of concentration. Risatti emphasizes that this means that art students in the B.F.A. program are not given a broad-based liberal arts education and that the curriculum comes "dangerously close to reducing art to an empty formal/technical exercise" (1991:22). Art students, he warns us, are not given the tools to be critical of what they are taught and are easily sidetracked by the glamour of the profession and superficial appeals to their rebellious spirit. While I agree with Risatti's criticisms, my own concerns focus on how the curriculum supports a larger colonial history and project.

The deconstruction of Western culture has been going on for some time now, but it seems to have eluded the art departments and institutions on the university level. These institutions, many of them still utilizing a NASAD-like curriculum, continue to think of themselves as bastions of "universal aesthetics" functioning to provide students with visual languages and techniques promoted as neutral conduits of experience. Although individual instructors may think otherwise, the overall system works, like the university itself, toward representing its knowledge as transcendent of cultural biases.

By promoting a curriculum informed by NASAD-like guidelines, the art department at the University of Hawai'i at Mānoa actively encourages its studio art students to use visual schemas and aesthetic knowledge developed elsewhere to inform their "local" visions. If one were to take into account the political and social history of the Hawaiian Islands, which includes the illegal overthrow of the Hawaiian monarchy in 1893, and accept the fact that Hawai'i remains under the colonial rule of the United States, the education of art students at the University of Hawai'i, I would argue, participates in an "aesthetic colonialism."

Against a history of colonialism, against the growing movement of Native Hawaiians for sovereignty, to teach modernist aesthetics in Hawai'i without considering how it participates in a legacy of colonialism is to unwittingly enact that legacy and to perpetuate the arrogant superiority it maintains over other forms of knowledge. Furthermore, the link between modernism and colonial enterprises has become increasingly difficult to ignore in light of recent scholarship. We can no longer think of Matisse in Morocco, for instance, as a simple painter on holiday in an exotic country, but as a French citizen in one of his country's colonies. Matisse's paintings of Riffian warriors become problematic once we are made aware that these warriors were subjugated by the French army a few years prior to the painter's arrival in Morocco; the modernist artist thus reworks the colonized into unthreatening figures of art. This does not mean that the paintings of

Matisse are any less important, but that our understanding of their meaning must be placed within an acknowledgment of France as a colonial empire. Art historian Roger Benjamin explains,

> It remains necessary to demonstrate that the great modernist painters like Matisse are by no means artists detached from the flow of history. . . . To maintain such detachment is to maintain a utopian reading of esthetic activity, to maintain that art can proceed without mounting up any debt in the sphere of the political (1990:211).

If we, as educators, believe that art is not simply reflective of social reality but also productive of it, then we need to take our pedagogical duties seriously. We cannot, as Benjamin says, naively think that art can proceed without "mounting up any debt." We need to heed the postmodernist critiques of modernist art practices that accuse the latter of ignoring the importance of issues of race, gender, and ethnicity. In fact, the formalist art curriculum's reluctance to discuss extra-aesthetic issues and colonialism's denial of history should be seen as no simple coincidence but an active *collusion* between two cultural practices that work to keep the past and the "local" at bay, away from the institutions of art.

We must also realize the harm we may inflict on our students when we promote an aesthetic from somewhere else that ignores the complexity of their "local" identities and invalidates many of their lived realities because of its preoccupation with form and its privileging of Euro-American culture. Ngũgĩ wa Thiong'o has eloquently explained the problems for indigenous (or local) people and for their sense of self-worth when they are forced to be educated in a language other than the one they were raised with. For Ngũgĩ, English was given priority over his native Gĩkũyũ in the colonial schools of Kenya, and it "became the measure of intelligence and ability in the arts, the sciences, and all the other branches of learning" (1981:12). His education, he says, progressively alienated him from his culture, first through the English language and then through the teaching of another culture centered in Europe.

As long as art students in Hawai'i are asked to speak in the visual languages of Euro-American culture, their agency will be mitigated and they will always be vulnerable to "being spoken by" languages that can never be as attentive to their needs as ones that are developed more locally. "A specific culture," Ngũgĩ warns, "is not transmitted through language in its universality but in its particularity as the language of a specific community with a specific history" (1981:15).

Since there is no established "local" visual language equivalent to the Hawai'i Pidgin English (called Hawai'i Creole English by linguists) spoken by a large percentage of the people living in the islands, art educators feel more than justified in introducing Western visual languages and modernist aesthetic structures as a foundation upon which other non-Western cultural forms may be incorporated. Art historian Judith Wilson refers to this type of thinking as "intellectual neocolonialism" because it "insists upon its own enlightenment in acknowledging the virtues of non-Western products. . . " (1990:130). In other words, Western art is used as the base from which all other cultural products are evaluated and into which they are assimilated. However, in regard to the latter, an unthinking appropriation of non-Western elements into Western structural forms may also participate in a problematic raiding of the cultures of already marginalized others. A call for the necessary fabrication of local, visual pidgins must therefore concern itself with larger political, economic, and social factors and avoid myopic visions focused exclusively on the aesthetic.

Art educators in Hawai'i should look to the work of contemporary artists of color who are already creating visual languages that speak of their hybrid identities and their efforts to straddle more than one culture. We also need to make these artists as familiar to our students as the "old white masters." But in presenting their work, we should also reveal how their art challenges the evaluative standards of a modernist aesthetic that privileges only certain kinds of formalist experimentations. This art should therefore be understood in terms of a cultural difference/hybridity that in itself constitutes a critique of other work. In this we need to be wary of efforts to assimilate the work as "equally different" from other kinds of Western art in a problematic process of cultural leveling.

In *Mixed Blessings: New Art in a Multicultural America* (1991), Lucy Lippard describes the dissatisfaction African American art historian Judith Wilson had as an adolescent with her drawings of the facial features of black women. Despite the benefit of extensive art classes, it was not until Wilson was given a book on the art of Nigeria, outside of school, that she was able to make a visual connection between the stylized elements of Gelede masks and the planes and angles on the faces of Yoruba people. This connection or visual realization helped her to finally "see" and satisfactorily draw the facial features of people of African ancestry (36).

Wilson's story underscores the deficiencies of an art curriculum which does not directly address the racial specificity of the student as artist or as the object of representation. It also confirms the insights of art historian

Ernst Gombrich who emphasized the importance of visual schema for artists in *Art and Illusion: A Study in the Psychology of Pictorial Representation*
(1960). Gombrich argued that without such a conceptual and aesthetic
framework, the visual world could not be represented. Wilson thus needed
the schema provided by the Gelede masks to "see" black facial features. To
understand and "see" non-white identities, I would also like to argue, requires new conceptual schemas, new ways of mapping the cultural and
racial difference of non-white local students. But mapping identity as cultural difference is no simple task.

The identities of our local students can never be understood in terms
of an essentialism or a simple adding up of discrete differences. According
to Homi Bhabha, such an identity will always be implicated in more than
one system of meaning, and more importantly, always interrupting, inter-
vening, and insinuating itself into the dominant "narrative" of a nation
(1990:291-322), or in the case of Hawai'i, the "narrative" of the state. In
other words, the cultural difference and identity of the non-white student
may be understood as the site of a transformative and retrospective knowledge. Identity as cultural difference can be used to reread a given national
narrative or the story of statehood to uncover the erasures and silences of
the minorities who have never been acknowledged in a nation's or a state's
"official" history, what Bhabha refers to as the "minus in the origin"
(1990:310).

It must be emphasized that this current discussion of identity is not a
return to the "identity politics" of the 1960s which was always seeking
some ground of "authenticity" or notion of a "true self." After Marx, after
Freud, and after Saussure, explains black British cultural critic Stuart Hall,
the old "logic of identity" is finished. The new identity is conceived as a
process, as something that is never complete and always in formation
(1991:42-47). Part of this formation is the result of the retrospective knowledge mentioned above, an identity that comes into being through the convergence of narratives of recovery, reconstruction, and a retelling of one's
history, in relation and, most often, in opposition, to the dominant culture's
narrative.

Hall calls this process of recovery and reaching into the past a "redis-
covery of ethnicity" (1991:37). It is the realization that one is grounded,
that one only speaks from a particular place and out of a specific historical
configuration. It is an "enormous moment" he says, when people begin
this retracing—a point at which the "world begins to be decolonized"

because people begin to retrieve their hidden histories (1991:35). They begin to tell other stories about themselves.

For non-indigenous peoples, acknowledging the histories that led us or our ancestors to Hawai'i is a necessary process. Not only will it help many of us who are non-White and living in the West to understand the heterogeneity, diversity, and contradictory aspects of our identities, it will also help us to place ourselves in relation to the indigenous people. The latter is critical for revealing to many of us who are non-indigenous how we have participated in (neo)colonial practices.

The political and cultural terrain in the Hawaiian Islands is extremely complex as it is almost everywhere. The return to the new "identity politics" is a way for all of us, educators and students, to locate ourselves and our partial perspectives so that we can acknowledge how we have been shaped by the trajectories of our own histories. It will also, I believe, help us to make our way through and out of the present configuration of colonialism in Hawai'i towards a more emancipatory society.

Let me end with a few words on art education. In order to counter the effacement of the "local visions" of art students in Hawai'i by a visual narrative from somewhere else, a critical pedagogy must develop practices that actively attend to the differences of our students—their gender, class, ethnicity, and race. It must also emphasize how each person is differently situated and positioned in relation to a historical past and a lived present. To this end it must challenge educational discourses that view schooling as a "decontextualized site free from social, political, and racial tensions" (Giroux 1992:118).

Notes

1. Statistic published by the Equal Employment Opportunity and Affirmative Action Office at the University of Hawai'i at Mānoa for the 1992 undergraduate class. The actual figure is 73.9 percent and reflects the ethnic distribution of Asian/Pacific Islanders, Blacks, and American Indians. It does not include Hispanic, Caucasian, and mixed ethnicities.

References

Benjamin, Roger. "Matisse in Morocco: A Colonizing Esthetic?" *Art in America* 78 (November 1990).

Bhabha, Homi K. "DissemiNation: Time, Narrative, and the Margins of the Modern Nation." In *Nation and Narration,* edited by Homi K. Bhabha. London: Routledge, 1990.

Giroux, Henry. *Border Crossings: Cultural Workers and the Politics of Education.* New York: Routledge, 1992.

Gombrich, Ernst. *Art and Illusion: A Study in the Psychology of Pictorial Representation.* New York: Pantheon Books, 1960.

Hall, Stuart. "The Local and the Global: Globalization and Ethnicity." In *Culture, Globalization and the World-System: Contemporary Conditions for the Representation of Identity,* edited by Anthony D. King. Binghamton: Binghamton University, Department of Art and Art History, 1991.

_____. "Old and New Identities, Old and New Ethnicities." In *Culture, Globalization and the World-System: Contemporary Conditions for the Representation of Identity,* edited by Anthony D. King. Binghamton: Binghamton University, Department of Art and Art History, 1991.

Lippard, Lucy. *Mixed Blessings: New Art in a Multicultural America.* New York: Routledge, 1991.

Ngũgĩ wa Thiong'o. *Decolonizing the Mind: The Politics of Language in African Literature.* London: James Curry, 1981.

Risatti, Howard. "A Failing Curricula." *New Art Examiner* 17 (September 1989).

_____. "Protesting Professionalism." *New Art Examiner* 18 (February 1991).

Wilson, Judith. "Seventies into Eighties—Neo-Hoodism vs. Postmodernism: When (Art) Worlds Collide." In *The Decade Show: Frameworks of Identity in the 1980s.* New York: Museum of Contemporary Hispanic Art, New Museum of Contemporary Art, Studio Museum of Harlem, 1990.

The Growing Asian Population in the American South: Defining the Process of Immigrant Community Development

William Sakamoto White

In 1990, Atlanta's total Asian population ranked nineteenth nationally, marking the first time a city from the "deep South" emerged as a major Asian population center (U.S. Bureau of the Census 1990). Of the top twenty Asian metropolitan areas in 1990, Atlanta had the highest percentage increase in Asian population, increasing by over 330 percent since 1980, adding nearly 40,000 Asians. Since the 1980s, Atlanta's attraction of ethnic immigrants and refugees has changed the racial composition of the Atlanta region from one that was predominantly Black to one where Hispanics and Asians are becoming increasingly significant (ARC 1992). Clearly, immigration has had a significant impact on Atlanta's urban space.

The Atlanta region's primary growth area for Hispanics and Asians has been DeKalb County with much of this growth occurring in a small area running north of Interstate 85 (I-85) and encompassing the cities of Chamblee and Doraville. Prior to 1990 this area was a predominantly white, middle-class Atlanta suburb with a commercial district along U.S. Highway 23 (Buford Highway) which included retail businesses, a county-owned general aviation airport, and some manufacturing sites. By 1990, the Chamblee-Doraville site had dramatically transformed into an ethnically and racially diverse business and residential area. The area's commercial district, known as the "Buford Highway Corridor," became a center of ethnic economic activity. This economic shift dramatized the ongoing racial changes in the area.

Many Asian immigrants and refugees make ethnic enclaves their first choice of residence in America. To be sure, several factors not necessarily in the newcomer's control account for this trend: family members reside in the enclave, support networks exist in the enclave area, and sponsoring agencies often associate enclave sites as appropriate residential locations for gradual assimilation into American society. Nonetheless, enclaves provide new immigrants with basic services, support networks, and labor opportunities that often do not exist outside the enclave. Enclaves also provide newcomers some insulation from a mainstream society that associates economic burdens and cultural deviance with the Asian immigrant and refugee.

The focus of this work analyzes how recent Asian immigrants and refugees influence Atlanta's spatial dynamics, specifically the process of how Atlanta's Asian immigrants are transforming the Chamblee-Doravill area and whether this area is an "Asian enclave." Though not addressed directly, this study will then explore the stages in community interaction in the enclave area today between these new Asian immigrants and the area's established residents. Framed in Kitano's (1991) sociological perspective of majority-minority relations, what does this process of community transformation imply for current and future relations between these two different groups?

This study relies primarily upon an analysis of existing data sources including the 1980 and 1990 Bureau of Census data, 1980 and 1992 *Haines Commercial Directory* information, and news accounts from the *Atlanta Journal-Constitution*. Through my participation in the local economy and civic activities of the Chamblee-Doraville Asian community, I obtained some preliminary observational data. I also held some informal discussions in the homes of recent Asian immigrants and with Asian business and social service leaders.

Census tracts with the largest numbers of Asian residents predominate in the I-85 highway corridor. Tables 1 and 2 illustrate the demographic changes occurring in DeKalb County and the Buford Highway Corridor between 1980 and 1990.

Table 1

Population Characteristics - DeKalb County
1980-1990

	1980	Percent of Total	1990	Percent of Total	Percent Change
Total Population	483,024	-NA-	545,837	-NA-	13.0%
Total Minority Population	144,095	29.8%	261,812	48.0%	81.7%
Total Asian Population	4,633	1.0%	16,150	3.0%	248.6%

Table 2

Buford Highway Corridor

	1980	Percent of Total	1990	Percent of Total	Percent Change
Total Population	113,094	-NA-	120,842	-NA-	5.4%
Total Minority Population	5,213	7.3%	32,495	26.9%	341.0%
Total Asian Population	2,009	1.8%	7,290	6.0%	245.8%

During the last decade, DeKalb County grew at a 13 percent rate while the Buford Highway Corridor area grew by only 6.9 percent. In total, the Buford Highway Corridor has not reproduced the same significant population growth as DeKalb County experienced over the last ten years. The data clearly shows, though, that a demographic transition is taking place. In 1980, the area was predominantly White (92.7%). By 1990, the percentage of white residents in the area had dropped to 73.2 percent. The total minority population in the area experienced a 341 percent increase during the decade. The number of Blacks increased by 370.7 percent, followed by Hispanics at 145 percent, and Asians with 132.3 percent. By 1990, this area represented 45.7 percent of DeKalb County's total Asian population, 52.2 percent of the total Hispanic population, and 7.3 percent of the black population. Over 31.1 percent of DeKalb's white population still resided in this area.

Table 3 describes the changes taking place in the Asian community during the last ten years.

Table 3

Buford Highway Corridor
Asian Population

	1980	Percent of Total	1990	Percent of Total
Total Asian Population	2,009	-NA-	7,290	-NA-
Chinese	558	27.8%	1,728	23.7%
Korean	507	25.2%	1,846	25.3%
Indian	534	26.6%	1,486	20.4%
Japanese	229	4.1%	256	.8%
Vietnamese	118	2.1%	1,767	24.2%
Other Asians	63	3.1%	207	2.8%

Though the total number of the Asians living in the area was small in 1980, it still represented 43.4 percent of DeKalb County's Asian population. In 1980, the fledgling Asian community consisted primarily of

Chinese, Indians, and Koreans. By 1990, the Buford Highway Corridor was home to over 45 percent of the county's Asian population. Koreans, Chinese, and Indians still dominate the area, but Southeast Asians (Vietnamese, Cambodians, Laotians, and Hmong) now represent over 24 percent of the community.

Clearly the area became a center for Asian population growth from 1980 to 1990. This growth appears to have stimulated a subsequent increase in the number of businesses catering to the Asian population along the Buford Highway commercial district. According to 1980 and 1992 comparisons of businesses operating in the commercial district, less than ten business and professional services in 1980 were owned or operated by Asians in this area (Haines 1980). Most of these services were small retail or restaurants. By 1992, this number had increased to over fifty-five and the variety of businesses and professional services ranged from groceries, video stores, doctors, attorneys, insurance agents, tailors, book stores, newspapers, travel agents, construction companies, herbalists, and clothing stores, as well as restaurants and other small retail shops (Haines 1992).

It appears from discussions with the area's Asian community leaders that a significant amount of investment capital came from Chinese and Korean investors. To a lesser extent, Vietnamese and Indian entrepreneurs also invest in this area's commercial district. But the driving capital force in the area seems to come from Chinese and Korean investors. This issue needs further examination in follow-up studies of this area.

The primary market groups vary among the area's Asian businesses. Some cater to one ethnic group while others attract a variety of ethnic Asians. For example, one commonly sees larger grocery stores stocking rental videos in Mandarin, Cantonese, and Vietnamese languages. Smaller retail shops and food stores, though, tend to cater to one Asian ethnic market. Asian restaurants appear to cater to many ethnic Asian groups and have emerged to serve populations outside the enclave. It is clear to see that the growth of the number of Asian owned and operated businesses in the area caters to the Asian community's "sheltered market," providing necessary and vital services not met outside the area.

Asians in the community appear to provide a good base for cheap labor both within and outside the community. Recent immigrants, especially Southeast Asians, are working in the local and regional service industry. In the enclave, they work in the larger stores and shops with other Asians. If they have access to transportation, they can work outside the local community. Some recent Asian immigrants commute one hour to work in the poultry industry in Hall County. Others commute to various service jobs such as hotels and restaurants just outside the community. Generally, these new immigrants are providing the local and regional economy with a source of low-skill cheap labor.

Though business activity represents a piece of the institutional process, perhaps a better measure of community solidarity and enclave establishment is the number of service organizations within the community. Table 4 highlights the service institutions located directly in the community.

Table 4

Asian Community Institutions

Religious
        Atlanta Buddhist Association
        Brookvalley Church of Christ (Cambodian)
        First Baptist Church of Chamblee (Cambodian)
        Shinjing Korean Presbyterian Church
        Southern Presbyterian Church (Korean)
        Sung Yahk Presbyterian Church (Korean)
        Rabha Saomi Satsand Beas (Indian)
Service Organizations
        Korean Community Services
        Chinese Community Center
        Refugee Resource Center
News Organizations
        Asia News
        Asia Printing
        The Korean Journal, Atlanta Edition
English as a Second Language Centers
        Cross Keys High School, International Center
        First Baptist Church of Chamblee, Adult ESOL Center
Other Organizations
        Pakistan Society
        Bangladesh Student Association
           Source: Atlanta Council of International Organizations.

The Chinese, Korean, and (to a lesser extent) Indian groups have created solid organizations within the community in all major institutional areas: religious, service, and news. The Southeast Asian group also has some institutions that focus on their needs. Since many Southeast Asians are new immigrants, these institutions are primarily resource organizations that help them adjust to life in America. Still, these institutions are even more important to the Southeast Asians. Given the lack of transportation resources within the Southeast Asian community, these institutions' close proximity to many Southeast Asians provide ease of service delivery.

Looking at the Buford Highway Corridor area, outsiders might initially conclude that an Asian enclave has fully developed here. It has a large Asian commercial/entrepreneur base, there appears to be a large amount of Asian capital investment in the area, new Asian immigrants seem to provide a source of cheap labor both within and outside the community, and there are large number of Asians living in the area, providing a sheltered market to access local goods and services. Structurally, the Asian community provides commercial services. It is also considered a source of cheap labor to the region's service industry. Relationships between Asian businesses and other established businesses do not yet appear to have reached a "problematic" state, but as the community becomes more visible to outsiders, conflict may emerge. Clearly, though, the community is concentrated and spatially identifiable.

What outsiders miss with this perspective are the many ethnic groups that make up the Asian community and the differing levels of "institutional completeness" attained by each group. What appears to be going on within the Buford Highway Corridor is a process where Asian ethnic groups work and live close together, but certain Asian groups have developed their own enclave economies. The Chinese and Koreans, for example, appear to have developed full enclave economies that not only cater to the needs of their own ethnic groups, but also provide services and opportunities to Asians outside these groups. More recent immigrants and refugees, including many Southeast Asians, exhibit more secondary sector economy characteristics while the more established or better financed groups exhibit more institutional completeness and enclave development.

Southeast Asians comprise a large portion of recent immigrants in the Buford Highway Corridor area. They are entering the area with very limited English language skills and are targets for cheap low-skill labor. These recent immigrants do not possess the capital nor the business expertise yet to develop into an enclave structure. However, early Vietnamese immigrants in the area provide limited capital and business expertise in the community. These first immigrants represented a primary sector immigrant community in the early 1980s. With the influx of new immigrants, the Southeast Asian community may be able to move towards establishment of an enclave setting. Indeed, certain entrepreneurs have emerged to attempt to develop the area's first Vietnamese "Town Center" (Fay 1993).

Currently, though, the Southeast Asian community lacks institutional completeness. Social service agencies that provide health care, recreational services, job skill training, and education do not exist yet for Southeast Asians in the Buford Highway Corridor. To be sure, churches and other organizations have volunteered to help this community develop English skills and direct individuals to jobs and housing. Also, there are a number of small businesses that cater exclusively to the Southeast Asian community. But Southeast Asians still represent a community that is in a primary/secondary sector typology that is moving towards an enclave type of community.

The Chinese and Korean communities have achieved a level of institutional completeness that the Southeast Asians have yet to experience. The Chinese community has attained the highest level of institutional completeness. The Chinese Community Center acts as the center for cultural, social, educational, and recreational activities for the Chinese community. In immediate proximity to the center is a commercial mall leased to predominantly Chinese businesses, but also to the Buddhist Association, an Asian news organization, professionals, groceries, small retail stores, and an herbalist. Chinese investors recently supplied a large amount of capital toward a new "Asiatown" commercial complex in the Buford Highway commercial zone. This complex will open up in 1993 and will provide more commercial and professional space primarily for the Chinese, Korean, and other Asian community groups. The Chinese community is relatively heterogeneous in ethnicity and class level. Recent immigrants from China represent political refugees, low-skill immigrants, and entrepreneurs. They all can find a niche within the community, and possess resources to make their adjustment to American society easier.

The Korean community has less institutional completeness and represents a community in the middle between primary sector and enclave economy typologies. There is strong reason to believe that they are moving toward developing the institutional completeness required of an enclave setting. The Korean Community Services Center, though not as expansive nor as full-service as the Chinese Community Center, provides the Korean community with a variety of services and referrals, and is primarily concerned with helping current Korean residents and new immigrants with finding social services for people in need. The next step toward institutional completeness would be for the community to create a community center that provides similar services to that of the Chinese Community Center.

The Chinese and, to a lesser extent, Koreans have developed ethnic enclave economies that serve not only their own communities but also other Asian immigrants. "To serve" does not imply affording opportunities for advancement across or within ethnic ranks between the "employer" and the "employee," though. My preliminary discussions with enclave entrepreneurs and employees seem to validate the findings made by Nee and Sanders (1987), Wong (1987) and Zhou and Logan (1980) that entrepreneurs, not enclave employees, are the major beneficiaries of participation in the enclave economy. What the Chinese and Korean businesses have been able to do is expand their consumer and employee market base beyond their own ethnic communities and into the greater Asian immigrant and refugee community. Some businesses have even expanded their market-bases into the non-Asian community, creating support within the Atlanta business community leadership for the development of an "International Village" in the Chamblee-Doraville area in time for the 1996 Olympics. The question that remains is whether new Asian immigrants who work in the enclave economy will be able to take advantage of opportunities to advance in the enclave or if they will remain, due to lack of opportunity, a permanent part of the enclave's working poor.

For the DeKalb County Board of Commissioners, the DeKalb Chamber of Commerce, and the cities of Atlanta and Chamblee, the Asian commercial expansion represents a new opportunity to revive what was a dying commercial and industrial area. Though relations between important political and business leaders in the Atlanta region and ethnic entrepreneurs appear truly positive, past research indicates that the enclave will enter a period of conflict in the near future (Wong 1989; Kitano 1991; Horton 1992). Doraville, for example, is feeling threatened by the growth of Asian businesses and the influx of new immigrants into its city. They are beginning to restrict "foreign" business development stating that the community needs to protect its "American" image. To complicate matters, I believe that conflict will emerge from a variety of fronts both outside and within the enclave.

The Chamblee-Doraville area, due to its attraction of many middle- to upper-class Asian immigrants, is likely to repeat the conflict that emerged in Monterey Park, California between Asian entrepreneurs and established residents who perceived their "valued resources" being "taken over" by the new Asian immigrants. We can measure and monitor this conflict as no-growth moratoriums, English-only campaigns, and other xenophobic and racially based initiatives directed against Asian businesses emerge. The South has historically been more nativist than other parts of the country, and there is no reason to believe that the attacks and strategies here would be any less reactionary than the anti-immigrant movement in Monterey Park.

Because the area is a large center of "secondary sector" Asian immigrants, a clash between different Asian classes is likely to occur. One must begin to fully explore the underlying issue raised by Nee and Sanders (1987) that within our own Asian community a certain level of stratification exists prohibiting certain working class poor immigrants the chance to elevate themselves within the enclave economy's opportunity scheme. Indeed, the clash may already be occurring. In recent negotiations between the Chamblee-Doraville business leadership and Asian enclave business owners to finalize the International Village concept, both sides have agreed to consider demolishing what they perceive is the largest blight in the area: a large area of substandard housing where many new Asian immigrants, primarily Southeast Asian and working class poor, currently reside. Many of these residents are full participants in the enclave economy, both as employees and consumers. Yet, the Asian business leadership appears willing to eliminate this sector of the enclave, providing no options for relocating these immigrants as residents back into close proximity to the enclave commercial area.

Finally, it is the image of the "foreign" immigrant that will lead to conflict at a larger level outside the community, especially if local residents do not positively receive the awareness programs initiated by local governments, the media, and Asians. As the presence of the enclave grows and as the community becomes more class heterogeneous, established residents will begin to question whether these new Asian immigrants are taking away resources "meant for long-time residents."

What is important currently, at this site, is that we identify the points where conflict situations may arise. From previous research, we have an idea how conflict will emerge in the Chamblee-Doraville area if left unchecked. If the last ten years are an indication of the future, Atlanta will not be the only new "site" for Asian immigration and enclave development. Conflict situations will continue to challenge the development of new Asian enclaves throughout the South in the coming years.

We need further exploration of the second level of conflict that appears to exist within our own community. Class stratification may be defining who will successfully adapt to American society in the coming years. We need to recognize the strong empirical proof that the enclave economy is perhaps only a mechanism for successful adaptation for an ever narrowing segment of the Asian immigrant community. These are the next challenges within our own community: to not only identify how Asian immigrants can coexist without conflict when interacting with American society but, perhaps most important, to also identify how to be our own critics and urge an examination of the conditions within the enclave economy.

References

Atlanta Council of International Organizations. *1991-1992 Directory of International Organizations*. Atlanta: ACIO, 1991.

Atlanta Regional Commission. *Atlanta Region Outlook*. Atlanta: ARC, 1992.

Banton, Michael. *Race Relations*. London: Tavistock Publications, 1967.

Bogardus, Emory. "A Race Relations Cycle." *American Journal of Sociology* 35 (1930):612-17.

Breton, Raymond. "Institutional Completeness of Ethnic Community and the Personal Relations of Immigrants." *American Journal of Sociology* 70 (1964):193-205.

Fay, Tim S. "Vietnamese Shopping Area to Open in Summer." *Atlanta Journal Constitution*, 22 April 1993.

Gordon, Milton. "Assimilation in America." *Daedalus* 90 (1961):263-85.

Guthey, Greig. "Asia Mall Likely to Hike Merchant's Competition along Buford Highway." *Atlanta Journal Constitution*, 2 January 1992.

Haines. *1980 Atlanta Suburban Directory*. North Canton: Haines & Co., 1980.

Haines. *1992 Atlanta Suburban Directory*. North Canton: Haines & Co., 1992.

Horton, John. "The Politics of Diversity in Monterey Park, California." In *Structuring Diversity: Ethnographic Perspectives on the New Immigration.*, edited by Louise Lamphere. Chicago: University of Chicago Press, 1992.

Hune, Shirley. *Pacific Migration to the United States: Trends and Themes in Historical and Sociological Literature*. Washington D.C.: Smithsonian Institution, 1977.

Jaret, Charles. "Recent Structural Change and U.S. Urban Ethnic Minorities." *Journal of Urban Affairs* 13 (1991):307-36.

Kitano, Harry H. L. *Race Relations*. Englewood Cliffs: Prentice Hall, 1991.

Lee, Sharon. "Asian Immigration and American Race Relations: From Exclusion to Acceptance?" *Ethnic and Racial Studies* 12 (1989):368-90.

Light, Ivan. *Ethnic Enterprise in America*. Berkeley: University of California Press, 1972.

____. *Cities in World Perspective*. New York: Macmillan, 1983.

Light, Ivan and Charles Choy Wong. "Protest or Work: Dilemmas of the Tourist Industry in American Chinatowns." *American Journal of Sociology* 80 (1975): 1342-68.

McInerney, Salley. "DeKalb Fast Becoming Melting Pot." *Gwinnett Daily News*, 15 January 1992.

Park, Robert E. *Race and Culture*. New York: John Wiley, 1950.

Portes, Alejandro and Robert D. Manning. "The Immigrant Enclave: Theory and Empirical Examples." In *Competitive Ethnic Relations*, edited by Susan Olzak and Joane Nagel. Orlando: Academic Press, 1986.

Ross-Sheriff, Fariyal. "Adaptation and Integration into American Society: Major Issues Affecting Asian Americans." In *Social Work Practice with Asian Americans,* edited by Sharlene Maeda Furuto. Newbury Park: Sage Publications, 1992.

Sanders, Jimy and Victor Nee. "Limits of Ethnic Solidarity in the Enclave Economy." *American Sociological Review* 52 (1987):745-73.

Scroggins, Deborah. "DeKalb's Melting Pot Is Bubbling." *Atlanta Journal Constitution*, 12 January 1992.

U.S. Bureau of the Census. *Asian and Pacific Islander Population of Metropolitan Areas: 1990 and 1980*. Washington, D.C.: U.S. Bureau of the Census, 1990.

Williams, Robin R. *Mutual Accommodation: Ethnic Conflict and Cooperation*. Minneapolis: University of Minnesota Press, 1977.

Wilson, Kenneth and Alejandro Portes. "Immigrant Enclaves: An Analysis of the Labor Market Experiences of Cubans in Miami." *American Journal of Sociology* 86 (1980):295-319.

Wong, Bernard. "The Role of Ethnicity in Enclave Enterprises: A Study of the Chinese Garment Factories in New York City." *Human Organizations* 46 (1987): 120-30.

Wong, Charles Choy. "Monterey Park: A Community in Transition." In *Frontiers of Asian American Studies*, edited by Gail M. Nomura, *et al.* Pullman: Washington State University Press, 1989.

Zhou, Min and John R. Logan. "Returns on Human Capital in Ethnic Enclaves: New York City's Chinatown." *American Sociological Review* 54 (1989):809-20.

Asiancy: Making Space for Asian Canadian Writing

Roy Miki

"People who feel invisible try to borrow visibility from those who are visible."—Robert Kroetsch (1989:6)

In Margaret Atwood's best-selling critical guide to Canadian literature, *Survival*, national literary politics located a methodological tool for constructing an Anglocentric history with Canada as victim of American imperialism. The privileging of the author's own subject position as "English-Canadian" reader, though advanced in the frame of liberal humanism, in effect banished "racialized" Canadians from public space, a gesture that denied them "identity" in her text of nationhood. In the climax to her critical narrative, at that moment when a liberated future for Canadian writing is posited, an astounding admonition appears in what is no more than an aside: "...the tendency in English Canada has been to connect one's social protest not with the Canadian predicament specifically but with some other group or movement: the workers in the thirties, persecuted minority groups such as the Japanese [sic] uprooted during the war. English Canadians have identified themselves with Ban the Bombers, Communists, the FLQ, and so forth, but not often with each other—after all, the point of identifying with those other groups was at least partly to distinguish oneself from all the grey WASP Canadians you were afraid you might turn into" (1972:242). For Canadians of Asian ancestry what is unsettling is the offhand, unabashed erasure of Japanese Canadians (who were not "Japanese," i.e. the "enemy") and the specific "Canadian predicament" of their mass uprooting, internment, dispossession, even deportation, as the direct consequence of racist government policy branding them "enemy alien" and stripping them of their citizenship rights.

The pervasive power of "English-Canadian" centrality—White and Anglo-Saxon—has acted as such a weighty cultural pall that the process of overcoming imposed representations, misrepresentations, and erasures has been an almost insurmountable obstacle for Japanese Canadians and other communities of color in Canada, until only recently. Of all the "isms" that have surfaced in the past fifteen years, perhaps feminism and post-structualism together have been the most instrumental theoretical positions to resist and critique the power of patriarchic nationalist forms and the normative ahistoricism of humanist beliefs in universality.[1] Although the debates are often engaged on the borderlines of literary and public institutions where all "isms" of any sort are still treated as hot potatoes, there are signs that writers and cultural workers of color have begun to create theories, texts, and visual works that foreground issues of representation, appropriation, race and ethnicity, and subjectivity.[2]

A brief example, May 1992: At the historic meeting of Canadian writers of color at a conference, "The Appropriate Voice," the issue of "cultural appropriation" was aligned with, among other consequences of colonialism, racial oppression, and exploitation, the "misrepresentation of cultures and the silencing of their peoples" (Racial Minority Writers' Committee 1992).[3] Asian Canadian writers too have begun to interrogate and undermine representations of their communities manufactured by outsiders, often liberal and sympathetic white writers, artists, and film-makers whose intentions may be sincere but who fail to account for differences based on subjectivity, language, and the problematics of appropriation. Instead of assisting Canadians of Asian ancestry, these products of white assumptions and biases have all too often confirmed and reinforced the systemic racialization process through which privilege and power has been maintained.[4]

American cultural critic Cornel West has pointed to an emerging theoretical awareness as "the new politics of difference" which has features including the desire "to trash the monolithic and homogeneous in the name of diversity, multiplicity and heterogeneity; to reject the abstract, general and universal in light of the concrete, specific and particular; and to historicize, contextualize and pluralize by highlighting the contingent, provisional, variable, tentative, shifting and changing" (1990:19). Within this evolving "new politics" is the contestation for positioning and the necessity for writers and cultural workers of color to assume responsibility for the frames of reference through which their subjectivities are reproduced in public discourses. In a time of imploding paradigms—and the temptation of riding on changing fads and fashions in theories and terminologies—the risk of compromise and co-optation hovers on the edge of every cultural fold. Who is speaking? For whom? Why? In the plethora of discourses formed to answer these simple but profoundly destabilizing questions, allegiances can become ambiguous, even misleading. For some establishment critics, the so-called "margin" (itself a critical construct for a prior "center") may even take on a curious exoticism, as a comment by Linda Hutcheon reveals: ". . . in this age of the postmodern re-valuing of borders and margins as preferred sites of articulation of difference, many feel that the margins are indeed where the action is: that resistance and contestation make for more exciting art than centrisms of all kinds (ethno-, phallo-, hetero-, and so on)" (1991:49). For those on the "borders and margins," for those oppressed by the "centrisms of all kinds," the question of preference is laughable at one extreme, and outrageous at the other. The paradigm of centrality in which the "other" is the necessary border/margin delimits the (assumed so unrevealed) discourse boundaries of Hutcheon's statement—a reminder of Trinh T. Minh-Ha's warning to be wary of those from the center who work from an authority that cannot leave a stone unturned and who, accommodating the language of humanism, may enact a kind of liberal "pilgrimage" to borderline sites in order to extend its dominant forms of power (1991:17).

Such a deterrent to the making of an historically-situated cultural space for Canadian writers of Asian ancestry, as well as for other writers of color, is all the more prevalent in a country such as Canada where the ideology of assimilation, despite the so-called "multiculturalist" lip service, still pervades dominant social values reflecting, by and large, white, male Anglo-European priorities. Whatever the varying contexts for understanding the federal government's "multicultural" policy, initiated in 1971 and enshrined in the Canadian Multiculturalism Act of 1988, at an explicit level it was meant to appease the rumblings of those "others" standing on the sidelines of the biculturalism and bilingualism policy. Indeed, it was the latter policy that was so necessary to solidify the English and French Canadian power base against the threat of growing demands for more recognition by Canadians who did not belong to those designated as charter ethnic groups. In Evelyn Kallen's words, the multicultural policy "was a technique of domination designed to entrench the power of the ruling Anglo élite when its superordinate, national position was threatened by

Quebec's claim to political power, on the one hand, and by the growing numerical and economic strength and increasing cultural vitality of immigrant ethnic collectivities, on the other hand" (1982:167-68).

However, by the early 1980s the strain and constraints of Canadian nationalist (read here "centralist") ideology with the "founding" priority given to the English and French colonist groups had become increasingly visible; the multiculturalism policy was perceived to be inadequate to deal with systemic racism and the specific problems of non-European minorities of color who, in turn, had begun to confront racism by foregrounding the historical framework of colonization and Eurocentricity still evident in Canadian institutions and public policies. That broader neo-colonialist perspective brought into view the inequality of representations of different subject positions in the body politic. The Japanese Canadian redress movement, a strategy to redress the injustice of internment in the 1940s, developed within that context, perhaps even thrived on the changes going on. Other communities of color, including Chinese Canadians, Afro-Canadians, and Natives, became more vocal in asserting their histories, which had thus far been neutralized, denied, or otherwise erased.

By the time of the Japanese Canadian redress settlement on September 22, 1988, the cultural spaces of Canada had radically transformed. In recent years, the new works and theories emerging from formerly excluded sites, from Natives, from writers of color, including Asian Canadians, have opened a network of articulations and theoretical concerns that not only undermine assimilationist pressures but also allow for provisional spaces where writers of color can navigate diversity within the specificity of histories, languages, and subjectivities. The struggle for such empowerment and liberation from the imposed signs of "race" is on-going, and may get even more tense in the years ahead. As the earlier rhetoric of a binary center (biculturalism) with its subordinate "others" in the margins (multiculturalism) has exhausted its credibility, reactionary voices have arisen sounding the alarm of the country's cultural disintegration, often pointing fingers at minorities of color as the cause. Indeed, the resistance of writers, cultural workers, and community activists of color has created the possibility of explosive conflicts with establishment institutions, making all the more urgent the need for terminology and theoretical speculations that avoid the pitfall of simply re-circulating the old systems of power.

A one-dimensional oppositional positioning is hardly an adequate basis for new cultural forms which can represent the localized subjectivities of writers of color. While such contests of will and confrontation may be a pragmatic strategy for certain instances requiring immediate intervention-ist action, they do not instigate the internal transformations necessary for moving beyond the constraints of racialization to make spaces where difference and diversity are constantly being (re)negotiated. For Canadian writers of color—and here I speak in (personal) terms of Japanese Canadi-ans—the internal "battle" to overcome the powerful effects of racialization may, finally, be the most formidable opponent. Assimilationist assumptions, mostly unspoken, continue to saturate the mass media, and the ideology of white, male, European-based values still reigns in literary institutions, in granting bodies, and in decision-making areas of the publishing world. In a climate where difference is pressed into sameness, and where "universality" implies white perceptions, many writers and artists of color internalize the propaganda of dominant aesthetic and cultural norms and never reach that critical threshold of having to decolonize themselves.

For writers of color, then, the new form of becoming invisible may be less visible as an ideology, because of the official rhetoric of multicultural-ism, but it still requires conformity to dominant representations, to so-cially determined "tastes," and to transparent literary expectations. Only the most vigilant can escape the temptations of power relations that gov-ern what gets to be judged of "national significance" and of "consequence"—reinforced as they are by an elaborate system of awards, rewards, media privileges, canonization, and ultimately, institutionalization.

Writers who become aware of the conflict between acceptance through conformity and resistance to co-optation undergo a paradigmatic internal-ized upheaval. Historically and even at present, the strain of a domineering exterior on the interior of those in the state of exclusion created/creates complicated networks of ambiguities, repressions, and compromises that infiltrate the language and geography of their subjectivity. Such a state of boundedness, of inhibitions, of imposed silences, at an extreme, kills cre-ativity altogether—but when interrogated, deconstructed, and entered, can constitute an exploratory process which may even necessitate the creative act. It can be a generative space analogous to what Trinh T. Minh-ha de-scribes when she speaks of that liminal consciousness betwixt and between, in the transitional zone of an inside-outside confusion: "The moment the insider steps out from the inside she's no longer a mere insider. She neces-sarily looks in from the outside while also looking out from the inside. Not quite the same, not quite the other, she stands in that undetermined thresh-old place where she constantly drifts in and out" (1990:374-75). Certainly, the "threshold place" is familiar to many writers, but for Asian Canadians, and perhaps for other writers of color, the experience of inner and outer is not merely an instance of a decontextualized, abstract binary, but vitally connected to a community-based positioning vis-à-vis—or contained by, or surrounded by—an overriding white majority from which it is estranged either by language, or by sociocultural values, or by the phenomenon of physicality, i.e., the appearance of the semiotic body as inscribed by the constructed signs of "race."

Françoise Lionnet says, while talking of the stance of postcolonial writers—substitute here, writers of color, in a Canadian context—"the individual necessarily defines him- or herself with regard to a community, or an ethnic group, and their autobiographical mythologies of empowerment are usually mediated by a determined effort to revise and rewrite official, recorded history" (1992:321). Let me, for a moment, consider the Japanese Canadian writer or artist as a case example to amplify the problems as well as the possibilities facing Asian Canadian and other writers of color.

The necessary tie to community establishes that ethnically-specific tension of inside and/or outside that Japanese Canadians have continued to inhabit as a matter of course. In the assimilationist, and even in the more recent integrationist model, on the one hand, the inside, or what in a familial realm of childhood may have assumed the shape of an interiority, is erased, rendered speechless, or so devoid of content that the subject does not or cannot even recognize its absence. For those who underwent the horrendous trauma of denial, estrangement, and ostracization during the internment period, the monolithic and unwieldy powers of the outside—the white Canadian public, the government, the media, and all the ethnocentric forces that together constituted the body politic of this country—decreed that Japanese Canadians were "enemies" in their midst who were incapable of speaking as subjects. The abrogation of citizenship and the subsequent degradation of subjectivity would have devastating effects on a community that had already suffered some fifty years of racism and exclusionist policies on the West Coast.

The group of Japanese Canadians who were interned adopted various poses in self-defense—silence, resignation *(shikata ga nai;* "it can't be helped"), and rationalization ("blessing in disguise"; forced assimilation got us out of our ghetto so we could finally enter the white mainstream). These are reactions evident in Japanese Canadian *nisei* (Canadian-born, second generation), a generation formed on the consciousness of doubleness: growing up between the ethnocultural and linguistic enclave of the *issei* (first-generation immigrants from Japan) and the Anglo-Saxon "westernized" democratic values of the Canadian majority. Had their lives not been so utterly stymied by the mass uprooting of 1942, the *nisei*, as is the pattern in other immigrant communities, may have developed aesthetic, political, and cultural strategies to promote their own expressiveness in visual and literary texts, but the radical discontinuity of internment at the hands of their own government severely shook their faith in democratic values—and threw them into a double bind. Their ethnicity, the very cultural and linguistic skin inherited from their parents, as they "entered" the dominant society in their dispersed state, became a negative that had to be translated into a positive, if they were to be accepted/adopted within white culture.

Significantly, though, for many *nisei*, the disintegration of community did not erase all of its traces, but forced that allegiance, now removed from the geocultural place on the West Coast, back into the privacy of familial ties, early friendships, local community organizations, all of which resulted in a "club" mentality. In other words, though the community bond was broken, community ties continued in diminished forms—even while, to all outward appearances, the assimilation process had occurred successfully. This is why many *nisei* see no contradiction in working with white Canadians all week long, then relating to their *nisei* friends in more intimate settings on the weekend. The two domains, though balanced in their minds, rarely coalesce in any significant way.

Such a doubleness does not characterize the *sansei*, the third generation, especially those born in internment or in the immediate aftermath of 1949, the year the restrictions were lifted. These *sansei* grew up, for the most part, in closely knit families and were witness to the debilitating effects of the internment but found themselves moulded by the dynamics of dispersal, the community in fragments, the language disappearing—and the more open road of assimilation as temptation for their future. The touchstone of community had slipped out from under, so no framework existed for reproducing, even identifying in meaningful self-critical patterns, a shared history. Instead, the weakening of community-based values often led to self-denial, self-effacement, passivity, and a fear of politics, qualities that aided in the stereotype of Japanese Canadians as the "model minority." Hardly the position out of which vital writing could arise. Before that could happen a reclamation process had to occur.

Japanese Canadians, as an ethnic group, in the 1950s and 1960s were characterized by the absence of writers. The exception is the lone figure, Roy Kiyooka, who was carving a place for himself in the art/literary world.

His first book, *Kyoto Airs* (1964),[5] is a landmark publication: a serial text written during a trip to Japan, in which Kiyooka confronts the manifestations of conflict and confluence between his Canadian-born mind and his Japanese ancestry. His text remains invisible, by-passed by his *nisei* peers and unknown by those *sansei* who might have been able to draw from it in the 1960s, and of course absent in national literary circles.

How, then, to begin to begin? On one extreme, in the tension between inside and outside, the inside can be so subordinated to the outside that it cannot recognize its specificity at all. Such an hierarchic determinacy almost inevitably results in a "self" in which the dominant values outside come to censor, repress, or otherwise propagandize the inside. Once the foundation of the "self" is undermined, however, as it is when a subject begins to mistrust its conditioned reactiveness, a process of reversals can come into play. There is, initially, the recognition that both poles in the interchange, inside and outside, are constructs dependent upon each other for their existence, and bounded by social, psychological, cultural, political, and historical constraints characteristic of a body politics in which minority subjectivities are denied or otherwise contained.

Once doubts and questions arise in the subject, the passageway between inside/outside (suddenly) transforms into a place of static, of noise, of perceptual destabilizations, including what Gloria Anzaldúa refers to as "linguistic code-switching" (1990:xxii), the disturbed subject/writer set adrift in a shifting space of vertiginous pluralities that awaken the desire to speak, to write. But where to begin? Feminist writer Gail Scott, commenting on the difficulty of articulating a female subject position that has had no space before, exposes an analogous beginning from scratch for writers of color:

> . . . We may use language our whole lives without noticing the distortions. Distortions and omissions. Surely the assertion of the inner self has to start with language. But what if the surfacing unconscious stream finds void instead of code? What if we often lack the facility to raise to the conscious level our unconscious thoughts? Due to our slant relationship with culture, therefore language, the words won't come. And without the words, the self. No capacity for separation (1989:17-18).

It is, for instance, out of such an inaugural crisis that the writing of *Obasan* by Joy Kogawa was "born," which is to say, called into being by the urgency to reclaim a repressed history—the urgency to speak back to the barrier of a denied personal and communal past. Alongside the overt narrative of the central character, Naomi, as she unravels the riddle of "herstory" as a Japanese Canadian, is the covert drama of the writer, herself the product of historical injustices, creating a fictional vehicle to recover, through documents, memories, and tales, the interior consequences of abuse and betrayal. The construction, then, is itself the movement into the inhibitions, ambivalences, and erasures that have underwritten the writer's psyche and which threaten, at each point in the unfolding narrative, to suck her back into silence, i.e., into the nothingness of non-speech. Much of the provisionality of *Obasan* inheres in the writing itself, in the very textuality through which the silenced history of Japanese Canadians is imagined[6] and re-configured.

As a novel written by an Asian Canadian, *Obasan* has enjoyed an unusual popularity, receiving great praise by reviewers and three awards, the *Books in Canada* First Novel Award (1981) and the Canadian Authors Association Book of the Year Award (1982), and the Before Columbus Foundation American Book Award (1982). Indeed, *Obasan* helped to make Kogawa into something of a celebrity, especially when its narrative entered the volatile context of the Japanese Canadian redress movement which gained momentum in the early 1980s. Academic articles appeared, magazines published profiles on the author, and *Obasan* was studied in many university courses across Canada.

The consensus from its commentators, for the most part white academics and journalists, has been that *Obasan* is a relevant literary work because, with it, Kogawa has written her way through the silence of the past to come to terms with Japanese Canadian internment. Academics who analyze the novel in detail, despite differences of approach, all tend to incorporate a resolutionary (not revolutionary) aesthetics in their overall critical framing of the novel. The agreement seems to be that Naomi resolves her silenced past, so establishes peace with the human rights violations that caused such havoc and grief to her, to her family, and to her community. Much is made of the immediate aftermath of Naomi's hearing of the translated letter disclosing the "facts" of her mother's disappearance, as she leaves Obasan's house wrapped in her militant aunt Emily's coat, and returns to the coulee—where the story began—where she sat with her uncle on the bank.[7] Here, as her grief is released to the landscape, the narrative ends with the faint scent of "wild roses and the tiny wildflowers" caught in a pose: "If I hold my head in a certain way, I can smell them from where I am" (Kogawa 1983:247). Quiescence, quietude, the absent presence of her uncle, all in the hushed silence of the coulee.

Still, Naomi's gesture and its fade-out does not close the novel, as many readers assume, but it is followed by a matter-of-fact document asking the government not to deport Japanese Canadians, signed by three white men. Why is this document here? Is it referentially necessary for readers to understand Japanese Canadian history? Is it simply meant to be read ironically? Naomi's story, beginning and end, does have the symmetrical balance of aesthetic closure, a novelistic convention that *Obasan* fulfills, and which many readers see as a sign of Naomi's resolution of the injustices, but the end document has an asymmetric relationship to its counterpart, the opening proem written out of the depth of the writer's struggle to dispel the silences that haunt her. At novel's closure, then, following Naomi's own private resolution, the silence still haunts in the absence of a Japanese Canadian name on this political document submitted to the government. The implication, in the materiality of the document, is that nothing has happened to change the social and political contexts of Naomi's experiences.

Naomi's tentative hold on her (now) unrecoverable past—only a scent remains of the memory of plenitude—stands in sharp contrast to the objectivity of the document signed by three men from the same white society that inflicted such violations on her family and community. And their comment that the dispersal of Japanese Canadians has worked and that the government need not "fear of [their] concentration on the Pacific Coast as in the past" (Kogawa 1983:249) sounds the eerie note of forced assimilation—not outrage at the destruction of the community, not outrage at the dispossession, only the objection to deportation of Canadian citizens who have not committed any crime or act of disloyalty. Is it not the social system talking back to itself, resolving its own contradictions through the disguise of petition and pleas? Where is the subjectivity of Japanese Canadians in this document? The last word is written in the rhetoric of dominant language. The silence of Naomi's gesture is speechless. It is as if, by clothing herself in Aunt Emily's warmer coat, she has absorbed her aunt's verbal outrage, in a sense drawing her voice back into silence. *Obasan*, then, instead of resolving the dichotomy between silence and speech, between repression and exposure, ends within a gap where private and public are dichotomized as a stasis. Japanese Canadians are still *spoken for*. "The voices pour down like rain but in the middle of the downpour I still feel thirst. Somewhere between speech and hearing is a transmutation of sound" (Kogawa 1983:245).

Language, the vehicle of power, is a contaminated site. Truth does not reveal itself in the voice of clarity and plenitude—so Asian Canadian and other minority writers of color, speaking out of the finitude of their subjectivities, have to be vigilant not to simply mime the given narrative, genre, and filmic forms through which dominant values are aestheticized. Minority subject matter, when encoded in forms adjusted to accommodate the expectations of the social majority, can willy-nilly lead to compromise, distortion, and misrepresentation. Formal disruptions, such as the generic crossing of fiction, history, autobiography, and documentary in *Obasan,* become strategies of resistance to norms. In terms of receptivity, these strategies relativize the reader's performance and draw her out to the subjective limits (hence the otherness) of the text where minority perceptions are encountered in their foreignicity.

Gilles Deleuze and Félix Guattari devise a useful term to describe the baffled textual screen characteristic of minority writing in its interface with dominant society: "deterritorialization." While they are talking about the strategies devised by Kafka, a Prague Jew whose first language was Czech but who had to write in the language of the majority, German, the term is appropriate for our discussion. By "deterritorialization," they point to a disturbed use of language that foregrounds its surface as a conflicted space. Minority writers, because of their subordinate position, must work in a language that disrupts the stability of conventional discourse and communication, by setting in opposition "a purely intensive usage of language to all symbolic or even significant or simply signifying usages of it" (Deleuze and Guattari 1990:61). This recourse to an opaque language is tied to the other two planes of minority writing identified by Deleuze and Guattari: its immediate political implications and its connection to a collective experience.

The act of "deterritorialization" through writing is perhaps a viable method for resisting assimilation, for exploring variations in form that undermine aesthetic norms, for challenging homogenizing political systems, and for articulating subjectivities that emerge from beleaguered communities—even at the risk of incomprehensibility, unreadability, indifference, or outright rejection. The ethical and artistic dilemmas faced by writers of color are considerable, given the burden of assuming the function of "writer" in various Canadian historical, political, social, and cultural contexts of colonization, marginalization, and discrimination. For Chinese and Japanese Canadians and Natives, these contexts would include the legacy of systemic racism imposed through the historic absence of rights (the right to vote, for instance), discriminatory immigration laws, the extreme of which were the Chinese Head Tax and Exclusion Act, the internment of Japanese Canadians during and after World War II, and the cultural genocide of Native communities. These are issues that cannot simply be wished away, but become an integral part of the responsibility of language, texts, and the theoretical underpinnings of writers and cultural workers of color.

In short, writers of color, as minority writers in Canada, cannot escape basic questions about the writing act: for whom do you write? for the majority? or for the more limited perspective of a community? These questions underlie the complicated relationship of the writer to the "reader," that vague unpredictable figure whose own subjectivity is conditioned by a multiplicity of determinants far beyond the intentionality of the text. To problematize the function of readership in current capitalist terms, that is, to transform the process of reading from passive consumption to critical interchange, the process of deterritorialization as a theoretical tool for Asian Canadian writers has to be, at the very least, carried out on two fronts simultaneously: (a) to generate the formal conditions so that the subjectivity of the writer, as a complex weave of internal and external pressures, can emerge in textual practice; and (b) to advance theoretical principles malleable enough to account for the foreignicity of texts and the enactment of subjectivities that cannot be codified by mainstream critical standards. Of course, both fronts implicate each other, though at present the former appears to be running ahead of the latter, at least in Canada.

The new wave of interest in so-called "minority" writing—with both positive and negative implications—is evident in the relative popularity of *Obasan*, and the more recent *Disappearing Moon Cafe* (1990), by Vancouver Chinese Canadian writer Sky Lee, and dramatically so in the production of anthologies. The anthology is, in many ways, a marketable container to present a "variety" of writers from one ethnic or cultural enclave, all at once as it were. In the past couple of years, for instance, there have been two native anthologies, *All My Relations* (1990) and *Native Literature in English* (1991); *Shakti's Words* (1990), poetry by South Asian Canadian women; *Voices* (1992), writing by African Canadians; and the focus of my closing remarks for this essay, *Many-Mouthed Birds* (1991), poems and stories by Chinese Canadians.

From the perspective of writers of color who are aligned through a shared history, ancestry, and culture, the anthology as mode of publication can be an empowering process and an opportunity for exchange, as general reader matter but also as educational texts that may penetrate the reading lists of institutions, such as in schools and universities. Nevertheless, the relative absence of theoretical awareness in minority groups has created complex risks of compromise and appropriation by publishers and otherwise well-intentioned editors and critics.

The old truism, "you can't tell a book from its cover," may once have been true, but in this design-obsessed consumerist era, the cover is often a tell-tale sign of power relations, stereotypes, and expectations. The cover of *Many-Mouthed Birds*, the dressing for the anthology, becomes a revealing text of the interface between a minority community and the sociocultural majority. It is the face that strikes the (potential) reader immediately: the exotic "Asian" soft featured feminized male face, appearing out of the dark enclosure of bamboo leaves. This photo by Chinese Canadian artist Chick Rice is part of a series on Tommy Wong shown in the exhibit, "Yellow Peril Reconsidered,"[8] but is here isolated and commodified for this anthology. In this decontextualized condition, the (appropriated) image evokes the familiar western stereotype of the Asian "othered," secretive and mysterious, a sign of "Chineseness"—Edward Said's "orientalism" *a la* Canadian colonialism. Framed by the capitalized territory of the cover, the face is stripped of the self-reflexivity, playfulness, and subtle eroticism of Chick Rice's photo series and becomes, instead, a more one-dimensional Eurocentric frame of reference. Here, in an iconized space, "Chineseness" is reproduced as an "inscrutable" pool of silence, one of the "many-mouthed birds," now speaking out, now coming out. The cover invites the reader in to eavesdrop, to become a kind of voyeur—to listen in on the foreign, the effeminate "Asian" of western fantasies. This reaction is reinforced in the blurb explaining the title on the flyleaf and repeated on the back cover: it is an anglicized version of a "Chinese expression used to describe someone who disturbs the peace, who talks out of turn, who is indiscreet," so these writers are the many-mouthed birds "breaking a long and often self-imposed silence." Self-imposed, given the history of discrimination against Chinese Canadians throughout the century? Who is speaking here? I am not denying or downplaying the empowering agenda of the anthology, the cultural objective of its editors to open a venue for writers of Chinese ancestry, but the framing process itself, the anthology as commodity, cannot be ignored as one aspect of the public space within which texts by writers of color are represented, received, codified, and racialized.

The critical treatment of *Obasan* and the cover of *Many-Mouthed Birds* are reminders of the need for reading approaches which respect the contexts of interpretation for writers of color. This may even be much more critical as their texts attract more attention as "insider" accounts of minority subjectivities. And as the "margins" constituted by centralization and dominancy become viable sites for domestication and normalization, particularly in economic and academic terms, the zone of conflict and transformation may very well become the theoretical spaces of writers and cultural workers of color—though the relationship is still asymmetric, since publishers, reviewers, and critics (mostly White) control the conditions of receptivity and interpretation.

Today we are moving through a shifting mine-field of terminological cross-dressing and theoretical instabilities. Now more than ever there is an urgency to devise malleable critical methodologies that can adjust themselves to difference and relativity. In the current intellectual climate in which the constructedness of ideas and methodologies has become apparent, the truth-value of statements is open to question, often measured against ideological constraints. Knowledge is no longer the stable end of a process of interrogation and experimentation, but a transitory site, as the late Canadian poet bp Nichol said, the "ledge" of what we "know" is always subject to alternate directions as the frames keep changing.

I realize that my own comments are subject to the destabilized situation of all positions in these destabilized times. What appears to be a solution today becomes tomorrow's problem. Perhaps, for the foreseeable future at least, the shaping of cultural theories (I emphasize the plural) to understand the workings of "racialization" in the production of texts must be an on-going negotiation process, in which the terminology and frames applied are open-ended and flexible enough to adjust to exclusions and blind-spots when these become visible. Perhaps the critical methodology that is called for at present is one that can articulate difference in such a way that the very notion of "otherness," which western thought has used to centralize "selfness" as source, as hierarchically prior, becomes obsolete as a way of defining people and cultures. What is important for a culture to thrive is a renewed belief in the viability of agency, so that writers from a diversity of subject-positions can develop the conditions in which social justice can be achieved through a language free from the tyranny of hegemonies of all kinds. It may be an impossible end, but the movement towards that "across cultural" end can initiate those heterogenous and indeterminate spaces (potentialities) where writers of color, including Asian Canadian writers, can negotiate their (non-totalizable) specificities—without looking over their shoulders for the coercive gaze of homogenizing discourses.

Notes

1. For a useful analysis of Canadian literary criticism and theory in the 1970s and early 1980s, see Godard (1987).
2. While Canadian literary theorists in academic institutions have been slow to undertake in-depth research on these issues, artists and writers of color have contested homogenizing ideologies that do not account for the historical legacy of racism, colonization, and white supremacist assumptions. Of a handful of magazines that provide space for protest and dialogue perhaps the most accessible is the Toronto-based *Fuse*. Philip's (1992) collection of essays also takes on the failure of Canadian institutions to face the conjunction of racism and culture behind the policies and practices that deny equality to writers and artists of color.
3. The conference, "The Appropriate Voice," was organized by the Racial Minority Writers' Committee, at the time an advisory committee to the Writers' Union of Canada. The motion passed on cultural appropriation was subsequently presented to the annual general meeting of the Writers' Union. It was accepted, though the term "appropriation" was changed to "misappropriation" against the opposition of the Racial Minority Writers' Committee, as reported by Val Ross in the *Globe and Mail*, 8 June 1992. The issue of terminological limitations is far from being resolved for Canadian cultural issues. For instance, the term "racial minority writer," used by writers of color in the Writers' Union of Canada, sounds out-dated because of its implicit origins in the problematic term, "visible minority," a bureaucratic invention now largely rejected by writers and cultural workers of color as a function of hegemonic discourse. "Racial" itself implies an essentialism that is blind to the historical constructedness of "race" signs in Canada; the term "racialization," as used in this discussion, is an effort to recognize the problematic ideological determination of "race" as an instrument of power. The term "minority," while rejected by many writers and cultural workers of color for its implied structural subordination and categorization, has been retained for its relative value: that is, despite the global facts of population distributions, in specific Canadian contexts the term reflects the unequal political, social, and cultural status for communities of color. The term "Asian Canadian" is also tentative and provisional, at least at this moment in Canadian cultural history. Many Canadians of Asian ancestry, if asked, would not relate to the generalization of commonalities implied, and would perhaps react negatively to such an alignment of communities from diverse source countries. Nevertheless, the term has assumed more theoretical importance among writers and cultural workers of Asian ancestry as a means of forging alliances necessary to develop a politics of cultural difference. Finally, the term "white" is not intended to erase differences among groups with ancestries in Europe or England, but refers to the dominant power system, historically shaping Canadian values and institutions, which has assumed the "racial" superiority and priority of British and European groups to both non-Whites and to Natives who suffered the barbarism of colonization and appropriation. As the cultural politics of Canada continues to unfold, no doubt terminology will undergo continuing obsolescence. Like sand castles, the words that look good today will (most likely) be swept away by the tides of interrogation.
4. One historical example for Japanese Canadians is Dorothy Livesay's dramatic poem "Call My People Home" (1968) written in the late 1940s, in which a documentary mode functions to turn Japanese Canadian subjects into racialized objects of white discourse. The appropriating gaze of the poem, operating under the guise of liberal empathy, circumscribes specificities of language, culture, history, and geography, ef-

fectively stripping away the subjectivities of those depicted. The thematic message conveyed to its non-Japanese Canadian readers (and listeners, since it was aired on the radio) is that internment and forced dispersal, despite the hardships, has "allowed" Japanese Canadians to assimilate. Rendered invisible and ahistoric, the sign "Japanese Canadian" is monumentalized and abstracted from the contexts of racism, political opportunism, and exploitation. Livesay's text, in other words, reinscribes itself as another site of internment, a site of containment, by which the white majority transposed "Japanese Canadians" into a model minority within a mainly Anglocentric political space.

5. This now rare publication was designed and printed by fellow *nisei* artist, Takao Tanabe.

6. The term "imagined" is here connected to the term "i mage" as used by Marlene Nourbese Philip in "The Absence of Writing or How I Almost Became a Spy," an introductory commentary to *She Tries Her Tongue* (1989). Colonized writers for whom "English" is the language of oppression and erasure have to recover denied localisms and specificities through the immediacy of image in the material conditions of memory.

7. Characteristically, Canadian critics foreground this "event" as a moment of transcendence: Naomi, and the novel too, rises above the politics of internalized racism to achieve a personal peace of mind; see, for instance, Gottlieb (1986) and Rose (1988).

8. The catalogue for this exhibit, which featured photo, film, and video work by twenty-five Asian Canadian artists, was published as *Yellow Peril Reconsidered* (1990), edited by Paul Wong.

References

Anzaldúa, Gloria. "Haciendo caras, una entrada." In *Making Face, Making Soul: Creative and Critical Perspectives by Women of Color,* edited by Gloria Anzaldúa. San Francisco: Aunt Lute Foundations Books, 1990.

Atwood, Margaret. *Survival: A Thematic Guide to Canadian Literature.* Toronto: House of Anansi, 1972.

Deleuze, Gilles and Félix Guattari. "What Is a Minor Literature?" In *Out There: Marginalization and Contemporary Cultures,* edited by Russell Ferguson, Martha Gever, Trinh T. Minh-ha, Cornel West. Cambridge: MIT Press, 1990.

Godard, Barbara. "Structuralism/Post-Structuralism: Language, Reality and Canadian Literature." In *Future Indicative: Literary Theory and Canadian Literature,* edited by John Moss. Ottawa: University of Ottawa Press, 1987.

Gottlieb, Erika. "The Riddle of Concentric Worlds in *Obasan." Canadian Literature* 109 (Summer 1986): 34-53.

Hutcheon, Linda. *Splitting Images: Contemporary Canadian Ironies.* Toronto: Oxford University Press, 1991.

Kallen, Evelyn. *Ethnicity and Human Rights in Canada.* Toronto: Gage, 1982.

Kiyooka, Roy. *Kyoto Airs.* Vancouver: Periwinkle Press, 1964.

Kogawa, Joy. *Obasan.* Penguin, 1983.

Kroetsch, Robert. *The Lovely Treachery of Words.* Toronto: Oxford University Press, 1989.

Lee, Bennett and Jim Wong-Chu, eds. *Many-Mouthed Birds: Contemporary Writing by Chinese Canadians.* Vancouver: Douglas & McIntyre, 1991.

Lee, Sky. *Disappearing Moon Cafe.* Vancouver/Toronto: Douglas & McIntyre, 1990.

Lionnet, Françoise. "Of Mangoes and Maroons: Language, History, and the Multicultural Subject in Michelle Cliff's *Abeng.*" In *De/Colonizing the Subject: The Politics of Gender in Women's Autobiography,* edited by Sidonie Smith and Julia Watson. Minneapolis: University of Minnesota Press, 1992.

Livesay, Dorothy. "Call My People Home." In *The Documentaries*. Toronto: Ryerson, 1968.

Philip, Marlene Nourbese. *Frontiers*. Stratford, Ontario: Mercury Press, 1992.

_____. *She Tries Her Tongue, Her Silence Softly Breaks*. Charlottetown: Ragweed Press, 1989.

Racial Minority Writers' Committee. "What We Accomplished at the Planning Session." *The Appropriate Voice* 1 (Winter 1992).

Rose, Marilyn Russell. "Politics into Art: Kogawa's *Obasan* and the Rhetoric of Fiction. " *Mosaic* 21 (Spring 1988): 215-26.

Scott, Gail. "Red Tin + White Tulle: On Memory and Writing." In *Spaces Like Stairs*. Toronto: The Women's Press, 1989.

Trinh, T. Minh-ha. "Not You/Like You: Post-Colonial Women and the Interlocking Questions of Identity and Difference." In *Making Face, Making Soul: Creative and Critical Perspectives by Women of Color*, edited by Gloria Anzaldúa. San Francisco: Aunt Lute Foundations Books, 1990.

_____. *When the Moon Waxes Red: Representation, Gender and Cultural Politics*. New York: Routledge, 1991.

West, Cornel. "The New Cultural Politics of Difference." In *Out There: Marginalization and Contemporary Cultures*, edited by Russell Ferguson, Martha Gever, Trinh T. Minh-ha, Cornel West. Cambridge: MIT Press, 1990.

Wong, Paul, ed. *Yellow Peril Reconsidered*. Vancouver: On Edge, 1990.

Part Two
GENDER

The Incorporation of Gender in Minority Discourses: Does the Body Play a Part?

Marilyn Alquizola

The chapters in this section on gender are quite varied in foci that range from literature to the law. The deployment of fashion, the popular construction of Hollywood images, and the modification of marriage via immigration, are but some of the specialized topics that touch on the need to re-negotiate the subjectivities created by the multiplicity of Asian American experiences. Given the particular circumstances of immigration, the different community histories, and the differential institutionalized treatments of heterosexual women and men, lesbians, and gays, the following discussions all implicitly demand that future perspectives should attempt to incorporate, rather than tokenize and discuss in passing, the aspect of gender, which is as much a part of the social personality as race, ethnicity, and class. (Because the issues of sexuality warrant their own section, papers regarding those topics are not included in this section.) In short, this section highlights the often muted topic, in the area of Third World concerns, of gender.

The chapter by Patricia A. Sakurai suggests that subsuming gender was a metaphorical sleight of hand, a cultural nationalist stratagem. (At this point, I should insert that although some might indeed consider that the cultural nationalist project formulated a viable beginning for Asian American studies, the cultural projects for current times could become more encompassing and inclusive without necessarily forfeiting points gained in the past.) Sakurai states: "Racism defined through gendered terms often gives the appearance of race as a separable issue, if not the issue, by in effect subsuming gender within issues of racial oppression." Sakurai incisively pinpoints what is a strategic cultural nationalist conflation of race with gender that has been quite prevalent since the 1970s. By implication, Sakurai emphasizes the need to differentiate between these notions, as well as to be cognizant that heterosexual identity of the Asian American male ironically may be unconsciously fashioned with the dominant white male stereotype as the determining paradigm. The notion of emasculation by a racist society implicitly buys into the tradition of heterosexual primacy, holding that tradition as a standard. In the possession paradigm that Sakurai deconstructs, the contest and dialogue exists and remains only between dominant and marginalized heterosexual males.

Marilyn Elkins begins her argument by acknowledging that Asian American women writers, in their prose and poetry, challenge the artificial binary, in which "attention to fashion indicates spiritual or intellectual vacuity." She goes on to conclude that Asian American women of the various communities, in their biculturality, have "mastered the metaphoric use of clothing as a subversive act." Drawing evidence from textual examples in Sasaki, Kingston, Tan, Jen, among others, Elkins argues that "Asian American women writers reject the oversimplification that regard for accoutrements constitutes a litmus test for character or for feminism." Elkins' argument, supported and vivified by the selected textual examples of the characters' aesthetic expressions of self is a strong mandate to recognize the discursive and cultural practices of Asian American writers in their own terms. Perhaps to do otherwise would be tantamount to missing or misreading what are significant acts of resistance or identity formation. These are acts that generate from what Elkins identifies as the intersection of race and gender.

Sau-ling Cynthia Wong examines the ironic situation that the legacy of exclusion has affected on the Chinese American community. In very literal terms, the repealing of the Exclusion Act logically might have precluded the conditions for worry over biological extinction of the community. The fear, however, of cultural extinction, to say the least, remains. Wong's chapter is particularly salient in its focus on the present and future conditions of communities as they concern the role and situation of Asian American men. It articulates a position that demands a current, contextual analysis of Asian American male subjectivity, one that goes beyond an understanding based on the historical past or on a reconstruction of identity based on that past.

Dolores de Manuel examines the fictional treatments of the institution of marriage, both affecting and affected by immigration. Looking at the works of authors, Jessica Hagedorn, Bienvenido Santos, and Linda Ty-Casper, de Manuel finds that there are differences based on gendered perspective, class position, and historical context. In the specific analyses of each literary situation, de Manuel illustrates the multiplicity of situations, in which characters must "rethink" the "rules" of marriage in order to "restabilize" its value, rendering marriage "productive rather than destructive." Thus, de Manuel strongly implies the importance of agency in the activity of reconstruction.

Vicki L. Ruiz analyzes both the public and private personaes of two Latina actresses, Dolores del Rio and Lupe Velez. While the on-screen sexual presence of both women was starkly different, both, nevertheless, "represented images of exotic 'female' carnal power on camera, images which required 'masculine' taming, symbolically and literally." In a retrospective juxtaposition of their careers, Ruiz discusses their activities in terms of cultural production, while paying close attention to both the elements of agency and material context. Although Ruiz strongly acknowledges that "[p]eople navigate across cultural boundaries as well as make conscious decisions in the production of culture[,]" she also tells us to be cognizant that "people of color have not had unlimited choice. Racism, sexism, imperialism, persecution, and social, political, and economic segmentation have constrained aspiration, expectations, and decision-making." Although Ruiz, in this article, does not attempt to discuss the effects of Americanization on Asian American experiences, general parallels may still be drawn, particularly with regard to the interfacing of dominant and minority cultures, as it affects the cultural production of minority culture.

By citing and explaining the specific situations of individual Korean immigrant women, Hyun Sook Kim illustrates how women of color are marginalized and virtually excluded by single-axis frameworks. These frameworks, albeit oppositional in their resistance to hegemony, oftentimes do not address the "multiple forms of oppression — economic, social, cultural, racial, and sexual systems of dominations inherent in the globalizing capitalist world . . . ." Furthermore, Kim posits that the theorizing that is necessary in order to make up for these theoretical deficits can and must be generated from specific life situations of women of color.

Like Kim, Kandice Chuh writes of the marginalizing and virtual oppression of Asian American women by the legal system. Hegemonic in nature, American law presumably exists on behalf of the lawful citizen, a universalizing notion in and of itself. In her chapter, however, Chuh brings into account the historical precedence in the legislative system that defined American citizen as white male, definitely to the exclusion of others. The genesis of racism in this country indeed had its legal basis, and still underpins the spirit of the law, if not the letter, in its sexist and legal ramifications. In analyzing the legislation, legal definitions, and descriptions of what constitutes the crime of rape, Chuh argues that in the judicial interpretation of rape, male sensibility is privileged at the same time female experience is nullified. Coupled with existing sexist stereotypes of the Asian American woman in dominant society, the Asian American woman, in legal terms, becomes multiply marginalized by virtue of gender, race, and ethnicity. In accordance with other writers in this section who discuss the nexus of race and gender, Chuh goes on to say that even institutional remedies such as affirmative action policies "only take into consideration one aspect of our identities at a time — women of color are women *or* of color" [emphasis added]. A total subjectivity of the woman of color seems not to be forthcoming in the American context. A re-negotiation that involves both a shift in perspective and paradigm is certainly in order.

Oftentimes, the oppositional thrust of minority discourses against hegemonic institutions is echoed in its own treatment of minorities, by virtue of power and/or number, within. This is unfortunate, as the imitation and deployment of dominant culture methods and strategies of silencing, muting, and trivializing in order to contain can and do result in resentment and separatism within the actual or symbolic borders of a given "community." Thus, Asian American political coalescence may be thwarted due to the silencing of multiple subjectivities, an unconscious imitation of the very activity of dominant discourse that minority discourses should desire to overcome.

The Politics of Possession: The Negotiation of Identity in *American in Disguise, Homebase,* and *Farewell to Manzanar*

Patricia A. Sakurai

In *American in Disguise* (1971), Daniel Okimoto, a second-generation Japanese American, describes his particular dating dilemma through a familiar paradigm of gendered race/class politics:

> In this white dominated society, it was perhaps natural that white girls seemed attractive personally as well as physically. They were in a sense symbols of the social success I was conditioned to seek, all the more appealing, perhaps, because of the subtly imposed feelings of self-derogation associated with being a member of a racial minority. In the inner recesses of my heart I resisted the seductive attraction of white girls because I feared I was being drawn to them for the wrong reasons. I was afraid that my tastes had been conditioned too centrally by white standards. Behind the magnetism there may have been an unhealthy ambition to prove my self-worth by competing with the best of the white bucks and winning the fair hand of some beautiful, blue-eyed blonde—crowning evidence of having made it (200-201).

Besides a certain awareness of the racism involved in his own socialization, what Okimoto recognizes here is the use of the white female body as "symbol," the very desirability of the white woman couched in her ability to materially signify male "social success," his "having made it." Here, under the terms of "white dominated society," the competitive relationship between men—in this case from different racial groups—is played out through the possession of the racially-defined female body.

The above passage articulates, then, the dominant version of what I would call the possession paradigm: the discursive use of heterosexual relationships described through race and/or class categories to both represent and negotiate race/class identities. It is a familiar paradigm, with widespread currency, strongly coded within white patriarchy and the compulsory heterosexuality on which it relies. In her essay, "Teaching the Differences among Women from a Historical Perspective: Rethinking Race and Gender as Social Categories," Tessie Liu examines the historical interconnections between race and class, tying the use of racial metaphors—historically shifting "[m]etaphors of common substance" (271)—to notions of kinship, lineage, and social/class status. She then considers the role of gender in these connections, stating:

> In a male-dominated system, regulating social relationships through racial metaphors necessitates control over women. The reproduction of the system entails not only regulating the sexuality of women in one's own group, but also differentiating between women according to legitimate access and prohibition. Considered in these terms, race as a social category functions through controlling sexuality and sexual behavior (271).

While Liu goes on to cite certain colonial societies, American slavery, and Nazi Germany as examples of such a system, and while differences between specific historical situations must be taken into account, I find Liu's essay helpful as she articulates the way in which the female body becomes inscribed within white patriarchy and interconnecting ideologies of race, class, gender, and sexuality—both materially and discursively, through childbearing and concepts of "legitimate access and prohibition";[1] Liu's observation not only informs the discursive use of the heterosexually-defined female body and categories of race and class within the possession paradigm, but serves to emphatically tie such discursive uses to their material expressions and consequences as well, situating this paradigm within the broader discourse of which it is part.

With these interconnections in mind, I turn to Sau-ling Wong's essay, "Ethnicizing Gender: An Exploration of Sexuality as Sign in Chinese Immigrant Literature." Here, Wong considers ways in which "ethnicity is, in some sense, always already gendered, and gender always already ethnicized" (126). In her examination of Chinese immigrant literature of the 1960s, she explores the commingling of ethnicity and gender and how "what appear to be merely self-contemptuous or insensitive gender stereotypes reveal, upon closer scrutiny, an intricate signifying practice at work" (111). This practice demonstrates, for one, how "ethnicized gender" at the site of sexuality is used in languages of nationalism, assimilation, and class status. Her work in this essay "shifts critical attention from content analysis—from determining the presence or absence of stereotypes within a text—

to a study of the semiosis whereby both stereotyping and counterstereotyping are made possible" (125).

Drawing from her essay, I find it helpful to likewise consider the possession paradigm "an intricate signifying practice" through/against which individuals attempt to negotiate their own identities, a signifying practice which produces meaning through identities based on race, class, gender, and heterosexuality—(re)producing, defining, and naturalizing these very identities in the process.[2] While I leave many nuances and areas unexplored, I hope to suggest the possession paradigm as a fruitful site at which certain constructs of race, class, gender, and sexuality might be critically engaged. I turn then to a discussion of several Asian American texts of the 1970s —*American in Disguise, Homebase,* and *Farewell to Manzanar*—and their particular responses to this paradigm.[3]

What I initially find interesting about *American in Disguise* is the degree to which Okimoto recognizes the dominant version of the possession paradigm as merely one way of reading his relationships with white women; he does not consider white women as inherently symbolic of success, but rather sees such practice as a matter of social conditioning (200).[4] Yet despite this and other political implications he attaches to interracial relationships, Okimoto treats his own eventual marriage to a white woman from "a middle class, Anglo-Saxon family in Idaho" (203) as a matter of individual transcendence of race and class; he grows determined "to rise above it all" (204), agreeing with his father, that "love was a matter of the heart and soul, not of culture and race . . ." (205). Though Okimoto might reject the particular meaning assigned his marriage by the dominant possession paradigm, thereby to some extent denaturalizing the meaning it attaches to the white female body, this effect is undermined by his own construction of and recourse to a sense of autonomous "personal" choice, his dismissal of rather than critical engagement with the dominant paradigm. More accurately, the racial identity of his wife, rather than being "erased" by love, changes from a sign of "social success" to one of Okimoto's "transcendence" of social conditioning, his marrying for the "right" reasons. Thus he leaves the paradigm's semiosis relatively in tact.

Considering the above, it might prove more fruitful to consider the possession paradigm in relation to certain implicit tensions and contradictions within Okimoto's text. To start, unstable and multiple definitions of terms such as "Japanese" and "American" produce numerous tensions of which Okimoto himself seems aware; he describes his own "obstinate problem of identity":

> . . . I wanted to be above all an 'American,' whatever meaning that may have had. But this attempt was doomed to failure, for I was not after all representative of the central figure of middle-class American mythology, the WASP in all his white-skinned, blue-eyed glory. In spite of that I was an American and hardly knew whether to love or hate that which I was and wanted to be (6).

The identity that the term "American" supposedly describes is destabilized as race-based definitions of nationality are placed in opposition to ideal notions of "colorblind" birthright and citizenship (the World War II internment of Japanese Americans looming as a particularly vivid example).[5] Okimoto's use of the term "schizophrenic" (142, 187) seems particularly significant, then, for it not only describes his anxiety over his contradictory position, but it also understands a single, stable identity as normative; Okimoto elsewhere describes his identity "problem" as "the psychological *neurosis* with which most minority races in America are *afflicted*" (172, emphasis mine). Thus the conflict arises within the text between Okimoto's efforts to "fix" and stabilize his sense of identity and the instability and multiplicity of the terms through which he attempts to achieve this.[6]

Further, the conceptualization of identity as a matter of individual struggle not only assumes that a unified, stable identity is indeed available through existing terms and that these terms are themselves stable and "real," but it also draws focus and responsibility onto the individual subject and attention away from broader cultural, economic, and political contexts— an effect contradicted within the text by Okimoto's concern with race/class politics. For one, Okimoto's objection to the use of Japanese American economic success to justify the socio-economic positions of other minority groups, particularly African Americans, rests on the conviction that individual "indolence and ignorance" (57) are *not* acceptable explanations for the inequalities he observes (chapter 6); he asserts that Japanese Americans did not succeed simply because they worked harder than other minorities (55) and criticizes "model minority" theories based on this assumption.[7] Okimoto seems aware, then, of a particular brand of individualism that facilitates the use of Japanese American economic success in mainstream mythology and serves to suppress the racist nature of socioeconomic stratification in America. "American society, as it now exists," he states, "is deeply racist" (57).[8]

There is a general tension, then, between Okimoto's construction of the "personal" and privileging of American individualism on the one hand (chapter 10), and his concern with the use of individualism in middleclass mythology to deny the existence of racial barriers on the other. This tension, in turn, brings attention to one of the characteristics of the possession paradigm itself: its suppression of the systemic interplay of race, class, gender, and sexuality by reducing these ideologies to terms of solely "personal" heterosexual relationships.

Moreover, Okimoto's dilemma of "schizophrenic" identity points to the way in which this paradigm also relies on and promotes normative conceptualizations of singular, stable identity: even though this paradigm presents itself as a means of articulating a shift in race/class identification, this shift is characterized as a move from an undesirable identity (or lack of one) to another supposedly singular and stable one. Considered in terms of this "change" in position, the possession paradigm also supports a certain kind of Horatio Algerism—the promise of individual class mobility and/or the transcendence of racial identity as marked by the symbolic white female body. Ironically, the possession paradigm at the same time reinforces notions of stratification through the concept of limited "access."

And then there is Okimoto's characterization of interracial marriage as the "key to final assimilation" (156) which places issues of assimilation and wide-scale class mobility in juxtaposition with the individual "miscegenation" involved in the possession paradigm and points to the interplay of race, class, gender, and sexuality within the paradigm itself. While strangely the possession paradigm might appear to admit, even encourage miscegenation as it heightens the desirability of the white female, it at the same time implicitly naturalizes intra-racial/intra-class relationships as unproblematic and reinforces concepts of "legitimate access and prohibition" that feed and are fed by a history of anti-miscegenist violence, legislation, and cultural taboo. Moreover, it naturalizes a race/class hierarchy topped by the materially successful white male as the order into which all strive to assimilate.

So while Okimoto's explicit response to the possession paradigm is rather limited, his text informs a discussion of the paradigm by implicitly pointing to some of its ideological characteristics and by-products: its naturalization of the categories it uses to produce meaning, its treatment of identity constructed through these categories as singular and stable, its use of and within certain middle-class assumptions and myths, its suppression of the systemic, interconnected nature of racism, classism, and heterosexism in its "personalization" of identity negotiation, and its naturalization of the hierarchy such a system entails. *American in Disguise*, while certainly problematic in its own assumptions and generalizations, inadvertently exposes these aspects of the paradigm via the contradictions and tensions named above.

Drawing on another text from the 1970s, I turn to Shawn Wong's *Homebase* (1979), a text which also informs and is informed by this paradigm as the narrator Rainsford, a fourth generation Chinese American, struggles with issues of national and ethnic identity. Aside from differences in narrative form (Okimoto's autobiography versus Wong's novel), the reaction to the possession paradigm presented in *Homebase* differs from that in Okimoto's text in several significant ways.[9]

For one, unlike the representation of the silent, passive white female in the dominant possession paradigm described by Okimoto, the white female in *Homebase* is assigned a more "active" though limited role in the narrator's search for identity:

> So now I take this fifteen-year-old blond-haired body with me on the road. She is the shadow, the white ghost of all my love life; she is the dream of my capture of America. . . . My patronizing blond-haired, whining, pouting bride of fifteen, known to me as "The Body," is my whole responsibility to America. She is America. She tells me things about me that I am not. America patronizes me and loves me and tells me that I am the product of the richest and oldest culture in the history of the world. She credits me with all the inventions of modern life, when in fact I have nothing of my own in America. But I stay with her to get what I can out of her (66).

As in the version before, the blonde, blue-eyed figure is at first understood as a sign of "making it"; Rainsford's "capture of America," illusory as it might be (a dream after all), is expressed through the capture of something of the white American male's domain—the white American female. But while Okimoto rejects this version of the paradigm by retreating to his sense of the "personal," Rainsford rejects it by disrupting the desirability of the white female body itself; Rainsford does not worry about wanting his dream bride for the "wrong reasons" as much as points explicitly to the limitations of the identity she grants him. The unsympathetic portrayal of the dream bride as the voice of a racist and ignorant mainstream renders her racial identity both reason for initially wanting and reason for ultimately rejecting her. Elaine Kim observes:

> Informed by the racial pride and ethnic consciousness that grew out of the Civil Rights Movement of the 1960s, *Homebase* targets the white woman and the white racism she symbolizes as impediments to the narrator's American selfhood, which he must find through his Chinese American forefathers (1990: 73).

Homebase, then, articulates a rewriting of the possession paradigm in which the blonde blue-eyed figure becomes a "negative" symbol of racism and exclusion rather than one of success, thus her use in signifying Rainsford's "lack" of an "American" identity.

Further, as Rainsford's attempts at mainstream national and cultural belonging fail (78), Wong's text also denies the dominant possession paradigm's promise of individual race/class transcendence; while in the version Okimoto names, the possession of the white female body potentially signifies "having made it," Wong's version denies the possibility of being fully accepted by the racist mainstream as an "American" and points to the prescripted role he is expected to play—the foreigner, the "Chinese." Here, there is no transcendence or recourse to the strictly "personal."

Indeed, as pointed out by critics such as Sau-ling Wong (1993:141-46) and Elaine Kim (1982:194-97), *Homebase* ties personal identity to a broader sense of historical collective identity through Rainsford's exploration not only of the American landscape but of his generational past as well; "haunted by the ghosts of the men of his great-grandfather's generation" (Kim 1982:194), Rainsford's search for identity comes to incorporate the historical legacy of which he is part: "And I knew then that I was only my father's son, that he was Grandfather's son and Grandfather was Great-Grandfather's son and that night we were all the same man" (86).[10] In this sense, Wong's text challenges the simplistic notions of individual identity offered by the possession paradigm.

Still, despite *Homebase*'s rejection of the dominant possession paradigm, it leaves the paradigm's semiotic use of the female body intact; even if a "negative" symbol, the dream bride serves a function similar to that of her "positive" counterpart as both are used to signify identity. Indeed, aside from his fifteen-year-old dream bride, Rainsford speaks briefly of his future return to a Chinese American woman in Wisconsin who "gave me part of her life back there early one summer when I was still dreaming about grandfathers, trying to pull all of my past together" (67); he describes this woman as "only the myth of the perfect day until I do get back to her home, she is the summit I must turn to in the end" (68). If the blonde dream bride is his failed "capture of America," the Chinese American woman, then, represents his recovery of identity, a final coming home through which, as Kim states, "Rainsford can affirm his American identity" (1982:196-97). Her role is a static one, her character synonymous with the stable identity she supposedly represents; she is locked in time, fixed in and defined through her relationship with Rainsford: "She tells me that it is bitingly cold in Wisconsin in the wintertime, but I know her only in early summer. When I'm on the road at night, she is that Wisconsin time" (67). It is the Chinese American woman, then, who becomes a "positive" symbol of Rainsford's finding place and home in America, marking yet another variation of the possession paradigm.

This considered, I turn to the issue of "voice" and the positions named within the possession paradigm and its variations. Interestingly enough, in the dominant version described by Okimoto, "winning the fair hand of some beautiful, blue-eyed blonde" (201) marks acceptance and relative empowerment within white patriarchy ("crowning evidence of having made it"), and the blonde symbol is appropriately inanimate and silent. Rainsford's "dream bride," on the other hand, is rendered undesirable precisely because of the racist, ignorant voice she embodies in the text, and it is his envisioned return to the "voiceless" Chinese American woman that affirms his sense of place and home.[11] That these characterizations are involved in issues of masculinity and femininity seems clear, as indeed certain assumptions about masculinity and femininity support and are generated by the heterosexual possession paradigm.

It seems useful, then, to look at the way these assumptions are voiced during this period in the often cited essay "Racist Love," by Frank Chin and Jeffery Paul Chan (the sentiments of which are repeated in the introduction to *Aiiieeeee!*). Here, the racial oppression of Asian Americans is equated with emasculation, the stripping of Asian American manhood:

> The white stereotype of the Asian is unique in that it is the only racial stereotype completely devoid of manhood. Our nobility is that of an efficient housewife. At our worst we are contemptible because we are womanly, effeminate, devoid of all the traditionally masculine qualities of originality, daring, physical courage, creativity. We are neither straight talkin' or straight shootin' (1975:68).

While keeping in mind the history of immigration and antimiscegenation laws, violence against and the oppression of Asian American men *and* women, Merle Woo points out that "[t]hese men of color, with clear vision, fight racism in white society, but have bought the white male definition of 'masculinity'" (1981:145).[12] bell hooks notes a similar practice within African American political discourse: "When words like castration, emasculation, impotency are the commonly used terms to describe the nature of black male suffering, a discursive practice is established that links black male liberation with gaining the right to participate fully within patriarchy"

(1990:76). Racism defined through gendered terms often gives the appearance of race as a separable issue, if not *the* issue, by subsuming gender within issues of racial oppression. Paradoxically, such dependence on certain assumptions about gender and sexuality for racism's very meaning indeed seriously calls into question the separability of race and gender altogether. I would argue, then, that by relying on a sign system that privileges men as actors and prescribes to women a passive role as objects of desire, by continuing to reinforce a compulsory heterosexuality and fixed categories of race, class, and gender to produce meaning, certain heterosexual variations of/reactions to the dominant version of the possession paradigm (such as the rejection of the white female body, or the rejection or seeking out of the Asian American female body), despite their "liberating" effects in some regards, ultimately risk upholding the same problematic signifying practice and discursive politics as the paradigm they set out to challenge.[13]

In *Farewell to Manzanar* (1973) Jeanne Wakatsuki Houston and James D. Houston use gendered language throughout their text as they call on the castration metaphor to describe Wakatsuki's father's experience during and after internment: "[A]nother snip of the castrator's scissors, and he never fully recovered . . ." (111). Still, the Houstons' text offers a response to the dynamics of interracial heterosexual relationships which I find significant, for it amplifies the way in which women, particularly women of color, are positioned within the discourse of the possession paradigm, pointing to the matrix of differences explicitly and implicitly drawn along gender and race lines. For one, while the narrator in *Homebase* actively uses the symbolic white female and Chinese American woman to negotiate his own sense of identity, the narrator in the Houstons' text is left attempting to negotiate her sense of identity by "trying on" pre-scripted, pre-constructed feminine roles in hopes of being literally (and passively) chosen and accepted, thus the masculine/feminine, active/passive construction within this discourse. Further, there are the racial differences drawn between women by the paradigm, differences articulated through these women's desirability and acceptance *as women* by a mainstream immersed in the value judgments of white patriarchy; Wakatsuki narrates:

> I see a young, beautifully blond [sic] and blue-eyed high school girl moving through a room full of others her own age, much admired by everyone, men and women both, myself included, as I watch through a window. I feel no malice toward this girl. I don't even envy her. Watching, I am simply emptied, and in the dream I want to cry out, because she is something I can never be, some possibility in my life that can never be fulfilled (123).

Within the confines of the possession paradigm, Wakatsuki cannot want, but rather can only want to be the admired and desired blue-eyed blonde. Unable to be or possess the white female, Wakatsuki considers her limited alternatives, for example, possession and acceptance *by* the white male.[14]

Wakatsuki describes her participation in her high school's carnival queen contest:

> I was among fifteen girls nominated to walk out for inspection by the assembled student body on voting day.
>
> I knew I couldn't beat the other contestants at their own game, that is, look like a bobbysoxer. Yet neither could I look too Japanese-y. I decided to go exotic, with a flower-print sarong, black hair loose and a hibiscus flower behind my ear. When I walked barefooted out onto the varnished gymnasium floor, between the filled bleachers, the howls and whistles from the boys were double what had greeted any of the other girls (124).

Here, "on voting day," her sense of being chosen on the basis of her assumed identity is quite literal. Further, she seems well aware of the interdependence of race, gender, and sexuality in her "staging" of the "exotic" Asian female as she submits herself to a white audience. She explains of her earlier adolescent years,

> At that age I was too young to consciously use my sexuality or to understand how an Oriental female can fascinate Caucasian men, and of course far too young to see that even this is usually just another form of invisibility. It simply happened that the attention I first gained as a majorette went hand in hand with a warm reception from the Boy Scouts and their fathers, and from that point on I knew intuitively that one resource I had to overcome the war-distorted limitations of my race would be my femininity (117).

If the white female body is a symbol of limited "access," indeed the woman of color is implicitly readily "accessible" to all; her sexuality is a given, a point reinforced by King-Kok Cheung's observation of the Asian American woman's "excess of 'womanhood'" (1990:236)—that is, her characterization as "only sexual" (1990:236). Here, Sau-ling Wong's discussion of "ethnicized gender" in immigrant Chinese literature and the function of sexuality in marking identity seems particularly relevant:

> In all of these [works], sexuality is represented as far more than a physical fact; rather, it constitutes one of the primary terms through which one's ethnic identity is understood, experienced and structured. . . . Gender roles, invested with strong emotions concerning what is "naturally fitting," become a convenient locus for testing out and codifying cultural meaning. Thus characters' actions, depicted along a spectrum of gender appropriateness, are assigned varying shades of "Chineseness" or "Americanness" to indicate their at-homeness in the adopted land (1992:113-14).

Though examining the specific situation of immigration, Wong's observation seems to inform Wakatsuki's "intuitive" understanding of her sexuality as tied to her sense of gender and racial acceptance; by playing out her expected role, Wakatsuki experiences a certain level of acceptance by her white peers, particularly her male peers, thus testifying to the extent to which the "exoticized" Asian female is indeed accepted as "naturally fitting." Yet it is exactly the nature of this "at-homeness" that Wakatsuki seems to be questioning.

Her performance of the orientalist stereotype of the "exotic" Asian female is named as "just another form of invisibility" (117). But then when she takes her place on the court, having decided to "be a white-gowned figure out of *Gone With the Wind*; I would be respectable" (128), the attempt fails miserably:

> I kept walking in my processional walk, thinking of all the kids who had voted for me, not wanting to let them down, although in a way I already had. It wasn't the girl in this old-fashioned dress they had voted for. But if not her, who had they voted for? Somebody I wanted to be. And wasn't. Who was I then? (129)

If her portrayal of the "exotic" Asian female allows Wakatsuki a certain amount of dubious "at-homeness," her attempt at playing the all-American girl allows her no sense of "at-homeness" whatsoever, further emphasizing the specific form of femininity and sexuality she is expected to enact as an Asian American woman. None of her attempted identities proves fitting.

While granted the narrative does in effect reinforce the privileged position of the white male as active choosing "audience," that Wakatsuki voices her dissatisfaction with her choices offers some criticism of her options for negotiating identity. The Houstons' text articulates, then, how heavily the Asian American female's acceptance within American culture relies on a particular model of sexuality and race/gender roles as located within the heterosexual possession paradigm.[15]

What seems clear, then, is that the possession paradigm, in its dominant form and its variations, is both product and apt producer of certain identities based on categories of race, class, gender, and sexuality. By examining certain texts of the 1970s in relation to this paradigm, this study's general aim has been to problematize the very way in which race, class, gender, and sexual identity are defined and described, pointing to the use of these identities within a certain signifying practice in which the practice itself—as much as the meanings produced—support and are supported by the discourse of white patriarchy; in this task, I hope this discussion of possession paradigm has been at least somewhat successful.

Notes

1. Indeed, Okimoto grows "annoyed" by the statements of classmates at Princeton who discourage him from dating white women and try to set him up with other Asian Americans, a practice "that suggested whites were the sole preserve of other whites" (201), or more accurately, white women who attended Ivy Leagues were the sole preserve of white men of similar background. Of "humble" beginnings himself, Okimoto touches on the way in which race/class relationships between men are discursively defined and maintained through concepts of "legitimate access and prohibition" and categories of race, class, and gender at the site of heterosexual relationships; while not under the same level of overt violent prohibition present in the situations Tessie Liu names, Okimoto nonetheless notes the cultural prohibitions against his dating white women in Ivy League circles.

2. This paper's own underlying assumptions about identity are informed by Lisa Lowe's essay, "Heterogeneity, Hybridity, Multiplicity," and her particular call for the (re)conceptualization of identity as unstable and unfixed. Noting the political uses of Gayatri Spivak's "strategic essentialism," she warns against lending permanence to essentializing definitions of particular identities: "The concept of 'strategic essentialism' suggests that it is possible to utilize specific signifiers of ethnic identity, such as Asian American, for the purpose of contesting and disrupting the discourses that exclude Asian Americans, while simultaneously revealing the internal contradictions and slippages of Asian American so as to insure that such essentialisms will not be reproduced and proliferated by the very apparatuses we seek to disempower" (1991:39).

3. My reasons for choosing texts of the seventies include their historical relation to the collective identity politics of the late sixties and early seventies and ways in which the possession paradigm functioned (or did not function) within this particular context.

4. Criticized in the past for his "dual identity" formula and generalizations about Japanese America's lack of individuality and inability to produce a writer of substantial worth [see for example Frank Chin, et al. (1975), Bruce Iwasaki (1976), and Joanne Sechi (1980)], Okimoto's text indeed launches some rather disturbing cultural generalizations and homogenizing assumptions about both the Japanese and Japanese Americans; while these issues are not my focus here, I do not mean to dismiss them either.

5. As James Tang notes, the term "Japanese" takes on several meanings in James Michener's patronizing introduction to Okimoto's text as well (Okimoto ix-x; Tang 7-8). Interestingly enough, while the coexistence of competing definitions are the source of irony and play for Michener, for Okimoto they are the source of anxiety and distress.

6. Okimoto's "dual identity" model, then, as much as it relies on terms that are themselves unfixed and unstable, seems on a continuum with, not an end to, Okimoto's "schizophrenia"; indeed, Okimoto himself states that his "feelings of profound ambivalence will probably never be permanently settled" (188). Moreover, what Okimoto's "dual identity" formula cannot take into account is his particular concern with issues of class; the reduction of identity to an issue of "Japaneseness" and/or "Americanness" lies in tension with other factors Okimoto brings into his struggle to identify concretely as an "American" (see, for example, chapters 7 and 8).

7. Okimoto is highly wary of the movement of Japanese Americans into the middle class and their acceptance of bourgeois values and mythology, arguing that "the successes of Japanese Americans have come at a price of rigid conformity to white middle-class standards of success and respectability" (54). He later states, "True, Japanese Americans have succeeded in securing a comfortable bourgeois life, an accomplishment for which we have earned the rousing commendation of the white majority. But this praise, it must be realized, has been based on value judgments that ultimately serve the purposes of the established social order" (152). Still, problematic here and at other points in the text is Okimoto's own assumption of homogeneous Japanese American economic success, an assumption that itself risks perpetuating "model minority" myths and holds serious implications for Asian Americans in general; while he mentions the effect of anti-Chinese sentiments on Japanese Americans in California (15), he fails to consider how his own generalizations about Japanese Americans might risk feeding assumptions that all Asian Americans have access to, let alone enjoy, such an "excess of success" (157).

8. Still, Okimoto often participates in a certain patriotism that treats democratic ideals as coterminous with "America." See for example chapter 14, "A Question of Loyalty."

9. While I do not pursue the point here, indeed these differences in narrative mode might fruitfully inform a discussion of other differences between these two texts.

10. While keeping in mind the historical ratio of Chinese American men to Chinese American women due among other things to immigration laws, the patrilineage invoked in Wong's text still seems worth noting.

11. My thanks to Linda Von Hoene and Sarah Murphy whose comments and feedback proved particularly helpful in bringing out this last point.

12. Others such as King-Kok Cheung and Elaine Kim make similar points.

13. While I do not explore the significance of homosexual variations of this paradigm in this essay, certainly such an investigation would be worth pursuing, indeed, necessary.

14. My thanks to the editorial collective of *Critical Mass* for pointing out the dual impulse of the narrator to both occupy the position of the white male observer and be object of his desire, the implications of which I unfortunately do not pursue here. Indeed, this essay as a whole has benefited immensely from their many comments and suggestions.

15. The fact that *Farewell to Manzanar* was written out by Wakatsuki's husband, James Houston, based on her taped recollections (Kim 1982:84) brings up a host of issues such as authorship, audience consideration and accommodation, and so forth; the mediated nature of the text problematizes assumptions about the Japanese American female voice in the text, an issue that complicates this study's own reading as well.

References

Cheung, King-Kok. "The Woman Warrior Versus The Chinaman Pacific: Must a Chinese American Critic Choose between Feminism and Heroism?" In *Conflicts in Feminism,* edited by Marianne Hirsch and Evelyn Fox Keller. New York: Routledge, 1990.

Chin, Frank, and Jeffery Paul Chan. "Racist Love." In *Seeing Through Shuck,* edited by Richard Kostelanetz. New York: Ballantine Books, 1972.

Chin, Frank, Jeffery Paul Chan, Lawson Fusao Inada, and Shawn Wong. "An Introduction to Chinese- and Japanese-American Literature." In *Aiiieeeee!* edited by Frank Chin, Jeffery Paul Chan, Lawson Fusao Inada, and Shawn Wong. New York: Anchor Books, 1975.

hooks, bell. *Yearning: Race, Gender, and Cultural Politics*. Boston: South End Press, 1990.

Houston, Jeanne Wakatsuki and James D. Houston. *Farewell to Manzanar*. New York: Bantam Books, 1974.

Iwasaki, Bruce. "Introduction." In *Counterpoint: Perspectives on Asian America*, edited by Emma Gee. Los Angeles: UCLA Asian American Studies Center, 1976.

Kim, Elaine. *Asian American Literature: An Introduction to the Writings and Their Social Context*. Philadelphia: Temple University Press, 1982.

_____. "'Such Opposite Creatures': Men and Women in Asian American Literature." *Michigan Quarterly Review* 29 (Winter 1990): 68-93.

Liu, Tessie. "Teaching the Differences among Women from a Historical Perspective: Rethinking Race and Gender as Social Categories." *Women's Studies International Forum* 14 (1991): 265-76.

Lowe, Lisa. "Heterogeneity, Hybridity, Multiplicity: Marking Asian American Differences." *Diaspora* 1 (Spring 1991): 24-44.

Okimoto, Daniel. *American in Disguise*. New York: Walker/ Weatherhill, 1971.

Sechi, Joanne Harumi. "Being Japanese-American Doesn't Mean 'Made in Japan.'" In *The Third Woman: Minority Women Writers of the United States*, edited by Dexter Fisher. Boston: Houghton Mifflin, 1980).

Tang, James D. "Gender Warfare in Disguise: The Autobiographies of Daniel Okimoto and Maxine Hong Kingston." ms., 5 May 1993.

Wong, Sau-ling C. "Ethnicizing Gender: An Exploration of Sexuality as Sign in Chinese Immigrant Literature." In *Reading the Literatures of Asian America*, edited by Shirley Geok-lin Lim and Amy Ling. Philadelphia: Temple University Press, 1992.

_____. *Reading Asian American Literature: From Necessity to Extravagance*. Princeton: Princeton University Press, 1993.

Wong, Shawn. *Homebase*. New York: Plume, 1979.

Woo, Merle. "Letter to Ma." In *This Bridge Called My Back: Writings by Radical Women of Color*, edited by Cherrie Moraga and Gloria Anzaldua. New York: Kitchen Table Press, 1981.

No More "Tight Red Cheongsams": Asian American Women's Treatment of Fashion

Marilyn Elkins

Mainstream feminists such as Naomi Woolf (1992) and Susan Faludi (1991) call for liberated women to create a revolutionary aesthetic which would ridicule and eliminate the "fashion-beauty complex."[1] They argue that fashion is a key ingredient in male domination and should be antithetic to feminists. However, as Ann Hollander suggests, the fiction that clothes are unimportant often seems generated by an inability to deal easily with "that intractable importance itself" (1993:450). The women writers of Asian American literature manage to treat the issue of fashion with the complexity that Hollander suggests it deserves, for they refuse artificial binaries which vilify or glorify their characters for attention to dress. They usually dismiss the assumption that a woman's attention to fashion indicates spiritual or intellectual vacuity.

   Much of Asian American women's poetry, fiction, and memoir suggests that fashion is inextricable from the intersection of race and gender and, therefore, from the very definition of self. Certainly, "American" fashion can be detrimental to self-esteem—especially when it rests upon white standards of beauty which may be difficult or costly to emulate.[2] When women feel forced to fit a popular image of the dominant culture, they often experience fashion as debilitating. In her poem "On Writing Asian American Poetry," Geraldine Kudaka's narrator recalls eating "rice/and langendorf bread/plates of/padded bras, blondes." She says "we learned racism/ and believed/blonds had more fun," while trains transported "kimono bodies/in suits and ties" (1983:122). "White" fashion standards force the speaker of the poem to see herself as other; her difference from the mainstream image makes her feel isolated and ghettoized.

But adopting Western clothing can also facilitate the search for autonomy and empowerment. Ann Hollander posits that in most Eastern countries visual sensibility is accustomed to the idea of human looks as abstracted into patterns, both by means of art and from direct experience of the clothing itself. She argues that such clothing as robes and kimonos take little account of the human body itself, and the robe has its own autonomy to which the wearer submits her "banal torso." While Western dress requires "the body to give clothes meaning," Eastern clothes aim at an ideal shape of their own to which individual bodies are subordinate (1993:336-37).

Roland Barthes insists that Western fashion has almost no social prohibition against the masculinization of women, pointing out the prominence of the "boyish look" and pant suits (1990:257). Perhaps Western fashion appears more empowering because it seems to pay attention to an androgynous-yet-individualized body and because it is worn by mainstream "American" women who are perceived as having relatively greater personal freedom than women from many other cultural groups.

"American" fashion can, therefore, afford Asian American women with an image which refuses the stereotypic role of the eroticized, exotic other; or the passive, obedient daughter and wife; or the "not boy." It can signal the rejection of an idea which Sucheta Mazumdar argues permeates all Asian cultures to some degree: the idea that men have greater worth than women (1989:15).

Consequently, many authors treat the affirming and crippling aspects of fashion in the same work, showing its complicated effect upon a single character. S. A. Sasaki's protagonist in the short story "The Loom" (1983) is initially victimized by the fashion complex. Never identified by any name other than daughter, wife, and mother, she has "muted her colors and blended in" (203). Sasaki uses clothing as a metaphor for the language that the protagonist spoke as a child with her parents: it is "like a comfortable old sweater that had been well-washed and rendered shapeless by wear . . . like a hole in one's sock, which was perfectly alright at home but would be a horrible embarrassment if seen by *yoso no hito*" (204). Like her Japanese American friends at Berkeley, the protagonist wants to reject her comfortable existence and be "a smart career girl in a tailored suit, beautiful and bold—an American girl," but racism, the depression, and eventually the internment camps, thwart her ambitions. Her dreams of selfhood seem to have vanished until, after the death of one of her daughters, she takes up weaving. As she threads "the warp with all the shades of her life," her remaining daughters discover the subtle colors she knits into their ostensibly brown mufflers: reds and greens which come alive in the sunlight (214). Through her weaving, their mother combines "diverse threads of life into one miraculous, mystical fabric" (214). Fortunately, she has not become "American," and now she selects details from her cultures and combines them into wearable art that provides her with a sense of self.

Maxine Hong Kingston's *Woman Warrior* (1976) uses fashion to help illustrate both the no-name woman's conflict with her role as a grass widow in China and the generational conflict her niece feels as a first-generation Chinese American woman.[3] Because the narrator's mother hints that a search for beauty may have been connected to the aunt's infidelity and subsequent rejection by her community, the narrator envisions the no-name woman as paying too much attention to her looks and rejecting ordinary loveliness. The narrator internalizes this lesson and tries to adopt the beauty and fashion standards of her community by becoming "American-feminine," a style that seems less confrontational toward mainstream society and, consequently, safer than her aunt's refusal to be "Chinese-feminine."

In her mother's recounting of the villagers' raid to punish the aunt's infidelity, they disguise themselves with white masks and bizarre hair styles, indicating that both the mother and the villagers understand the concealing aspect of clothing. They rip up most of the no-name woman's clothing, tear her cloth from the loom, and take only unbroken bowls (perhaps symbolizing their interpretation of the "correct" condition for a grass widow's womb during her husband's protracted absence) and the clothes which they have not torn. Why do her persecutors destroy some clothes and reserve others for their own use? Perhaps only those garments are considered appropriately modest. The reader is left to ponder this gap, for the narrator confesses she is powerless to ask for more information and, therefore—within the didactic guidelines of talk-story—additional guidance: "If I want to learn what clothes my aunt wore, whether flashy or ordinary, I would have to begin, 'Remember Father's drowned-in-the-well sister?' I cannot ask that. My mother has told me once and for all the useful parts" (6). The protagonist's imagination eleaborates upon this elliptical story, hoping to discover what her own feminine demeanor and dress should be.

So the issue of clothing remains in her mind. When she imagines how her aunt met the man who impregnated her, she thinks that "perhaps he sold her the cloth for the dress she sewed and wore" (7). In the scenario that the narrator invents to speak the unspoken, her aunt "often worked at herself in the mirror, guessing at the colors and shapes that would interest [her lover], changing them frequently in order to hit on the right combination" (10).[4] Her hypothesis suggests that the no-name woman seemed eccentric, unlike the other women whose plain hair never "blew easily into heart-catching tangles" (10). Even though she probably raised and altered her hairline in the traditional way, using a depilatory string,[5] her aunt, the narrator suggests, "combed individuality into her bob." The narrator's hope that her aunt's lover "appreciated a smooth brow, that he wasn't just a tits-and-ass man" (11) reflects the narrator's suspicion that men usually have more regard for the sexual parts of a woman's anatomy.

The narrator's insistence on filling the gaps of her mother's version of the no-name woman's story with questions about her style of dress and the story's placement at the book's beginning demonstrate Kingston's sense of the importance of fashion for female self-construction.[6] The book also acknowledges that appropriate dress and, therefore, in the lexicon of the novel, self-creation are frought with special treachery for Asian American women. The narrator fears that by making herself "American pretty" she will be unable to make "attraction selective," and will perhaps attract a male of another race. So she opts for an exterior that she characterizes as "sisterliness, dignified and honorable" (14).

Later she uses her knowledge about the social construction of sexual attractiveness to avoid the FOBs her parents want her to marry. She affects a limp: donning open shoes, she flaps "about like a Wino ghost" (225) to frighten away possible arranged husbands. The narrator converts her knowledge of fashion and its link to a woman's perceived sexuality and/or sexual value into a weapon to subvert her parents' intentions and to liberate herself from a traditional, gender-defined role. Ironically, this is not the moral her mother hoped to teach with the story of the no-name woman. The narrator surmises that anti-fashion can be empowering and closes her book by reiterating the importance of knowing the language of clothing to avoid becoming "a slave or a wife" (234). As Lovely Orchid's story illustrates, being too pretty is dangerous: she escapes from kidnappers when they desert her for "a prettier one" (241).

Amy Tan also employs fashion as a literary trope to illustrate generational conflict. *The Joy Luck Club* (1988) dramatizes the effect of the American fashion beauty complex through the Shirley Temple image which shadows Jing-Mei, a nine-year-old girl whose mother insists upon a child prodigy as a way of partaking in the mythical American dream. Seeking Shirley Temple curls for her daughter, the mother takes her to a beauty training school. When Jing-Mei's hair is frizzy and burned, she feels alienated from her mother and decides that she will become the "angry, powerful" girl who she sees in her mirror, a girl who has "new thoughts, willful thoughts" and will not allow herself to "be what I'm not" (144). After the frizz has been cropped, she emerges with a new hair style "the length of a boy's, with straight-across bangs that hung at a slant two inches above" her eyebrows. This pleases Jing-Mei and, temporarily, makes her believe that she is capable of the perfection she feels her mother demands. After all, the hairdresser assures her that the Peter Pan look is very popular.

Western fashion as empowerment is evident in *The Kitchen God's Wife* (1991) as well. Wei-Wei's mother tries on and discards three Chinese dresses before she returns to the initial, green, Western-style dress she dons for her afternoon jaunt with her daughter and what seems to be an assignation with her lover. Perhaps Western dress appears more appropriate for what is viewed as primarily a Western activity: a married woman's adultery. Tan's narrator seems to approve, rather than judge, the clandestine actions of Double Second. The various versions of her mother's fate allow both Wei-Wei and the reader to assign the mother whatever punishment, or reward, they deem appropriate.

As Gish Jen points out in *Typical American* (1991), Western fashion can also offer compensations to Chinese American immigrants: Theresa Chang has less difficulty finding attire, for she is a "giantess—five-seven! With feet that entered rooms before she did" (47).

A look at the shoes that Theresa wears to be viewed by prospective husbands in both worlds illustrates the way Jen uses fashion. In China, Theresa's mother despairs of her "gait"; to be viewed by her intended, Theresa is forced to wear a "pair of silk shoes a size too small, the idea being not so much to make her feet more acceptable but to help her maintain a more ladylike step," and to carry a shell-pink parasol (49). Consequently, she minces "as though her toes had been bound with fire-strips" (51). When Janis arranges for her to meet Grover Ding in New York, Theresa buys

> Vermilion high heels, the voluptuously curvy kind, shoes [that] had snagged her—so vital . . . that they did not look like shoes so much as some highly adapted life form, mimicking shoes the way lizards mimicked desert rocks. Whereas the shoes she'd had on were plainly the real thing: worn out, dried up, cracking. Like their owner—her reflection in the window was spindly and stiff, separated just this way, by a pane of glass, from some more vibrant world. At the center of her image, the red shoes had seemed to pulse, like her own true heart (90-91).

Theresa purchases red shoes, the traditional color for shoes worn by Chinese brides (Garrett 1987:43), as her visa for "American" society and, perhaps, a Chinese American husband; they also reflect her vibrant interior. But these heels are too "American"; paired with her blue-black qipao,[7] they border on desperate pink, thus losing their power to provide marital fortune; their height makes Theresa totter. Her choice, despite the information she has received about Gordon's five-foot-four stature, hints that at some unconscious level she is ambivalent about marriage. Once again, she presents herself to a prospective mate on shaky footing that disguises her confident stride. Perhaps she wants a husband who can admire her height without interpreting it as "masculine"; perhaps she does not want an "arranged" partner; or perhaps she is using fashion as a method for subverting patriarchal expectations. Theresa's footware lends itself to all of these possible interpretations—and more.

Typical American, at times, seems to have a shoe fetish. When Callie starts kindergarten, Helen buys her "Buster Browns with such perfectly smooth pale tan leather soles that Callie wouldn't wear them home from the store" (161). These shoes were made popular by early television commercials which maintained that Buster Brown and his dog lived happily in a shoe, playing off the European nursery rhyme about the old woman who lived in a shoe which was overcrowded with children. An androgynous fashion icon for children, the Buster Browns are so important to Callie that she sleeps with one hand in each. When the jealous Mona steals one and refuses to tell where it is hidden, Callie is forced to begin kindergarten wearing one old shoe and one new, perhaps symbolizing her biculturalism.

Jen uses another telling fashion allusion to end her novel. As Ralph holds up his arm to hail a taxi to visit his recovering sister, he remembers that "he hadn't even known Theresa owned a bathing suit. An orange one! Old Chao's was gray, a more predictable choice." In the language of clothing, the image reassures us that the resilient Theresa will survive. She seems to have suffered enough for her affair with Old Chao and will not, like Kingston's no-name woman, die as punishment for her sexuality. While the swimsuit seems an unlikely component of the matched-and-muted, Western wardrobe she now owns and which her nieces carefully pack, its color seem to reflect Theresa's "own true heart," her inner vibrancy. She is courageous enough to combine parts of her Chinese self with selected "American" elements to create her Chinese American self. She discovers that she can be a successful doctor and enjoy her love affair.

The liberating aspect of self-creation is also treated in Diane Mei Lin Mark's poem "Suzie Wong Doesn't Live Here" (1983). Her narrator rejects "tight red cheongsams/embroidered with peonies" and "downcast eyes" to celebrate liberation from the stereotypes of "Madame Butterfly/and the geisha ladies." What emerges are women who are "stepping on/without downcast eyes, /without calculating dragon power" and without the "silence/that you've come to/know so well" (187). For Mark, rejecting traditional fashion is a necessary step to rejecting the role of sex object in both the Asian American and mainstream cultures. She refuses to be either passive wife and mother or eroticized, exotic other. In her new-found feminist sisterhood, "seeing each other at last," she usurps the power of the gaze from males, proclaiming strength in being "born female in Asian America" (187).

As Sucheta Mazumdar stresses, arrival in America is often liberating for Asian women because "societal norms of the majority community frequently provide greater personal freedom" (1989:15). The key problem of bicultural existence becomes, as Esther Ngan-Ling Chow points out, selecting elements from both cultural worlds "to make the best adaptation according to the demands of social circumstances" (1989:368). This accommodation and incorporation is quite naturally reflected in a woman's dress. Naseem Khan suggests that, in fact, contemporary fashion is really about those issues involved "in the shifts and squeezes that go on when one race locates itself in the midst of another" (1993:73).

Choosing to adopt mainstream fashion may signal the construction of a bicultural self or it may simply provide the necessary camouflage for an easier entry into the workplace. Asian American women writers reject the oversimplification that regard for accoutrements constitutes a litmus test for character or for feminism. Instead, they convert the fashion system into a literary trope for accommodating and celebrating their biculturality. They have mastered the metaphoric use of clothing as a subversive act.

Notes

1. I have taken the image and spelling for my title from Diane Mei Lin Mark's poem "Susie Wong Doesn't Live Here." Valery M. Garrett points out that the traditional Chinese *sam*, a Chinese adaptation of the Manchu's flowing robes fashioned from animal skins, was worn by both male and female; eventually the overlap on the *sam* was dispensed with by males and replaced by a center-front opening. These differences became essential demarcations of gender (1987:6). By the 1930s the *cheung sam* referred to a tight-fitting woman's dress with side slits reaching "right up to the thigh" (Garrett 1987:18). Emma Louie, the editor of *Gum Saan Journal* which is published by the Chinese Historical Society of Southern California, believes that Madame Chiang

Kai-shek helped to popularize the dress with Chinese Americans. After the Communist takeover in 1949, the *cheung sam* disappeared for a while in mainland China although it continued to be worn in Hong Kong (Garrett 1987:18). In the United States, the film *Suzie Wong* imbued the dress with qualities of eroticized exoticism for members of the mainstream culture.

2. For expediency, I consistently place the term "American" in quotation marks to indicate fashion of the United States of America as it is institutionalized in media imaging and do not intend to lessen the importance of all countries of the Americas.

3. I follow the suggestion of King-Kok Cheung (1992) in distinguishing between Kingston's "re-vision" of her historical self and Kingston as author; therefore, I refer to the subject of Kingston's memoir as "narrator" or "protagonist."

4. Barthes interprets fashion as an "image system constituted with desire as its goal" (1990:xii), an assumption which Kingston's narrator seems to share.

5. Garrett points out that this procedure was a typical wedding preparation to give the bride "a more open-faced look." Called *hoi min,* literally "opening the face," the process was done by a "fortunate woman with many sons" to ensure that the bride would be "similarly blessed" (1987:38). Perhaps Kingston mentions the process for irony; no-name woman's pregnancy is not a blessing.

6. David Leiwei Li points out that the multiple stories of this text "unfold a message that the ethnic woman cannot authorize herself without a full recognition of the shared stories of her gender and her race" (1992:329). I suggest that fashion serves as a trope that actualizes the narrator's authorization in a visible, public way.

7. The use of *qi pao* as appellation for Theresa's clothing, rather than *cheung sam*, indicates that she and Ralph have emigrated from northern China, for *qi pao* is the term used outside of south China (Garrett 1987:18).

References

Barthes, Roland. *The Fashion System.* Trans. Matthew Ward and Richard Howard. Berkeley: University of California Press, 1990.

Cheung, King-Kok. "'Don't Tell': Imposed Silences in *The Color Purple* and *The Woman Warrior.*" In *Reading the Literature of Asian America,* edited by Shirley Geok-lin Lim and Amy Ling. Philadelphia: Temple University Press, 1992.

Chow, Esther Ngan-Ling. "The Feminist Movement: Where Are all the Asian American Women?" In *Making Waves: An Anthology of Writings by and about Asian American Women,* edited by Asian Women United of California. Boston: Beacon Press, 1989.

Faludi, Susan. *Backlash.* New York: Crown, 1991.

Garrett, Valery M. *Traditional Chinese Clothing in Hong Kong and South China, 1840-1980.* Hong Kong: Oxford University Press, 1987.

Hollander, Anne. *Seeing Through Clothes.* Berkeley: University of California Press, 1993.

Jen, Gish. *Typical American.* New York: Penguin, 1992.

Khan, Naseem. "Asian Women's Dress: From Burqah to Bloggs—Changing Clothes for Changing Times." In *Chic Thrills: A Fashion Reader,* edited by Juliet Ash and Elizabeth Wilson. Berkeley: University of California Press, 1993.

Kingston, Maxine Hong. *The Woman Warrier: Memoirs of a Girlhood among Ghosts.* New York: Random House, 1977.

Kudaka, Geraldine. "On Writing Asian American Poetry." In *Breaking Silence, an Anthology of Contemporary Asian American Poets,* edited by Joseph Bruchac. Greenfield Center: Greenfield Review Press, 1983.

Li, David Leiwei. "The Production of Chinese American Tradition: Displacing American Orientalist Discourse." In *Reading the Literatures of Asian America*, edited by Shirley Geok-lin Lim and Amy Ling. Philadelphia: Temple University Press, 1992.

Louie, Emma. Telephone interview. 29 April 1993.

Mark, Diane Mei Lin. "Susie Wong Doesn't Live Here." In *Breaking Silence, an Anthology of Contemporary Asian American Poets,* edited by Joseph Bruchac. Greenfield Center: Greenfield Review Press, 1983.

Mazumdar, Sucheta. "A Woman-Centered Perspective on Asian American History." In *Making Waves: An Anthology of Writings by and about Asian American Women,* edited by Asian Women United of California. Boston: Beacon, 1989.

Sasaki, R. A. "The Loom." In *Making Waves: An Anthology of Writings by and about Asian American Women,* edited by Asian Women United of California. Boston: Beacon, 1989.

Tan, Amy. *The Joy Luck Club.* New York: Ballantine, 1989.

_____. *The Kitchen God's Wife.* New York: Ballantine, 1992.

Wolf, Naomi. *The Beauty Myth: How Images of Beauty Are Used Against Women.* New York: Doubleday, 1992.

Chinese/Asian American Men in the 1990s: Displacement, Impersonation, Paternity, and Extinction in David Wong Louie's *Pangs of Love*[1]

Sau-ling Cynthia Wong

The year 1993 marks the fiftieth anniversary of the repeal of the 1882 Chinese Exclusion Act, the legislation that deliberately thwarted the formation of families in Chinese American communities for decades. Earlier in the year, the organizers of a commemorative conference at San Francisco State University sent out a "Call for Papers" on the effects of Exclusion on various aspects of Chinese American life, including literature. When I pondered whether the marks left by Exclusion had persisted in contemporary Chinese American literature, I immediately thought of David Wong Louie's *Pangs of Love* (1991), with its stories of anxiety over paternity, progeny, extinction—until it occurred to me that the world of *Pangs of Love* is hardly the world of the "old-timers" with direct links to the Exclusion era.

Over a quarter of a century after the 1965 reform that allowed large-scale Asian immigration, the Chinese American community is no longer a "bachelor society"; families with young children are no longer a rare sight in Chinatowns. In fact, the term *Chinatown* itself—if it refers to the ghettoized urban communities that initially formed in response to discrimination—can no longer adequately epitomize Chinese American demographic patterns.[2] It stands to reason, therefore, that the figure of the heir-obsessed patriarch found in works such as C. Y. Lee's *Flower Drum Song* (1957); Louis Chu's *Eat a Bowl of Tea* (1961); Jeffery Paul Chan's "Jackrabbit" (1974); Monfoon Leong's "New Year for Fong Wing" (1975); and Frank Chin's *The Year of the Dragon* (1981) likewise can no longer encompass the concerns of Chinese American men of the post-1965 generation.

Indeed, the fictional world of *Pangs of Love* seems light-years away from the grimy Chinatown streets memorialized in early Frank Chin. Louie's characters are apparently well-assimilated, and the author's sensibility appears to have little in common with the literalist realism of a Louis Chu or a Monfoon Leong. On the surface, Louie's characters exist in a world from which legislative, political, economic, and cultural injunctions against Chinese American men have been removed, freeing them to reproduce without fear.

The world of *Pangs of Love* is a seemingly egalitarian world of consumerist multiculturalism and ethnic diversity, a world of Italian-style cafes, sushi bars, Cuisinarts, and Swedish rye bread no less than baseball and apple pie (though soy-sauce chicken does make a guest appearance). Male yuppies heavily populate it, some identifiably Asian, some stereotypically gay. Only in a few of the stories is the Chineseness of the characters foregrounded; elsewhere male characters are of indeterminate or ambiguous ethnicity, giving the impression that hegemonic cultural fluency has exempted them from the need to be preoccupied about emasculation and marginality. The Chinese men are commercial artists, cafe owners, corporate chemists, and designers of home video games. They know their way around the America of the Reagan-Bush era, use its products, speak its lingo; they drive expertly and not only sleep with white women but break up with them with regularity. Unlike their "old-timer" predecessors, they cannot be described as "emasculated," biologically (lack of offspring) or otherwise, by restrictive laws, political disenfranchisement, economic constraints, geographic isolation, linguistic barriers, or "cultural illiteracy" in the Euro-American tradition.

The stories in *Pangs of Love* evince not only a recognizably contemporary content but also a distinctive voice and sensibility. The language has a sharp edge to it; it is hip, literate, and oblique, with frequent flights of dark humor and surreal fantasy. Narrative structure is sophisticated; a story like "One Man's Hysteria—Real and Imagined—in the Twentieth Century" exemplifies postmodern metafiction to an extent guaranteed to warm an English graduate student's heart. Ironic control, not reactive spontaneity, is the dominant characteristic of the volume's form and prose.

Nevertheless, beneath the observable, sociologically accurate "improvements" in the Chinese American male subject's condition, *Pangs of Love* is anxiety-ridden. Problematic paternity and prospects of extinction are especially prominent themes—in biological and not merely "metaphorical" terms. The question then arises: if collective biological extinction is no longer a serious threat for Chinese Americans, why the unremitting heir-obsession? An answer is hinted at when the themes of paternity and extinction are examined in conjunction with two other recurrent figures—displacement and impersonation—in *Pangs of Love*. What emerges from this examination with startling clarity is the connection between gender concerns and the cultural project promulgated by the *Aiiieeeee!* group in the late 1960s and early 1970s. That project, anti-essentialist vis-a-vis white culture, has opened up deconstructive possibilities greatly at odds with a patrilineal concept of cultural transmission to which the *Aiiieeeee!* authors subscribed and which they modified only under duress. The contradiction might have gone unremarked when adverse historical conditions highlighted the resistance aspect of literary production. However, when the Chinese American population changed in its composition and positioning in American society, and when the kind of open-ended cultural definition of "Chinese Americanness" once boldly envisioned as an alternative to biological procreation is proving to be realizable, the male fear of heirlessness resurfaced.

While my analysis pertains to Chinese Americans, the issues can be generalized to Asian Americans to some extent. Not only were exclusionary policies directed against all Asian groups at one time or another, to varying degrees, but the *Aiiieeeee!* claims are pan-ethnic. Furthermore, the male voices heard in the *annus mirabilis* of 1991—among them Frank Chin *(Donald Duk)*; Gus Lee *(China Boy)*; David Mura (*Turning Japanese: Memoirs of a Sansei*); Jeffery Paul Chan et al. (*The Big Aiiieeeee!*); and Peter Bacho *(Cebu)*—all address gender and culture in some interrelated fashion. Of this group, David Wong Louie has perhaps looked the most unblinkingly at the possibility of identity extinction.

Displacement, which is the title of one of Louie's short stories in *Pangs of Love*, often takes the form of a character finding himself (or less frequently, herself) in the wrong place, usually the wrong house.[3] Mrs. Chow and her husband in "Displacement" are immigrants living as maid and caretaker in a white widow's house; they are restless to move out to their own apartment but the search is discouraging. Like Mrs. Chow, Mrs. Pang in "Pangs of Love" is an immigrant displaced to America; the speaker of the story has been "volunteered" by his brothers to live in the apartment of their widowed mother. In "Birthday," Wallace Wong barricades himself in the bedroom of his white ex-girlfriend's son and tries to fend off the biological father of the boy (i.e., the ex-girlfriend's ex-husband). The two have gotten back together again, leaving the would-be adoptive father out of the picture. In "Social Science," a man separated from his wife continues to live as a renter in their house, which has been put on the market; in his effort to get even by deliberately misleading potential buyers, he ends up trying to get another man to take over his former life and wife. In "The Movers," a couple trying to revive a precarious relationship move into an empty house and wait for the Salvation Army to deliver their furniture. After the woman walks out on him, the man stays alone in the deserted house, feeling like an intruder. When the former owner's son sneaks in for a tryst with his girlfriend, the new renter fends off the girl's father by pretending to be the boy's father. In "Bottles of Beaujolais," there is a displaced animal, an otter kept in a climate-controlled tank in a sushi restaurant. The captive creature's life seems to parallel that of its keeper, a restaurant employee who is yet another hapless male unable to court or keep a white woman. Throughout David Wong Louie's dark comedies of displacement, someone who should be the rightful inhabitant of a place feels or acts like a guilty intruder, or else an intruder tries but fails to become the rightful inhabitant.

Even though explicit references to ethnicity and identity politics are rare in Louie's stories, the fact that displacement figures so prominently in them raises an inevitable question: is a man considered an intruder because he is Chinese/Asian? Does a rightful inhabitant vacate his place because, as a Chinese/Asian American man, he is unable to sustain the kind of relationship with a white woman that legitimizes his position in this society? (I should add that the woman's ethnicity is almost always spelled out.) In a few of the stories, a dwelling is heavily identified with a woman, so that issues of ownership or occupancy could apply to both. Such a reading is encouraged by certain tantalizingly muted but unmistakably deliberate details let drop by the author. For example, the speaker in "The Movers" is humiliated by the delivery men, who make rude homosexual jokes, dismiss his claim that he is Suzy's boyfriend, and refuse to let him sign for the furniture. Why? Only a tangential reference elsewhere—to the speaker's morbid fantasy of lying in a morgue in China—confirms the possibility that racism is responsible for the outrageous treatment. In "One Man's Hysteria," a minor character speaks to the male protagonist's white girlfriend even when he is the one asking the question: later on, we find that the couple's son has black hair, which is the only clue that Asian ethnicity might have played a role in a story where the principals recite obscure Metaphysical poetry to each other from memory.

As the house imagery suggests (sexual connotations aside), the idea that an ethnic subject can be liberated into universal humanity through acculturation is but a myth: a full American identity is not something one comes to possess through internal self-alteration, but a position one is or is not authorized to inhabit. Fluency in the hegemonic culture, including superb mastery of the Western literary canon, is no guarantee of authority. When assumed by someone with the "wrong" skin and hair color, it is mere impersonation, mimicry, occupation of a subject position that is not yours, or can be yours only through acts of fakery, like the synthetic sprays concocted by the Chinese chemist in "Pangs of Love." To keep his Vassar-educated girlfriend Amanda Millstein, the protagonist "jump-starts" her by spiking their food and drinks with an aphrodisiac, Musk 838/Lot No. 191443759413 (81). The protagonist's efforts at denerdification remind one of the upbeat, revisionist construction of male sexuality in a well-known contemporaneous cultural project, the 1991 Asian Pacific Islander Men calendar (De Castro), in which six college-educated male models are shown in two poses each, one dressed, in the work setting; and one stripped, in "beefcake" postures. Pang's two personas—"dress for success" "model minority" at the office, wild animal in the bedroom—are shown to be tenuously held together, at worst even fraudulent and self-deceptive.[4]

The story "Love on the Rocks" further illustrates how precarious the model minority position is. When global recession causes video game designer Buddy (Beijing) Lam to be fired, his marriage to the Vassar-educated white dreamgirl, Cookie, falls apart, and he ends up killing her and preserving her body on ice in the bathtub. Without his job, the best he can do now is to continue wearing his wool suit while pursuing an affair of dubious carnal reward with Miriam, a brown-skinned professional shopper for a supermarket impressed by his appearance of affluence. Sexual contempt from those both socially above and socially below the Asian American man thrives on. Cookie's father says of Buddy: "When they walked down the street, Cookie towering over him, people rubbernecked as if they just saw Jackie O. pass with Arafat on her arm" (105). As for her Miriam, her girlfriend advises: "Face it, girl, so what if he's not the best-looking guy on the street. A quarter of the world looks like him and none of them's got his kind of dough" (104). When Miriam orders him to "keep low" in her delivery car, "Buddy, who's short, folds neatly into his predicament" (101). So much, then, for denerdification.

"Real or imagined"—a phrase embedded in the title of "One Man's Hysteria . . . in the Twentieth Century"—presents an interpretive dilemma which tests a male Chinese/Asian American subject's interpellation by the dominant ideology. Is the legitimizing power of cultural competence real or imagined? Is your authority real or imagined? Is your sense of belonging real or imagined? Is your personal inadequacy real or imagined? Is American racism in the twentieth century real or imagined? What mainstream society terms paranoia may be ethnic consciousness, and vice versa. Clues to this choice of perspective cannot be found in "improved conditions."

Given Louie's treatment of ethnicity, the concern with problematic paternity and extinction in *Pangs of Love* takes on all the more poignancy. In the stories, all of the identifiably Chinese men and Chinese women, and most of the possibly Asian men, are preoccupied with the question of whether or not having children is possible or desirable.[5] Wallace Wong loses Welby to his biological father, a white man. His parents are not sympathetic, however, since they do not want their only son "adopting a used family" (6).

> I tried to imagine myself as a condor at the dead end of evolution. In my veins I felt the primordial soup bubbling, and my whole entropic bulk quaked as I gazed at the last females of my species. I knew I was supposed to mate, but I wasn't sure how. Yeah, I'd probably have to start by picking a partner. But which one? I looked them over, the last three in creation; she'd need to have good genes. Finally, after careful consideration, I chose—her, the bird with blond tail feathers. Then I heard my father's voice: "No, not that one, that one" (7).

Mrs. Pang in *Pangs of Love* tries to send all her three sons on "bride safaris in Hong Kong" (87). She is distraught over the speaker's loss of his Mandarin-speaking Jewish girlfriend, the perfect compromise if one *had* to outmarry. She is kept from knowing that one of his sons, Bagel, is gay and therefore a bad candidate for procreation. Bagel evades her pressing questions by joking, "I'm already married to my cat." "'Such crazy talk,' [Mrs. Pang says]. 'What kind of life is that, hugging a cat all the time. She give you babies?'" (88) The last story of the volume, "Inheritance," features a Chinese family whose patriarch sports the ill-advised English name of Edsel; sure enough, he loses his entire family except for a younger daughter, who feels increasing pressure to have a baby so that the family name and bloodline can be carried on. Even in the ethnically unmarked, or minimally marked, stories, the male characters are preoccupied with fatherhood. The speaker in "The Movers" impersonates a father, but the delivery man tells him "You don't sound like anyone's father" (131). In "One Man's

Hysteria," the speaker invents (or has) a son, who is, however, named Todd, German for "dead."

The intensity with which misgivings over displacement, impersonation, paternity, and extinction are expressed in David Wong Louie's *Pangs of Love* is thought-provoking. While Exclusion, anti-miscegenation, and other discriminatory laws first prompted a concern for familial and communal continuance among Chinese American men, that concern has not been eliminated by the lifting of these laws or the gradual replacement of "bachelor societies" by families. Nor has the dominant society's construction of Chinese/Asian American male desire been significantly modified by the apparent success of the male "yappie." An obvious conclusion that one might draw from this is that racism persists under changing material circumstances, making ceaseless vigilance necessary. Acknowledging that political necessity, however, does not explain a further paradox: if collective biological extinction is no longer a serious threat for Chinese Americans, why the "hysteria" over the issue of extinction?

On this point, the principle of "pain displacement" mentioned in "Displacement" may be helpful. "[Mrs. Chow] had read in a textbook that a malady in one part of the body could show up as a pain in another locale—sick kidneys, for example, might surface as a mouthful of sore gums" (20). I submit that fear of biological extinction in *Pangs of Love* may actually be a displacement of the fear of *identity extinction*, and that the visions of *global* environmental disaster or nuclear holocaust that haunt "One Man's Hysteria" and "Inheritance" mask a male anxiety over *patrilineal transmission*. By "identity" I refer here specifically to the notion of a uniquely Asian American identity—a kind of "third entity" that cannot be captured or accounted for by Asian and dominant American cultural formulations—first articulated in the *"Aiiieeeee!* project," my shorthand term for the Asian American cultural enterprise as defined in the 1960s and early 1970s by predominantly male writers associated with the *Aiiieeeee!* anthology. I avoid collocations like *cultural identity, ethnic identity,* or *cultural extinction* in this discussion because the unresolved question is precisely *what* delimits this Asian American identity that appears so menaced.

The *"Aiiieeeee!* project" attempted (among other things) to meet the challenge of building a viable culture on the basis of a "bachelor society." Though immigration laws changed in 1965, the Asian American movement took place at a time when the effects of the new legislation were just beginning to be felt, and the aftermath of Exclusion was still very visible in Chinatowns and Manilatowns. As Frank Chin's short story "The Only

Real Day" shows, if biological reproduction is impossible for Chan, the old waiter from the Exclusion era, his only hope for cultural transmission lies in revising the descent-based notion of the Chinese family to include a biologically unrelated male child, the American-born, English-speaking Dirigible. It is, in part, the predicament of males like Dirigible that calls for the cultural tenets informing the *Aiiieeeee!* Introduction: since genetic patrilineality is unfeasible, culture must be dissociated from blood, and the concept of an ever-evolving Asian American culture unencumbered by expectations of "authenticity"—whether of pedigree or of cultural practices—must be allowed to flourish.

In a much more literal, physical sense than that in which Edward Said (1986) uses the terms in "Secular Criticism," this renunciation of bloodline to create a larger community is a turn from *filiation* to *affiliation* (615), a response to "the pressure to produce new and different ways of conceiving human relationships":

> [I]f biological reproduction is either too difficult or too unpleasant, is there some other way by which men and women can create social bonds between each other that would substitute for those ties that connect members of the same family across generations? (614)

In Said's analysis, failure to bear children is first and foremost a metaphor standing for a general societal affliction—that of cultural exhaustion; the predicament of "real" individuals is of corollary significance.[6] In the case of Chinese Americans, however, obstructed filiation was a historical fact legislated into existence. Thus the development of affiliation might be a much more urgent task than if the impending extinction were primarily spiritual.

Yet the unspoken end of this putatively open-ended project to replace filiation with affiliation is in fact to ensure that some form of patrilineal cultural transmission proceeds uninterrupted. In Monfoon Leong's story, Fong Wing's willingness to adopt the legless veteran after the death of his sons is predicated on the utter unthinkability of considering his surviving daughter a true heir. *Eat a Bowl of Tea* is a comedy of successful affiliation only because Mei Oi gives birth to a baby boy; if the illegitimate child had been a girl, her arrival would not even have amounted to a temptation for the male elders to stretch the boundaries of the family. In Frank Chin's "The Only Real Day," when Chan attempts to educate Dirigible in the heroic tradition by offering to buy him Chinese comic books, his aim is to lure him away from competing cultural claims and ensure that the boundary between Chinese and non-Chinese remains demarcated even after his own death as an issue-less bachelor. Chan's proffered "adoption" of Dirigible is again a gendered act. Thus the anti-essentialist cultural enterprise of 1960s Asian America is, at heart, a means to recuperate essentialism in some disguised or attenuated form: a compromise with the realities of the threatened patriline for which *traceability* is a prerequisite.[7] A filiative impulse lurks beneath the persuasive general logic of affiliative theory.[8]

Books like David Wong Louie's *Pangs of Love* are made possible by the achievements of the "*Aiiieeeee!* project" to legitimize what was previously illegitimate. If the spirit of the project were realized to its logical limits, marrying white women and reading Gerard Manley Hopkins should be no less Asian American than being American-born and Anglophone, which in Dirigible's case is deemed acceptable. However, once the threat of collective biological extinction for Asian Americans is no longer present in history to serve as a lightning rod for male anxieties, the makeshift and amorphous nature of the redefined Asian American sensibility and community becomes painfully apparent. By being inclusive, the concept of an Asian American identity, initially constitutive, may end up deconstructing itself. In theory, no Asian American cultural imperative prevents Wallace Wong from adopting his white girlfriend's white son to create a family. The only remaining barriers from this nightmare of patriarchy are pressure from the immigrant parents (who will die sooner or later) and the abiding disdain of white society, which one would hate to use as the sole basis for drawing a community's boundaries.

This nightmare of interrupted patrilineality is not confronted either by Frank Chin in *Donald Duk* or by Gus Lee in *China Boy*. The former sidesteps the question by looking backward to the railroad building days when biological extinction was a real menace, and by devising a narrative mechanism whereby traditional Chinese myth, Chinese American history, and one individual Chinese American boy's dream conveniently coincide to guarantee Donald's induction into the male line of succession. Gus Lee adopts a similar past-oriented strategy, focusing on his own childhood. The poverty of Kai Ting's world provides a ready excuse for not addressing the implications of upward mobility out of the ghetto. Furthermore, by adopting a naturalized testosteronic code of equal-opportunity male violence, the vexed issue of community boundaries is dispatched. In contrast, David Wong Louie's *Pangs of Love* looks ahead to confront the disturbing possibilities raised by the problematic positioning of Chinese/Asian American men in a racialized and gendered society.

Notes

1. The possibility that Frank Chin's concern with cultural purity might be gendered was first raised by Vivian Chin in an unpublished paper on mistranslations in *The Woman Warrior* that she presented at my graduate seminar on Asian American literature at U.C. Berkeley, Spring 1993. My analysis of the *"Aiiieeeee!* project" has been profitably influenced by this idea, and I thank Vivian for permission to make use of it here. I have also benefited from discussions with Cynthia Liu and other members of the seminar.
2. Fong's study of Monterey Park in southern California (1993) examines one important aspect of the new Chinese American demographics.
3. The female gender of some of the characters discussed here is not necessarily a problem for my thesis, since the principle of "pain displacement," as explained later in this essay, appears operative in *Pangs of Love.*
4. The ambiguities in the 1991 calendar project to rehabilitate Asian American manhood are discussed in Wong (1993).
5. The question facing female Chinese characters like Mrs. Chow or Edna is whether to fulfill their culturally mandated feminine role by getting pregnant. In other words, the concern is still patriarchal and patrilineal.
6. Said's categories of "childless couples, orphaned children, aborted childbirths, and unregenerately celibate men and women" are derived first from high modernist literature—from the works of Joyce, Eliot, Mann, and others—then applied to "individual men and women" (614). Except for a brief allusion to Lukacs on reification and alienation, Said fudges the exact relationship between literal and spiritual infertility and specific historical bases for the former.
7. I am indebted to Vivian Chin for this felicitous term. Note that in everyday language, *fathering* and *mothering*, ostensibly parallel terms, have entirely different connotations. Traceability is inherent in the meaning of *fathering:* one can father a child without doing anything with it afterwards. Mothering, on the other hand, usually implies a caregiving act which is readily extendable to biologically unrelated individuals.
8. In this perspective, Frank Chin's defense of cultural "authenticity" in the controversy regarding Maxine Hong Kingston, Amy Tan, and David Henry Hwang is not as surprising as it may first seem; rather than a change of heart or a lapse in intellectual consistency, it represents an unfolding of the contradictions latent in the *"Aiiieeeee!* project."

References

Bacho, Peter. *Cebu.* Seattle: University of Washington Press, 1991.

Chan, Jeffery Paul. "Jackrabbit." In *Yardbird Reader 3*, edited by Shawn Wong and Frank Chin. Berkeley:Yardbird Publishing, 1974.

Chan, Jeffery Paul, et al. *The Big Aiiieeeee! An Anthology of Chinese American and Japanese American Literature.* New York: Meridian, 1991.

Chin, Frank. *The Chickencoop Chinaman and The Year of the Dragon: Two Plays.* Seattle: University of Washington Press, 1981.

———. "The Only Real Day." In *The Chinaman Pacific & Frisco R.R. Co.* Minneapolis: Coffee House Press, 1988.

———. *Donald Duk.* Minneapolis: Coffee House Press, 1991.

Chin, Frank, et al. *Aiiieeeee! An Anthology of Asian-American Writers.* Washington, D.C.: Howard University Press, 1983.

Chu, Louis. *Eat a Bowl of Tea*. Seattle: University of Washington Press, 1961.

De Castro, Antonio. *Asian Pacific Islander Men: 1991 Calendar*. San Francisco: Human Ties Production, 1991.

Fong, Timothy. *The First Suburban Chinatown*. Philadelphia: Temple University Press, 1993.

Lee, C. Y. *Flower Drum Song*. New York: Farrar, Straus and Cudahy, 1957.

Lee, Gus. *China Boy*. New York: Dutton, 1991.

Leong, Monfoon. "New Year for Fong Wing."In *Number One Son*. San Francisco: East/West Publishing Company, 1975.

Louie, David Wong. *Pangs of Love*. New York: Knopf, 1991.

Mura, David. *Turning Japanese: Memoirs of a Sansei*. New York: Pantheon, 1991.

Said, Edward W. "Secular Criticism." In *Critical Theory since 1965*, edited by Hazard Adams and Leroy Searle. Tallahassee: Florida State University Press, 1986.

Wong, Sau-ling Cynthia. "Subverting Desire: Reading the Body in the 1991 Asian Pacific Islander Men's Calendar." In *Critical Mass: A Journal of Asian American Cultural Criticism* 1:1 (Fall 1993): 63-74.

"Across That Ocean Is . . .": Trans-Oceanic Revaluations of Marriage in Filipino American Fiction

Dolores de Manuel

What does marriage signify in Filipino American fiction? A number of stories and novels, spanning several decades, can be read as addressing the question, both directly and indirectly. The answers constitute a discourse on the economy of marriage, an attempt to determine whether the institution is by nature productive or destructive, fertile or sterile. In working out the equation of value, the fiction of Jessica Hagedorn, Bienvenido Santos, and Linda Ty-Casper quickly brings many factors to the surface. The meaning of marriage depends on where the protagonists have located themselves, and whether this act of self-positioning is conceived in terms that are geographical, racial, cultural, or emotional. It depends on the type of redefinition of social and gender roles that takes place in the act of marriage and union, and whether that redefinition is seen as positive or negative.

The movement of the immigrant's inner relocation can be situated within a larger process in Asian American literature that Shirley Geok-Lin Lim has noted: "the paradigm of conflict and ambivalence reflected . . . in internalized alienations and in external racial discrimination and violence, will be transformed into a productive multivalence" (1992:28). In the process of revaluation and transformation charted in Filipino American fiction, as male and female, east and west collide and redefine each other, both casualties and survivors emerge.

In reading the work of Filipino American fictionists as a running commentary on the economy and imperatives of marriage in the trans-oceanic, cross-cultural setting, a quick definition of traditional Filipino marriage is in order; the easy formula "love, honor, obey" should be supplemented. While noting the high value ascribed to marriage, one should posit, in addition, a code of unspoken, unwritten cultural rules that exist over and above the legal and religious restrictions, including family stability, loyalty, and female subordination. In each work of fiction examined in this paper, one finds that the meanings ascribed to marriage at home in the Philippines shift their ground, as characters move into new territory and come to redefinition.

This shift is most simply and graphically illustrated in Jessica Hagedorn's *Dogeaters* (1990). Rio Gonzaga, a narrator, grows up in the Philippines as an observer of a procession of failed or bizarrely dysfunctional marriages. Her mother, after being humiliated by her husband's flagrant infidelities, attacking him with a pair of spike heels and seeking refuge in the company of homosexual friends, finally moves to America to escape her marriage; Rio comes with her. Her last comment on her own uneasy progress to maturity is "I never marry" (247). For both mother and daughter, the effects of a bad marriage are lasting. Geography is their escape; the ocean between insulates them from the cultural norms of home and enables them to devalue marriage. The novel leaves one questioning whether codes of behavior, gender roles, and social conditions within a macho culture have made marriage in the Philippines an impossibly destructive institution for women, and whether failure is actually an inescapable precondition of its existence.

Although this question is never addressed directly, the novel's conclusion seems to imply that since the rules of marriage are too complicated, it is easier to just get out of the game. Placing oneself outside of the confines of marriage is facilitated by the literal crossing; in this novel America is the escape hatch, the position off the playing board where the rules need not be obeyed. The physical movement allows Rio to step away from the system of value. But the simplicity of this unbinding and redefinition is illusory and deceptive, since decentering and relocation also carry the price of personal destabilization. Rio's description of herself implies a sense of disorientation: "I am anxious and restless, at home only in airports. I travel whenever I can" (247). The act of relocation outside the domain of marriage may imply a permanent dislocation.

However, not everyone can step so far out of these bounds, nor does everyone want to; avoidance is not always a viable way of dealing with the question of marriage, especially when the institution is regarded as practically a categorical imperative, a social construction of inherent value. Unlike in Hagedorn's novel, where America is an escape, the American experience adds another layer to the mandates of marriage as described in

Bienvenido Santos' work. To the Filipino frame of reference is added another set of codes that need to be confronted, and when the complications of interracial factors enter the equation of value, the possibility of a complete and clean repositioning becomes minimal.

This complication is demonstrated in two of Bienvenido Santos's early stories. The first, "Scent of Apples," set in the 1940s, is very widely anthologized in the Philippines. One probable reason for its popularity there is its reversal of race relations in its portrayal of Ruth, an American woman, heroically risking her life and working uncomplainingly for Fabia, her Filipino husband, who in praise compares her to the tradition of "our own Filipino women" (28). However, the positive reception of the story by the Filipino audience does not fully take into account the fact that Fabia, as a Filipino, has placed himself in a position in which his personal roots are of marginal value, both socially and economically. In fact his Filipino origins actually devalue him; Ruth knows nothing of his background, saying with disbelief "there's no such thing as first class Filipino" (24). While he sees in her a support and kinship with his roots, his isolation and distance from his Filipino identity is more striking. Fabia hopes that his young son will be better than him, taller—in other words, more American than Filipino (24). As "just a Filipino farmer out in the country" (22), he is pathetically lost in the Midwest, and when asked about making contact with his home town, recognizes his distance from his roots: " 'No,' he said softly, sounding very much defeated but brave, 'Thanks a lot. But you see, nobody would remember me now'" (29).

Fabia's sad comment reveals the condition of his repositioning: his life in America is something of a success, with a happy marriage and growing son, but at the cost of his sense of Filipino selfhood. His devoted wife is an unwitting collaborator in this devaluation of his Filipino identity. Her naive assessment "there's no such thing as first class Filipino" reflects her absorption of the values of the colonial master/servant relationship. While she may be personally dedicated to Fabia, recognizing his positive qualities as husband and provider, she cannot help but categorize him as a marginal other in the scheme of socioeconomic and racial stratification that she knows. She herself is simple and uneducated; it may be her recognition of her own low status that alerts her to Fabia's even lowlier position.

Santos's "Scent of Apples" is quite benign when compared to another story of the same period, "Woman Afraid," which, in its grim picture of the prejudices surrounding interracial marriages, shows the possible dangers of attempted redefinition. The story opens with a young couple, Alice, an American, and Cris, a Filipino, happily in love after first overcoming the misery of having to hide their relationship from fear of public disapproval. At the start of their relationship they are apprehensive about even walking together on the street, but after a few months they have reached a point of stable happiness, finding that they are accepted and that their relationship is recognized by the community as one of genuine love. They spend peaceful evenings in the simple pleasures of music and laughter; their lives are vital and fulfilled. When Alice has overcome her initial doubts that "people might think you are colored" (130), she accepts all of Cris's Filipino qualities as desirable, delighting in his warmth and affection, which she sees as a trait of his "lovely people" (139). Even his dark skin is a quality that makes him look "like a God" to her; she hopes that their future children may look just like him (139). She has bought into the ideals of Filipino culture, and has made a successful repositioning, at least temporarily. It is important to note that in this story the American wife, while physically on home territory, is the one who has made the crossing. However, this reverse acculturation is inherently unstable because of its physical and social site; it sets the stage for a painful confrontation with the dominant culture.

The climate of the marriage becomes ominous when Alice hears about another Filipino-American intermarriage that has ended in disaster. The American wife, Marge, a friend of the couple, has crumbled under the "slow torture" of constant prejudice (138). The taunts of Marge's neighbors who call her half-Filipino children "monkey boys" drive her to insanity; she drowns the boys in the bathtub, screaming "Now, you can leave me alone. The monkeys are dead. Now, you leave me alone!" She attempts to kill herself and is taken away to an institution (139). The failure of Alice's own marriage is more gradual and not as spectacular; as the story of Marge preys on her mind, it undermines the stability of her position in the marriage and erodes her confidence in the relocation and cultural crossing that she has made.

Alice finds that she is still bound by the codes of racial superiority/inferiority that she had initially seemed to transcend in the happiness of the marriage. She refuses Cris's sexual advances, shuddering with the fear that she might become pregnant and have a "monkey" child; gradually she wilts away like a dying flower. The ocean crossing in this marriage has been only partially successful; Marge's story shows Alice a large gulf that her original redefinition cannot bridge. A fatal dysfunction becomes apparent in the juxtaposition of the traditional gender role of male superiority and the assumed racial hierarchy of white superiority, and the dilemma implied in the subordination of a white woman to a non-white man. The story thus shows a violent collision of codes; in this marriage, the elements of race and gender have so misshapen and debased its economy that physical fertility has become deadly. In this distorted system it is self-destructive for a white woman to bear "monkeys" sired by inferior non-white men, while presumably white men may beget such children on inferior non-white women with impunity.

While the story "Woman Afraid" may appear dated in this era of supposedly greater racial tolerance and of birth control, the pattern of self-imposed sterility in the confrontation with a competing set of codes is one that continues to resonate in contemporary Filipino American fiction. To recall Hagedorn's *Dogeaters* briefly: the novel ends Rio Gonzaga's story with her reflections on her own psychic emptiness.

It is not only intermarriages that provide the opportunity for either sterility or fertility; arranged marriages, in their confrontation with another set of codes, may be in their own way destructive or productive. The implications are both political and cultural, because these are not the family-arranged and socially sanctioned marriages of traditional practice; instead they are arranged by the individual concerned. They take place to acquire a green card, as a defense against deportation by the U.S. government, an attempt to circumvent a rigid legal code and to make the ocean crossing more possible and more permanent. However, to some this use of marriage is a source of guilt over the contravention of a moral code, exposing a form of inner death.

Linda Ty-Casper's novel *Wings of Stone* (1986) shows the conflict in its protagonist, who has married to acquire a green card: "it was fake, his conscience outfaced him: outright fake based on a phony marriage. He, Johnny F. Manalo, had undermined the system by importing corruption. Intending to liberate himself in the United States, he had fouled it instead for himself and for everyone who lived there" (12). Johnny Manalo's over-scrupulous sense of guilt comes from the ideals he has learned from his father, a doctor who has dedicated his life to treating the poor. He has no reason to feel culpable towards Rose Quarter, his wife, whom he treats well and wishes he could love; he calls the marriage "fake" but in many senses it is a real one. Instead, his guilt arises from his having married without love and at remaining in a marriage with a woman who is incapable of sustaining a loving relationship. In this equation of value, the ideal Filipino marriage is seen as one which is based on love and whose purpose is to beget children, not one for a blatant legal purpose. The arranged marriage in Ty-Casper's novel thus becomes a representation of an inner sterility that ensues from the incomplete crossing.

The emptiness of the arranged marriage is personified in the description of Rose Quarter, who leads "a life that seemed full of stillborn hopes" (68). She is psychologically handicapped, on medication "to control her thoughts and emotions" (69). Johnny has thought that he can help her: "For some time he believed that if Rose Quarter had someone she loved, who could make her want to, she would become a butterfly instead of a moth" (69). But he has come to realize that there is no hope for change. He finds this out through his relationships with two Filipino women: Sylvia, whose vitality gives him the impression that "she could just as well have sprouted wings" (64), and his dead mother, whose loving relationship with his father seems to have set his ideals for marriage. The sterility of Johnny's relationship with Rose Quarter shows that he is still bound by the codes of Filipino marriage, that he has not made the crossing; the emptiness of his "fake" marriage is representative of the hollowness of the American experience for him. He has redefined himself in a way that is wrong and repugnant to him. Ty-Casper's analysis of the marriage shows that if the crossing is incomplete and the reconstruction of the self is flawed, then the marriage that takes place within an unstable value system cannot work.

For Filipinos in America, one way to restabilize the value of marriage, making it productive rather than destructive, is to rethink some of their rules. This is one view of the arranged marriage as a possibility, seen in recent fiction. "Not Philippine girls," is the first reaction of the horrified Antonieta Zafra in Bienvenido Santos's "Immigration Blues"; Philippine "girls" are supposed to be special, and telling men that they want a marriage of convenience is an unthinkable act, "degrading, an unbearable shame. A form of self-destruction" (12). However, for Antonieta it works instead as an action of successful self-construction, since she finds in an arranged marriage not just an escape from the immigration authorities but a solution that has given her stability and happiness. In time her views so change that she comes to see her marriage as "a miracle . . . her friend God could not have sent her a better instrument to satisfy her need" (13). It turns out, somehow, to be congruent with the religious beliefs she prizes, and thus acceptable to her sense of self.

While Antonieta's marriage is a failure in Filipino terms, since she has no children, its relative success is evident instead in American terms of self-actualization, being productive and fertile in the satisfaction she has gained by reshaping her life and values. She has successfully overcome her initial scruples, saying she has "no regrets" (14), a phrase that is typically American, and definitely not Filipino, in its assertive tone. Antonieta has managed to disengage herself from the Filipino frame of reference; in her new context she patterns her life after what she perceives as an American model, repositioning herself in terms of sociocultural and gender norms so that she attains a site where she can accept her actions. Her younger sister Monica, contemplating the same step, is similarly reticent at first, but spurred by fears of deportation, by economic expedience, and the desire for independence, finds herself moving towards the same position of insertion into the American experience, and in so doing appears more active, less cringing, more alive.

Alipio Palma, the story's protagonist, has himself found satisfaction in an arranged marriage and looks back on his late wife with affection. He is happy to see the possibility of making another such marriage with Monica; having already accepted the revision of the role of the dominant male, he is not ill-pleased with being the passive, receptive object of women's proposals: "talk of lightning striking the same fellow twice" (19). With mingled wistfulness and contentment, he reflects on the physical and cultural relocation of Filipinos in California: "The waves. Listen. They're just outside, you know. The breakers have a nice sound like at home in the Philippines . . . across that ocean is the Philippines, we're not far from home" (7).

Although Alipio speaks of the pleasant sound of the waves as a reminder of home, the pleasure also reconciles him to his new position on the other side of the world. At the core of "Immigration Blues" is the awareness of the many distances that its characters have traveled; the journey over the ocean has moved these Filipinos onto new ground, where relocation within a new system of meaning becomes not merely possible, but productive. Garrett Hongo's words in celebration of the work of Asian American poets are also an apt tribute to these Filipinos who have survived the crossing and revalorized their lives:

> We are already upon the shore of this land, though, undeniably, there have been losses and lands left behind. We will not forget them . . . . The people are running and shouting on the grassy hills above the strand where the wreckage of a boat bounces in foaming surf higher than our knees. We lift our voices, bodies from the sand, and call (1993:xiii).

References

Hagedorn, Jessica. *Dogeaters*. New York: Penguin, 1990.

Hongo, Garrett, ed. *The Open Boat: Poems from Asian America*. New York: Doubleday, 1993.

Lim, Shirley Geok-Lin. "The Ambivalent American: Asian American Literature on the Cusp." In *Reading the Literatures of Asian America*, edited by Shirley Geok-Lin Lim and Amy Ling. Philadelphia: Temple University Press, 1992.

Santos, Bienvenido N. "Immigration Blues." *Scent of Apples: A Collection of Stories*. Seattle: University of Washington Press, 1979.

_____. "Scent of Apples." *Scent of Apples: A Collection of Stories.*. Seattle: University of Washington Press, 1979.

_____. "Woman Afraid." *You Lovely People*. Manila: Bookmark, 1991.

Ty-Casper, Linda. *Wings of Stone*. New York and London: Readers International, 1986.

"La Malinche Tortilla Factory": Negotiating the Iconography of Americanization, 1920-1950

Vicki L. Ruiz

During his 1828 visit to the far-flung province of Tejas, Mexican artillery officer José Mariá Sánchez wrote an unflattering appraisal of Tejano settlers. "Accustomed to the continued trade with the North Americans, they have adopted their customs and habits, and one may say truly that they are not Mexicans except by birth, for they even speak Spanish with a marked incorrectedness" (Weber 1973:80-81). One could argue that Mexicanos continue to harbor similar attitudes toward their cousins to the north. At present there exists a plethora of social science literature on the topic of Americanization among Latinos in the United States. Acculturation scales, standards, and typologies peg people's identification within a finite spectrum. Do you know the difference, for example, between "bicultural" and "cultural blend"?[1] I admit having little interest in neat categorizations of identity. I am, however, captivated by the processes of Americanization, particularly during the early decades of the twentieth century. What images and through what mediums have images of an "American life" filtered into the barrios of the Southwest? More importantly, how have Mexican immigrants and their children appropriated, resisted, and transformed these images?

Individual and community consciousness form the crux of any discussion attempting to theorize border culture. Does the iconography of Americanization represent cultural imperialism or cultural invigoration? Articulating the invigoration model, Malaysian scholar Shreedhar Lohani explains that "it is an acknowledged fact that a very healthy impact of foreign culture on individual national cultures is that each nation becomes more conscious of its own heritage and wishes to reinvigorate its own cultural roots after exposure to the culture of other countries" (Lohani 1992). I take a more cautionary tone. I prefer to examine elements of both imperialism and regeneration which permeate the processes of cultural production, especially with regard to the configurations of gendered identity. Selected visual representations of popular culture, as transmitted through education and the mass media, provide both the frame and the fuel for this examination. As George Lipsitz reminds us in *Time Passages*, ". . .hegemony is not just imposed on society from the top; it is struggled for from below, and no terrain is a more important part of that struggle than popular culture" (16).

In 1910, 100,000 Mexicans lived in small towns and cities throughout the Southwest. Their numbers increased tenfold as over one million Mexicanos migrated northward. Escaping the devastation of the Mexican Revolution and lured by the prospect of jobs in U.S. agriculture and industry, they settled into the existing barrios and created new communities both in the Southwest and Midwest. Los Angeles, for example, in 1900 had three to five thousand Mexican residents; by 1930 approximately 150,000 persons of Mexican birth or heritage had settled into the city's expanding barrios. Mexican immigrants resided side by side with those whose parents had arrived from Mexico a generation earlier and with others whose roots went back three centuries.[2]

Despite regional, class, and generational differentials within Mexican barrios, outsiders to the communities tended to view the residents as a monolithic group of unassimilated immigrants. From Los Angeles, California to Gary, Indiana, state and religious-sponsored Americanization programs swung into action. Imbued with the ideology of "the melting pot," teachers, social workers, and religious missionaries envisioned themselves as harbingers of salvation and civilization.[3] Targeting women and, especially, children, the vanguard of Americanization placed their trust "in the rising generation." As Pearl Ellis of the Covina City schools explained in her 1929 publication, *Americanization through Homemaking*: "Since the girls are potential mothers and homemakers, they will control, in a large measure, the destinies of their future families." She continued, "It is she who sounds the clarion call in the campaign for better homes" (preface).

A growing body of literature on Americanization in Mexican communities by such scholars as George Sánchez, Sarah Deutsch, Gilbert González, and myself suggest that church and secular programs shared common course offerings and curricular goals. Perhaps taking their cue from the regimen developed inside Progressive Era settlement houses,

Americanization projects emphasized classes in hygiene, civics, cooking, language, and vocational education (e.g. sewing and carpentry). Whether seated at a desk in a public school or on a sofa at a Protestant or Catholic neighborhood house, Mexican women received similar messages of emulation and assimilation. While emphasizing that the curriculum should meet "the needs of these people," one manual proclaimed with deepest sincerity that a goal of Americanization was to enkindle "a greater respect . . . for our civilization" (Ellis 1929:13).[4]

Beyond class work, the proponents of Americanization used dance recitals, plays, and music to further their goals. Writing in 1933, sociology graduate student Clara Smith explained the importance of these public performances. "No activity helped the Mexicans to participate in the activities of the community more than the pageants" (104). These staged events typically valorized U.S. history, holidays, and European roots writ large. For example, Methodist missionaries at the Rose Gregory Houchen Settlement House in El Paso, Texas orchestrated elaborate recitals for children enrolled in their music and dance classes. Missionaries outfitted young girls in European folk garb complete with yoked peasant dresses, lace aprons, and liederhose (Smith 1933:104-14; Ruiz 1991:41).

In contrast, a teacher affiliated with an Americanization program in Watts sought to infuse a multicultural perspective as she directed a pageant with a U.S. women's history theme. Clara Smith (1933) described the event as follows:

> Women, famous in the United States history as the Pilgrim, Betsy Ross, Civil War, and Covered wagon women, Indian and Negro women, followed by the foreign women who came to live among us were portrayed. The class had made costumes and had learned to dance the Virginia Reel. . . . They had also made costumes with paper ruffles of Mexican colors to represent their flag. They prepared Mexican dances and songs (104).

Despite such an early and valiant attempt at diversity, the teacher did not think it necessary to include the indigenous heritage of Mexicanas. Indeed, stereotypical representations of the American Indian "princess" (or what Rayna Green [1990:15-21] has termed "the Pocahontas perplex") supplanted any understanding of indigenous cultures on either side of the political border separating Mexico and the United States. Dressed in Pocahontas-style outfits, Mexican women modelled popular images of "Indian maidens," images which persist to the present in the realms of butter cartons, china plates, and even museum displays (Smith 1933:113).

While these pageants may have lacked the didactic power of the dramatic productions staged by Franciscan friars in New Mexico over three centuries before, their impact on identity and consciousness could also foster an internalization of oppression. Like the Pueblo peoples of New Mexico, Mexican children who attended settlement programs in El Paso heard the messages of colonization. Sometimes subtle, sometimes overt, the privileging of race, class, culture, and color taught by women missionaries had painful consequences for their pupils. Relating the excitement of kindergarten graduation, Houchen instructor Beatrice Fernandez included in her report a question asked by Margarita, one of the young graduates: "'We are all wearing white, white dress, slip, socks and Miss Fernandez, is it alright if our hair is black?'" (Ruiz 1991:48)[5]

Exploring the attitudes and activities expressed by the advocates of Americanization makes a good case for the model of cultural imperialism. Although motivated by what they perceived as humanitarian ends (and certainly Houchen missionaries can be credited with providing the first professional health care to barrio residents in El Paso), they could not grasp the personal and at times excruciating impact of their cultural ideations.

Despite these attempts at "inner colonization," "whispers of resistance," to quote Genaro Padilla (1991:43-60), developed within the hearts and minds of Mexican children.[6] Remembering her El Paso school days, award-winning choreographer of ballet folklorico, Rosa Guerrero remarked, "'The school system would teach us everything about American history, the colonists, and all of that. Then I would do a comparison in my mind of where my grandparents came from, what they did, and wonder how I was to be evolved and educated'" (Ruiz 1987:222).

With few exceptions, such as Houchen which still exists as a Methodist community center, most Americanization programs, whether state or church-affiliated, faded from the barrios within a few years. Historians generally agree that these efforts made little tangible headway in Mexican neighborhoods. However, Gilbert Gonzalez contends that the curriculum, which emphasized domestic and vocational training, reinforced the economic stratification of Mexican immigrants and their children (1990:60).[7] One could also argue that teachers and missionaries left behind another legacy—that seductive cultural ideation known as the American dream. As one Mexican American woman related, "We felt that if we worked hard, proved ourselves, we could become professional people" (Mulligan 1983).

During the 1920s, the ethic of consumption became inextricably linked to making it in America.[8] The message of affluence attainable through

hard work and a bit of luck was reinforced in English and Spanish language publications. Mexican barrios were not immune from the burgeoning consumer culture. For instance, as I have related in previous work, the
icon of the flapper engendered considerable intergenerational conflict between parents and daughters. The society pages of Spanish language newspapers promoted acculturation through the venues of fashion layouts, advice
articles, celebrity news, and advertisements. One week after its inaugural
issue in 1926, *La Opinion*, the influential Los Angeles-based newspaper,
featured a Spanish translation of Louella Parsons' nationally syndicated
gossip column. Advertisements not only hawked products but offered instructions for behavior (Ruiz 1992:61-80). As historian Roberto Treviño
related in his recent study of Tejano newspapers, "the point remains that
the Spanish-language press conveyed symbolic American norms and models to a potentially assimilable readership" (1991:460).

Advertisements aimed at women promised status and affection if the
proper bleaching cream, hair coloring, and cosmetics were purchased. A
print ad [in English] for Camay Soap carried by *Hispano America* in its 2
July 1932 issue reminded women readers that "Life is a Beauty Contest."[9]
Flapper fashions and celebrity testimonials further fused the connections
between gendered identity and consumer culture. It is important to keep
in mind that Spanish language newspapers filtered to its readers not only
the iconography of U.S. popular culture, but also their perceptions of gender relations within that culture. For example, an advertisement for
Godefroy's "Larieuse" hair coloring featured an attractive woman in profile smiling at the tiny man cupped in the palm of her hand. The diminu-
tive male figure is shown on bended knee with his hands outstretched in
total adoration. Now did this hair coloring promotion found in the 8 February 1938 issue of *La Opinion* relay the impression that by using this
Anglo product, Mexican women will exert the same degree of power over
their men as their Anglo peers supposedly plied?

These visual representations raise all sorts of speculation as to their
meaning, specifically with regard to the social construction of gender. While
I cannot identify the designers of these layouts, the architects are less important than the subtle and not-so-subtle messages codified within the
text. Mexican women interpreted these visual representations in a myriad
of ways. Some ignored them, some redefined their messages, and others
internalized them. The popularity of bleaching creams offers a poignant
testament to color consciousness in Mexican communities, a historical

consciousness accentuated by Americanization through education and popular culture (R. García 1991:118-19; Treviño 1991:459-60).

Reflecting the coalescence of Mexican and U.S. cultures, Spanish-language publications promoted pride in Latino theatre and music while at the same time celebrating the icons of Americanization and consumption. Because of its proximity to Hollywood, *La Opinion* ran contests in which the lucky winner would receive a screen test. On the one hand, *La Opinion* nurtured the dreams of "success" through entertainment and consumption while on the other, the newspaper railed against the deportations and repatriations of the 1930s.[10] Sparked by manufactured fantasies and clinging to youthful hopes, many Mexican women teenagers avidly read celebrity gossip columns, attended Saturday matinees, cruised Hollywood and Vine, and nurtured their visions of stardom. A handful of Latina actresses, especially Dolores del Rio and Lupe Velez, whetted these aspirations and served as public role models of the "American dream." As a 2 March 1927 *La Opinion* article on Lupe Velez idealistically claimed, "Art has neither nationalities nor borders."[11]

Dramatic art relies on visual representation. With the birth of the motion picture industry, actors found themselves on a public stage twenty-four hours a day. Performance did not end with the credits, as reporters, photographers, and publicists kept audiences abreast of the private lives of popular entertainers. As a result, actors developed off camera personas which coincided or contradicted the fictional characters they portrayed. The most visible Mexicana film stars, Dolores del Rio and Lupe Velez chose very disparate paths in crafting their "real life" figurativeness for public consumption.[12]

The publicized rivalry between the two women accentuated the tensions embodying the madonna/whore dichotomy in Mexican culture. For instance, *Photoplay* defined del Rio's beauty as reaching an "'unhuman loveliness,'" but characterized Lupe Velez as a "'Human Pepper Pot (Rodríquez 1992:4, 34).'" While *Photoplay* cannot be considered the torchbearer of *Mexicanidad*, the popular fan magazine was part of the Hollywood machine and as Ana López has emphasized in her elegant essay, "Are All Latins from Manhattan?" Hollywood was an important "ethnographer . . . creator . . . and translator of otherness" (1991:406).

To what extent did the two celebrities actually choose their own on and off screen personas? And did their agency matter? In addressing these issues, class must be taken into consideration. Alicia Rodríquez, in her richly-detailed study of del Rio and Velez, brings out their differences in family background. A child of wealth, Dolores Asúnsolo de Martínez, at the age of sixteen, married Jaime del Rio, a man many years her senior but her equal in status and financial resources. On the other hand, María Guadalupe Villalobos, had an upper middle-class upbringing. Her father was a military officer, her mother an opera singer. With her father's death during the Mexican Revolution, the family's economic situation declined to the extent that young Villalobos worked as a clerk in a department store and at the age of fifteen as a dancer. Their tales of being "discovered" in Mexico City further reveal their differences in class—del Rio at an elegant afternoon tea and Velez on a chorus line (Rodríquez 1992:35-36, 50; Carr 1979:3-4; Slide 1973:166).

As a starlet in 1925, del Rio conformed in her dress to Hollywood conceptions of a Latin American beauty. However, a few years later as an established celebrity, del Rio shed the ethnic imagery and emerged as an international fashion diva. Indeed, in one interview del Rio insisted that she always possessed a sense of style but during her first years in Hollywood, she was not allowed to dress as she wished. Even her home reflected "modern" tastes with its "walls of mirrors" and "gleaming linoleum." Although her Santa Monica residence was as "modern as tomorrow's newspaper," del Rio could not quite pass as a quintessential representation of modernity, for in describing her home, a fawning reporter noted that "Every line, every detail, every stick of furnishing were worked out in the brain of that ace interior decorator and master of the household, Cedric Gibbons, as the perfect background for his exotic and darkly lovely wife" (Hadley-Garcia 1990:40, 43, 59; Rodríquez 1992:18-20; Carr 1979:20).

In 1928, a columnist described Lupe Velez as a "wild Mexican kitten." During her seventeen year career, Velez would personify "Carmelita," "The Mexican Spitfire." She made the original film and seven sequels with titles such as *The Mexican Spitfire Out West* and *The Mexican Spitfire Sees a Ghost*. Even as she grew older, she clung to her "ethnic volcano" image. From product endorsements to starring roles to publicized escapades, Velez played her tumultuous image to the hilt (Rodríquez 1992:31-32, 51, 59; Lopez 1991:412-14).

As Alicia Rodríquez has noted, both women played active roles in creating and shaping their on and off screen images. As an established star, del Rio became much more selective in her choice of roles. She turned down the lead in *Broken Wing* because of the script's depiction of Mexicanos. The role was then offered to and accepted by Lupe Velez. Film scholar Ana López has argued that del Rio typically starred in films in which she portrayed aristocratic, exotic women of Latin American, ethnic European, or Asian origin. This codified figurativeness carried over into her private life. Dolores del Rio crafted a persona of a cosmopolitan, high born Castilian beauty— a symbol of Hollywood glamour. del Rio, however, did not live the staid lifestyle of a sheltered socialite turned movie star. Though she weathered two divorces, a nervous breakdown, and a highly publicized affair with a younger man (Orson Welles) during her Hollywood career, her image as a "lady" remained intact. Perhaps del Rio used this persona as a way to gain respect and artistic control. Chicana artist and art historian Amalia Mesa Bains constructed in 1984 an elaborate public altar, *An Ofrenda for Dolores del Rio* as a testament to del Rio's cinematic performances and "institutional clout" (Carr 1979:20; Rodríquez 1992:42-43, 48, 63-64; *La Opinion* 24 May 1931; Griswold del Castillo, McKenna, Yarbro-Bejaramo 1991:plate 63; López 1991:410, 414). In 1942, frustrated by the vehicles offered her, del Rio returned to Mexico where for over two decades, she reigned as the grand dame of Mexican cinema. Before leaving Hollywood, del Rio wistfully remarked, "But someday I would like to play a Mexican woman and show what life in Mexico really is" (Carr 1979:32, 44).

In juxtaposition (perhaps intentionally so) to del Rio, Lupe Velez fashioned herself as a liberated Mexicana, full of "smoldering sexuality." As she told one reporter, "'I am not wild. I am just Lupe.'" With an exaggerated accent, Velez gave the impression of a madcap, yet sultry, señorita. One *Photoplay* columnist suggested that Velez deliberately fused her performances with her private life as a way to promote her career. "There is never a moment when she is not emoting—putting on a show. . . [like] a vaudeville performer before a filled house" (López 1991:413; Hadley-García 1990:45, 54; Rodríquez 1992:1, 54). Certainly Velez demonstrated few qualms about accepting roles which pandered to stereotypes. As she grew older, the spicy ingenue became more difficult to play. Velez dyed her hair blonde and further embellished her comedic talents. While typecasting may have worked as a strategy of self-promotion during her early years, Velez may have internalized her image with tragic results. At the age of thirty-six, Velez faced the end of the "Spitfire" sequels and possibly the end of her Hollywood career. George Hadley-García uses the ungenerous term "washed up" in reference to Velez (1990:45, 85-88). Five months pregnant and jilted by her young lover, Lupe Velez took her life in 1944 (López 1991:413; Parish and Taylor 1974:620-23).

Dolores del Rio and Lupe Velez held out very different conceptions of sexual presence. Yet, both women represented images of exotic "female" carnal power on camera, images which required "masculine" taming, symbolically and literally. An evocative dance sequence in the 1934 film *Wonder Bar,* starring del Rio, raises a series of possibilities regarding subliminal (actually overt) texts of domination and conquest. As part of the dance, del Rio reclines on the floor with one arm shielding her face as her dashing leading man, dressed as a gaucho, threatens to strike her with his bull whip. For Lupe Velez, life imitated art. Jane Hampton in a 1934 issue of *Photoplay* trivialized scenes of domestic violence in the Velez-Weissmuller household. (Yes, "The Mexican Spitfire" was briefly married to "Tarzan.") Referring to their battles as "gorgeous" and "hilarious," the reporter related that "Lupe will show anyone at any time the scars left from Custer's Last Stand." Hampton continued, "To think that Hollywood's fiery little pepper pot, its snapping little firecracker, its exploding little tamale is a tamed and chastened woman! Positively, it's the scream of the year!" (Carr 1979:19; Hampton 1934:58, 98). However, one can still hear Velez's crafted persona within the narrative:

> I say, "yes, darling," "yes darling" . . . to everything Johnny say. Everyday but Sunday. . . . On Sunday I say, "No, you blankety . . . ." And so I let Johnny win the fight, because when I say "yes" he does what I want to do anyhow (Hampton 1934:98).

But even this piece of seeming resistance still embodies a code of stereotypes. The conniving, manipulative, and volatile Latina—the imprimatur of Velez's cinematic performances resonate throughout this disturbing text.

The messages of Americanization seemed to seep into the barrios from every direction—the public schools, Spanish language newspapers, and motion pictures (to name a few). Conflicting cultural ideations, sprinkled with stereotypes, which the films of Dolores del Rio and Lupe Velez embodied and transmitted can be discerned within the barrio itself. The 1940s photographs of Russell Lee capture the cultural landscape of Mexican American communities in Texas. A former Farm Security Administration photographer, Russell Lee documented both the dignity of the human spirit and the daily routines of life.[13] Indeed, his photographs convey "the performative power of the image," and to use Michael Charlesworth's phrase, "transgresses . . . the theoretical limits of its own power" (1991:49, 56).[14] Lee's photograph of the La Malinche Tortilla Factory in Corpus Christi starkly exemplifies the melding of "American" and "Mexican" cultural constructs. Born of Aztec nobility, La Malinche (Malinalli Tenépal) was sold by her mother into a state of slavery at the age of eight. Six years later, she

was given to Hernán Cortés who soon made use of her linguistic and diplomatic skills. La Malinche would also bear him a son. Viewed as a traitor
to her people, La Malinche remains "the Mexican Eve" or *"la chingada"*
(Mirandé and Enríquez 1979:24-31; Paz 1961:65-87).[15] The neon sign in
Lee's photograph, however, hardly reflects the image of an Aztec princess,
rather she has become transformed into Pocahontas. This imposition of
American iconography represents a bifurcation of consciousness where the
boundaries blur to the point that cultural codes converge.

While the imposition of Pocahontas as La Malinche may be interpreted as a violation of Mexican culture, other examples of cultural coalescence reveal the ways in which Mexicans in the United States appropriate
"American" goods and symbols to reinforce cherished cultural practices.
Home altars lovingly decorated with dime store trinkets symbolize in a
literal sense how people create their own expressions of religious belief.
Each family has its own special saints and feast days, often originating as
remembrances for favors granted.[16] Arizona native Socorro Felix Delgado
fondly recalls preparing the home altar for Christmas with her mother and
grandmother:

> She [her grandmother] covered the little table with beautiful embroidered
> cloths that my great-grandmother made. . . . We hung sheets on the wall and
> pinned a lot of paper flowers on them. . . . And then she would buy four big
> candles at the cathedral. . . . I used to buy things at Kress'—little birds and
> bells . . . and Manina would supervise. . . . It was a *big spending* (Martin
> 1992:62).

Delgado continued, "Under the altar table she had hidden little gifts—
a little doll or a little car. . . ." Her grandmother then informed the children "that the baby Jesus had left it here because we had been good." "We
didn't know Christmas trees; we didn't know Santa Claus" (Martin 1992:66).

Russell Lee documented the great pride with which Mexican women
cared for their home altars in his photography. Tinsel, glass ornaments,
and garland become incorporated into the pageantry of a home altar. In
her study of Texas folk art, sociologist Cynthia Vidaurri emphasized the
importance of home altars and yard shrines in articulating Texan-Mexican
cultural identity.

The mix of religious iconography, family photos, and popular ephem-
era nestled atop a dresser or night stand represents a historical tableau, one
which locates the family within communities and cultures. A 1984 photograph by Alex Harris offers a glimpse into the cultural placements of a
northern New Mexican family (Harris 1993:55). The broken television set

serves as a frame for a pageant of religious statues while a much smaller, working television sits on top. In this instance, tradition supersedes technology. However, as Barbara Brinson Curiel (1989:64) playfully acknowledges in her poem "Recipe: Chorizo Con Huevo Made in the Microwave":

> I won't lie.
> It's not the same.
> . . . .
> There's no eggy lace
> to scrape from the pan.
> No splatters of grease
> on the back of the stove.
> Everything is clean:
> vaporized
> dripless.

Sorting through the strands of cultural imperialism and invigoration, I am reminded of the words of George Lipsitz, "Images and icons compete for dominance within a multiplicity of discourses." He continues, "consumers of popular culture move in and out of subject positions in a way that allows the same message to have widely varying meanings at the point of reception" (1990:13). Or as Indonesian poet, Nirwan Dewanto stated, "the struggle for our survival in the information era is not to be won where information originates, but where it arrives" (1992). The imposition, appropriation, and transformation of American iconography within the borderlands of Chicano culture come together in a process of cultural coalescence. As I have noted in previous work, immigrants and their children pick, borrow, retain, and create distinctive cultural forms. There is not a single hermetic Mexican or Mexican American culture, but rather permeable *cultures* rooted in generation, gender, region, class, and personal experience. People navigate across cultural boundaries as well as make conscious decisions in the production of culture. But, bear in mind, people of color have not had unlimited choice. Racism, sexism, imperialism, persecution, and social, political, and economic segmentation have constrained aspiration, expectations, and decision-making.

Cultural coalescence encompasses both accommodation and resistance as Mexicanos/Chicanos/Latinos (and even Hispanics) negotiate the iconography of Americanization.[17] Chicano intellectuals are not immune from this process. Literary theorist Angie Chabram Dernersesian admonishes us to reconsider our own ethnographies:

. . .[we] must acknowledge the pre-institutional histories of Chicano academics, histories that originate in the fields, the border, the family, the oral tradition, factories, public institutions, and research designs . . . we must acknowledge the active presence of our sociocultural formation and class origins, origins that continue . . . to linger in our talk . . . and our cultural traditions as we live them and as we contextualize them . . . we must be willing to recognize . . . that the 'differences' which mark our condition as social beings in the academy are not the product of contemporary literary critical or anthropological discourse, but the product of an historical condition, inaugurated by conquest and domination, and propelled by our present social realities (1990:234-35).

Simply stated, we are all the children of the La Malinche Tortilla Factory.

Notes

1. Examples of this literature include: Flores-Ortiz, (1991); and Keefe and Padilla (1987:81).
2. For more information on twentieth-century Mexican American history, see: Camarillo (1979 and 1984); García (1980); García (1989); Montejano (1988); Romo (1983); and Ruiz (1987). Population statistics are taken from Romo (1983); and Camarillo (1979).
3. Recent scholarship on Americanization programs aimed at Mexican communities include: Sánchez (1990); Deutsch (1987); González (1990); Crocker (1987); and Ruiz (1991).
4. While critical of the Eurocentric tone and condescension typical of Americanization programs, scholars have recognized the value of education and at times health care services rendered by teachers, social workers, and missionaries. See Gonzalez (1990:60); and Ruiz (1991:42).
5. For more information on the Franciscans, see Gutierrez (1991).
6. I use the term "inner colonization" within the framework developed by philosopher Jurgen Habermas. My understanding and application of the ideas of Habermas have been informed by the following works: Habermas (1990); Seidman (1989); Fraser (1989); and Benhabib and Cornell (1987).
7. See also, Deutsch (1987:64-66, 85-86); Sánchez (1990:259-61); and Crocker (1987:121).
8. The best elaboration of this phenomenon can be found in Marchand (1985).
9. *Gracias a* Gabriela Arredondo for sharing this advertisement with me, an advertisement she included in her seminar paper (1991).
10. For examples, see *La Opinion* 23, 24, 27, 30 September 1926; 4 June 1927; 27 February 1931; and 17 August 1931. Between 1931 and 1934, an estimated one-third of the Mexican population in the U.S. (over 500,000 people) were either deported or repatriated to Mexico, even though many were native U.S. citizens. For more information, see Acuña (1981); Hoffman (1974); and Balderrama (1982).
11. For an elaboration of this theme, see Ruiz (1992).
12. My understanding of the careers of Dolores del Rio and Lupe Velez is informed by López (1992), and the many conversations I have had over the past two years with Alicia Rodríquez, Ph.D. candidate in history and American Studies at The Claremont Graduate School. Rodríquez is currently reworking a seminar paper on Dolores Del

Rio and Lupe Velez for publication. Her essay, "Dolores del Rio and Lupe Velez: Images On and Off Screen" will appear in Armitage and Jameson (forthcoming).

13. For more information on Russell Lee, see Curtis (1989:91-122).

14. *Gracias a* Robert Dawidoff for providing me with this citation.

15. Feminist on both sides of the border have challenged this pejorative rendition of La Malinche. See Alegria (1975); Del Castillo (1977); and Gutiérrez (1993).

16. My discussion of home altars has been informed by the following works: Martin (1992); Jasper and Turner (1991); Vidaurri (1991); and of course, my own experience growing up with home altars.

17. Indeed, as Gutiérrez (1991) demonstrates so persuasively, contestation and negotiation of cultures is not a twentieth-century phenomenon, but one which traces back to the very roots of Chicano ethnogenesis.

References

Acuña, Rodolfo. *Occupied America*. New York: Harper and Row, 1981.

Alegría, Juana Armanda. *Psicologia de las Mexicanas*. Mexico City: Samo, 1975.

Arredondo, Gabriela. "'Equality' for All: Americanization of Mexican Immigrant Women in Los Angeles and San Francisco through Newspaper Advertising, 1927-1935." Seminar paper, San Francisco State University, 1991.

Balderrama, Francisco. In *Defense of La Raza* . Tucson: University of Arizona Press, 1982.

Benhabib, Seyla and Drucilla Cornell. "Introduction: Beyond the Politics of Gender." In *Feminism as Critique*, edited by Seyla Benhabib and Drucilla Cornell. Minneapolis: University of Minnesota Press, 1987.

Camarillo, Albert. *Chicanos in California*. San Francisco: Boyd and Fraser, 1984.

____. *Chicanos in a Changing Society*. Cambridge: Harvard University Press, 1979.

Carr, Larry. *More Fabulous Faces*. New York: Doubleday, 1979.

Chabram, Angie. "Chicana/o Studies as Oppositional Ethnography." *Cultural Studies* 4 (October 1990).

Charlesworth, Michael. "Rhetoric of the Image: Charles Collins' 'Convent Thoughts' and a Photograph by Gertrude Jekyll the Garden Designer." *Word and Image* 7 (January-March 1991.

Crocker, Ruth Hutchinson. "Gary Mexicans and 'Christian Americanization': A Study in Cultural Conflict." In *Forging a Community: The Latino Experience in Northwest Indiana, 1919-1975*, edited by James B. Lane and Edward J. Escobar. Chicago: Cattails Press, 1987.

Curiel, Barbara Brinson. *Speak to Me from Dreams*. Berkeley: Third Woman Press, 1989.

Curtis, James. *Mind's Eye, Mind's Truth: FSA Photography Reconsidered*. Philadelphia: Temple University Press, 1989.

Del Castillo, Adelaida R. "Malintzin Tenépal: A Preliminary Look into a New Perspective." In *Essays on la Mujer*, edited by Rosaura Sánchez and Rosa Martínez Cruz. Los Angeles: UCLA Chicano Studies Publications, 1977.

Deutsch, Sarah. *No Separate Refuge: Culture, Class, and Gender on the Anglo-Hispanic Frontier in the American Southwest, 1880-1940*. New York: Oxford University Press, 1987.

Dewanto, Nirwan. "American Kitsch and Indonesian Culture: A Sketch." Paper presented at the Third Annual International Symposium: American Studies in the Asia-Pacific Region, "The Impact of American Popular Culture on Social Transformation in Asian Countries," 3 April 1992, Tokyo, Japan.

Ellis, Pearl Idella. *Americanization through Homemaking*. Los Angeles: Wetzel Publishing, 1929.

Flores-Ortiz, Yvette. "Chicana Workers, Level of Acculturation, Marital Satisfaction, and Depression: a Psychological Perspective." *Aztlan* 20 (1991) 151-73.

Fraser, Nancy. *Unruly Practices: Power, Discourse, and Gender in Contemporary Social Theory.* Minneapolis: University of Minnesota Press, 1989.

García, Mario T. *Desert Immigrants.* New Haven: Yale University Press, 1980.

____. *Mexican Americans.* New Haven: Yale University Press, 1989.

García, Richard A. *Rise of the Mexican American Middle Class: San Antonio. 1929-1941.* College Station: Texas A & M Press, 1991.

González, Gilbert. *Chicano Education in the Era of Segregation.* Philadelphia: Balch Institute Press, 1990.

Green, Rayna. "The Pocahontas Perplex: The Image of Indian Women in American Culture." In *Unequal Sisters: A Multicultural Reader in U.S. Women's History,* edited by Ellen Carol DuBois and Vicki L. Ruiz. New York:Routledge, 1990.

Griswold del Castillo, Richard, Teresa McKenna, and Yvonne Yarbro-Bejarano. *Chicano Art: Resistance and Affirmation 1965-1985.* Los Angeles : UCLA Wight Art Gallery, 1991.

Gutiérrez, Ramón. "Community, Patriarchy, and Individualism: The Politics of Chicano History and the Dream of Equality." *American Quarterly* 45 (March 1993):44-72.

____. *When Jesus Came, the Corn Mothers Went Away: Marriage, Sexuality, and Power in New Mexico, 1500-1846.* Stanford: Stanford University Press, 1991.

Habermas, Jürgen. *Moral Consciousness and Communicative Action,* translated by Christian Lenhardt and Sherry Weber Nicholsen. Cambridge: MIT Press, 1990.

Hadley-García, George. *Hispanic Hollywood: The Latins in Motion Pictures.* New York: Carol Publishing Group, 1990.

Harris, Alex. *Red White Blue and God Bless You: A Portrait of Northern New Mexico.* Albuquerque: University of New Mexico Press, 1993.

Hoffman, Abraham. *Unwanted Mexican Americans in the Great Depression.* Tucson: University of Arizona Press, 1974.

Jasper, Pat and Kay Turner. "Art among Us/Entre Nosotros: Mexican-American Folk Art in San Antonio." In *Hecho en Tejas: Texas-Mexican Folk Arts and Crafts,* edited by Joe S. Graham. Denton: University of North Texas Press, 1991.

Keefe, Susan E. and Amado Padilla. *Chicano Ethnicity.* Albuquerque: University of New Mexico Press, 1987.

Lipsitz, George. *Time Passages: Collective Memory and American Popular Culture.* Minneapolis: University of Minnesota Press, 1990.

Lohani, Shreedhar. "Sivilize Me? I Can't Stand It." Paper presented at the Third Annual International Symposium: American Studies in the Asia-Pacific Region, "The Impact of American Popular Culture on Social Transformation in Asian Countries," 3 April 1992, Tokyo, Japan.

López, Ana M. "Are all Latins from Manhattan? Hollywood, Ethnography, and Cultural Colonialism." In *Unspeakable Images,* edited by Lester D. Friedman. Chicago: University of Illinois Press, 1991.

Marchand, Roland. *Advertising the American Dream: Making Way for Modernity, 1920-1940.* Berkeley: University of California Press, 1985.

Martin, Patricia Preciado. *Songs My Mother Sang to Me: An Oral History of Mexican-American Women.* Tucson: University of Arizona Press, 1992.

Mirandé, Alfredo and Evangelina Enríquez. *La Chicana: The Mexican-American Woman.* Chicago: University of Chicago Press, 1979.

Montejano, David. *Anglos and Mexicans in the Making of Texas.* Austin: University of Texas Press, 1988.

Mulligan, Rose Escheverria. In *Rosie the Riveter Revisited: Women and the World War II Work Experience*, edited by Sherna Berger Gluck. Long Beach: CSULB Foundation, 1983.

Padilla, Genaro. "Imprisoned Narrative? Or Lies, Secrets, and Silence on New Mexico Women's Autobiography." In *Criticism in the Borderlands: Studies in Chicano Literature, Culture, and Ideology*, edited by Hector Calderón and Jose David Saldívar. Durham: Duke University Press, 1991.

Parish, Robert and T. Allen Taylor, eds. *The RKO Gals*. New York: Arlington House, 1974.

Paz, Octavio. *Labyrinth of Solitude: Life and Thought in Mexico*. New York: Grove Press, 1961.

Rodríquez, Alicia. "Dolores del Rio and Lupe Velez: Images On and Off Screen." In *Toward a Multicultural Women's West*, edited by Susan Armitage and Elizabeth Jameson. Norman: University of Oklahoma Press, forthcoming.

_____. "Dolores del Rio and Lupe Velez: Imagery On and Off Screen, 1925-1944. " Seminar paper, University of California, Davis, 1992.

Romo, Ricardo. *East Los Angeles*. Austin: University of Texas Press, 1983.

Ruiz, Vicki L. *Cannery Women, Cannery Lives: Mexican Women, Unionization, and the California Food Processing Industry, 1930-1950*. Albuquerque: University of New Mexico Press, 1987.

_____. "Dead Ends or Gold Mines?: Using Missionary Records in Mexican American Women's History." *Frontiers* 12 (1991): 33-56.

_____. "Oral History and La Mujer: The Rosa Guerrero Story." In *Women on the U.S.-Mexico Border*, edited by Vicki L. Ruiz and Susan Tiano. Winchester: Allen and Unwin, 1987.

_____. "'Star Struck': Acculturation, Adolescence, and Mexican American Women, 1920-1940." In *Small Worlds: Children and Adolescents in America*, edited by Elliot West and Paula Petrik. Lawrence: University of Kansas Press, 1992.

Sánchez, George J. "'Go after the Women': Americanization and the Mexican Immigrant Woman, 1915-1929." In *Unequal Sisters: A Multicultural Reader in U.S. Women's History*, edited by Ellen Carol DuBois and Vicki L. Ruiz. New York: Routledge, 1990.

Seidman, Steven, ed. *Jürgen Habermas on Society and Politics: A Reader*. Boston: Beacon Press, 1989.

Slide, Anthony. *The Griffith Actresses*. South Brunswick and New York: A.S. Barnes and Company, 1973.

Smith, Clara Gertrude. "The Development of the Mexican People in the Community of Watts." M.A. thesis, University of Southern California, 1933.

Treviño, Roberto R. "Prensa Y Patria: The Spanish-Language Press and the Biculturation of the Tejano Middle Class, 1920-1940." *Western Historical Quarterly* 22 (November 1991).

Vidaurri, Cynthia L. "Texas-Mexican Religious Folk Art in Robstown, Texas." In *Hecho en Tejas: Texas-Mexican Folk Arts and Crafts*, edited by Joe S. Graham. Denton: University of North Texas Press, 1991.

Weber, David J., ed. *Foreigners in Their Native Land: Historical Roots of Mexican Americans*. Albuquerque: University of New Mexico Press, 1973.

Theorizing Marginality: Violence against Korean Women

Hyun Sook Kim

In *Yearning: Race, Gender, and Cultural Politics* (1990) and *Feminist Theory: From Margin to Center* (1984), bell hooks discusses marginality as a "position and place of resistance" which is crucial for oppressed, exploited, colonized people.[1] For hooks, theorizing about the experience of living on the margins provides a critical and radical cultural practice; that is, marginality is the site of radical possibility, a space of resistance (1990a:150-51). In her own words, "It was this marginality that I was naming as a central location for the production of a counter hegemonic discourse that is not just found in words but in habits of being and the way one lives" (1990b:341).

I begin with this quote from bell hooks in order to incorporate the notion of "marginality" into our theoretical understanding of violence against Asian women, and to break down their invisibility. The stories of violence discussed in this article involve Korean women who speak limited English, and who are first-generation immigrants, poor, single mothers, unemployed, with young children, without friends and family support systems, and homeless. For survival on the economic, social, and cultural margins, the women rely on defiance, false compliance, and feigned ignorance.[2] Resistance, in this sense, is understood as "ordinary weapons" women employ to defend their interests and to survive on the margins.

By violence, I refer broadly to the forms of violence rooted in systems of racial, class, and gender domination. For the purpose of my analysis, the multiple systems of domination refers to the following configurations: *class or economic discrimination*—whereby poor, working immigrant women are positioned at the bottom of the labor market; *state domination and discrimination in the legal system*—whereby the police, the court system, and the laws control, define, and target poor, working class, immigrant communities and women of color for engaging in "criminal" activities; and *cultural, racial, and gender discrimination*—whereby women of color who work and live on the socioeconomic margins are punished for stepping outside of the traditionally assigned white, middle-class, female roles. In short, violence, as used throughout this study, refers to abuse, discrimination, and exploitation, including domestic violence, which Korean immigrant women experience because of their location in the intersecting systems of domination.

In this essay, I discuss two situations—a murder case in North Carolina and police raids on New York Korean massage parlors. First, the case of *State of North Carolina v. Chong Sun France* illustrates how the state and courts have framed the case of a Korean woman who was found guilty of murdering her son. I will provide a brief review of the case which reveals the ways the courts misinterpreted her defense while ignoring the mitigating circumstances. Second, recent newspaper reports of Korean massage parlors will be examined in order to discuss how law enforcement officials categorize, criminalize, and control Korean women caught up in the massage parlor industry. The negative stereotyping about Korean women as hookers and devious mama-sans and the criminalization of these women, portray the violent and discriminatory treatment Korean women receive from law enforcement officers. Finally, the study returns to a discussion of marginality as a site of violence and survival. The analysis of marginality, in my view, provides "an opening in a discursive fabric" (Smith 1990:12): that is, an entry into a range of everyday practices and activities of Korean women who have been denied, repressed, subordinated, and absent in our understanding of the state, race, and gender intersections. Thus, this study adopts a reflexive approach to understanding the everyday experiences and standpoints of Korean women who live and work in the margins.

On December 14, 1987, Chong Sun France was convicted of second degree murder and felonious child abuse of her son, Moses Krystowski. Chong was sentenced to twenty years imprisonment, and was sent to the Correctional Institution for Women in Raleigh, North Carolina.[3] The difficult circumstances surrounding Chong's life actually began in Korea. When Chong was twenty years old, she met an American soldier, Danny France, and after marrying him, moved to Los Angeles. Shortly thereafter, the marriage ended in a divorce. Later, Chong met Edmond Krystowski, moved with him to Aberdeen, Maryland (Appeals Trial Transcript:19). Chong and Krystowski had two children, Moses, born December 11, 1984, and Esther, born February 13, 1986.

In spite of the financial, cultural, and language difficulties she faced, Chong said she tried to rear her two children as best she could, but because of Krystowski's abuse of Chong emotionally and physically, she was forced to stay away from her home on numerous occasions. In her trial, she stated,

> I go back to my husband. I pray to God everytime so, you know, everything is going to be fine and ok, so I went home again and I went home again and for a while everything is fine and we, you know, happy family. Then we got a little problem again (Appeals Trial Transcript:232).

Krystowski's mother also abused Chong. According to Chong, the mother-in-law "bothered her about all kinds of things" and threatened to send Chong back to Korea. To escape from the constant harassment from Krystowski's mother and the physical and emotional abuse from Krystowski, one day in May 1987 Chong left her Maryland home. With her two children, she moved to Jacksonville, North Carolina, where she was told by a Korean friend that she could find a job. A single mother with two young children, with limited job skills and without much knowledge of English, Chong desperately looked for a job. After a few days in Jacksonville, she found work as a bartender, not too far away from a motel where she was staying temporarily. During the hours she had to work, Chong put her two children to sleep in bed, turned on the television so as not to disturb other tenants in case her children cried, and locked the room door (*Carolina Korean News*: March 1992). Chong did not have any friends or family in Jacksonville, nor any money to hire a babysitter while she went to work.

On May 28, 1987, Chong returned to her room from work around 2:00 a.m. and found her son, Moses, dead. According to Chong, when she returned to her room she found her daughter asleep on the bed and her son's body on the floor. She found Moses's lower body enclosed inside the lower drawer of a dresser; both the television, which was on top of the dresser, and the dresser toppled over on Moses. Chong telephoned Edmond Krystowski in Maryland for help but no one answered. Not knowing what to do, Chong says she knocked on the door of a downstairs tenant. She then called the police. Before the police arrived, Chong placed the dresser upright, placed the television on top of the dresser, and swept up the shards of broken mirror from the floor. Fearful that a social worker from the Child Welfare Agency would take her daughter away, as her neighbors had told her, Chong cleaned up the room.

When the police arrived, Chong said the death of her two-year-old son was accidental. But in grief, she also screamed, "I killed my son."[4] Moreover, when she was being taken to the county jail, she continued to cry,

> I did it. I did it. Ok, you stupid idiot. He [police detective] thinks I did it, huh? . . . you guys are sick. Why don't you get out of here. Can you kill your son, huh? Can you kill your son? I'm crazy. You know I killed my son. I'm crazy (Appeals Trial Transcript:183).

When she uttered these words, she was speaking out of anguish and desperation. This self-blaming reflects a mother's grief and guilt for having left her children alone; not for the actual killing. The self-blaming and self-accusation for the loss of her son is common for women who feel personally responsible for their children and family. For Chong, a Korean, immigrant woman who was forced into socioeconomic marginalization, her guilt represents an additional psychological effect of a woman who lost familial and cultural ties.

On the other hand, the above statement also reflects Chong's resistance to the authorities. Showing outrage, Chong resists the police officers' arrest and their charge of her for the murder of her son. Chong calls the officers, "you stupid idiot," and, in disbelief, asks them, "Can you kill your son?" When Chong becomes conscious that the officers equates her feeling of a mother's guilt for a murderer's guilt, she shows defiance and anger against the police officers. This struggle, to be understood on her terms, is further evidenced in Chong's trial testimony.

The police officers' judgment of Chong as a murderer was based on gender, cultural, and communication biases. Additionally, the officers' mistreatment of Chong reveals their racial and misogynist contempt. For example, when the first police officer arrived at the motel, the officer called Chong "an oriental woman" whom he presumed was "asleep sitting on the floor in the hallway" (Appeals Trial Transcript:183). He described Chong as "sick," "crazed," "hateful," and "very hysterical" (Appeals Trial Transcript:57). Later, a female police officer arrived at the scene and also stated it was impossible to understand how the incident occurred because of "Chong crying and use of broken English." At the trial, both officers insisted that Chong must have killed her son before she left for work and that she staged the incident to "look like an accident." They argued that the dresser was too heavy and large for a two-year-old child to move it or make it fall on his own (Appeals Trial Transcript:57).

Chong was criminalized and convicted because of the police officers' bias and misunderstanding. Similarly, the state, courts, and jury ignored cultural differences and could not see past the language barrier. For example, the court clerk who prepared the trial transcript stated that Chong's spoken English was most difficult to follow and noted as such in the transcript. The prosecution and defense attorneys also stated that they could not comprehend Chong's statements. Regardless of this serious language barrier, the trial proceeded without providing a court interpreter for Chong. According to the *Raleigh News and Observer* of December 31, 1992, the prosecution concluded that Chong asphyxiated Moses by slamming him inside the drawer and then tried to make it look like an accident. With such accusations and assertions, Chong was presumed guilty prior to her actual testimony (which could not be understood by the court). Chong was effectively made culturally incomprehensible and invisible.

The court did not have sufficient evidence to prove the alleged murder was based on her actions (what she did). However, it found her guilty based on an assessment of the "kind of" mother and woman she was assumed to be. Instead of questioning her motives or substantiating the necessary evidence for murder, the law enforcement officials viewed Chong as *doubly dangerous*. First, the trial transcript shows the police officers' and the court's assumption that Chong was an irresponsible, inadequate, and negligent mother who did not care for her young children (e.g. references to the "dirty" room, wet laundry, abandonment of children, and so forth). Second, Chong was represented as an angry, opportunistic, conniving, promiscuous woman (e.g. obtaining a visa and residency in the U.S., leaving marriages, and so forth).[5] Within the embodiment of a masculinized state hierarchy, the law enforcement officials, in this case, successfully delimited the boundaries of personal/domestic violence by criminalizing Chong Sun France as a "deviant" and stigmatizing her as an "unfit mother."

Moreover, the state, court, and law enforcement officials failed to recognize the mitigating circumstances—such as Chong's experiences of physical and psychological abuse, socioeconomic hardship, and cultural and language differences. In more than one way, therefore, the state failed to protect or to recognize Chong's rights. The legal system failed her not only when a court interpreter was not provided, but more specifically, when it effectively subordinated a poor, marginalized immigrant woman to the state and police officers' will.

In short, repressive state actions were deemed necessary to punish and make inaudible an immigrant woman on several grounds: for not being a "good mother" and not practicing the traditional Anglo-American standard of "proper" parenting, and for not behaving as a "good woman." To Chong, excluded from both Korean and American communities, separated from her families, relegated to the lowest end of the labor hierarchy, as well as having lost her child, the actual imprisonment represented another form of systemic violence. On the other hand, in Chong's story we find the strength and resilience of a Korean-military-bride-turned-single-mother who, living alone without friends and family in a country "foreign" to her, tried to carve out a place for herself and her children. She also courageously exited from a situation where both her husband and mother-in-law were abusive, and her husband, additionally violent. In a broader context, however, Chong's circumstance represents, as one Korean woman minister laments,[6] "the same pain felt by all of us who live in a culturally different and racialized America."[7]

I have focused my analysis on Chong Sun France's case to show the ways in which the state acts as a primary organizer of relations of race, class, and gender as reflected in one Asian woman's story. However, the state also regulates race, class, sex, and gender in the street. While the street is not commonly thought of as an institution, R. W. Connell (1987) rightly suggests that the street is a "setting for much intimidation of women, from low-level harassment like wolf-whistling to physical manhandling and rape" (1987:132). What then happens to immigrant women who are forced to work and live on the streets as prostitutes? Next, I will discuss massage parlor prostitution in New York City and examine how Korean women have been particularly victimized and attacked by law enforcement officials.

In New York City, law enforcement officials have carried out crack-downs on Korean massage parlors for their alleged links to the new "organized criminal rings." Raids on massage parlors have escalated since the mid-1980s, and in May 1993 the New York City Mayor's Office of Midtown Enforcement and the police waged a new war on massage parlors in midtown Manhattan. When the police shut down the operation of five massage parlors, they ejected the johns without imposing any punishment but arrested and fined the women for promoting prostitution.[8] At the Pinocchio Club, according to the May 17, 1993 issue of the *New York Daily News*, seven Korean women were forced into the streets, including an older woman called "Ajuma" who cooked, cleaned, and dispensed condoms for women. One Korean woman was forced out of the parlor with only a pair of jeans and a T-shirt in a plastic bag as her belongings.[9] She became instantly homeless. She said she was formerly married to an American serviceman, came to the United States with him in 1982, and began work in massage parlors in August 1992. Thrown out of a raided parlor, she cried, "I need a place to go. . . . If I don't find a job today, I'll have to sleep in the park."

There are similar stories of Korean women forced to work in massage parlors who experience numerous incidents of police harassment, arrests, fines, and criminal charges imposed on them for promoting prostitution (Henican 1989). The stories of many Korean women who turn to the massage parlor industry for wages actually begin in Korea.

Jinhee's[10] story represents a common experience of Korean women's alienation, marginalization, and exclusion in the United States. According to the *Newsday* report Jinhee met an American military police officer who was stationed in Korea with the 82nd Airborne Division. Within a month, they lived together near a military base; shortly thereafter, Jinhee followed her husband-to-be to the United States on a "fiancee visa." A year later, they married and lived in Indiana. After that, they moved to Massachusetts, Georgia, Maryland, and North Carolina from one military base town to another. In the fall of 1985, Jinhee and her husband moved to Ft. Bragg, North Carolina, where he was assigned to the 21st Military Police Company; she had a kitchen job on the Army post. While it is unclear what their marriage was like, Jinhee left home to look for a job at a "health club" which paid "big money." According to the same newspaper report, Jinhee moved to Greenboro, North Carolina, to Philadelphia, then to New York City to work in massage parlors.[11]

The newspaper reports can be read to identify the ways in which authorities routinely arrest and criminalize numerous Korean women (Sullivan 1992). From Kansas City to Philadelphia to Atlantic City to New York City, the police conduct raids of suspected massage parlors for fronting prostitution; but it is the prostituted women who are charged with bribery, fined for promoting prostitution, and arrested for the unlicensed practice of massage. When unlicensed parlors are raided and shut down, the law enforcement officials actually invoke the state education law and the city's nuisance-abatement and morality laws which place the blame on prostitutes for corrupting the community. As one Nassau County police officer states, "There was no public outcry. . . . It was just a concept we were not pleased with, euphemistically speaking. We don't want to be known as a hot hooker haven" (Lickman and Young 1988). The illegal status of prostitution has led the police to criminalize the prostituted Korean women while tolerating the johns and procurers. It is the women who are arrested for victimless crimes because they have violated traditional stereotypes about how women in Anglo-American society "should" behave. The police define the poor, immigrant Korean women who work in massage parlors as dangerous, aggressive, and amoral, thus "criminal"; they do not define the patrons or johns as criminal despite their participation in the same acts.

Since the police officers, prosecutors, and judges have not taken the rape, physical abuse, and battering of women seriously (especially the rape and abuse of women of color), there is little reason to think that they will protect prostituted Asian women. In fact, the police, the Immigration and Naturalization Service (INS), and local politicians control and shape the operation of massage parlors by tolerating the trade but punishing the prostitutes (Klausner 1987:289; Sullivan 1992). Furthermore, the enormous growth of the parlor industry in New York City since the 1970s has, in fact, served to reinforce the indispensability of industry attorneys.[12] The role of attorneys in the massage parlor industry provides one of the clearest examples of the interplay between parlor-prostitution and legal culture. As reported in the *Daily News* of May 17, 1993, attorneys work to provide "legal advice" to victimized women and to bridge the gaps between the law enforcement officials and parlor operators. A Manhattan lawyer, William Knisely, for example, has "represented" and profited from more than 200 Korean women arrested for promoting prostitution.

According to one attorney, Korean women arrested for parlor-prostitution claimed that they have not "done anything wrong" but they "plead guilty to a lesser charge of disorderly conduct to expedite their cases" (Lickman and Young 1988). Women do not feel they are guilty of promoting prostitution or of breaking the state education law; however, they consciously comply to a lesser charge. As explained by attorney Knisely, the women "don't feel they have the ability, time or money to fight the system. The reality is, it's going to be their word against the word of one, two or three police officers. The likelihood of success is not great" (Lickman and Young 1988). In other words, Korean women who maintain their livelihood by working in massage parlors resort to false compliance and feigned ignorance of the New York state education and nuisance abatement laws in order for them to survive on the margins.

The reports of the prostituted Korean women covered in the newspapers are not disconnected or isolated events. Rather, the stories of the women shed light on the ways in which they are caught in the systems of domination—racial, sexual, and socioeconomical—as well as illuminating the ways in which the women survive and endure exploitation and criminalization. For example, it is not difficult to understand the numerous reasons why Korean women would turn to massage parlor trade. In my work in Korea and the U.S. with Korean women's groups directed against sexual violence against women, I have learned that there have been over 200,000 intercultural marriages between Korean women and American servicemen since the Korean War, and separation and divorce cases are as high as 80 percent. Divorced Korean women often find themselves alone, without financial and other resources. They experience battering and violence in the home, and they lose custody of their children when they leave their marriages. Without language or job skills, they are forced into low-paying service jobs. In cases where women are still married, Korean women might turn to massage parlor work because the thriving sex trade, both locally and internationally, lures women with promises of good money. Massage parlor prostitution thus provides a seemingly logical solution, particularly for younger and more vulnerable women.

Korean women working in massage parlors become scapegoats on multiple levels. On the individual level, women are abused and blamed by their husbands and usually by their husbands' families for socioeconomic problems. At the same time, they bear the burden of cross-cultural miscommunication. On the institutional level, people in positions of power, such as johns, the madams who operate the parlors, the police, and lawyers, blame and/or target women working in parlors for lowering the morality of the community. Media representations like the newspapers sensationalize Korean massage parlors and stereotype women working in the parlors both as "money grabbers" and as "exotic hookers." Beneath the scapegoating, however, lies the complicated material situation of working-class Korean women, who met American servicemen in clubs and bars in military camptowns in Korea, married them, and arrived in the United States without any resources. In some cases, women are lured to the United States by the promises of traffickers who trade in women for the international prostitution industry. In recent years, marriages to American servicemen and signing up with "entertainment groups," for example, have been used as two common methods by which procurers smuggle women from Asia to the United States (McQuillan 1993; Gambardello 1993). The women arriving in the United States through the international prostitution rings, however, end up caught in a slavery situation from which it is difficult to escape. The women are forced to sign contracts promising to work in massage parlors until their debts are paid off. Once in the parlors, the women are charged room and board fees, and exaggerated prices for toiletries and other necessities which compound their debt.

The women caught in massage parlors, therefore, illustrate the experience of racial, class, and gender violence. Whether these forms of violence occur in the home or in the street, they might be seen as results of the contradiction inherent in the globalized capitalist system. In such situations, the women's ethnicity, class position, cultural difference, and sex, articulate with the labor and market logic in a particularly insidious manner.

In short, the situations discussed in this study illustrate very frequent and common experiences of repression and violence faced by Korean immigrant women. Because of the location of these women on socioeconomic and cultural margins, their daily survival involves a subversion of the roles and norms assigned to traditional middle-class women, both in American and Korean cultures. For deviating from the middle-class norm of femininity, the women are viewed as "dangerous." This treatment is revealed in how the authorities stigmatize, denigrate, and categorize the women as "fallen women" or "throw-aways." The women's stories reveal how women are caught in the contradiction between the culture of the place of their birth and the culture of liberal American society. Thus it is important to highlight the ways in which the women who live on the margins rely on their resourcefulness, flexibility, and creativity for survival, both physically, materially, and culturally. Women on the margins, survive by struggling from within—they are not only victims of structural violence, but they manage to survive in the segregated and stigmatized sectors of society.

Theoretically and politically, there are several approaches to domination and resistance that are relevant to Korean and Asian women. Each perspective has been incorporated into social movements; each is narrowly defined and rooted in a single-axis[13] framework such as on capital/class, gender/patriarchy, or race/ethnicity. First, the traditional Marxist perspective, which has been incorporated into Third World radicalism or anti-imperialist movements, defines resistance as those actions which are organized, systematic, principled, and selfless, and refers to the embodiment of revolutionary ideas that negate bourgeois class interests, private property, and capitalism.[14] This perspective of class-based domination and resistance has not problematized the racial or the sexual bases of violence that Asian women experience everyday.

Second, feminist theories of gender oppression locate women's situation directly in relation to male power and patriarchy, in which men control, use, subjugate, and oppress women. Central to radical and liberal feminist analyses is, therefore, the image of patriarchy as violence practiced by men. Violence, in other words, results from the exploitation and control of women in male-dominated organizations in, for example, standards of beauty, ideals of motherhood, chastity, sexual harassment, rape, sexual abuse, sexual slavery, incest, pornography, and domestic violence. Patriarchy exists as a universal social form in which men ultimately practice violence against women and control resources.[15] How does feminist theory explain what constitutes women's resistance to patriarchy? Violence against women is viewed as distinct and separate from other forms of institutionalized and societal violence. As in Third World radicalism, feminist theory ignores the ways in which racial, class, cultural, and gender bases of domination contribute to differential experiences of violence for Asian women and women of color. By essentializing categorizations of all men as abusers and all women as victims, the existing radical and liberal feminist theories fundamentally misconstrue the economic and political bases of the struggles conducted daily by subordinate groups and classes, including women of color. For Asian immigrant and refugee women, their subordination, discrimination, and in turn their consciousness[16] are inextricably linked to the conjuncture of ethnicity/race and gender. In other words, they experience violence as Asian *and* female.[17]

The third approach to resistance focuses on oppression based on race and ethnicity. While feminist theories have excluded or ignored the race and ethnic based forms of domination and violence, the anti-Asian violence analysis has, thus far, excluded sex/gendered basis of violence in their organizing and theoretical framework. Since the 1980s, for example, the anti-Asian violence movements in the United States have shed light on hate crimes and racist violence targeted against Asians because of their race/ethnicity. The anti-Asian violence movement groups have successfully articulated how race and ethnicity are used to subordinate, discriminate, and bring physical violence against Asians. However, this movement has yet to address violence targeted against Asian women which is based on both race/ethnicity and sex. Addressing this point, for example, a group of Asian and Pacific Islander women based in San Francisco have recently produced a collaborative document entitled "Violence against Asian Women, Document to Share with the Anti-Asian Violence Movement."[18] This group is concerned with the invisibility of violence when Asian women are victims of hate crimes, whether based on race, national origin, sexual orientation, religion or any combination of these "protected classes." The document states: "We want the anti-Asian violence movement to work with us to identify the causes of this invisibility." The group calls for a collective effort to recognize the multiple forms of violence targeted against Asian women.

Since the theoretical perspectives and political movement approaches view domination and resistance premised on a single-axis, none adequately addresses violence against Asian immigrant women. It still remains a challenge, both locally and internationally, to broaden the definitions and frameworks of social movements by factoring in the issues of race, class, and gender.[19] An adequate theoretical and political framework requires a more complete picture of how violence against Korean and Asian women results from their "multiple jeopardy."[20] That is, how multiple forms of oppression—economic, social, cultural, racial, and sexual systems of domination inherent in the globalizing capitalist world—marginalize Korean and Asian women, and other women of color.

To articulate the dynamics of repression and resistance as experienced by marginalized Asian women and women of color, it is necessary to analyze the complex relations of domination and power. On Third World women and feminism, Chandra Mohanty (1991) provides new insights into the way that feminist politics could move. Extending Dorothy Smith's (1987) notion of historically specific "relations of ruling,"[21] Mohanty (1991:14) locates Third World women's resistance and struggles in systems of domination which operate in multiple contexts—e.g., of colonialism, class, gender, race, state, citizenship, racial formation, and multinational production, as well has hegemonic mode of discursive practices. Therefore, in Mohanty's view, multiple forms of domination intersect to locate women differently at particular historical junctures. At the same time, however, women also resist by insisting on "the dynamic opposition agency of individuals and collectives and their engagement in daily life." It is this focus on dynamic oppositional agency that clarifies the intricate connection between systemic relationships and the directionality of power (Mohanty, Russo, and Torres 1991:13). Clearly, systems of racial, class, and gender domination, as pointed out by Mohanty (1991), do not have identical effects on Anglo-American women, Asian women, African American women, Latinas, or in general, on women in Third World contexts.

In sum, I have argued for broadening our theory and politics to address the everyday forms of resistance of Asian women in marginal positions, as well as of articulating the ways in which violence experienced by Asian women results from the multiple systems of domination. The understanding of everyday forms of violence and resistance from the position of marginality compels us to break down the invisibility of Asian women in the current politics of feminism and racism. A broadened theory also pushes us to re-think about how each of these systems of domination—race, class, gender, and culture—intersect in the actual conditions under which women live. Instead of privileging a single-axis structure, it is necessary to shift our analysis of violence, repression, and resistance to the periphery, where Asian women, and other women of color, struggle to survive.

Notes

1. This article represents a segment of my larger project on resistance, repression, and violence. I would like to thank Susan Dearing, Louise Tilly, Letti Volpp, and Wendy Weiss for their comments on this paper.
2. These forms of resistance have been first analyzed by Scott (1985). For him, the ordinary weapons of powerless groups, such as peasants, include Brechtian forms of class struggle: for example, "foot dragging, dissimulation, false compliance, pilfering, feigned ignorance, slander, arson, sabotage, and so forth" (29).
3. Since 1988, a group of Koreans residing in North Carolina have tried to rally support on behalf of Chong. However, it was not until January 1992 when the "Free Chong Sun France Campaign" was mobilized by a broadly-based network of women's groups and concerned individuals in the United States and in South Korea that Chong's case received public attention. While the campaign was based in New York City, a petition with over 3,000 signatures were gathered to demand Chong's freedom. A year-long pressure on the governor of North Carolina finally led to clemency, and Chong was released on parole on December 31, 1992. During the six years she served in prison, a place that held mostly women of color imprisoned for breaking the normative definition of standard behavior, Chong was not allowed to receive any letters or newspapers written in the Korean language. Chong's sentence would not have been commuted without the unrelenting protest mobilized by the Free Chong Sun France Campaign, and the campaign successfully built grassroots-based linkages across international borders.
4. In the life story of Esperanza, anthropologist Ruth Behar discusses the power and meaning of rage as a "culturally forceful state of consciousness" and explains that rage can be viewed as "diffused anger that oppressed people feel in colonial settings" (1990:241).
5. Tijerina (1990) sheds light on her own experience of state oppression and violence targeted against her. Incarcerated on numerous occasions when she was sixteen years old, and having been sent to an experimental maximum security institution upon a

plea bargain, she describes how a prison psychologist viewed her as "dangerous to society and to herself." Tijerina writes, "Dangerous to tell the violence I am. Dangerous to release the anger I am. Dangerous to write the truth of the source of oppression. Dangerous to name it—name the person, the myth and the props. Dangerous to be who I am. Dangerous to the social make-up of this country. Dangerous to write it. Dangerous to myself" (171).

6. Reverend Henna Han founded the Rainbow Church on Long Island, New York, to provide support to Korean women married to American servicemen and their interracial families, and has helped to organize the Free Chong Sun France Campaign. Since last year, she, Chong Sun France, and other Korean women have been working to create a women's house called the Rainbow Center in Flushing, New York, where Korean women come to meet each other for emotional, psychological, social, and cultural support.

7. *The Central Daily* (Choong Ang Ilbo), 16 April 1992.

8. William Daly, director of the Mayor's Office of Midtown Enforcement, closed twenty-two massage parlors during the first five months of 1993 under the state education and public morality laws. According to Captain Michael Brooks, head of the police public morals division, in 1992 alone 3,097 women were arrested, many Korean, for practicing in unlicensed parlors and for promoting prostitution *(Daily News,* 17 May 1993).

9. Only two weeks prior to this crackdown, this same woman was thrown out of another club. Sex clubs and massage parlors routinely advertise in *The Village Voice* and *Screw* magazine. My review of the club advertisements in the March 30, 1993 edition of *The Village Voice* were still printed in the April 20, 1993 edition of the paper, along with new advertisements for several new parlors and clubs. The frequent changes of club names and addresses indicate constant relocation of the parlors due, probably, to police crackdowns. Moreover, the objectification and violence against Asian women are explicit in the racial and sexual stereotypes of Asian women constructed in advertisements found in *The Village Voice.* For example, the Pinocchio Club advertises "Grade A #1 Very Hot Steamy Oriental Girls"; the Sensational/American Touch Club promises "the Best looking Oriental Girls"; the China Doll Club promises "Beautiful Oriental Hostesses"; the Oriental Star Club advertises "Friendly Oriental Woman with Big Smile and Noisy Laugh"; and the Oriental Paradise advertises "Come Feel the Excitement as Our Young Oriental Hostess Melt You to Ecstasy."

10. This is a pseudonym. Her story is covered in *New York Newsday,* 19 March 1989.

11. Jinhee's ex-husband, Timothy Cook, blames his wife for leaving him for no reason and states: "She could be dead today, for all I know." Cook has since remarried another Korean woman and states that his marriage to Jinhee " . . . is something from the past . . . I can't see any reason to dwell" *(New York Newsday,* 19 March 1989).

12. In the 1970s, Kassner and Detsky were the two biggest New York City attorneys who controlled the daily operations of their clients' massage parlors. According to Patricia Klausner, they also provided information on how to successfully design and manage massage parlors involved in the international traffic in women (1987:283).

13. Kimberlé Crenshaw suggests that feminist theory and antiracist politics privilege gender or race, respectively, and excludes and erases black women in conceptualization of race *and* sex discrimination. By challenging us to recognize the multidimensionality of black women's experience of violence and discrimination, rooted in race and sex intersections, Crenshaw argues for broadened feminist and antiracist analyses (1989).

14. Scott (1985) provides a lucid and compelling analysis of everyday forms of peasant resistance by refuting theoretical objections to both Marxist and bourgeois notions of political action. I have been inspired by his analysis, but have also expanded his frame-

work of resistance of subordinate classes to include poor, working-class, Third World immigrant women. According to Scott, for example, the problem with the existing concepts of resistance is such "sociologically naive insistence" to distinguish "self-indulgent," individual acts from "principled," selfless, collective actions, while, at the same time, excluding what constitutes everyday forms of "real resistance" (294-95).

15. Radical feminists such as Barry (1979), Dworkin (1976), Griffin (1979), Millet (1970), Rich (1976), and MacKinnon (1989) have done significant research to support this thesis about violence and cruelty against women resulting from patriarchy.

16. While recognizing differences in Asian women's location and multiple forms of oppression, sociologist Esther Chow (1987) argues that Asian American women are invisible and have not engaged in American feminist politics because Asian women lack feminist consciousness. I find this argument limiting because it assumes lack of agency and consciousness on the part of Asian women, and accepts the parameters of feminist politics as defined by white, middle-class feminism. Asian American women are indeed, in my view, conscious of the multiple forces which oppress them, and they struggle to subvert and to resist the forces which systematically overpower them. Yet, the difficult challenge is that they must fight on more than one location/site. We cannot, therefore, presume a lack of consciousness, but must come to an understanding of multiple consciousness of women of color, which recognizes their location in more than one axis.

17. The immigration and nationality laws, and the racial and gender basis of granting American citizenship, illustrate the continuity between the relationships of colonization and white, masculine, capitalist state rule. Historically, for example, white feminist movements have not been concerned about the gendered/sexualized/racialized nature of immigration and nationality which affect immigrant women. See discussion of this point in Mohanty (1991:23).

18. This document points to the invisibility of Asian women both in the feminist and anti-Asian violence movements. Leti Volpp presented this document on a panel discussion, "Intersectionality of Violence Against Women," at the 1993 Association for Asian American Studies conference at Cornell University.

19. For discussion on racism in feminist politics, see Joseph and Lewis (1981).

20. King (1988) addresses the theoretical invisibility of black women and their experiences. King states that discussions of black people tends to focus on black men, and discussions about women tends to focus on white women. As a corrective, King pushes us to move towards an analysis of "multiple jeopardy"—which recognizes the interdependent control systems of racism, classism, and sexism.

21. By posing a "women's standpoint theory," Smith argues for a feminist sociology which challenges the assumed standpoint of men and which reveals the everyday world of "ruling" as problematic. In Smith's words, "'Relations of ruling' is a concept that grasps power, organization, direction, and regulation as more pervasively structured than can be expressed in traditional concepts provided by the discourses of power" (1987:3).

References

Anzaldúa, Gloria, ed. *Making Face, Making Soul.* San Francisco: Aunt Lute Foundations Books, 1990.

Barry, Kathleen. *Female Sexual Slavery.* Englewood Cliffs: Prentice-Hall, 1979.

Behar, Ruth. "Rage and Redemption: Reading the Life Story of a Mexican Market Woman." *Feminist Studies* 16 (Summer 1990): 223-58.

Chow, Esther. "The Development of Feminist Consciousness among Asian American Women." *Gender and Society* 1 (September 1987): 284-99.

Collins, Patricia Hill. *Black Feminist Thought: Knowledge, Consciousness, and the Politics of Empowerment.* New York: Routledge, 1991.

Connell, R. W. *Gender and Power.* Stanford: Stanford University Press, 1987.

Crenshaw, Kimberlé. "Demarginalizing the Intersection of Race and Sex: A Black Feminist Critique of Antidiscrimination Doctrine, Feminist Theory, and Antiracist Politics." *Legal Forum* . Chicago: University of Chicago, 1989.

Dworkin, Andrea. *Our Blood: Prophecies and Discourses on Sexual Politics.* New York: Perigee Books, 1976.

Gambardello, Joseph. "International Sex Slave Free." *New York Newsday,* 1 May 1993.

Griffin, Susan. *Rape, The Power of Consciousness.* New York: Harper & Row, 1979.

Henican, Ellis. "Parlors Lured a Wife Away from Army Life." *New York Newsday,* 19 March 1989.

hooks, bell. "Marginality as Site of Resistance." In *Out There: Marginalization and Contemporary Cultures,* edited by Russell Ferguson, Martha Gever, Trinh T. Minh-ha, and Cornel West. Cambridge: MIT Press, 1990 (b).

_____. *Yearning: Race, Gender, and Cultural Politics.* Boston: South End Press, 1990 (a).

Joseph, Gloria I. and Jill Lewis. *Common Difference: Conflicts in Black and White Feminist Perspectives.* Boston: South End Press, 1981.

King, Deborah K. "Multiple Jeopardy, Multiple Consciousness: The Context of a Black Feminist Ideology." *Signs* 14 (Autumn 1988): 42-72.

Klausner, Patricia. "The Politics of Massage Parlor Prostitution: The International Traffic in Women for Prostitution into New York City, 1970-Present." Ph.D. diss., University of Delaware, 1987.

Lickman, Steven and Gwen Young. "Fronts." *Newsday,* 30 July 1988.

MacKinnon, Catharine. *Toward a Feminist Theory of the State.* Cambridge: Harvard University Press, 1989.

McQuillan, Alice. "Kidnapped Sex Slave Drags Suspect into Station." *The Gazette,* 3 May 1993.

Millet, Kate. *Sexual Politics.* Garden City: Doubleday, 1970.

Mohanty, Chandra. "Cartographies of Struggle: Third World Women and the Politics of Feminism." In *Third World Women and the Politics of Feminism,* edited by Chandra Mohanty, Ann Russo, and Lourdes Torres. Bloomington: Indiana University Press, 1991.

Mohanty, Chandra, Ann Russo, and Lourdes Torres, eds. *Third World Women and the Politics of Feminism.* Bloomington: Indiana University Press, 1991.

Rich, Adrienne. *Of Woman Born: Motherhood as Experience and Institution.* New York: Bantam, 1976.

Scott, James. *Weapons of the Weak: Everyday Forms of Peasant Resistance.* New Haven: Yale University Press, 1985.

Smith, Dorothy. *The Conceptual Practices of Power, A Feminist Sociology of Knowledge.* Boston: Northeastern University Press, 1990.

_____. "Women's Perspective as a Radical Critique of Sociology." *Sociological Inquiry* 44 (1987): 7-13.

Sullivan, Ronald. "Ex-Policeman is Charged in Protection of Brothels." *New York Times,* 5 June 1992.

Tijerina, Aleticia. "Notes on Oppression and Violence." In *Making Face, Making Soul,* edited by Gloria Anzaldúa. San Francisco: Aunt Lute Foundations Books, 1990.

White, Evelyn C. ed. *The Black Women's Health Book: Speaking for Ourselves.* Seattle: Seal Press, 1990.

Race, Gender, and the Law: Asian American Women and Rape

Kandice Chuh

Control over Asian American women's sexuality is an often invisible and powerful part of our legal system. In this paper, I will interrogate the relationship among gender, race, and the law as it pertains to Asian American women. I hope to demonstrate the ways in which the law's claim to gender- and race-neutrality, in combination with stereotypes defining Asian American women's sexuality,[1] creates a socio-legal environment which is not only unfriendly to Asian American women,[2] but which in fact locates us outside of the very realm of juridical subjectivity. I will argue that the intersection between racism and sexism does not reside merely in the realm of literary and other cultural artifacts, but rather, that a parallel can be drawn between those cultural texts and the law.

Like stereotypes, behavioral mores, and cultural expectations, our legal system seeks to describe and regulate what behavior is and is not socially acceptable. It does so largely based on understandings and enforcement of boundaries between and among individuals. As Martha Minow (1990) states, "[t]raditional legal rules presume that there is a clear and knowable boundary between each individual and all others" (7). She explains that tort, contract, and constitutional law are sets of legal rules based on boundary transgression, the presumption of the existence of distinct parties, and the rights of an individual, respectively (7-8). Minow suggests further, that "[l]egal rules . . . historically have drawn a boundary between normal and abnormal, or competent and incompetent people" while also seeking "to define the boundaries of each person's obligations to others" (8). The law, then, focuses on the governance and maintenance of these boundaries, rather than on the individuals—the people—involved. What Minow attempts to do in *Making All the Difference* (1990), is to shift the emphasis of legal reasoning away from boundaries and toward relational understandings between and among individuals. That is, she examines not (only) the boundaries established by the law themselves, but, the *differences* delineated by these boundaries. It is Minow's work on difference which I find helpful for the purposes of this study.

Minow poses what she terms "the dilemma of difference" as a problem which, because of the law's "preoccupation with boundaries" (9), the legal system is ill-equipped to handle. Minow suggests that: "The dilemma of difference grows from the ways in which this society assigns individuals to categories and, on that basis, determines whom to include in and whom to exclude from political, social, and economic activities. Because the activities are designed, in turn, with only the included participants in mind, the excluded seem not to fit because of something in their own nature" (21). Thus, because of the categorization of individuals based on singular traits and characteristics, inclusion and exclusion become not only possibilities, but realities. The deployment of boundaries in the law turns the dilemma of difference into a problem for the "different" individual. For example, if Asian Americans face White American racism in this country,[3] it is because we are different/abnormal/incompetent, and not because of the construction of Whiteness as normative.[4] Stereotypes could be conceived of, in Minow's terms, as categories through which we "structure the world and show that the order we impose reduces anxiety and lends an appearance of legitimacy and self-evident truth to what we have invented" (179). In other words, these categories allow us to naturalize and thereby make invisible the constructedness of aspects of our society. White, as already in power, legitimizes its own position by using stereotypes to identify who is different and how.

According to Minow, legal resolutions to the dilemma of difference result in a reification of the same system of boundaries and categorization. "[P]osed as a choice between integration and separation . . . similar treatment and special treatment . . . or . . . neutrality and accommodation" (20-21), adjudication means the making of an either/or choice, and that choice consequently reemphasizes difference, located in the "different" individual, as the problem. This self-perpetuation is made possible, Minow argues, because of unquestioned and invisible assumptions of the law.

Minow identifies five "Unstated Assumptions" which, when made visible, reveal the inclusionary/exclusionary nature of the legal process. Briefly, these are: (1) difference is intrinsic and not derived through comparison (50; 53+); (2) the norm is simply assumed and need not be stated (51; 56+); (3) the observer sees without a perspective (52; 60+); (4) other perspectives are irrelevant (52; 66+); and (5) the status quo is natural, uncoerced, and good (52; 70+). Thus, the law assumes a starting point of neutrality and normality against which difference is determined, but that point takes on a cloak of naturalness and universality which, in turn, makes these assumptions invisible. The law, through this assumption of universality, conceives of itself as being completely objective, as being, for example, race- and gender-neutral. If we adopt Minow's assertions, however, it is clear that the seemingly natural point of reference against which the "unnatural" is judged is, in fact, the perspective of the already empowered Subject.

Similarly, Patricia Williams suggests that not only does our legal system rely on and believe in the existence of an objective Truth, but that it also relies on/believes in the "pure" expression of that Truth through vehicles such as judges: "'Theoretical legal understanding' is characterized, in Anglo-American jurisprudence, by . . . [t]he existence of transcendent, acontextual, universal legal truths or pure procedures . . . [and by] . . . [t]he existence of objective, 'unmediated' voices by which those transcendent, universal truths find their expression" (8-9). Williams goes further to assert that "the supposed existence of such voices is also given power in romanticized notions of 'real people' having 'real' experiences—not because real people have experienced what they really experienced, but because their experiences are somehow made legitimate—either because they are viewed as empirically legitimately . . . or, more frequently, because those experiences are corroborated by hidden or unspoken models of legitimacy" (9) (emphasis in original). Consider what is revealed, for example, by the historical example of the Supreme Court's decision in *U.S. v. Bhagat Singh Thind*, 261 U.S. 204 (1923).

Classified as Caucasians, the immigration and naturalization status of Asian Indians posed a unique "problem" for the U.S. Government early in this century. According to historian Ronald Takaki, the Asiatic Exclusion League, formed in 1905 by White American workers who feared competition from Asian immigrant laborers, and whose organization's constitution stated that "[t]he Caucasian and Asiatic races are unassimilable . . . . The preservation of the Caucasian race upon American soil . . . necessitates the adoption of all possible measures to prevent or minimize the immigration of Asiatics to America" (Takaki 201),[5] created a definition of Whiteness in order to exclude Asian Indians from the category of Caucasian—a definition subsequently adopted by the Supreme Court in the *Thind* decision. The point of law in question in this case was the eligibility of Asian Indians for U.S. citizenship, based on a 1790 federal law which reserved "naturalized citizenship to 'whites' only" (Takaki 298). Takaki explains that:

> [T]he Supreme Court ruled that Asian Indians were ineligile to naturalization. Arguing that the definition of race had to be based on the "understanding of the common man," the Court held that the term "white person" meant an immigrant from northern or western Europe. For the "practical purposes" of the statute, the term "race" must be applied to a "group of living persons *now* possessing in common the requisite characteristics . . . . The law "does not employ the word 'Caucasian' but the words 'white persons,'" the Court explained, "and these are words of common speech and not of scientific origin . . . . Thus Asian Indians, while they were "Caucasian," were not "white." The intention of the Founding Fathers was to "confer the privilege of citizenship upon that class of persons" they knew as "white" (299) (emphasis in original).

By setting aside ethnological classifications, the Supreme Court revealed the constructedness of the supposedly natural assumptions made by the law. The "common" or "average" man in the Court's opinion is clearly White. The Court's choice to embrace and adopt the Asiatic Exclusion League's definition of Caucasian demonstrates the un-naturalness of White as being normative: White had to be *created* or constructed as such in response to a particular situation. The perspective and experiences of the Asian Indian were cast aside as irrelevant and illegitimate, compared to a standard of the relevant and legitimate American as being W/white. The universal "truth" appealed to in this decision is the truth of the White, male "Founding Fathers." Thus, the Supreme Court resolved this manifestation of the dilemma of difference by choosing to exclude Asian Indians from the subjective position of citizen, thereby defining the juridical Subject as being—as appearing—White.

In relation to sex and gender, this dilemma of difference translates into the perpetuation of "the deeply entrenched social institutionalization of sex difference" (Okin 1987:43). As Susan Moller Okin (1987) asserts in discussing the relative valuation of "women's work" and "men's work" within family settings, "[w]e live in a society in whose past the innate characteristic of sex has been regarded as one of the clearest legitimizers of different rights and restrictions, both formal and informal. While legal sanctions that uphold male dominance have been to some extent eroded within the past century . . . tradition, combined with the effects of socialization . . . still work powerfully to reinforce roles for the two sexes that are commonly regarded as of unequal prestige and worth" (42). In essence, though the imbalance of power between men and women has become less extreme, it continues to be maintained through the invocation of supposedly inherent differences between the sexes. Okin argues that "gender hierarchy is determined by a single value—sex—with maleness taking the place of . . . purity" (57). That is, using sex as the category for measurement, historically, man has been assumed to be normative while woman was then oppositionally defined as different.

The maintenance of this gender or sex differentiation has borne troublesome effects as women have sought formal equal protection and rights under the law. Some feminists have argued, and I agree, that the claim to gender neutrality must necessarily be false, given the hegemonic position of men in our society: "'rules formulated in a male-dominated society reflect male needs, male concerns, and male experience'" (Olsen 1984:396) (citation omitted).[6] Feminist examinations of the laws defining and governing the crime of rape make clear the male-oriented nature of the law, and it is these examinations to which I now turn.

Historically, the criminal justice system has reflected and, indeed, codified sexist assumptions regarding the seriousness of rape to women. Requirements necessitating corroboration and proof of resistance, exemptions for marital rape, and the admissibility of the woman's prior sexual behavior were common elements in the handling of rape cases. Largely due to the efforts of feminists, rape legislation has moved away from these misogynous practices (Searles and Berger 1987:25). Much of this collective effort has been directed toward reconsidering the definition of rape.

Legally, the traditional definition of forcible (as opposed to statutory) rape differentiates it from sex because of the presence of force or coercion and the lack of mutual consent prior to penile penetration of the vagina, or intercourse (MacKinnon 1989:172; Searles and Berger 1987:26). Both coercion and lack of consent are necessary for an act of sex to be considered the crime of rape.

The problem with the concept of consent here is the underlying assumption that the parties are equally empowered. Yet, if the threat of force from one party is even a possibility, how can we consider the parties as possessing equal power? In U.S. society, women live under and within phallogocentric constructs; we are constantly faced with the threat of force. We find ourselves in a society in which pornography eroticizing aggression against women and representing them as objects against whom violence is not only acceptable, but titillating, proliferates.[7] Catharine MacKinnon (1989) goes so far as to state that "under conditions of male dominance," there is little distinction between rape and heterosexual intercourse (174). Clearly, an assumption of equal empowerment between the sexes is false.

According to MacKinnon (1989), rape law divides women into "spheres of consent according to indices of relationship to men" (175). These categories are: "the virginal daughter and other young girls, with whom all sex is proscribed, and the whorelike wives and prostitutes, with whom no sex is proscribed. Daughters may not consent; wives and prostitutes are assumed to, and cannot but" (175).[8] In general, wives and prostitutes, because they are in constant states of consent, are therefore effectively unrapable.

For an adult woman, her relationship with the accused is used as an indicator of consent. "The exemption for rape in marriage is consistent with the assumption underlying most adjudications of forcible rape: to the extent the parties relate, it was not really rape, it was personal" (MacKinnon 1989:176). What goes on between husband and wife is seen as a private matter to be dealt with in the domestic sphere. Though marital rape statutes differ from state to state, it is possible to note commonalities among them. For example, as of the late 1980s, only twelve states had no statutory exemptions for spouses, and as many as six states had no exceptions to the marital exemption (Searles and Berger 1987:28; 34). However, as MacKinnon (1989) states: "although the rape law may not now always assume that the woman consented simply because the parties are legally one, indices of closeness, of relationship ranging from nodding acquaintance to living together, still contra-indicate rape. In marital rape cases, courts look for even greater atrocities than usual to undermine their assumption that if sex happened, she wanted it" (176). Spousal impunity from rape prosecution is particularly telling of the misogynous nature of rape legislation. This exemption is traceable to a seventeenth-century English jurist, Lord Hale, who wrote that a "husband cannot be guilty of rape committed by himself upon his lawful wife, for by their mutual matrimonial consent and contract the wife hath given up herself in this kind unto her husband, which she cannot retract" *[People v. Liberta,* 64 N.Y.2d 152, 162, 474 N.E.2d 567, 572, 485 N.Y.S.2d 207, 212 (1984)]. In other words, the rape laws which purport to protect and defend women's right to determine women's sexualities are, in actuality, far less based on consent or nonconsent, but rather, on the *presumption* that certain women/females "always" say yes or no.

Related to consent is the concept of the *mens rea,* the criminal mind. Legally, the accused must have had at the time of the alleged crime the intent to commit the crime. "The man's mental state refers to what he actually understood at the time or to what a reasonable man should have understood under the circumstances" (MacKinnon 1989:180). The consent defense asserts that if the accused *honestly believed* that the accuser consented to sexual intercourse, then he is not guilty. And, "[w]hile the presence of reasonable grounds for such a belief must be considered by the jury, it is *not a necessary condition* for a successful defense" (Los 1990:166) (emphasis in original).

According to MacKinnon (1989), the problem with applying *mens rea* as an element necessary to the crime of rape is that though "the injury of rape lies in the meaning of the act to its victim . . . the standard for its criminality lies in the meaning of the act to the assailant" (180). In other words, the man's perceptions of the woman's will—of the nature of her consent—determines whether or not she has been raped. Her experience is effectively nullified.

Assessing the criminality of sexual intercourse solely from the assailant's perspective, in addition to unjustly privileging male sensibility, assumes that there is a single, essential event which cannot be interpreted in different ways—that there is only one answer to the question of "what really happened," or, that there is an objective and universal truth which can be uncovered through the supposedly transcendent perspective of the "reasonable" man. In the reality of lived experience, however, rapes involve "both honest men and violated women" (MacKinnon 1989:183). This seeming paradox is possible because men's notion of consent differs significantly from women's: Men may believe that "a woman's resistance often presents a challenge, an invitation to 'rough sex,' or a sign that she must yet be shown what she really wants" (Los 1990:166). Or, they may believe that actions as seemingly innocuous (at least from the woman's perspective) as accepting a ride or sharing a meal are indicators of consent (Los (1990:166). The acceptability/usability of the consent defense signifies the reification of men's right to define women's sexuality; it allows men to claim authority over—to control—women's desire and will.

Efforts to classify rape solely as a crime of violence—as sexual assault—prove similarly harmful to the victim/ survivor. Rape falls squarely on the intersection between sex and violence. "Equating rape with other assaults . . . for assault is, 'by definition, something to which the victim does not consent'" (Searles and Berger 1987:26), evades the larger issue of women's sexual autonomy. Sexual assault is defined in gender-neutral terms. This desexualization of rape negates the argument that "rape is a unique crime in that it involves predominantly the victimization of members of one gender group by members of the other" (Los 1990:166). By redefining rape in gender-neutral terms, we lose sight of the institutionalized control men have over women's sexuality. In MacKinnon's (1989) words, "[t]he view that derives most directly from victims' experiences . . . construes sexuality as a social sphere of male power to which forced sex is paradigmatic. Rape is not less sexual for being violent. To the extent that coercion has become integral to male sexuality, rape may even be sexual to the degree that, and because, it is violent" (173). Shifting the terminology of rape in the direction of violence-not-sex effectively (re)centers the assailant's motives while simultaneously distorting the experience of rape as a sexual violation (Los 1990:167). The victim/survivor of rape cannot remove the element of sex from the experience of rape, and for this reason, neither should the laws determining its criminality.

In sum, gender-neutrality in rape laws effectively skews the scales of justice in the favor of men. The laws defining this crime, having as their unstated and universal perspective the actual, situated point of view of the male assailant, deny women juridical subjectivity. That is, the experience of the victim/survivor is of secondary importance in the eyes of the law: the primacy of the assailant's perspective centers the male experience and sensibility while simultaneously marginalizing and illegitimizing the female.

So, what does all of this mean for the Asian American woman in relation to rape? Cultural expectations and stereotypes work together to construct the "normal" Asian American woman as a submissive being, whose very nature describes her as sexually and otherwise oriented toward the purpose of serving men. Literary and other mediated images of the Asian American woman describe and define women only in relation to men; women's very identities are proscribed as complete only in the (sexual) service of men. As such, the Asian American woman, regardless of marital or employment status, falls into MacKinnon's classification of some women as being "unrapable." This class of women—wives and prostitutes, to be exact—cannot be raped because they are presumed to be always already consenting to (hetero)sexual intercourse. This, in combination with the law's exclusion of women and of Asian Americans of both sexes from juridical subjectivity—its casting of women and Americans of color as "different" and thus not-normal—creates an environment in which Asian American women are perceived as safe to rape. The gender- and race-neutrality of the law in effect leads to prejudicial and disparate protection of and by the law.

A new and better legal system would recognize and incorporate the existence and dynamics of the disproportionate distribution of power along lines of race, class, age, gender, and sexualities, among others. It would, in a sense, conceive of justice in relational terms, as Martha Minow (1990) might argue. As Nancy Hartsock (1992) suggested, feminists (of color) need to "think about what a gendered legal system might look like" and work toward a system which does not operate "on the basis of 'individuals' who are assumed to have no race and no gender." Those who construct and create law must be made to understand the falsity and negative impact of this assumption. In some ways, the legal system has attempted to remedy the disparate impact of the law on women and on people of color of both sexes. For example, the recent federal court decision in *Ellison v. Brady*, 924 F.2d 872 (9th Cir. 1991) "established that the standard by which sexual harassment in the workplace would be judged was no longer the reasonable man or even the reasonable person but rather the reasonable woman" (Sanger 1992:1411). This shift in perspective prioritizes the experience of women over that of men. And, affirmative action policies have attempted to redress socio-historical differences in power between White Americans and Americans of Color, as well as between men and women of all races. These remedies, however, only take into consideration one aspect of our identities at a time—women of color are women *or* of color; the *Ellison* decision fails to consider the impact of race in relation to gender and/or sex. Much feminist legal theory, too, has come under criticism by those who believe it has ignored or neglected race and class as they inform and construct subject positionality.[9] We need to stop looking at race or gender as if they were discrete and autonomous. By considering these issues together, in combination with other elements which structure identities and identifications, we can formulate better—more encompassing, more realistic—understandings of the world at large.

At the individual level, Asian American women must recognize that "because of cultural values that we as Asian American women are brought up with and cherish, we are frequently agreeable, gentle, and willing to please others before ourselves" (Chan 1987:13). With this recognition as a starting point, we can begin to protect and empower ourselves against the socio-legal structures which code us as unrapable.[10]

Notes

1. Issues of and discussions around race and racism in this country are most often conceived of as being between African and White Americans. While I recognize the importance of the discourse between those groups and communities, as a kind of metatextual project, I want to focus specifically on race relations between Asian and White Americans. That is, I am pushing for readers to recognize that race and racism

are not only limited to "Black" and/versus "White." I want to emphasize the need for and importance of centering Asian Americans in at least some of the dialogue around race and racism. For these reasons, I have not worked to differentiate specifically the experiences of and/or stereotypes about Asian Americans from those of other "minority" groups in this country.

2. Some comments on my use of "Asian American": For the purposes of this paper, "American" should be understood to refer to anyone who desires and plans to make the United States his or her permanent domicile. I would also like to note that I do not conceive of the term and/or the individuals and communities denoted by it to be static entities, nor do I mean to represent the views and opinions of all Asian Americans. And finally, I use the term "Asian American" without hyphenation in order to emphasize both the adjectival use of "Asian" and our subject positions as "Americans."

3. "White," here, denotes an attitude which is related to being "white" or having "white skin." That is, "White" is the unconscious assumption of normativity, the un-self-reflexive assurance of a natural position in society, and an unawareness of privilege associated with "white skin." "White America" stands as the institutional version of the above description; an attitude and an episteme of unconscious superiority and naturalness.

4. I am not calling for mass assimilation here. "Majorification" or assimilation does not seem to me to be the solution to the problem of continued exclusion of Asian Americans from full participation in society. In fact, what I am suggesting is that the strategy of assimilation would, in any case, inevitably fail, because Asian Americans can never be(come) truly "W/white."

5. For an explication of the history of Asian Americans, see, generally, Takaki (1990).

6. See also Colker (1986).

7. For thorough discussions of the consequences of (heterosexual) pornography on women, see: Kappeler (1986), MacKinnon (1987), and Williams (1989).

8. As Vivyan Adair has pointed out, this passage seems to suggest that "virginal daughters and other young girls" are not, in actuality, raped. It is important to note that MacKinnon presents these categories as those of "presumed consent"; that is, if a female child has sexual intercourse with any man, she is presumed by rape law to have said no.

9. Marlee Kline (1989) convincingly reveals some of the places at which feminist legal scholars, including MacKinnon, have used as their "unstated assumptions," a White, middle-class American woman as the norm.

10. Many thanks to Nancy Hartsock, Vivyan Adair, and Phebe Jewell, whose comments greatly assisted in the redrafting of this paper, and especially, to Carolyn Allen, for her invaluable suggestions and guidance, and her supportive encouragement.

References

"The Asian Bride Boom." *Asiaweek,* 15 April 1983.

Chan, Connie S. "Asian-American Women: Psychological Responses to Sexual Exploitation & Cultural Stereotypes." *Asian American Psychological Association Journal* 12 (1987): 11-15.

Clark, Anna. *Women's Silence: Men's Violence.* London: Pandora Press, 1987.

Colker, Ruth. "Anti-Subordination above All: Sex, Race, and Equal Protection." *New York University Law Review* 61 (December 1986).

Ellison v. Brady, 924 F.2d 872 (9th Cir. 1991).

Frug, Mary Joe. *Postmodern Legal Feminism.* New York: Routledge, 1992.

Hartsock, Nancy. Personal communication, March 1992.

Hoff, Joan. *Law, Gender, and Injustice.* New York: New York University Press, 1991.

Kappeler, Susann. *The Pornography of Representation.* Minneapolis: University of Minnesota Press, 1986.

Kline, Marlee. "Race, Racism, and Feminist Legal Theory." *Harvard Women's Law Journal* 12 (1989).

Lim, Shirley Geok-lin, Mayumi Tsutakawa, and Margarita Donnelly, eds. *The Forbidden Stitch: An Asian American Women's Anthology.* Corvallis: Calyx Books, 1989.

Lorde, Audre. "The Master's Tools Will Never Dismantle the Master's House." In *This Bridge Called My Back,* edited by Cherrie Moraga and Gloria Anzaldua. New York: Kitchen Table Press, 1983.

Los, Maria. "Feminism and Rape Law Reform." In *Feminist Perspectives in Criminology,* edited by Loraine Gelsthorpe and Allison Morris. Philadelphia: Open University Press, 1990.

MacKinnon, Catharine A. *Feminism Unmodified: Discourses on Life and Law.* Cambridge: Harvard University Press, 1987.

____. *Toward a Feminist Theory of the State.* Cambridge: Harvard University Press, 1989.

Minow, Martha. *Making All the Difference.* Ithaca: Cornell University Press, 1990.

Okin, Susan Moller. "Justice and Gender." *Philosophy and Public Affairs* 16 (1987).

Olsen, Frances. "Statutory Rape: A Feminist Critique of Rights." *Texas Law Review* 63 (1984).

People v. Liberta, 64 N.Y.2d 152, 474 N.E.2d 567, 485 N.Y.S.2d 207 (1984).

Rapada, Marilou and Emilina Ragaza-Garcia. "The Bride Trade." *Asiaweek,* 10 June 1983.

Russo, Ann. "'We Cannot Live without Our Lives': White Women, Antiracism, and Feminism." In *Third World Women and the Politics of Feminism,* edited by Chandra Mohanty, Lourdes Torres, and Ann Russo. Bloomington: Indiana University Press, 1991.

Sanger, Carol. "The Reasonable Woman and the Ordinary Man." *Southern California Law Review* 65 (March 1992): 1411-17.

Schneider, Elizabeth M. "The Dialectic of Rights and Politics: Perspectives from the Women's Movement." *Harvard Women's Law Journal* 12 (1989).

Searles, Patricia and Ronald J. Berger. "The Current Status of Rape Reform Legislation: An Examination of State Statutes." *Women's Rights Law Reporter* 10 (1987): 25-41.

Spender, Dale. *Man Made Language.* London: Routledge and Kegan Paul, 1980.

Sunday, Suzanne R. and Ethel Tobach, eds. *Violence against Women: A Critique of the Sociobiology of Rape.* New York: Gordian Press, 1985.

Takaki, Ronald. *Strangers from a Different Shore.* New York: Penguin Books, 1990.

U.S. v. Bhagat Singh Thind, 261 U.S. 204 (1923).

Waugh, Dexter. "More Efforts Needed to Expose & Treat Domestic Violence in U.S." *New York Asian News* 1:4 (1991): 1+.

White-Parks, Annette. "Women's Force: Between Image and Reality of Chinese Immigrant Women in Literature." In *Frontiers of Asian American Studies,* edited by Gail M. Nomura, Russell Endo, Stephen H. Sumida, and Russell C. Leong. Pullman: Washington State University Press, 1989.

Williams, Linda. *Hard Core: Power, Pleasure, and the "Frenzy of the Visible."* Berkeley: University of California Press, 1989.

Williams, Patricia J. *The Alchemy of Race & Rights.* Cambridge: Harvard University Press, 1991.

Wong, Nellie. "When I Was Growing Up." In *This Bridge Called My Back,* edited by Cherrie Moraga and Gloria Anzaldua. New York: Kitchen Table Press, 1983.

Yamada, Mitsuye. "Asian Pacific American Women and Feminism." In *This Bridge Called My Back,* edited by Cherrie Moraga and Gloria Anzaldua. New York: Kitchen Table Press, 1983.

Part Three
SEXUALITY AND QUEER STUDIES

Introduction

Dorothy Fujita Rony

I recently asked a professor of Asian American literature for some advice about a poem for a wedding.[1] I wanted to find a poem written by an Asian American author that talked about love, commitment, and community. But, there was a catch. The poem was to be read by the father of the bride as part of the wedding ceremony. And, in deference to the unspoken rules between immigrants and their children in which certain topics are just not spoken about, particularly in public, the poem was not to make overt mention of sex. So, four of us sat there at the dining room table, all Asian American studies people, and tried unsuccessfully to think of an appropriate poem. In many respects, it was a silly exercise. For after all, if marriage celebrates the passage of two "children" into adulthood, did it really matter what other people thought about the poem's contents?

I reflected upon the contradictions of this story as I sat down to write the introduction to this anthology's section. Not all of us come from immigrant families, and not all of us would feel the same constraints of expression when faced with a ritual, inter-generational ceremony. But the story made me realize that topics of sexuality are regularly shrouded in particular forms of silence in the Asian American community. It is "understood" that you do not bring up the topic of sex in polite conversations without risking the disapprobation of community elders. We negotiate these kinds of issues on an everyday level, both in our private lives and in our professional careers.

These issues about silence are also applicable on a similar level to Asian American studies. In this regard, the 1993 Association for Asian American Studies conference was an historic event. Not only did we have the usual scattering of papers concerning sexuality throughout the conference, but we also deliberately positioned sexuality as a central topic in a conference "mega-session." This prominence of "sexuality" as a conference theme in 1993 heralded a new cultural moment. It indicated the arrival of a generation of Asian American studies people whose coming-of-age had been informed by the AIDS crisis, as well as by a greater "acceptance" of gay and lesbian issues. The relative youth of the participants in the sexuality mega-session was widely mentioned, as was the general absence of senior people. Again and again, I heard people comment about the lack of "out" senior professors, a visible reference to the difficulties of being gay, lesbian, bisexual, or transgender in our supposed "home" of Asian American studies. As a reflection of the "cutting edge" nature of this field of sexuality and Queer studies, the bulk of the contributors herein are graduate students, and only one professor is included among the authors.

The 1993 conference was, in addition, notable because of the organization of two Queer studies panels. The significance of these panels is referred to by the titling of this section "Sexuality and Queer Studies." Here, I want to emphasize that our intent as editors is not to conflate "sexuality" and "Queer studies," but to name them as two separate "sites." To place Queer studies papers solely within a "sexuality" context is to view the pieces in a one-dimensional way—they are about "sexuality" because they do not conform to a heterosexual norm. At present, "sexuality" is often used as a code word for gay and lesbian studies, in the same way that "gender" might signal women's issues while assuming the male experience as center, and "race" might be a reference to the experience of people of color while "whiteness" is left as an unmarked category. Queer studies, however, has a much broader scope than as a sexuality subtopic. As Eric Reyes writes in his essay concerning the definition of "queer," in this case the use of "queer" by the Asian Pacific group at the 1993 March on Washington:

> In using "Queer," the marchers stated a specific position of not only homosexual, which is referenced to heterosexual and binarily gender- coded, but transgressively sexual; we claim the right to choose our boundaries of expressing our sexual desire. "Queer" claims and defines a space to speak, act, and live through, about, and to.

Thus, Queer studies refers to a field with its own integrity.

Despite representing an advance in the discipline, this section is clearly less than complete. Additional papers could have included discussions about subjects like teenage pregnancy and global prostitourism. Yet another problem with this section as constituted is the perennial issue of Asian American studies: insufficient representation of all Asian Pacific groups. Although the marginalization of South Asians is discussed within Alice Hom's paper, South Asians are again little mentioned, as are Pacific Islanders. Bisexuals, transgenders, and heterosexual women are also not focused upon. Southeast Asians are represented in Martin Manalansan's discussion of Filipinos, but other Southeast Asian groups are under documented. One point to note, however, is that this section is truly interdisciplinary. The authors here write from the fields of urban planning, anthropology, history, literature, and American studies.

Both the successes and the problems of this section are a reflection of the fact that the configuration of these issues is relatively new to Asian American studies. This is not to say that "sexuality" has not been an important topic within the field, particularly in the areas of representation and work. But until the present time, these issues have primarily been couched through an overwhelmingly heterosexual framework. For example, in looking through the 1971 anthology *Roots: An Asian American Reader,* sexuality as presented in the "Identity" section included pieces about interracial dating, the relationships between Asian American men and women, and the impact of the Vietnam War on sexual images of Asian American women.

The essays in this anthology's section reflect their cultural times, and are implicitly and explicitly in dialogue with one another. Hence, rather than separating them into the two sections of "sexuality" and "Queer studies," the papers have been placed together as parts of one "converation."

First, Eric Reyes's piece "Asian Queer Spaces" not only sets the stage for the difficulties of posing sexuality as a category of analysis, especially within the context of Asian American studies, but also deliberately unsettles preconceptions about the possibility of "containing" sexuality. In his essay, Reyes's conception of "space" strives to preserve the dynamism and complexity of our multi-faceted identities. In Speaking about Asian Pacific Queer space, Reyes offers to us the problematic of naming oneself as an Asian Pacific Queer, where "Queer" signifies "an *idea(l)* of sex and desire" and "Asian Pacific" refers to "an *idea(l)* of place," Reyes asks:

> For Asian Pacific Queers then, the difficulties lie in how these ideals of place and sex generate contradictory spaces of absence: How are Asian Americans recognized in Queer contexts? How are Queers recognized in Asian American contexts?

By arguing for "the space in between" which recognizes multiple and often contradictory identities, Reyes thus challenges us to conceive of a culture in which all of the different parts of ourselves can be recognized, even as they continually change depending on the context. The "traveling citizen-ship" that he ultimately proposes would maintain the integrity of an individual's identity, but also allow for movement, change, and exploration.

In Mona Oikawa's poem "Exclusion\Inclusion," Oikawa articulates the difficulty of both claiming and gaining recognition for her multiple identities. Oikawa's essay "Locating Myself within Histories of Disloca-tion" is a powerful personal statement about the challenges of being posi-tioned, and positioning oneself, among many different identities in her work as a documenter of the Japanese Canadian internment experience, and as an Asian lesbian poet. Tokenization, "othering," and silencing are all part of her lived experience. She writes: "The tension between the lived realities of oppression and the threat of loss, on the one hand, and the internalization of this oppression, on the other, is something I continue to live with and negotiate in my work."

Jennifer Ting's essay, "Bachelor Society: Deviant Heterosexuality and Asian American Historiography," indicates new theories and methodolo-gies that are transforming Asian American studies, particularly cultural studies. Ting argues that historical writing about the pre-World War II experience of Chinese immigrants has conceptualized Chinese Americans within a deviant heterosexuality. She unveils the "common sense" of this notion through a close examination of two important Asian American stud-ies texts: Mary Coolidge's *Chinese Immigration* (1909) and Paul C. P. Siu's *The Chinese Laundryman: A Study in Social Isolation* (1953). As she ex-plains in her conclusion, "Accounts of the past shape our politics in power-ful ways; we historicize everything but sex at our peril."

Jeff Nunokawa's "Oscar Wilde in Japan: Aestheticism, Orientalism, and the Derealization of the Homosexual" and Martin F. Manalansan IV's "Dissecting Desire: Symbolic Domination and Strategies of Resistance among Filipino Gay Men in New York" explore the role of Orientalist discourse in the production of desire in very different ways. Nunokawa's piece offers Asian Americanists a comparative discussion about the pro-duction of desire by delving into Oscar Wilde's work. Nunokawa examines the expression of "light desire" in Wilde's *The Importance of Being Earnest* which "partakes of a late Victorian climate of manufactured and manipu-lable passion associated with Wilde in particular, and Aestheticism, in gen-eral." Nunokawa argues that this "desire-lite" is also shaped and produced by conceptions of Japan. As Nunokawa remarks about Wilde's piece "The Decay of Lying," " . . . his account, which begins by noticing the skill of Japanese artists, and ends by celebrating all of Japan as a work of art, locates the land of the rising sun as a site, more generally, for the process of aestheticization."

Manalansan's ethnographic discussion of Filipino gay men in New York examines how this community may "negotiate, contest, resist, and refigure stereotypical (Orientalized) representations of the body with their understanding and constructions of themselves as individuals and as a collective." Using Joseph Itiel's *Philippine Diary: A Gay Guide to the Philippines,* a "stereotypical 'Orientalized' gay narrative about Filipino gay men written by a Caucasian man," Manalansan exposes representations of Filipino gay men to provide a backdrop for life narratives of his informants. For example, Manalansan reports that the phrase *paglaruan ang mundo* or, "to play with the world," is often used by Filipino gay men to characterize strategies like cross-dressing, playing "scripts" in which they appropriate and exploit stereotypes, and the employment of "swardspeak," Filipino gay slang. Despite apparent acquiescence with stereotyped roles, the men may also be engaging in resistance, and subverting these stereotypes.

Alice Hom's piece provides analysis on "differences" within the Asian Pacific Lesbian Network, a group organized in 1988 after the 1987 March on Washington for Gay and Lesbian Rights. In her essay, Hom uses "differences" to mean "diverse ethnic and cultural backgrounds, class statuses, and regions." Specifically, Hom presents documentation from organizers and participants in the 1989 Asian Pacific Lesbian Network's national retreat, "Coming Together, Moving Forward," held in Santa Cruz, California. While this conference offered an important community space for Asian Pacific lesbians, power and privilege were also divisive forces. In particular, ethnic hierarchies emerged as a barrier to the formation of community. As a result, ten South Asian women protested their invisibility in the conference programs and materials, providing important constructive criticism about issues of equity within the organization.

Taken as a group, the studies in this section offer not only valuable documentation, but also new theoretical advances for Asian American studies. While tentative and exploratory, they reflect positive growth within the discipline, particularly in the arena of Queer studies. I hope that readers will understand that the problems and compromises of the organization of this section are part of the "growing pains" of the field. In the coming years, we have much to look forward to—and much work to do—in not only the increasingly sophisticated ways our field approaches these topics, but also in how we may be more inclusive as a discipline. As suggested by Hom's work on the Asian Pacific Lesbian Network, confronting our "differences" will be a constant and often painful struggle for the Association for Asian American Studies. But it will be an absolutely necessary task if we are to adhere to the founding ideals of the civil rights movement, in which this Association was formed. In conclusion, I would like to quote at length from Mona Oikawa's piece, which I think, provides a fitting and eloquent challenge for all of us, and gives us sustenance for the task we have ahead:

> How will we speak of the Association for Asian American Studies conference of 1993? Perhaps these conferences and workshops we participate in can never reflect our work and ourselves in our wholeness and complexities. But as resisting thinkers and writers, maybe we can create spaces that support our different sites of home, and where all of us can be interacting subjects in our resistant and relational histories.
>
> I would like our academic institutions and our political movements to be connected to each other, and to be places where we can locate our sites of difference and learn from them, bringing us to common sites of struggle. I believe, this work may always entail people who live in sites of resistance sharing their insight with those in sites of privilege. But I would hope that it will also result in work where we interrogate economic divisions on an individual and global scale, where white people interrogate the construction of whiteness, where heterosexuals interrogate the construction of heterosexuality, where men interrogate the construction of masculinity, and where people of color interrogate our relationships to each other in our varying sites of commonality, difference, and privilege.

Note

1. Although all mistakes are my own, many people have helped me to edit this section. For their advice and counsel, special thanks are due to the following individuals: Martin Manalansan, Eric Reyes, Alice Hom, Norma Timbang, Gary Okihiro, and Tom Fujita Rony.

Asian Pacific Queer Space

Eric Estuar Reyes

The effect of mass migrations has been the creation of radically new types of human beings: people who root themselves in ideas rather than places, in memories as much as in material things . . .

In using this quote from Salman Rushdie's *Imaginary Homelands*, the editors of the gay Asian and Pacific Islander male publication, *Lavender Godzilla*, suggest a shift in how we define our relationship with a place.[1] This shift references our movement as cultures and communities that have traveled, been dislocated and/or displaced by ourselves (and others). "What is our relationship to this place, America?" is a question that forms a stream of thought in Asian American Studies. Indeed, our efforts to root ourselves to physical sites, to locate and dislocate identities in representations (literary or otherwise), or to construct some kind of class indicators are different strategies for defining "community" and "culture." We, as individuals with Asian and Pacific Islander heritages, have sought to create our spaces here through remembering and documenting our journeys to a place.

In this discussion, I would like to examine a dimension of these journeys for and from the position of Asian and Pacific Islanders who construct their sexual identity as homosexual, lesbian, gays, bisexual, transgender, or Queer. As academics and members of multiple communities, we have focused on how our places and placemaking relate to one another.[2] However, what of "the spaces in between"? In constructing places, whether through reclaiming memory or taking actual sites physically, what space do we use to reclaim and take those places? This is "the space in between" of examining our individual and social processes of "rooting ourselves." There are dimensions to this process which I believe can provide us with a different viewing of the social constructions of multiple identities based on ethnicity and sexuality. In doing so, perhaps we can begin to see that the spaces in between are not places to take or reclaim, but spaces in which, as multiply marginalized and differently rooted human beings, we can meet for a moment outside our borders.

(in)Visible Spaces

> Every language is located in space. Every discourse says something about a space (places or sets of places); and every discourse is emitted from a space. Distinctions must be drawn between discourse *in* space, discourse *about* space, and the discourses *of* space (Lefebvre 1991:132).[3]

Many writers use "space" to refer to a place, a location, a time, an illusion, or as a metaphor.[4] "Space" is very much like "community" and "culture." These words themselves mean so much that they sometimes mean nothing, and in so doing encompass everything. I do not presume to discuss everything (or nothing). Rather, I would like to suggest a movement toward "someplace." In using "space," I am moving away from the universalized tendency of using physical place (as a mapped location), physical site, and material inventory as the characteristics of establishing presence and territory. When I say "space," I mean more than "over there, not here" or "a place with the following x, y, and z characteristics existing in such and such quantities." In using "space," I also include the tension of simultaneous multiple positionalities. Within this tension are different dimensions of, from, and about the mental spaces of experience and perception and, importantly, the social spaces of interaction. Thus, space encompasses more than the territoriality of physical ownership or control, but includes other dimensions that are transitory, contextual, and simultaneous. An unfortunate example is how the act of driving through West Hollywood shouting "all fags die!" changes that place through the space of that homophobic intervention.[5] Or, consider a gay bar in Chinatown. Is Chinatown then an "Asian Queer Space"?[6] Thus, the relationship between space and place is often demonstrated by an intervention of some kind such as a physical site, verbal incident, or socially disruptive event. These interventions create that space in between which is often sensed as the "not here, or there" feeling.

The language of physical mapping is about space. Mapping generates a representation of *visible* viewpoints. The identification of space as Asian, Pacific Islander, Queer, Gay, or Lesbian cannot be revealed as easily as showing a dot density map of location.[7] These dot density mappings visually mask the dynamic spatial dimensions of place-making and destruction by individuals and groups that happen every day in the city. This analysis of place geography leads to a materialist question of "how many dots does it take to make it a Place?" One, ten, or one hundred? Quantity is not the point but how that one, ten, or one hundred generates interaction or isolation, visible or not. We should ask not only who is at the table or how many, but who is not even invited.

Yes, the myth of universal heterosexuality is shattered everyday in places like West Hollywood, the Castro District, and other "gay places." And similarly, Manila Towns, Chinatowns, and Little Saigons, and Little Tokyos disrupt the myth of a singular American cultural landscape. Yet within these gay, Asian, and other places, there are sites of sexisms, racisms, ageisms, looksisms, AIDSphobias, dragphobias, and classisms that interact with larger contexts that reinforce or even create the isolation or concentration of these "isms."[8] The ordering of space on one scale produces and perpetuates spatial distinctions for what is and what is not "appropriate" behavior, attitude, and existence on many different scales.[9]

The shattering of one myth does not erase the mythology of the landscape. By becoming visible, place can be established, but this physical place, discursively or physically ghettoized through an academic discipline or neighborhood, is not enough. For as marginalized individuals whether on the basis of ethnicity or sexuality (or otherwise), we understand how we can be here in this place, but not here in this space.

Asian Queer: Queer Asian—Closets of Scale

Spatializing through individual and collective acts, perceptions, productions, and purchase, we constitute and reconstitute our living realities as our daily life experiences. Within these living realities, we manipulate selectively our Queer and Asian Pacific viewpoints. Queer identity has been constructed through the current narratives of everyday and discursive actions as based on a primary visibility. This strategy for establishing presence is in response to the dominating invisibility of a presumed universal heterosexuality. So, one strategy to acknowledge that one is not heterosexual is to be vocal, visible, and to be out. Queer.

"Coming out of the closet" in our Asian and Pacific Islander contexts, in the white male-dominated gay culture, or somewhere in between, are the choices for confronting visible sexual orderings of place. This degree of visible sexual identity marks the boundaries of our private closets of desire. Yet, what are the boundaries of these places? In claiming a "public closet" in coming out and superimposing an imposed private sexuality onto the "Public," the distinction between public and private individual space is destroyed. On another scale, at the 1993 March on Washington, one of the slogans flashed on the large multimedia boards was, "We are the public." Yet, I ask, "Which one?"[10] In stating a universal "we" with a singular "public," the subtext displays the assumption that there is a "one unified public." Thus, what exactly does a demonstration through "public space" accomplish when, as people of color, we are denied the full recognition of being part of "that public" that this government and society supposedly reflects? What space are we, as Queers of all color, manipulating when we march through our various gay ghettoes which are not colored? What space are we subjected to when we arrive home for the wedding banquets of cousins and siblings? What spaces do we generate when we produce discursive explorations into the meaning of sex and sexuality in our many Asian and Pacific Islander communities? How can we read these "texts" of space? How did the March on Washington as a Queer intervention into the national "democratic" and patriarchal heterosexual space of Washington, D.C. articulate our relationship, as Asian Pacific Queers, to this "national space"? The "we" seems to be someone else out there.

"Asian/Pacific, Queer 'n Proud" proclaimed the banner for the Asian Pacific-identified contingent at the March on Washington.[11] In using "Queer," the marchers stated a specific position of not only homosexual, which is referenced to heterosexual and binarily gender-coded, but transgressively sexual; we claim the right to choose our boundaries of expressing our sexual desire.[12] "Queer" claims and defines a space to speak, act, and live through, about, and to. However, in this articulation "Queer" masks several other orderings of space. Just as physical mappings veil social and mental orderings of space, socially constructed signifiers often envelop physical orderings such as race, class, and gender. For example, the issue of class in Queer studies has seen very little attention while representation studies such as literary theory and film studies form a core of Queer intellectualization. In using "Queer" as a signifier of space, we reference an idea(l) of sex and desire that appropriates a historically stigmatized identifier and situate ourselves in the present. We center our positionality not as a margin to reify or a new center (or panopticon) to displace another center.[13] Rather, we establish "Queer" as another positioning of human difference amid a sexual landscape of experience and action, not a tightrope with heterosexual and homosexual endpoints. Desire has more than two dimensions.

The many terms imbedded in "Asian American" such as Asian, Pacific Islander, Asian Pacific, East Asian, or South Asian do not refer to the same processes as the Queer construction. In using "Asian American," we reference an idea(l) of place—a mentally perceived, imagined, and created space with possible social and physical projections in our daily lives. "Asian American" references a geographical location—"a continent over there, over here." For Asian Pacific Queers then, the difficulties lie in how these ideals of place and sex generate contradictory spaces of absence: How are Asian Americans recognized in Queer contexts? How are Queers recognized in Asian American contexts? The matters of scale and simultaneous self-replication of hegemonic interventions cannot be ignored. In fighting for civil rights based on our experiences as Queers and/or Asian Americans, we have had to choose a movement and a context.[14] Within space there is always a place, but within places there are not always spaces. In other words, in establishing sites of intervention, are we not, all of us, creating borders?

Again, I return to the 1993 March on Washington as a site that can be called "Queer." The contingencies were organized both by indices of action and location. Yet, as a Queer Filipino graduate student from California, should I march with the "Asians"? "California"? Or "Students"? Our spaces of intervention even within our interventions are ordered by these and other specific spatial indices. Is my intervention among these hundreds of thousands of lesbians, gay men, bisexuals, Queers, supporters, and spectators (both friendly and not), more significant as an identified Californian, student, or Asian/Pacific? Scale matters and I marched with the other Asians and Pacific Islanders. Many of us did and many of us did not. Closets are not the same in all places.

Mapping other Spaces

Queer spaces are not just spaces for homosex. Asian spaces are not "dim sum palaces." Asian Queer Spaces are not "rice bars."[15] They are the spaces of otherness that allow us to confront and reject the alienation and division by forces that manipulate our everyday spaces. These are the forces that create the impossible choice between our many and one selves. To be Queer-identified forces us to confront the privileged white gay male position of power. To be Asian-identified is to confront the power of a racist society. For Asian Queers this produces the contradiction of choosing space over place. To claim Queer is to de-locate oneself from the place and rootedness of home, family, and community to the idealized space of a "Queer community." Creating memory, ideas, and space, we have had to learn the process of locating and dislocating not the physical place of continent but the spatial sites of desire.

Where is this Asian Pacific Queer Space? In the course of completing my M.A. thesis in urban planning, I facilitated several discussions with Queers of various ethnicities in which I asked individuals about their daily spaces, as Queers, Asians, people of color, and as residents of Los Angeles. I also asked them to draw these spaces. In one of these conversations about Queer spaces, I asked JT, a twenty-four-year-old Pilipino[16] Chinese gay male, to draw his living spaces. JT had drawn an image of his Queer space as a figure in Buddha-esque repose with eyes, nose, mouth, forehead, heart, crotch, hands, and feet in red while he exclaimed,

> You can't draw one! Geographically it's so flowing in Los Angeles. All of LA, at all times, queer is something that's in here [pointing at himself] not out there. For example a straight bar can easily become a queer space. Making tangible something that isn't, it isn't possible. It's everywhere. Trying to represent it is immediately inaccurate. It's difficult and dangerous because the white queer establishment and bureaucracy will always try to draw it and it is West Hollywood and ghettoize it. This fills the order of the het[17] counterpart, to ghettoize, because once you ghettoize it is easy to put them in place. Space in Los Angeles. Safe spaces, no, I got it here. Safe space in here in red. Everything you choose to see, if you use your eyes, heart and mind. You really have to love yourself. If you do, then every place is a safe space. There are no guarantees. Physical safety itself is an illusion. It's in your hands, feet, and genitals whether you decide to fuck or not to.

JT had shifted the problematic from a place-based spatiality to one that seeks to locate a position that is based on the spaces generated by individuals and the spaces in between. He inferred something altogether different: spaces travel and travelers move spaces.

In revealing this dimension, I think we can begin to see how Queer, in acting as a spatial intervention, assumes it/we intervene into a "universal space" of heterosexism, racism, and other orderings of space. However, Asian Americans, and perhaps any Person of Color have always resisted other interventions, namely the eurocentric interventions of colonization. These interventions are resisted on a different scale figuratively, literally, and most definitely spatially. In our daily migrations, we manipulate our rootedness to place in order to survive. This is citizenship. To fulfill our desires we instead generate rootedness to the ideals of spaces of sexuality, ethnicity, and perhaps other ideals of difference. This is how we attach meaning to our existence. Across many scales of collective or individual boundaries, I believe that we need sites and sitings, but perhaps for Asian Queers, we are concerned more with how we shift these borders as we travel through the webs of rootedness to place.

Site Seeing

Where is Asian Pacific space? Where is Queer space? What is an academic conference but the destination of a mass migration of people rooted to ideas, memories, and the realm of witnessing possibilities past, present, and future? Underlying our efforts as "witnesses" is our endeavor to "uncover" the absence of past memories, fill them with our own, and in so doing redefine "the public" to include "us." Considering this discussion of visibilities and closets of scale, the question now arises of how are we creating or recreating "domains of citizenship"? The production of place through political, economic, or social ordering is critically related to the production of social, mental, and other spaces of meaning. "American democracy" is rooted in its emphasis on the belief of universal access to place whether through heritage or ownership. Yet, as we begin to understand that for many of us, the significance of place is shifting, what is a citizenship based on the spaces in between?

As individuals subject and subjected to spatial orderings based on heterosexisms, homophobias, racisms, and other discriminations, we travel certain pathways. Do we need these mappings of space, or do we need more space? This seems to be the next critical step in our endeavor to establish our relationship with our place here whether it is our Asian Pacific, Asian Pacific Queer, Queer, or other communities. For Asian Pacific Queers, I think we are exploring and creating traveling identities and essentials. We are generating nations, ghettos, and neighborhoods of varying visibility and scale. Perhaps for us, we should now examine the notion of a "traveling citizenship" based on space. In this effort, perhaps we can begin to map the spaces in between not only Asian Pacific contexts and Queer contexts, but other similarly constructed domains. We can take the next step beyond borders and can go to other spaces, to speak, generate, and listen for the answers to the question: "What is our relationship to place when our spaces move?"

Notes

1. *Lavender Godzilla*, Summer 1992. Filled with prose, poetry, and other visual texts, this is a 'zine published and produced by a group of gay Asian men in San Francisco affiliated with the Gay Asian Pacific Alliance. This issue was devoted to examining "home" and how we create it.
2. By multiple communities, I am referencing not only ethnically, place-based, or academic/non-academic communities. I suggest that we have multiple agendas. For ex-

ample, even if we prioritize one identity over another, heterosexual men always, consciously or not, are subject to and benefit from an institutionalized patriarchal and heterosexist system.

3. I have drawn the majority of my thoughts on spatiality from Lefebvre (1991).

4. For examples of spatial analyses see: Cooper Marcus (1986); Downs and Stea (1973); Jackson (1989); Sack (1980); Tuan (1977).

5. West Hollywood is similar to other well-known concentrations of gay men (and to some extent lesbians and bisexuals) such as the Castro District in San Francisco. Recently, the numerical dominance of white gay men has been diminishing somewhat as more African American, Asian and Pacific Islander (API), Latino, and other men of color seem to be coming to West Hollywood. Whether this is due to the advent of some raised consciousness or openness, increasing economic access, better marketing by West Hollywood businesses, or some other factor are questions for future research.

6. As far as I know, there are no gay bars in Los Angeles' Chinatown. However, there is a gay bar in an old Japanese restaurant in Hollywood which is often frequented by Asian men here on business trips.

7. In my M.A. thesis, "Queer Spaces," I identified 1,138 sites of advertised locations from a variety of Queer media sources, including newspapers, magazines, and "yellow pages." These mappings revealed certain concentrations of locations that advertise to Queer populations of Los Angeles County. Yet, are these Queer neighborhoods, and are they any different from neighborhoods of ethnic segregation? What space is being manipulated here? Are concentrations of locations identified by ethnic or Queer association subject to the same process of economic production of space such as urbanization processes that are subject to societal and institutional patriarchy, racism, sexism, and so forth. Just as specific ethnic yellow pages and newspapers are distributed selectively, the sources that I used for these Queer mappings are circulated carefully. This type of mapping of place reveals a tension between the economic and social production of space.

8. Looksisms refers to the ordering of space by some aesthetic hierarchy. For example, in American gay male culture, this can be seen in the number of pictures of blond, blue-eyed, muscle-bound, well-proportioned, tall, and well-off men there are in gay media as opposed to the reality of the demographics of the gay male population. A heterosexual counter-example can be easily drawn from the reader's own experiences.

9. For a discussion on differing scales of "location," see Probyn (1990).

10. In the last weekend of April 1993, hundreds of thousands of individuals converged on Washington, D.C. to rally for lesbian, gay, bisexual, transgender rights.

11. The various individuals and groups of API Queers who attended the March on Washington marched together under this banner as one of the contingents. The banner was one of many others that displayed other regional API gay male, lesbian, and bisexual groups.

12. The use of "Queer" is not without controversy. Many APIs consider "Queer" to be in reference to the mainstream (read: white gay male) movement, and counter to APIs interests as part of a people of color gay/lesbian/bisexual movement.

13. For a discussion on marginality as a site of resistance, see hooks (1990). In essays on sites of resistance, such as "Homeplace: A Site of Resistance" and "Choosing the Margin as a Space of Radical Openness," she discusses how the basis and destination of social action should move from eurocentric patriarchal heterosexist-focused movement to one that seeks "our" space on the margins of the so-called center. My caution is that we forget that there are many margins to "a center." In prioritizing our margin as our center, we should be careful not to infringe on other margins as other people seek their space.

14. For a discussion of the "queer movement," see Duggan (1992), and for a discussion of radical democratic movement, see Winant (1990).
15. A "rice bar" is a bar in which the patrons are predominantly API and with "rice queens" of various ethnicities. A "rice queen" is an individual who prefers Asian or Pacific Islander men as partners. The terms "rice bar" and "rice queen" are alternatively used descriptively or derogatorily to describe explicit and implicit racist dimensions of sexual relationships. Or as Ming Ma states: "It's where men are 'sushi' or 'spring rolls' or 'chicken adobo,' the sexual equivalent of a Third World restaurant adventure, where the dynasty of Orientalism is in full power and the contributions of cultures living in civilization for thousands of years are reduced to erotic tricks with strings of pearls." See Reyes (1990).
16. These discussions were part of my M.A. thesis. I had asked each participant to self-identify using their own terms. JT prefers to use Pilipino with a "P."
17. "Het" refers to heterosexuals.

References

Cooper Marcus, Clare. *Home-as-Haven, Home-as-Trap: Explorations in the Experience of Dwelling.* Proceedings from the 74th Annual Meeting of the Association of Collegiate Schools of Architecture, 1986—The Spirit of Home.

Downs, Roger and David Stea. *Image and Environment, Cognitive Mapping and Spatial Behavior.* Chicago: Aldine Publishing Company, 1973.

Duggan, Lisa. "Making It Perfectly Queer." *Socialist Review* 22 (January-March, 1992):11-32.

hooks, bell. *YEARNING: race, gender, and cultural politics.* Boston: South End Press, 1990.

Jackson, Peter. *Maps of Meaning, An Introduction to Cultural Geography.* London: Unwin Hyman, 1989.

Lavender Godzilla. The Homelands Issue. Edited by Pablo Bautista, et al. San Francisco: Gay Asian Pacific Alliance (GAPA), Summer 1992.

Lefebvre, Henri. *The Production of Space.* Translated by Donald Nicholson-Smith. Oxford: Basil Blackwell, 1991.

Probyn, Elspeth. "Travels in the Postmodern, Making Sense of the Local." In *Feminism/Postmodernism,* edited by Linda J. Nicholson. New York : Routledge, 1990.

Reyes, Eric Esuar. "Queer Spaces, The Spaces of Lesbians and Gay Men of Color in Los Angeles." Master's thesis, University of California, Los Angeles, 1993.

Reyes, Nina. "Common Ground, Asians and Pacific Islanders Look for Unity in a Queer World." *Outweek,* 22 May 1990, 32-37.

Sack, Robert David. *Conceptions of Space in Social Thought, A Geographical Perspective.* Minneapolis: University of Minneapolis Press, 1980.

Winant, Howard. "Postmodern Racial Politics: Difference and Inequality." *Socialist Review* 20 (January-March 1990): 121-47.

Tuan Yi-fu. *Space and Place, The Perspective of Experience.* Minneapolis: University of Minnesota Press, 1977.

Exclusion\Inclusion

Mona Oikawa

I don't know any Asian lesbian writers . . .
One Asian lesbian in this anthology,
in this course curriculum meets our quota,
states the publisher, editor, teacher, academic . . .
           I read out lines of poetry, prose:
           Word pictures spun soft, angry, proud,
           make me imagine countries where women lie
           with each other, their skin golden and brown
           and mixtures of all our womenly colours.
           Lines penned by twenty-five Asian lesbian
           sisters, published in fourteen different
           sources.[1]
           Search and you will find them.

I didn't know Japanese Canadians were interned in Canada, says my
new Sansei American friend.
           22,000 Japanese Canadians were interned
           between the years 1942 to 1949, I answer.[2]
           Joy Kogawa, author of *Obasan*,[3] was in the
           same camp as my mother. Two girl children
           waiting to go home. Sisters and brothers
           north of the U.S. border. How much stronger
           we would be to know each other's pain and
           laughter and survival.

Why aren't you doing a thesis on Asian lesbians? People already know about the internment.

> I need to hear the stories of Japanese
> Canadian women, lesbian, bisexual, and
> straight, interned during WWII. I want to
> see how they lived how they loved how they
> felt. This history is one root of women-
> loving in me.

I'm glad I'm working with a heterosexual feminist scholar, not with a lesbian. You know, lesbians don't have normal family lives, my Nikkei elder tells me. I want to write Nikkei women's history. They have been so excluded.

> Whose histories are you writing? What about
> our Nisei sister who was interned, as you
> were, during the war? Her women-loving helps
> to heal her scars. What about me, Sansei
> daughter, who loves you as my elder. But
> must I hide my women-living ways to be loved
> by you, to be included in your history? . . .
> You will always be a part of mine.

Exclusion/Inclusion.
Disentangle these lines of geography and history.
Redefine borders between us.
Different and alike,
tell our histories as one.

Notes

1. I am referring to a talk I gave on the "Identity, Visibility, Activism: Asian/American Writers" panel at the OutWrite 92 Conference in which I read a compilation poem of work by Asian lesbian writers. Writer Tamai Kobayashi has told me she has compiled a list of forty-five published Asian lesbian writers. See also, Karin Aguilar-San Juan. "Landmarks in Literature by Asian American Lesbians." *Signs* 18:4 (Summer 1993): 936-943.
2. For the historical literature on Japanese Canadians and the internment, see, for example, Ken Adachi. *The Enemy That Never Was.* Toronto: McClelland and Stewart, 1976; and Ann Gomer Sunahara. *The Politics of Racism.* Toronto: James Lorimer, 1981.
3. Joy Kogawa. *Obasan.* Markham, Ontario: Penguin, 1981. For historical accuracy, it is important to note that Joy Kogawa is writing about a Japanese Canadian internment experience given some writers' practice of describing her as "American." See, for example, Shirley Geok-Lin Lim. "Japanese American Women's Life Stories: Maternality in Monica Sone's *Nisei Daughter* and Joy Kogawa's *Obasan.*" *Feminist Studies* 2 (Summer 1990): 288-312. Also, Ruth Yu Hsaio. "A Practical Guide to Teaching Asian-American Literature." *Radical Teacher* 41 (Spring 1992): 22. For a commentary on this American appropriation of Kogawa, see, Ruth Roach Pierson. "International Trends in Women's History and Feminism: Colonization and Canadian Women's History." *Journal of Women's History* 4:2 (Fall 1992): 145.

Locating Myself within Histories of Dislocation[1]

Mona Oikawa

In this essay, I will explore questions of exclusion/inclusion and the spaces in between. I would like to raise several questions: "How do our various and interconnected identities as Asian North Americans get taken up, and how do we take them up in the many sites in which we do work, including the site of the academy?" "What parts of ourselves, if any, are being silenced or are we silencing in our intellectual activities?" "And how do we engage in truly interactive work in the academy where specialization, even in disciplines resulting from critical pedagogies,[2] may isolate us from each other and distance us from political communities in which many of us have worked and developed our theoretical perspectives on oppression?"

In a world divided by economic and social hierarchies, organizing from our knowledge of oppression is a political necessity. This entails our active naming of sites of oppression such as gender, race, class, sexuality, and ability. It is the representation of these categories, and how they are variously construed in my work and my public presentation of myself, that I would like to connect with your experiences as writers and documenters of history and culture.

From what I have seen in my work as a writer, student, and member of different political communities, identities become fragmented and marginalized in settings when they are treated as minority, exotic, unique, even perverse. This is done through processes that either render them invisible or emphasize them as larger than life, where only part (or parts) of us are called upon to be seen or to speak.[3] This results in the extremes of not talking about certain parts of our analytical frameworks, like not addressing heterosexism and homophobia in the Japanese Canadian community. Or it is manifested in the expectation that a lesbian of color in a women's studies course should "spill her guts" and educate women through an all-inclusive analysis of gender, race, class, and sexuality while some women, including some professors, talk about gender alone, isolating issues in what are often still racial and class biased feminist discourses.

One of the many examples of this contradictory positioning of visibility/invisibility occurred for me when I spoke at a lesbian and gay studies workshop in Toronto. I had agreed to talk about how I use history in my work as a creative writer.

When I arrived at the workshop, I realized that I was the only lesbian of color to be speaking. I raised this observation with the audience. What ensued was a defensive response from some of the organizers of how "so and so" had been asked and had declined. Two white gay men then proceeded to describe their work on gay men of color. I became conscious that once again as a "lesbian of color," I was introducing race into the discourse of yet another meeting. Although I could have chosen not to articulate this observation, my very presence at the workshop and my presentation on writing as a Japanese Canadian lesbian were racialized positions within a context where white people spoke from non-problematized positions as lesbians and gay men, whose race was not considered consequential nor made explicit in their work.

My response to the audience was that while I did not expect or even necessarily want gay and lesbian white people to construct the histories of gay and lesbian people of color, it would be nice for once to feel that the burden of talking about racism was not being placed upon me or any person of color. I challenged them with the thought that maybe it was time for white people to begin to analyze how they become constructed as White.

I also realized during this panel discussion how we can become fragmented in the eyes of our audiences and to ourselves when we adhere to the discourses proposed to us, talking about parts of ourselves at the exclusion of the others. This fragmentation is already inherent in processes whereby we are asked to speak or write in public places in order to meet the organizer's or publisher's specific identity or identities criteria.

At this same workshop, I talked about how I was committed to documenting different forms of Asian lesbian political organizing through my creative writing, but when I began to discuss my academic research, which is on the internment of Japanese Canadian women during World War II, I was asked by a white lesbian in the audience to talk about Japanese Canadian lesbians: Had I found any? She elaborated upon her question by saying she was unable to find any "older" Asian lesbians to interview for her research.

Although finding elder Japanese Canadian lesbians is a compelling personal, political, and academic project for me, I felt discomfort in sharing my sources with someone who seemed so incredulous as to their existence. I answered her question by saying my research was at a preliminary stage, all the while thinking that the audience did not want to hear about the internment experience of Japanese Canadians, but just about "lesbians and gay men." While I am hoping to learn more about the historical construction of sexuality, including same sex practices among Nikkei North Americans interned during World War II, I know that much of my knowledge and analysis of oppression comes from my learning about the internment of all Japanese Canadians. This leads me to ask the question: "Is queer history, and more generally, queer studies, only about queers?"

I believe the answer to this question is "no." As Asian lesbian and gay peoples, our knowledge of our histories is informed by our lived experiences of difference—of sexuality, but also of race, class, gender, and disability. These are sites of difference that we share with people of diverse sexual identities.

Some of the questions raised in my participation at this gay and lesbian workshop have haunted me as I considered speaking at this Asian American Studies conference. "How will the 'out' presences of Asian lesbians and gay men disrupt and inform the discourses at this conference?" I wondered. Will sexuality be put on the agenda because lesbians and gay men identify ourselves in our written and spoken texts? We do it and say with whom we do it, and theorize the political necessity of saying it within a context where heterosexuality, even though never explicitly articulated, is part of a system of dominance. Our presence as Asian lesbian and gay academics and creative workers in this setting is challenging the dominant paradigm of heterosexuality in Asian North American intellectual history.

While I can think of numerous occasions where I have felt tokenized by individuals' "othering"[4] practices—like when a straight Canadian feminist author recently asked me to be on a panel because she wanted a "lesbian of color who writes about sex" to finish her complement of writers, while at the same time admitting she had never read any of my work—I want to look at my own self-silencing practices in sites that are of crucial social, political, and emotional importance to me.

I participated in perpetuating the silence on sexuality in Japanese Canadian history when I presented a paper at the HomeComing 1992 Conference in Vancouver.[5] On a panel entitled, "Japanese Canadian Women's Experience," I talked about historical work that I had completed in 1986 for my M.A. thesis, which examines government policy as it was applied to the forced resettlement of Japanese Canadians to southern Ontario (Oikawa 1986).

The panel was the only "women's panel" in the conference proceedings, thus emphasizing the gender specificity of the work to be presented.[6] Although I was the only panelist to state I was a feminist and that I used a feminist approach in my work, I did not come out as a lesbian. More importantly, my paper, and those of my co-presenters, did not in any way problematize sexuality. Although there is a general lack of discussion or acknowledgment of any kind of sexuality in the Japanese Canadian historical literature, the dominant discourse of heterosexuality, of the past and of the present, was left unchallenged in that conference room.

I do feel it is also important to recognize some of the many acts of resistance at the HomeComing conference. The gathering together of people who had fifty years earlier been forced from their homes into camps and then dispersed across Canada, and their speaking about their experiences, were courageous and inspiring moments to witness. The existence of a panel of Nikkei women doing historical work on women, in the face of histories dominated by the telling of men's activities, was a challenge to male historical hegemony. And lastly, it also must be noted that a group of Japanese Canadian lesbians formed a caucus and met by the indoor pool, demonstrating lesbian resistant activism in a context filled with references to familial ties, and the real presence of members of our families and extended families.

This scenario, however, underlines a tension I feel as an Asian lesbian writer/scholar who wants to document my various histories, yet also fears losing one of my cultural and political communities because some members do not accept other sites of home in my life—in this case, the lesbian site. Despite my wanting to own up to my decision to selectively present myself, I must also recognize that I am doing this in a world where there are always serious consequences for challenging relations of power. But, in re-thinking my own participation in these locations, I am trying to revision my own work and how I present it to different audiences. The tension between the lived realities of oppression and the threat of loss, on the one hand, and the internalization of this oppression, on the other, is something I continue to live with and negotiate in my work.

Ironically, or perhaps fittingly, in Vancouver during the week following the conference, I participated in one of the first public Asian lesbian readings in Canada.[7] My creative writing is a site where I choose to write about loving women, including sexual expressions of this love. And in this work, I often feel the least fragmented, allowing myself, more and more, to discover and be all of who I am.

How will we speak of the Association for Asian American Studies conference of 1993? Perhaps these conferences and workshops we participate in can never reflect our work and ourselves in our wholeness and complexities. But as resisting thinkers and writers, maybe we can create spaces that support our different sites of home, and where all of us can be interacting subjects in our resistant and relational histories.

I would like our academic institutions and our political movements to be connected to each other and to be places where we can locate our sites of difference and learn from them, bringing us to common sites of struggle. I believe, this work may always entail people who live in sites of resistance sharing their insight with those in sites of privilege. But I would hope that it will also result in work where we interrogate economic divisions on an individual and global scale, where white people interrogate the construction of whiteness, where heterosexuals interrogate the construction of heterosexuality, where men interrogate the construction of masculinity, and where people of color interrogate our relationships to each other in our varying sites of commonality, difference, and privilege.

Notes

1. I would like to thank Kari Dehli and Ann Decter for their comments and discussions related to this paper.
2. Here I am referring to disciplines such as feminist studies, ethnic studies, and gay and lesbian studies.
3. In referring to the common practice of inviting one person of color to speak on panels as tokenization, Barbara Smith states: "Tokenizing is a form of silencing too because . . . it is not possible to share the range of her or his creativity when she or he is objectified and isolated" (1990:98).
4. I am using the term "othering" to denote practices that result in objectifying people who do not share various sites of dominance. For work that exposes these practices, see, for example, Chow (1989); and Bhabha (1983).
5. The HomeComing 1992 Conference was held on 9-11 October to commemorate the fiftieth anniversary of the internment of Japanese Canadians and was attended by more than 700 people.
6. Although this panel was the only one specifying "women" in its title, women did participate actively in the organization of the conference and on most of the panels.
7. "Asian Lesbian Writers: An Evening of Readings" took place on 17 October 1992 at Octopus Books in Vancouver, Canada.

References

Bhabha, Homi K. "The Other Question . . . " *Screen* 24:6 (November-December 1983): 18-36.

Chow, Rey. "'It's you, and not me.'" In *Coming to Terms: Feminism, Theory, Politics,* edited by Elizabeth Weed. New York: Routledge, 1989.

Oikawa, Mona. "'Driven to Scatter Far and Wide': The Forced Resettlement of Japanese Canadians to Southern Ontario, 1944-1949." Master's thesis, University of Toronto, 1986.

Smith, Barbara. "The NEA Is the Least of It." *The American Voice* 21 (Winter 1990).

Bachelor Society: Deviant Heterosexuality and Asian American Historiography

Jennifer Ting

In the world according to Asian American studies, families are separated or reunited by migration (when they do not immigrate together); families and systems of kinship organize labor, enclave businesses, and loan opportunities; families reproduce Asian America by passing on names, histories, and recipes: by socializing us.[1] Asian American studies organizes theories, histories, and imaginative representations around the idea of family.[2] Since "family" is always (but not exclusively) about gender and sexuality, the Asian American studies discourse on family is also a discourse on sexuality. How then can we attend to what Asian American studies has been saying about sexuality?

Part of my project here is to establish "sexuality" as a category for analysis rather than as an attribute (to use Judith Butler's term). In other words, I want to go beyond questions of the sexualities with which Asian American studies invests its subjects, because such a model relies on a subjectivity constituted beyond, or prior to, sexuality (Butler 1990). I am more interested in the kinds of sexualities through which Asian American studies constructs its subjects. By moving sexuality to the conceptual center, I want not only to render visible the narratives about sexuality already present in Asian American studies, but also to take the category of sexuality as enabling certain kinds of analysis for questions of long-standing importance in the field. I approach the history texts discussed as a kind of writing, a kind of representation engaged in the construction and dissemination of narratives and meanings, rather than as competing accounts of (past) reality. I am arguing that this writing constructs pre–World War II Chinese immigrants in terms of a specific kind of heterosexuality, which I locate within the critical category of "deviance."

This essay has three sections. The first section discusses the under-theorized relations between the sojourner mentality and the bachelor society. The importance and complexity of these relations becomes clear in the second section, which examines the bachelor society trope in two historiographically important texts. This section emphasizes the importance of sexuality in the conceptualization of "the family" in the writing on the bachelor society. The final section introduces the notion of deviance in order to enable a critical discussion of the continued reproduction in Asian American history writing of the bachelor society trope.

The complex historiographic relationship between the figures of the sojourner and the bachelor should be taken up as a research question in its own right. I will simply point out the interdependence of the two: Asian American history cannot discuss one without reference to the other. *The Dictionary of Asian American History* (1986) illustrates this point, repro-ducing the standard use of the bachelor society in historical narratives on early Chinese immigrants. These lines from the *Dictionary*'s description of early Chinese American social organization enact a series of juxtapositions which render the sojourner and the bachelor almost interchangeable: "In America the Chinese lived in an abnormal society full of young males—wandering sojourners. . . . The Chinese population was almost totally tran-sient, and there was a great scarcity of females" (Tsai 1986:4-5). This passage takes for granted the historiographic equivalence of the sojourner and the bachelor. In fact, these two ideas must be collapsed, or the sentence, "The Chinese population was almost totally transient, and there was a great scar-city of females," is a *non sequitur*. This interdependence suggests that the texts usually read as theorizing the sojourner are also theorizing the bach-elor. For example, Mary Coolidge's *Chinese Immigration* (1909) and Paul C. P. Siu's *The Chinese Laundryman: A Study in Social Isolation* (1987), most often associated with the development of an Asian American studies discourse on "the sojourner," theorize the problem of the "bachelor soci-ety." I am emphasizing the word "theorize" here to undermine the com-mon-sense notion that the sojourner mentality is an explanatory model, while the bachelor society is a description of historical fact. If we take the "bachelor" metaphor too literally, we not only lose sight of the economic units these men were part of, but we risk describing family ties solely in terms of cohabitation. I will show that the bachelor society trope depends on a particular model of sexuality; it does ideological work on the histori-cal features it describes.

The sojourner mentality is taken to be a constituting feature of the bachelor society: Chinese men neither emigrated with their wives nor sent for wives after reaching the U.S. because they intended to return to their households in China. Yet the interrogation of the sojourner mentality has not led to a critical re-evaluation of the bachelor society and its relation to the sojourner mentality. For example, Sucheng Chan's, *Asian Americans: An Interpretive History* (1991) can be read as a critique of the sojourner model which privileges capitalism's demand for cheap labor over migrants' intentions to settle or return. Chan annexes the bachelor society as part of this critique: "Parents of emigrant sons believed that keeping the latter's wives in China ensured that they would faithfully remit money home to support their extended families" (104). Although here the absence of wives from the U.S. ensures the return of money, rather than the return of the emigrant, even Chan's refusal of the sojourner mentality must take up the imbrication of bachelor and sojourner.[3]

Coolidge's *Chinese Immigration* is generally referred to as one of the foundational texts for Asian American history writing. Coolidge follows the historian H. H. Bancroft's lead in linking anti-Chinese agitation, labor history, and California state and statehood politics. Methodologically the book locates itself at the intersection of political history and sociology, drawing heavily from contemporary newspaper accounts, published proceedings of various state and federal government bodies, and California state census tables and tax records. Coolidge refers frequently to earlier descriptions of Chinese immigrant social institutions and cultural practices, although no one section of *Chinese Immigration* is devoted to an account of immigrant "society."

Coolidge's fiercely anti-exclusionist book provides two distinct and competing arguments for free immigration, each of which depends on her notion of family. Coolidge sees family as more than kinship—it is an emotional, financial, and cultural tie between the immigrant and China that ensures the labor migrant's return. For her, the existence of a family (conjugal or filial) in China constitutes the emigrant as a sojourner. Yet she also insists that the cultural values of respect for these ties and responsible fulfillment of duty toward one's family make Chinese immigrants a more productive, more assimilable workforce than the spendthrift, overly proud, greedy, white miners and laborers of the anti-Chinese movement.

The tension between Coolidge's sojourner and assimilationist arguments for unrestricted immigration is staged in three accounts of Chinese immigrant men's sexuality—celibacy, marriage, and prostitution.[4] Together, these accounts allow us only two categories for thinking sex—conjugal heterosexuality and non-conjugal heterosexuality. Coolidge insists on the legitimacy of Chinese marriages apart from the presence or absence of wives as part of her argument that sojourning immigrants will return to their families in China. To make these family ties intelligible as marriages, she discusses married Chinese immigrants as monogamous—that is, as celibate. Those workers who emigrated as unmarried men and did not return to China are forced into celibacy by the exclusion of Chinese women and antimiscegenation laws. In other words, the heterosexual assumption leads Coolidge to state that the absence of both wives and potential wives disallowed any sexual activity at all in the immigrant community. Coolidge also suggests that their celibacy makes the Chinese desirable settlers:

> There are thousands of families in California who have counted Chinese tradesmen and employees as friends; there are hundreds of women on lonely ranches who have been indebted to Chinamen for their safety, their comfort, even for nursing of themselves and their children when no other help was to be had; for in the country districts, the only common man with whom as a class, a woman is perfectly safe, is the Chinaman (455).

The Chinese men in this passage can have intimate relationships with (white) families precisely because of their celibacy, their lack of sexual interest in white women and, conversely, the unlikelihood that they will arouse the sexual interest of white women. The sexual pun here reveals what makes this interracial intimacy tolerable. The image of a Chinese man "nursing" a white woman and her children is written in terms of celibacy: first the potential for miscegenation is downplayed by the implication that physical contact between white women and Chinese men is sought only in emergency situations ("when no other help was to be had"), and then Coolidge assures us that there is no threat of sexual assault by Chinese men. Following this highly sexualized praise of celibacy, the passage continues:

> Californians will tell, most appreciatively, stories of the generosity, kindness, devotion, and integrity of individuals whom they have known, but the moment the question of exclusion is broached, they insist, without apparent consciousness of inconsistency, that the Chinaman is a dangerous creature, that he will not assimilate and that therefore, he must go! They are unaware or they ignore the fact that a few thousand Chinese have already assimilated here and that the children of those who have families here are as much Americanized as the children of other foreigners who were not born to the English tongue (455).

In another twist on Coolidge's connection of marriage and celibacy, suddenly the celibate Chinese men of the first part of the paragraph have families and children. Within the terms of Coolidge's rhetoric in this particular passage, both the celibacy and the families are evidence of the immigrant's worthiness, indeed, of his *fait accompli* assimilation.

Coolidge's text is reluctant to cede any non-conjugal sexuality. Chinese prostitutes (or, as she writes, "lewd women") pose a problem for her tactics because their presence in the U. S. is highly publicized, and because they represent, in this text, the sole sexual activity available outside of marriage. She obscures the most visible site of Chinese heterosexuality in the U.S. by focusing on the invisible, hypothetical Chinatown wife and the dutiful, assimilable family man. Coolidge's anti-exclusion arguments rest on the construction of Chinese women as wives. She insists that Chinese women have not immigrated in significant numbers (the sojourner aspect of her anti-exclusion argument), only to suggest that many women are concealed within Chinatown (the settler aspect):

> The more respectable a Chinawoman is . . . the less she will be mentioned in conversation and the less she will be seen in public. It would be absolutely impossible for any employee of the city or state or any reporter to procure information about the wives and daughters of decent men in Chinatown (420).

This passage concludes:

> Under these circumstances and with the general California tendency to enhance anything adverse to the Chinese, it would be inevitable that the number of lewd women would be greatly exaggerated and the number of wives underestimated. The figures given by different writers for the same periods are indeed so wholly contradictory that no reliance can be put upon them (420).

This attempt to disallow discussion of prostitution in what she repeatedly claims is a population of heterosexual men indicates the degree to which her anti-exclusion arguments rely on an ideological reduction of Chinese sexuality to conjugal sexuality.

I have demonstrated that the coherence of Coolidge's depends argument on a certain kind of heterosexuality in order to show the logical importance of sexuality to a debate which disguises it as "common sense." The importance of sexuality in Paul C. P. Siu's *The Chinese Laundryman* may be seen without such interpretive work. Siu not only devotes an entire chapter to "Sex and Personal Disorganization," he also includes sections such as "Wanted—Either Money or Man" in a chapter on "The

Laundryman's Folks in China" and "Interracial Marriage" in a chapter entitled "Out-group Contacts and Deviant Types."

For Siu, the racism of U. S. society determines to a large degree the opportunities and experiences available for Chinese immigrants. Researched during the 1930s and completed in 1953, his book recognizes the legal structures affecting Chinese immigration to and residence in the U. S., yet as a sociologist, he is interested primarily in the social psychology of the ethnic enclave. Despite his careful rehearsal of a series of structural impediments to assimilation, he presents—in the manner of his discipline — the sojourner as a "personality type." Thus, Siu's work participates in the debate over whether the sojourner's apparent failure to assimilate was due to his desire to remain Chinese, or to the systematic prevention of Chinese assimilation by a racist society.

In describing the sojourner personality type and its effect on immigrant life, Siu describes the cultural practices and social institutions which developed around the figure of the bachelor sojourner. Coolidge's two categories for thinking sex, conjugal heterosexuality and non-conjugal heterosexuality, inform Siu's argument even though his account of immigrant life and immigrant sexuality is very different. "Sex maladjustment" characterizes Siu's bachelor, yet "maladjustment" and "vice" (Siu's euphemism for gambling and the patronage of prostitutes) are understood in terms of non-conjugal heterosexual activity. What is maladjusted about the sexualities Siu describes is not act or object choice, but the fact that sexuality occurs outside of the confines of the family: "Some laundrymen, preoccupied with sex, neglect the duties of supporting their family, lose interest in the return trip to China, and eventually lost their social status among their fellow countrymen" (265). At stake is the sojourner mentality itself: "Others could not go home because of immigration problems and sex maladjustments"(298).

Unlike Coolidge's text, which posits the immigrant's family as both present in and absent from the U.S., Siu's text differentiates between the immigrant's true family in China, to whom well-adjusted immigrants return, and the kind of family formulated in the U.S. By constructing China as the site of normal family and heterosexuality, Siu inverts the anti-naturalization claim that Chinese immigrants are inherently deviant and therefore unassimilable. When families are not allowed to immigrate together, the basic unit of "family" itself becomes "disorganized" and "maladjusted."

This inversion forecloses the notion that the bachelor society has developed a new kind of all-male family, although this new family is implicit in his description of the bachelor society. For example, Siu writes about the elaborate mechanisms for the illegal immigration of "paper sons" as a result of the same exclusion laws which created and maintained the bachelor society. The phenomenon of "paper sons" seems to arise from a securely heterosexual, all-male system of economic exchange and resistance to oppression, based on kinship and community alliances. Yet it is also a kind of reproduction, which generates new meanings about kinship and sexuality. "Fictive" kinship networks such as the paper sons or even Siu's clan associations appear fictive only in terms of a model which privileges biological reproduction.

One of the most striking things about the bachelor society trope is that it has not changed much in almost one-hundred years of history writing, despite profound changes in the cultural context for this writing. Between the appearance of Coolidge's book in 1909 and the publication of the *Dictionary of Asian American History* in 1987, U.S. culture's conceptualization of the relationship between race, citizenship, and the people we now call "Asian American" has undergone interrogation and change. Yet the features of the bachelor society have remained constant, raising some serious questions: Why has this concept not been elaborated, challenged, or replaced? Why has it been so consistently reproduced and recirculated within the historiography?

It is quite striking that this history writing insists on both the absence of Chinese women in the U.S. and the exclusive heterosexuality of Chinese immigrant men. Although it seems unlikely that bachelors never touched each other sexually, I am not arguing here about the accuracy or inaccuracy of these accounts of the past. Instead, I am interested in taking seriously the effects of heterosexism on Asian American history writing by looking at the sexualities described by these texts. As the examples of Coolidge and Siu demonstrate, "heterosexuality" and "normal sexuality" are by no means synonymous in Asian American historiography. For Coolidge and Siu, bachelor sexuality is described as deviant: non-reproductive and non-conjugal. Historians of sexuality have repeatedly shown that deviance constitutes a norm in opposition to itself. As we have seen in Coolidge and Siu, deviant heterosexuality is differentiated from the normative heterosexuality it points towards.

By introducing the idea of "deviant heterosexuality" here, I mean to point out that "heterosexuality" is not a monolithic category. However, this is not to suggest a heterosexual pluralism. Rather, to say that "heterosexuality" is determined by more than object choice is to say that not all heterosexualities will be equally privileged by heterosexism, precisely because sexualities are implicated in power relations and cultural logics. In other words, the particular kind of heterosexuality constructed within the historiographic tradition of the bachelor society is working, at the level of representation, to develop, secure, and reproduce certain cultural logics (such as those underpinning the racial and class meanings of Asians and Asian Americans or ideas of U.S. national identity). I have already suggested readings of Coolidge and Siu which use deviant and normative sexualities to think about the political debates that history texts participate in. Interestingly, the *Dictionary of Asian American History* describes the passing away of the bachelor society:

> With the repeal of the exclusion laws and naturalization prohibition, more and more Chinese could and did build normal lives in America. The old sojourner's bachelor society was being replaced by a better structured social order and family system that was to become a mainstay of Chinese stability and distinctiveness (Tsai 1986:5).

This passage enacts a complex double move: it contrasts past deviant heterosexuality with present "normal" heterosexuality, and locates the transition from old to new order at the moment when legal impediments to assimilation were removed. There is no suggestion here that assimilation was inherently impossible for the Chinese; rather, it was prevented by the exercise of power. Like the bachelor society, impediments to assimilation are a past condition, rather than a present reality. Thus, deviant heterosexuality marks out a past, an historical oppression now overcome. "Normal" heterosexuality here is a not only a marker of assimilation achieved, it is itself a means to assimilation.

As I hope I have demonstrated, Asian American studies can no longer afford to relegate "sexuality" to the realm of "common sense." Accounts of the past shape our politics in powerful ways; we historicize everything but sex at our peril. The bachelor society trope is not adequate to the consideration of crucial historical questions, such as: How is Asian American sexuality constructed? How does it construct a norm? What norms are in play in different periods? What is the relation between the construction of these normative and deviant sexualities and competing racial meanings? Taking these questions seriously gives us a new angle of vision on "the family" and the reproduction of all-male immigrant communities in Asian American history. The concept of deviant heterosexuality enables these questions, while making visible the politics of history writing.

Notes

1. An earlier version of this paper was given at the 1993 Association for Asian American Studies conference. My thanks to Nancy Armstrong, Mark Cooper, Bob Lee, Gary Okihiro, Ezra Tawil, Leonard Tennenhouse, my students in "Producing Asian American Sexuality," and the editors of this volume for their helpful comments.
2. Asian American studies privileges an "extended family." Yanagisako's (1985) valuable insight that the "extended family" has no defined features except its opposition to the nuclear family suggests that we should be suspicious of both this binary and the racial economy inscribing it.
3. Although I believe that any attempt to critique the sojourner mentality alone cannot succeed, I do not mean to imply that Marxism is inadequate to a critique of the sojourner/bachelor problem. Indeed, it is a small step from Chan's (1991) position to say that the scarcity of Chinese households in the U.S. was related to capitalism's demand for a labor force with a minimal cost of social reproduction.
4. George Peffer (1992), in his article on the historiography of Chinese immigrant women, has pointed out Coolidge's remarkable ignorance of laws restricting the immigration of Chinese women. Coolidge claims Chinese cultural norms and gender roles as solely responsible for the prevention of wives accompanying their husbands (note the inscription of gender within marriage). By aligning this absence of women with "culture," Coolidge constructs exclusion laws as relevant only to men, who are the focus of her anti-exclusion argument.

References

Butler, Judith. *Gender Trouble: Feminism and the Subversion of Identity.* New York: Routledge, 1990.

Chan, Sucheng. *Asian Americans: An Interpretive History.* Boston: Twayne, 1991.

Coolidge, Mary. *Chinese Immigration.* New York: Henry Holt, 1909.

Kim, Hyung-chan, ed. *Dictionary of Asian American History.* Westport: Greenwood Press, 1986.

Peffer, George. "From under the Sojourner's Shadow: A Historiographical Study of Chinese Female Immigration to America, 1852-1882." *Journal of American Ethnic History* (Spring 1992): 41-67.

Siu, Paul C. P. *The Chinese Laundryman: A Study in Social Isolation,* edited by John Kuo Wei Tchen. New York: New York University Press, 1987.

Tsai, Shih-shan Henry. "Chinese in the U.S." In *Dictionary of Asian American History,* edited by Hyung-chan Kim. Westport: Greenwood Press. 1986.

Yanagisako, Sylvia Junko. *Transforming the Past: Tradition and Kinship among Japanese Americans.* Stanford: Stanford University Press, 1985.

Oscar Wilde in Japan:
Aestheticism, Orientalism, and the
Derealization of the Homosexual

Jeff Nunokawa

The story is simply this . . . . Two months ago I went to a [party] . . . after I had been in the room about ten minutes, talking to . . . tedious Academicians, I suddenly became conscious that someone was looking at me. I turned halfway round, and saw [him] for the first time. When our eyes met, I felt that I was growing pale. A curious sensation of terror came over me. I knew that I had come face to face with someone whose mere personality was so fascinating that, if I allowed it to do so, it would absorb my whole nature, my whole soul, my very art itself. I did not want any external influence in my life . . . . I have always been my own master; had at least always been so, till I met [him] . . . . Then—but I don't know how to explain it to you. Something seemed to tell me that I was on the verge of a terrible crisis in my life. I had a strange feeling that Fate had in store for me exquisite joys and exquisite sorrows (Wilde 1891:11).

For all of its terror, the attraction confessed in this passage from *The Picture of Dorian Gray* is common to us; the coerciveness that characterizes desire in Wilde's telling of it, a coerciveness that, defeating initial efforts at containment ("*if I allowed it to do so*, it would absorb my whole nature, my whole soul, my very art itself") eventually "master[s]" the subject it invades, makes his story difficult to distinguish from one closer to home. If this passage sounds like the confession of a modern homosexual, it is not because the man who admits his desire for another gains identity, but rather because he loses self control. Whatever else separates the love featured in the contemporary coming out story, where desire is taken as the signature of its subject, from the one pictured in Wilde's text, where it disperses rather than defines him, they are united by the power to compel. Conceptions of desire as different from one another as the centrifugal from the centripetal, as an aesthetic of impersonality from a politics of identity, share a conviction that the shape of our passions, no less than the place of our birth, or the sources of our illnesses, is quite out of our hands. A fear of desire powerful enough in late nineteenth century texts like *The Picture of Dorian Gray* and *Dr. Jekyl and Mr. Hyde* to become indistinguishable from desire itself, has its cause in its capacity to compromise the will of the subject confirmed or vaporized by it; a fear of desire no less hard at work in the late twentieth century than in the late nineteenth inhabits the common sense that what attracts coerces.

But however powerful the drive of desire may seem, the testimony of the merest whim will indicate that it is not pervasive. It is altogether absent for example in *The Importance of Being Earnest*, first published in 1899, where the frightening passion Wilde calls the enthralling effects of Dorian Gray, and others before and after chart as the progress of primordial or viral forces, becomes faced in the daylight into a desire which, like the occasional cigarette, the weekend escapade, or the momentary reverie, are determined entirely by the subject who indulges them.

Such governance is administered by a variety of management styles in and beyond *The Importance of Being Earnest*, beginning with the familiar strategy of the double life, well outfitted here with false names and alibis. A tactic defined in the late nineteenth century by the difference between Dr. Jekyl and Mr. Hyde, between Dorian Gray and his portrait, and in the late twentieth by the difference between the wholesome heroine of the situation comedy, and her dark cousin, leaves the pursuit of pleasure to the discretion of its subject:

> You have invented a very useful younger brother called Ernest, in order that you may be able to come up to town as often as you like. I have invented an invaluable permanent invalid called Bunbury, in order that I may be able to go down into the country whenever I choose (Wilde 1988:224).

But the manipulation of desire in Wilde's comedy exceeds what is normally accommodated by the double life. The dandy that speaks in this passage is unusually modest in the account he furnishes of his *modus operandi*: the power he possesses over his wishes is more than the capacity to choose when he gives in to them; as half the labor performed by the term "Bunbury" indicates, a fiction which names both the "friend" who gives the pursuit of pleasure its excuse, as well as the pleasure itself ("Bunburying"), Algernon determines not only the timing of his capitulation to his wishes, but also their very character.

Comprehending everything from cradle to grave in *The Importance of Being Earnest*, where characters are commended or condemned for the conditions of their birth, the circumstances of their death, and the state of their health, the spirit of volunteerism is never more striking than when it casts "an irresistible fascination" as an act of caprice: "For me you have always had an irresistible fascination . . . my ideal has always been to love some one of the name of Ernest" (229). This speech may put us in mind of the familiar testimony of the modern sexual subject, who might "respect" a member of the unpreferred gender, "might admire" his or her "character," but cannot offer "undivided attention" (259), but a gap as wide as the gulf between free will and fate divides Wilde's character from the one inducted by a more recent discourse of desire. For despite the claim that her preference for the name of Ernest is irresistible, it is readily abandoned. In the rush to the altar that concludes *The Importance of Being Earnest*, we may forget that Cecily is content with a man whose name she had earlier declared would disqualify him as the object of her "undivided attention"; we may forget that for fully fifty percent of the *Ernestosexual* community, being Ernest proves not so important after all. Freed from any responsibility to an anterior condition that can be ignored or concealed but hardly wished away, the subject of desire, like the masochist who knows the ropes better than the master who applies them, or a diarist whose record of events is a work of fantasy, paradoxically chooses what she cannot resist, and is thus just as free to choose to be released from it.

The light desire that governs *The Importance of Being Earnest* partakes of a late Victorian climate of manufactured and manipulable passion associated with Wilde in particular, and Aestheticism, in general. When Cecily describes the diary of her fictional devotion Ernest as "a very young girl's record of her own thoughts and impressions, and consequently meant for publication" (256), she embraces the exhibitionism that Gilbert and Sullivan, in their parody of the Aesthete's pretenses, arraign as Wilde's own most prominent feature. The character in *Patience* that everyone recognized as Aestheticism's self-styled spokesman confesses that his "languid love for lilies," "Lank limbs and haggard cheeks," "dirty greens," and "all one sees/ That's Japanese," is a sham affection, "born of a morbid love of admiration!" (1976a:168)

And if the passion championed by Wilde in *The Importance of Being Earnest*, the pre- or extra-marital proclivities contrived and controlled by the subject who entertains them circulated more broadly in the culture of his day, other versions of it are rehearsed in our own. Wilde's brand of desire-lite will be both familiar and unfamiliar to those schooled in contemporary theories of dissident sexualities. Familiar because of its egregious artificiality: cutting itself off from Nature where defenses of passions eccentric to the marriage plot from Whitman's to those of recent gay essentialists have found their grass roots support, asserting itself not as a fact of life, but as a work of art, such desire may put us in mind of the performances of gender and sexuality that recent theorists have celebrated. Familiar because of the optimism of the will that defines it—Carole Ann Tyler has argued that recent reviews of generic and sexual performance appeal to their actors' intentions to separate theaters of insurrection, from rituals of conformity:

> [I]f all identities are alienated and fictional, then the distinction between parody, mimicry, or camp, and imitation masquerade, or playing it straight is no longer self-evident. What makes the one credible and the other incredible when both are fictions? The answer, it seems, are the author's intentions: parody is legible in the drama of gender performance if someone meant to script it, intending it to be there (1991:54).

Wilde's light passion becomes unfamiliar though when we consider that this performance of desire works not to subvert heterosexual normativity, but rather to cooperate with it. Confined to the moment and from the materials of whimsy, the "irresistible attraction" for the name of Ernest is abandoned when it proves discordant to the wedding march; the desires embodied in Bunbury are made to disappear like so much smoke at the first sound of wedding bells.

Dwelling all in fun and easily put aside before the altar, the airy passion of *The Importance of Being Earnest* is thrown into relief by the escalating anxiety about certain extra-marital pleasures that defined Wilde's cultural situation, an escalating anxiety marked and arranged by the scandals and legislation that crowded the decades during which he wrote, an escalating anxiety which culminated in the show trial where he found himself cast as the star witness for a love that he had spent considerable wit to avoid having to name. An acquired passion, less like an infectious disease than a love of the dance, the desire that, for all its lightness, moves more than the plot of *The Importance of Being Earnest* is no apology for dissident sexualities: it is rather an effort to prevent the need to make one.

To recognize that Wilde is never more a good citizen than when he flouts the conventions of referentiality is to notice again that social effects cannot be neatly collated with linguistic categories. But I want to suggest that the light passion that dwells on the surface of *The Importance of Being Earnest* does more to enhance our appreciation of the complexity of desire than encourage a by now common apprehensiveness about certain poststructuralist efforts to align resistance to reference, with resistance to the Law. I want to suggest that desire-lite, the domesticated passion that we have sampled in *The Importance of Being Earnest*, sometimes has a surprisingly foreign source; I want to suggest that this house brand of libido is often produced with foreign help.

Frantz Fanon describes an association of eros and exotic ethnicity more familiar than the one we will investigate here in his canonical account of the western sexual imagination; already active in the late nineteenth century, the association Fanon outlines has only intensified with the passing years: "One is no longer aware of the Negro, but only of a penis: the Negro is eclipsed. He is turned into a penis. He *is* a penis" (1970:120). For all its raciness, the condensation of psychiatrist locates in the waking dreams of Whites about Blacks is as routine as a man in a polyester suit. Fanon's bold eye resolves the image of a cultural figure whose staying power has spanned several centuries, an image uncovered recently both by Robert Mapplethorpe's explicitness, and by the often perfect integration of racial and sexual aversion that has attended it.

As its obtrusiveness in Mapplethorpe's photograph suggests, the threat of sexuality commonly embodied in the black man, as the black man, dwells in its undeniability; an undeniability rendered vivid by the failure to cover it. While the artful passions featured in Wilde's comedy turn on a dime, or on a dictate of chapel and hearth, while "irresistible attractions" there disappear the instant they prove inconvenient to the regime of Church and State, the desire in and for what will not be contained by the polyester suit is itself too compelling to respect the white collar requirement of nine to five.

The field of color where appetites coercive enough to refuse the impressive demands of marriage plot or work place extends beyond the skin tone recorded in the Mapplethorpe photograph. If the black man and black woman are typically cast as figures of a sexuality too compelling to be stopped by red lights, time clocks, or the check points of apartheid, other races, such as those who attend the opium den which Dorian Gray frequents, are attached to other no less coercive strains of desire, cast either as their subject or object. Those addicted to what, in an irony of imperialism, was called a Chinese drug, "grotesque things that lay in . . . fantastic postures on the ragged mattresses" (224) are themselves "crouching Malays," whose nationality, like the "odour of opium," is absorbed by the den's clientele, generally: "A crooked smile, like a Malay crease, writhed across the face of one of the women" (225).

But if the dark compulsions clothed in the polyester suit of the black man, or housed in the opium den are sometimes affiliated with exotic races, the desire that concerns us here sometimes take their light from the land of the rising sun. In order to assess the labor done by the figure of Japan to promote safer passions, we need first to recall that this malleable desire is first and foremost a work of art. Whatever it is not, the work of art is the domain of the artist's will. If art, according to Wilde's famous meditations, evades the constraints of mimesis, it is all the more the servant of the artist; if Wilde frees art from its bondage to accuracy, he makes it the compliant medium of the artist's will.

Wilde's account of the work of art recalls the child's play recorded by Freud, in which the infant masters what elsewhere masters him. "I don't want to be at the mercy of my emotions," Dorian Gray declares in a fit of pique: "I want to use them, to enjoy them, and to dominate them." Such power is achieved only when emotions, and desire chief among them, are spirited away from the element of blind compulsion that Wilde, in the following passage, calls "action":

> There is no mode of action, no form of emotion, that we do not share with the lower animals. It is only by language that we rise above them, or above each other. . . . [Action] is a blind thing dependent on external influences, and moved by an impulse of whose nature it is unconscious (1968a:359).

If Wilde's account of "action" resembles our own ideas about the vicissitudes of sexuality, this is not only because of its animal and unconscious elements, but also, and most importantly, because it is driven by "external influences" and "impulse[s]." As much as anything else, Wilde's aversion to the outdoors, his distaste for the natural is a dislike for the coercions of desire that he finds there. Only when desire migrates to the house of art does it acquire the pliancy necessary to render it safe for Church law and family movie.

In the figure of Japan, the artfulness of desire-lite finds agreeable surroundings. When, in their litany of Aesthetic tastes, Gilbert and Sullivan mention the "longing for all one sees that's Japanese" they refer to a style as central to the 1880s as the color black was to the 1980s. A part of a long line of fashions given over to the celebration of the artificial, the rage for things Japanese was, as much as anything else, a longing for an exoticism removed from the realm of the real. In an early instance of Japanese exceptionalism, the land of the rising sun, in contrast to the various regions of the non-occidental world that imperial cartography mapped as a wildlife park, was apprehended by Western eyes as a palace of art. Starting with its "opening" to the west in the middle of the nineteenth century, Japan had become a storehouse for English, American, and French artists and collectors—the Impressionists, for example, located Japan as the home of their signature styles.

"Now, do you really imagine that the Japanese people, as they are presented to us in art, have any existence? If you do, you have never understood Japanese art at all," Wilde declares in a famous oriental travelogue sandwiched into "The Decay of Lying" (1891)—less a travelogue, really, than an explanation of why no such thing is necessary: "The Japanese people are the deliberate self-conscious creation of certain individual artists" (1968:315).

The deliberate self-conscious creation of certain individual artists such as Gilbert and Sullivan, whose cartoon rendering of Japan was never intended to fool anybody—Chesterton speaks the commonest sense in his review of *The Mikado* ["I doubt if there is a single joke in the whole play that fits the Japanese. But all the jokes in the play fit the English" (Baily 83)]. Its ostentatiously theatrical character relies upon and reproduces Japan's reputation as pure artifice—a reputation supported by Rudyard Kipling in his musings on Japan:

> It would pay us to establish an international suzerainty over Japan: to take away any fear of invasion and annexation, and pay the country as much as ever it chose, on condition that it simply sat still and went on making beautiful things . . . . It would pay us to put the whole Empire in a glass case and mark it *Hors Concours*, Exhibit A (1900:455).

Japan sets the stage for a story of love which, partaking of the general character of the light opera form that Gilbert and Sullivan stirred into the modern musical, is all show. When in *The Mikado*, the two lovers enact as mere performance the intercourse denied to them in deed by a law that prohibits all flirting, the comedy derives from the impossibility of keeping the fiction of love separate from the fact of it in the world they inhabit:

> Nanki-Po: If it were not for the law, we should now be sitting side by side, like that. [Sits by her]
> Yum-Yum: Instead of being obliged to sit half a mile off, like that. [Crosses and sits at other side of stage]
> Nanki-Po: We should be gazing into each other's eyes, like that. [Gazing at her sentimentally]

[Sighing and gazing lovingly at him]
Nanki-Po: With our arms round each other's waists, like that. [Embracing her]
Yum-Yum: Yes, if it wasn't for the law.
Nanki-Po: If it wasn't for the law.
Yum-Yum: As it is, of course we couldn't do anything of the kind.
Nanki-Po: Not for worlds! (1976b:312)

The joke that Yum-Yum and Nanki-Po play here takes in more than the general ontology of the theater; it alludes to a whole nation cast as a work of art. Everything in *The Mikado*, most importantly the safe desire that propels its plot, is established by the chorus of Japanese nobles who introduce it:

> If you want to know who we are,
> We are gentlemen of Japan;
> On many a vase and jar—
> On many a screen and fan,
> We figure in lively paint . . .
> Perhaps you suppose this throng
> Can't keep it up all day long?
> If that's your idea, you're wrong (299).

The throng of artificial Japanese continue their song until the end of the play: all of its action is contained by it. Like the oriental objects that one "can touch and handle," the "lacquer-work," and "carved ivories" that Dorian Gray calls a means of inculcating "the artistic temperament," the floating world of *The Mikado* supplies local habitation and a name for passions light enough to carry on stage, and agreeable enough to be left at the church door. (For all its fun, the passion performed in *The Mikado*, like the pleasures of Bunburying and the passion of the Ernestosexual cooperate utterly with the demands of the law, here resolved into a single edict forbidding "non-connubial affection." When love proves inconvenient for the successful resolution of the plot which enforces this edict by rendering it unnecessary, the lover simply drops the subject.)

And if the aesthetic character of Japan renders it a suitable theater for the production of desire-lite, the process of its aestheticization supplies a paradigm and a catalyst for its production. In his guide to Japan, Wilde remarks upon not merely Japan's aesthetic character, but the process of its aestheticization:

> If you set a picture by Hokusai, or Hokkei, or any of the great native painters, beside a real Japanese gentleman or lady, you will see that there is not the slightest resemblance between them. The actual people who live in Japan are not unlike the general run of English people; that is to say, they are extremely

commonplace, and have nothing curious or extraordinary about them. In fact, the whole of Japan is a pure invention. There is no such country, there are no such people. One of our most charming painters went recently to the Land of the Chrysanthemum in the foolish hope of seeing the Japanese. All he saw, all he had the chance of painting, were a few lanterns and some fans. He was quite unable to discover the inhabitants . . . . He did not know that the Japanese people are, as I have said, simply a mode of style, an exquisite fancy of art. And so, if you desire to see a Japanese effect, you will not behave like a tourist and go to Tokio. On the contrary, you will stay at home, and steep yourself in the work of certain Japanese artists, and then, when you have absorbed the spirit of their style, and caught their imaginative manner of vision, you will go some afternoon and sit in the Park or stroll down Piccadilly, and if you cannot see an absolutely Japanese effect there, you will not see it anywhere . . . (1968b:315-16).

As he proceeds in this passage from the modest claim that Japan as it is depicted in art does not actually exist outside of it, to the bolder announcement that Japan only exists there, Wilde records the wholesale exodus of Japan into the region of Japanoisme. If the misguided tourist who goes to Tokyo in the hope of discovering Japan finds the place abandoned, that is because the entire population has left town to take up residence in or on paintings, fans, and tea cups, or in the style that is implied there.

As usual, Wilde's cheek is only the nerve and lucidity to pronounce an ideological operation that others do not think to say out loud. Like the belief that the Japanese are great technicians, a belief which expand metonymically into the sense that the Japanese are technology, themselves, Wilde's account, which begins by noticing the skill of Japanese artists, and ends by celebrating all of Japan as a work of art, locates the land of the rising sun as a site, more generally, for the process of aestheticization.

We can catch the Japanese contribution to the aesthetization of desire on the first page of a text famously obsessed with the subject. Here is the opening of *The Picture of Dorian Gray* (1891):

> The studio was filled with the rich odour of roses, and when the light summer wind stirred amidst the trees of the garden, there came through the open door the heavy scent of the lilac, or the more delicate perfume of the pink-flowering thorn.
> From the corner of the divan of Persian saddle-bags on which he was lying, smoking, as was his custom, innumerable cigarettes, Lord Henry Wotton could just catch the gleam of the honey-sweet and honey-coloured blossoms of a laburnum, whose tremulous branches seemed hardly able to bear the burden of a beauty so flame-like as theirs (7).

The safety of the studio, filled with the luxuries of art and artifice, is compromised by its exposure to the outdoors—the heavy scent of the lilac intrudes through the open door, but more importantly, so does the sight of the laburnum, caught in a tremulous embrace of a flame like beauty, not unlike that of a young man destined by the dictates of nature to fade. (Yes, there would be a day when his face would be wrinkled and wizened.) This arboreal analogue to a passion for the novel's show stopping hero is displaced, as the passage continues, by figures of art:

> Lord Henry Wotton could just catch the gleam of the honey-sweet and honey-coloured blossoms of a laburnum, whose tremulous branches seemed hardly able to bear the burden of a beauty so flame-like as theirs; and now and then the fantastic shadows of birds in flight flitted across the long tussore-silk curtains that were stretched in front of the huge window, producing a kind of momentary Japanese effect, and making him think of those pallid jade-faced painters of Tokio who, through the medium of an art that is necessarily immobile, seek to convey the sense of swiftness and motion (7).

Retreating from the involuntary tremblings of a compelling passion, the first thing to be seen in the safety zone arranged by the pains of the aesthetic is a "Japanese effect," a wholly fantastic figure, as removed from "the burden of a [natural] beauty so flame-like" that it would burn anyone who seeks to play with it as a "medium of an art that is necessarily immobile" from "the sense of swiftness and motion."

More than that though: put in mind of "those pallid jade-faced painters of Tokio" as he removes himself from the vicissitudes of the elements that his author placed outdoors, Lord Henry is put in the mind of a culture that renders the countenance of Japan as faces in jade. If the indoor landscape of the aesthetic features the familiar figures of the floating world, the journey there is guided and fueled by the impulse to artifice that defines more than Oscar Wilde's vision of Japan.

References

Fanon, Frantz. *Black Skin, White Masks*. London: Paladin, 1970.
Gilbert and Sullivan. *The Mikado*. In *Complete Plays*. New York: W. W. Norton, 1976b.
_____. *Patience*. In *Complete Plays*. New York: W. W. Norton, 1976a.
Kipling, Rudyard. *From Sea to Sea*. London, 1900.
Tyler, Carole-Anne. "Boys Will Be Girls: The Politics of Gay Drag." In *Inside/Out: Lesbian Theories, Gay Theories*, edited by Diana Fuss. New York: Routledge, 1991.
Wilde, Oscar. "The Critic as Artist." In *The Artist as Critic: Critical Writings of Oscar Wilde*, edited by Richard Ellmann. Chicago: University of Chicago Press, 1968a.
_____. "The Decay of Lying." In *The Artist as Critic: Critical Writings of Oscar Wilde*, edited by Richard Ellmann. Chicago: University of Chicago Press, 1968b.
_____. *The Picture of Dorian Gray*. London, 1891. Reprint edited by Donald L. Lawler. New York: W. W. Norton, 1988.
_____. *The Importance of Being Earnest*. In *Complete Plays*. London: Methuen, 1988.

Dissecting Desire: Symbolic Domination and Strategies of Resistance among Filipino Gay Men in New York

Martin F. Manalansan IV

As more gay Asian men come out of their personal and intellectual closets, representations long prevalent in both the mainstream and gay communities are increasingly being interrogated. The Song Liling of *M. Butterfly* fame and the image of Sum Yuhn Mahn of gay male porn[1] are being framed within the borders of critical theory and subjected to the scrutiny of those that they supposedly represent.

This paper attempts to provide another alternative critique of prevailing stereotypes of Asian gay men while at the same time, extending the discussion into a more sustained micro-analysis of "Orientalized" figures, symbols and counter-discursive practices. Previous studies of representations of Asian gay men in the popular media have concentrated on film, and have privileged a particular kind of iconological reading (Fung 1991; Wong 1991). The kind of reading prevalent among such works is anchored to abstract notions of spectatorship and reception as well as to simplistic notions of racial, economic, and sexual oppression and hegemony. These studies largely deny (consciously or unconsciously) the agency of Asian gay men and overlook the discontinuities or disjunctures between representations and dynamics of their everyday lives.

Using two years of ethnographic fieldwork interviews with more than fifty Filipino[2] gay men in the greater New York City area, [3] I will attempt to show how this group of men negotiate, contest, resist, and refigure stereotypical (Orientalized) representations of the body with their understanding and constructions of themselves as individuals and as a collective. I juxtapose presentations and interpretations of various cultural forms such as print media with the life narratives of these gay men in order to provide a more dynamic picture of how hegemonic representations of race, sexuality, and gender are creatively confronted.

The fifty Filipino informants' ages ranged from 22 to 60 years. A majority of these men immigrated to the U.S. when they were adults (21 years or over). All of those who immigrated as adults were born and raised in the Philippines. Those who immigrated as adults came to New York primarily because of job opportunities particularly in the medical professions (e.g. nurses, doctors, physical therapists), theatre, art, fashion, and business. In addition, New York was seen by most of these men as the quintessential American city as well as "the" gay mecca. Those who were born and raised in the U.S. were from California. Over a third of these men lived in Manhattan. Others lived in Queens, Brooklyn, and Jersey City (New Jersey).

Previous works have tended to examine texts, novels, paintings, photographs, and films produced by privileged individuals. Presenting how Filipino gay men react to Orientalized narratives through their words and experiences bridges the rupture between representations and "lived" lives even if provisionally, and enables a more creative understanding of the dynamics of race, sexuality, and gender.

In analyzing these issues, I find the theory of resistance set forth by James Scott (1990) to be particularly illuminating. For Scott, power differentials between superiors and subordinates are played out in everyday life by the use of two kinds of scripts, the public or official transcripts and the private or "hidden" transcripts. The former is a performance of "misrepresenting" the actual asymmetry between the powerful and the powerless. In the latter script, this asymmetry is subverted by disguised and clandestine acts of resistance by subordinates such as gossip, sabotage, arson, dissimulation, and rituals of inversion. I am interested in the ways Filipino gay men perform such clandestine or "offstage" acts of resistance in relation to hegemonic Orientalized narratives. In other words, I am interested in the dramaturgy of race and desire in the American gay scene as viewed through the experiences of Filipino gay men.

I will first present a stereotypical "Orientalized" gay narrative about Filipino gay men written by a Caucasian man. This is to set the stage, so to speak, for the interviews and stories of Filipino gay men. Through Filipino gay men's narratives, I will attempt to discern the sites of resistance, and the struggle for symbolic domination by this group of men. In the final section, I will analyze the implications of these acts of resistance to conventional notions of "Oriental" stereotypes.

Travelogues and travel guides are informative texts because not only do they provide glimpses of people and places for touristic delectation, but they also raise deep insights about the authors and the social milieu in which such genres are produced. The narrative in question is *Philippine Diary: A Gay Guide to The Philippines* by Joseph Itiel.[4] This is not so much an actual diary but a catalogue of cruising places and people. It is intended for men who "like Asians and [who] wouldn't go to the Philippines if [they] didn't."

For these kinds of men, Itiel offers a connoisseur's tips in establishing, maintaining, and controlling an encounter or relationship with Filipino gay men. He offers interesting insights about Filipino gay men based on his "relationships" with several of them—which he chronicles haphazardly in the book. Among such gems is his observation that Filipino gay men have unstable personalities. "Filipinos may be very patient," he writes, "but if they are pushed far enough, they snap completely and are capable of extreme violence" (1989:15). His other observations about Filipino gay male traits include: a childish fascination for telephones, an inability to manage sums of money, noisiness, a penchant for gossip, intellectual shallowness, and a disdain for any intellectual conversations. Among his other interesting assertions is that behind the smiling Filipino faces "lurks a deep melancholy, an unresolved sorrow that is almost always associated with their family relationships" (1989:23).

Despite being a guide for "rice queens" going to the Philippines, Itiel extends his analysis to include Filipino gay men everywhere including those in the United States. "Rice queen" is a term in gay slang used for men who are attracted to Asian men. The stereotypical profile of such men include being Caucasian, old, unattractive, and socially inept. He maintains that there are particular "immutable traits" of Filipino gay men that do not change regardless of place of birth and socialization. The "transplanted" Filipino gay man in the U.S. displays the same "child-like" qualities he observed among his "companions" in the Philippines. Although he said that the Filipino gay male may actually change some of his habits, he will only do so for survival and individual gain.

Itiel emphasizes that a Filipino gay man's family and class background do not matter. He asserts that a Filipino gay man, whether from the slums of Manila or educated at Harvard, possesses specific immutable characteristics. Despite the global mobility of Filipinos, Itiel incarcerates the Filipino

gay male into an essentialized and exoticized island of cultural primitive-
ness and pre-adult developmental limbo. Itiel's narrative connects itself to
the dominant Orientalized stereotypes by asserting that anything Filipino,
be it person, object, or idea belongs and is rooted to that locale of imagined exotic alterities—the Orient.

It will be too easy to provide an *ad hominem* diatribe against this text,
however, such is not the intention here. I would take this text as a spring-
board for Filipino gay men's narratives. The text may be an overt form of
the "rice queen" syndrome, but the images constructed in the texts are the
same ones that confront Filipino gay men when they enter the shores of
the American gay community.

Before presenting the narratives of Filipino gay men, I would like to
reconstruct the "Orientalized" notions of the Filipino (and Asian) male
body from Itiel's text and from other texts such as personal ads and stories.
In these scenarios, "Orientalized" stereotypes dichotomizes "East" and
"West" to female and male. The oriental body is always female or feminized. This construction is then extended to the passive and active axes,
and rooted to corporeal characteristics that involve feminized, androgynous, and pedophilic dimensions. For example, popular "Orientalized"
signifiers would include hairlessness, boyish/feminine qualities, slimness,
and a gentle mien. It is this fixed and static notion of the body that will be
disputed by the narratives of Filipino gay men. I will provide several sites
of resistance such as drag or cross-dressing, forms of dissimulation, and the
use of specialized argot and rituals.

One of the phrases that I have found to be emblemmatic of Filipino
gay men's resistance to Orientalized images is *paglaruan ang mundo* or to
"play with the world." This phrase was often uttered by Filipino gay men
who were in drag. For many of my informants, cross-dressing was one way
of manipulating the situation.

If resistance is veiled subversion of existing power asymmetries (Scott
1990), then drag or cross-dressing is the quintessential example of this
process. Drag, as the most important act of resistance among Filipino gay
men, marks and codes power differentials in race and gender while at the
same time re-configuring these social hierarchies within various places and
sites from gay bars to the domestic front.

For example, during the New York City Halloween parade in 1991,
two Filipino drag queens in bright Las Vegas attire were shocking and delighting crowds on Christopher Street in Greenwich Village. They came
up to me and my friends, and one of them said, "Oh it is so much fun

playing with these people. We have fooled the world once again"[5] When I asked if he meant that the people or the audience were fooled into believing they were women, one countered, "It really has nothing to do with their believing that we are women or not, it has more to do with creating an aura—you know—atmosphere."

This was basically the same statement that other Filipino drag queens on different occasions have told me. The basic premise of this strategy of resistance is less about tricking people into believing they are women than about reinventing the world around them and taking control of the situation.

To illustrate this contention, I cite the case of a Filipino gay man, who went by the name of Exotica while competing in a drag context. During the contest which he eventually won, he was introduced to the audience as "an exotic beauty hailing from the exotic island of Java." When I interviewed Exotica, I asked him why he used the nom de plume and the hyper-exoticized persona. He claimed that he was just trying to get ahead of the game. Since he did not resemble the muscular blond hunks lionized in the gay media, he could be the mysterious and yes—exotic creature from Java. He thought that Java sounded more remote and alluring than Manila where he grew up. He said, that in this "game," one needed a gimmick or a unique way of selling oneself.

When I asked some of my drag queen informants if they felt they were perpetuating the myth that Asian gay men were all effeminate drag queens, all of them seemed not to mind. One in particular said that being in drag and being effeminate had nothing to do with dominance and submission. In fact, he pointed out that even if most of the Filipino drag queens set out to play degraded and/or notorious "Oriental" female characters like Kim in the Broadway play *Miss Saigon* or Imelda Marcos, such practices have nothing to do with who is dominant in the relationship.

Successfully looking the part, as affirmed by the recognition and applause of any audience in the streets or in the clubs, is in the perception of these drag queens playing with or reconfiguring the world. One informant said, "When I look beautiful and look the part of Miss Saigon, then I can make people believe and appreciate my work and my body. During Halloween or in any drag contest, most people know that I am a man in drag, but if my get-up enables them to suspend that knowledge and marvel at my beauty—then I have succeeded."

In everyday life, the cross-dressing informants emphasized that it was the biggest myth that the masculine (mostly Caucasian) men who courted them were in any way dominant. In fact, one informant said that this was the biggest secret that female accoutrements (like a wig or a beaded gown) are able to hide or disguise.

One Filipino cross-dressing informant said that while he had a smaller body, assumed the "wifely" duties of cooking and cleaning and the like, and was the passive bed partner, he was in no way subservient to his big hunky white lover. He reported that it was he who dominated the relationship by controlling finances, making most of the decisions for both of them, and was also emotionally stronger than his partner. He said, "I may wear the skirt in this relationship, but when I snap my fingers, darling, he [the lover] snaps into attention."

There are other ways by which Filipino gay men resist stereotypes. One of the most direct ways is to develop muscles and subscribe to one of the activities of mainstream gay lifestyle—going to the gym. One informant said that he went to the gym and did not cross-dress precisely to counter the prevailing image of Asian drag queen. He said that there were quite a number of Filipino gay men who go to the gym, and many of his Filipino gay friends have stopped considering bodybuilding as peculiar and too "masculine." Several of his Filipino gay friends both cross-dressed and went to the gym. For him, growing muscles was like drag, a way of controlling the game or situation. He said, "With my new lean, buffed body, I have become very successful in cruising. It [going to the gym] has paid off."

Other Filipino gay men perform other kinds of "scripts" such as "FOB" or "fresh off the boat." My informants reported that pretending to be the innocent waif from some Asian country who just emigrated for the benefit of a non-Asian suitor was one way of controlling the situation. The non-Asian suitors would usually assume the role of benefactor, providing gifts and other financial and emotional support. They were quite aware of the prevailing image of Asians as a largely immigrant population and not culturally belonging in America. In addition, these Filipinos were also cognizant that many non-Asians see the Filipinos and other Asians as "looking" younger. Orientalist narratives such as Joseph Itiel's support stereotypes of Filipino gay men as being childishly innocent, helpless, and ignorant.

In other situations, Filipino gay men have exploited such images to suit their particular interests. For example, when one of my informants met a Caucasian man in a bar who was about his age, the Caucasian assumed that my informant was considerably younger than he and was new to the gay scene in New York. My informant did not correct him. He said that such an age disparity worked in his favor despite the rather patronizing attitude of the Caucasian man. He said that the Caucasian catered to his every whim and allowed his idiosyncrasies.

Another form of resistance is through the use of Filipino gay slang or "swardspeak." Filipino informants noted that speaking in this argot was one way of getting together with other Filipino gay men and having a kind of secret code. Most of their non-Filipino lovers whom I also interviewed noted that this was a source of annoyance since this practice would exclude them.

An informant said that the use of swardspeak was one arena where their lovers do not have the upper hand, unless they learned Pilipino and the mercurial lexicon of swardspeak which was unlikely. Using swardspeak, Filipino gay men are able to gossip about everything including non-Filipino men who they either desire or despise. For non-Filipino men whom they hate, some Filipino gay men create vicious rumors about these men's promiscuity (*sawsawan ng bayan* or the "town's/country's dipping sauce" is the usual term for such men) or their physical shortcomings. Filipino gay men are therefore able to put these men down and laugh at them even if they are within hearing distance.

The various sites of resistance that I have very briefly presented all have several features in common with other strategies laid out in Scott's book. Foremost of these is the enactment or performance of such acts away from the direct surveillance of those in power. For example, the exclusionary power of using swardspeak or the Filipino gay argot is one effective counter-discursive situation which attempts to subvert the racial, cultural, and even economic difference between Filipino gay men and their non-Filipino lovers.

Another important feature that runs through all these sites is the preoccupation with disguises and appearances. The need for disguised and euphemistic practices means that Filipino gay men do not directly assault the hegemonic discourses of Orientalism. Rather, they are able to gain both symbolic and material dominance by appropriating symbols of either the mainstream gay community such as bodybuilding or from traditional forms of discourses such as swardspeak. In fact, the sites of resistance were stronger in practices or situations where Filipino gay men deployed the very materials and ideas that make up Orientalism such as femininity, innocence, and being childlike because they were performed under the guise of consent and subservience. The euphemistic nature of the acts enable Filipino gay men to present the popular and accepted images while acting upon the discursive situation at the same time.

The body provides the arena and the site for most of these strategies. Drag and bodybuilding, among others, refigure the seemingly frail, boyish, and docile bodies of the Filipino gay men into agents who return the gaze of spectators and actively participate in their own re-presentations. Female attire, muscles, and innocent mien provide the tactical codes necessary to hide the ongoing manipulation of power hierarchies between the valorized Caucasian masculine gay men and themselves. Furthermore, these "materials" or props allow the disruption of the naturalized, seemingly "immutable" connections between bodies, ideas, and practices to Asian gay men.

These acts of resistance are not valorized among the increasingly politicized Asian gay and lesbian groups. In many popular discussions about "Oriental" stereotypes and narratives in these circles, there is a tendency to simplify the discussion into a dichotomy between good and bad images of Asians (Ogasawara 1993). Being a sexual bottom, wearing native costumes, cross-dressing, and dating Caucasians are seen by many to be symptomatic of political misguidance and self-hatred. Asian gays and lesbians who are "guilty" of performing such acts are disparaged by those who believe that showing a strong, visibly confrontational stance is the only way to change what to them is a monolithic system of ideas and practices.

However, the idea of a static and stable system of Orientalism and the notion of "good and bad" Asian images reify the very foundation of Orientalist stereotypes and narratives that this kind of activism seeks to subvert. Lisa Lowe perhaps said it best when she noted that, "[A]lthough orientalism may represent its objects as fixed or stable, contradictions and noncorrespondences in the discursive situation ultimately divulge the multivalence and indeterminability of these fictions" (1991:x).

The same kind of idea about the fixed or "immutable" notions of Orientalized images brings into question not only the nature of Orientalist practices, but also the agentive abilities of Filipinos and other Asians who are subordinated by such ideological arrangements. Filipino gay men, as I have presented, are cognizant of the images that supposedly represent them and other peoples "like" them. However, in maintaining their own individual and collective interests, they are able to (unwittingly or wittingly) displace and subvert the stereotype by appropriation and inversion of meanings and symbols.

Filipino gay men as a subordinate group are able to attain both symbolic and sometimes material dominance in various discursive situations through the veiled or clandestine nature of such acts of resistance and by undermining the instability of Orientalist ideology. Scott noted this when he wrote:

> what permits subordinate groups to undercut the authorized cultural norms is the fact that cultural expression by virtue of its polyvalent symbolism and metaphor lends itself to disguise. By the subtle use of codes one can insinuate into a ritual, a pattern of a dress, a song, a story, meanings that are accessible to one intended audience and opaque to another audience the actors wish to exclude" (1990:158).

In sum, I have very briefly presented the contours of Filipino gay men's "hidden transcripts." Such scripts of resistance centralizes the role of Filipino gay men and other subordinate groups as actors in the formation of discursive situations. Such acts of veiled defiance, to go back to the words of my Filipino informants, are ways of "playing with the world" of racial, economic, and cultural disparities and winning (at least provisionally) in the "game" of racialized desire.

Notes

1. Song Liling is the protagonist in the play, *M. Butterfly*, (Hwang 1986) and Sum Yuhn Mahn is an actor of Indochinese extraction in gay porn film (see Fung 1991). These characters represent mainstream critique and marginal gay versions of "Oriental" men respectively.
2. I use the term "Filipino" and not "Pilipino" not as a political act but to be sensitive to the way most of my informants define themselves. In addition, the spelling acknowledges the manner in which the people of the Philippines use either of the term. Filipino is used for citizenship or identity while Pilipino is used for the national language. This acknowledgment reflects the fact that most (except for three of my informants) were post-1965 immigrants who either grew up as adults in the Philippines and/or still maintains close ties with practices, ideas, and relationships in the homeland.
3. In addition, I had informal interviews with about a hundred Filipino gay men from the New York City area, Los Angeles, San Francisco, and Washington D.C. The term, "greater New York area," is to be inclusive of informants who resided in southern New Jersey and Long Island. The names of informants mentioned in this paper have been changed to protect their privacy.
4. Joseph Itiel is a hypnotherapist and travel writer who is based in San Francisco. The extent of his travel writing include this book, a book about gay tourism in Mexico, and a novel. A great part of this book is devoted to descriptions of tourist spots and helpful tips for gay travelers. In between these sections are anecdotes of his own experiences with young Filipino males where he provides his so-called "psychological profile" of these men.

5. All of the conversations were in Taglish or code-switching between Tagalog and English. I have translated these into English except when appropriate.

References

Fung, Richard. "Looking for My Penis." In *How Do I Look?* edited by Bad Object Choices. Seattle: Bay Press, 1991.

Hwang, Henry David. *M.Butterfly.* New York: Plume, 1986.

Itiel, Joseph. *Philippine Diary: A Gay Guide to the Philippines.* San Francisco: International Wavelength, 1989.

Lowe, Lisa. *Critical Terrains: French and British Orientalism.* Ithaca: Cornell University Press, 1991.

Ogasawara, Dale. "Beyond the Rice Queen: Different Politics, Varying Identities." *Color Life.* 1 (1993):1, 11-28.

Scott, James. *Domination and the Arts of Resistance.* New Haven: Yale University Press,1990.

Wong, Lloyd. "Desperately Seeking Sexuality: A Gay Asian Perspective on Asian Men in Film." *Rites,* May 1991.

Addressing Differences: A Look at the 1989 Asian Pacific Lesbian Network Retreat, Santa Cruz

Alice Y. Hom

In her opening comments at the first national retreat sponsored by the Asian Pacific Lesbian Network in Santa Cruz on September 1-4, 1989,[1] Filipina activist Trinity Ordoña welcomed participants by explaining the importance of the retreat:

> We recognize the absence of our reflection in the lesbian community. We recognize the denial of our presence in the Asian American community. As long as we exist in a homophobic and racist society, we will always have this need to be together. We are here for all different reasons, but we have decided to do something about our needs. This is an important event because we are doing something about our presence (1989).

Many women applauded, responding, "Yes" and "That's right." They felt her words deeply, having experienced that type of invisibility as Asian Pacific[2] lesbians. This 1989 retreat "Coming Together, Moving Forward" heralded the first national attempt to organize and bring together Asian Pacific lesbians from across the United States. The event gave Asian Pacific lesbians the opportunity to have their identities validated, to build and expand personal networks, and to gain a forum within which to define their own history. Over 180 women participated in the retreat, with ethnic backgrounds including Chinese, Japanese, Korean, Filipino, Indonesian, Malaysian, mixed race, South Asian, and Pacific Islanders.

As an important marker in the development of the Asian Pacific lesbian movement, the retreat provides us with an opportunity to reflect on both the achievements and the continuing problems of political work within the Asian Pacific community. This essay presents some of my research on the Asian Pacific Lesbian Network, an organization formed in 1988 after

the March on Washington for Gay and Lesbian Rights in 1987.[3] My purpose in this essay is to use the Santa Cruz retreat to discuss "differences"
within the Asian Pacific lesbian community. "Differences" in this context
refers to diverse ethnic and cultural backgrounds, class statuses, and regions.

On a grand scale, the retreat participants were able to come together
under the rubric of "Asian Pacific lesbians." But like most labels, this head-
ing served to erase the variations and diversity within the group. The term
"Asian Pacific lesbian" encompasses a number of ethnic groups with varying immigration patterns, generational identities, class statuses, ethnic heritages, and historical perspectives. But, as retreat participants discovered,
being a part of the Asian Pacific lesbian movement did not guarantee recognition of the complexity of people's backgrounds. Lisa K. Yi, an artist
from New York of Chinese and Korean heritage, explained, "You can't expect just because they are Asian lesbians they are going to be better than a
white man" (1991).

Why was it so difficult to talk about these "differences" at the Santa
Cruz retreat? Perhaps, one reason was because there were high expectations
for participants about coming together with other Asian Pacific lesbians,
and women did not want the "feel good" atmosphere to be disrupted.
Many of the women interviewed said that the participants who attended
the Santa Cruz retreat had the feeling of finally "coming home." When
asked why she got involved with the Asian Pacific Lesbian Network, Joan
Varney, an educator of mixed Japanese and Irish heritage, provided a common response: "It was to move out of isolation and satisfy needs that weren't
being met; doing Asian American organizing where the lesbian community was very white." She further commented: "I was very validated [at the
retreat] as a lesbian of mixed heritage...because there are so many other
people like me. Just to really even visually see how many APLs there are,
that alone is just a beautiful experience, how beautiful we are, how varied
we are. . ." (1991).

Milyoung Cho, a Korean American organizer of the retreat, explained:
"Because we shared being API [Asian Pacific Islander] lesbians and having
that affirmed by all these women there was a reality [add context] for that
moment. It was empowering; you got that certain part, that was always
being fucked over [and] denied, being affirmed" (1991). Cho's description
of "reality" stresses a "moment" when the multiple identities of Asian Pacific lesbians were acknowledged in totality rather than in fragments. Referring to the overwhelming euphoria commonly experienced during that
weekend, Tacy Urian, a Filipina health care worker, remembered: "I felt

like I was high the whole time I was there. It was just so energizing the whole time" (1991).

These expectations were heightened by the risks faced by people openly identifying as Asian Pacific lesbians. Nancy Otto, who is of mixed Japanese and European heritage, was in her first lesbian relationship at that time. She said, "I remember walking towards the registration table and feeling terrified. You don't know these people, everybody is a stranger and you are supposed to get along great. It was scary and wonderful at the same time" (1991).

Even if women had lived in areas highly populated by Asian Pacific Islanders, internalized oppression might have deterred them from formally identifying with each other. Joan Varney explained some of the reasons behind her hesitation: "To have that visual thing of 200 of us all in one place was really . . . scary. It was scary and at the same time it was exciting. . . . All the vulnerability . . . was sort of right there. Am I going to fit in, do I really belong. . . ? (1991) Zoon Nguyen, a Vietnamese political organizer, also had friends who were unwilling to attend the retreat, deterred perhaps by factors such as internalized racism, internalized homophobia, or an ambivalence caused by having a white lover. Zoon remarked: "A lot of people, I think, took risks by being there and I hope that those people felt like they did belong somewhere and were able to hook up with friends they could be pen pals with or sleeping partners or whatever the case may be" (1991). As an example of the continuing danger in just having Asian Pacific lesbians come together, a would-be participant from Amsterdam was detained by the Immigration Service and deported (Islam 1989).[4]

Yet, despite the desire to achieve unity, many participants felt isolated from the general group. "Differences" emerged as established hierarchies continued to divide participants. For example, class issues emerged as one area of contention. In all probability, the majority of the participants were mostly middle class and college-educated. There was some concern about the cost of registration for the retreat, based on a $100-$150 sliding scale, as being too high for some people. Although the organizers tried to fundraise, there were not many scholarships and travel grants available to help everyone. This might have meant that working-class and regional issues were not addressed in this retreat because some women might not have been able to attend due to financial constraints, especially if they lived in the Midwest and East Coast.

Perhaps the most visible difference was ethnic. During the retreat the experiences of East Asians born in the United States were dominant, which left the experiences of immigrants, South Asians, Southeast Asian, and Pacific Islanders on the margins. Willy Wilkinson, a lesbian of mixed Chinese, Scottish, Irish, and English heritage commented:

> Certainly, the issue of racism was up and . . . was not dealt with in any sound way. The Asian sisters really had to be called to the carpet to look at what our privilege is in terms of looking at dynamics of how long we have been in this country, what are our socioeconomic status . . . . It's primarily Chinese and Japanese American. Those sisters are called the mainstream when you say Asian in this country. Those girls were not at all dealing. They would say, "Oh well, we don't have to get down to ourselves for this. We're oppressed too." How many times do we hear that from white girls? How many times have we heard it from men . . . ? (1992)

As Wilkinson argued, it was important to identify the power and privilege enjoyed by some participants and not others.

Those who voiced the most concerns were the South Asians and Pacific Islanders who felt invisible in a crowd dominated by Chinese and Japanese Americans. V. K. Aruna, a South Asian born and raised in Malaysia and one of the South Asian organizers, recalled: "I was able to see quite painfully something that I had thought only existed in Malaysia, that is the cross-racial hostility in the APLN." As Aruna reported: ". . .We felt invisible in the slide show, in the brochures and in the t-shirts. There were not images that looked like us and it just accumulated." Aruna recalled the difficulty the ten South Asian lesbians had in coming up with a statement that included remarks about their invisibility in the slide show and on the speaker's panel for the important last plenary, "Coming Together, Moving Forward." She explained:

> It was a risk because of the friendships involved. It was hard, painful and we got some flak for the way we did it but they needed to know. We broke the silence [and] it was very powerful for us. We [South Asians] had never made a big deal about it [invisibility] before, but we're glad it happened. Many in the audience felt sad and sorry. They were supportive and said "hopefully it will not happen again" (1992).

Despite the difficulties of confrontation, Aruna recalled the South Asian criticism: "Much time went into figuring out what would be said and how it would be said so that our criticisms would be offered in the spirit of raising awareness rather than lashing out" (1990:5). Doreena Wong, a Chinese American attorney, concurred with the spirit of the confrontation: "It was constructive criticism; it wasn't like negative criticism like we're going to walk out of here, forget you. It was saying we want you to know this is the problem and do something about it and hopefully, they will help us do something about it" (1991).

Clearly, the organizers and the participants did not anticipate the type of critical remarks expressed by the participants who felt alienated from the retreat. Milyoung Cho tried to explain possible causes for the tension: "This is why it was so explosive because people had these expectations that this conference was going to be inclusive. This was going to be a safe space. This is where we can let our guard down and feel accepted by people, but of course that's not going to happen" (1991). June Chan, a Chinese American and one of the original creators of the network, reacted strongly to the unexpected charges of isolation and tokenism: "I couldn't say anything. People were angry, people were defensive, people were crying . . . . There was a whole big misunderstanding" (1991).

Some organizers were defensive because they had tried their best to include everyone and to be sensitive to the needs of the attendees. One woman thought that the organizers had expended considerable effort to have South Asian lesbians participate and was surprised by their feeling left out (Chan 1991). Another organizer believed participants might have felt the blame even though they might not have been responsible (Cho 1991). Although some things were not within their control, she acknowledged the ownership of the blame in not doing more in terms of outreach to different communities (Cho 1991). The practical limitations of organizing were mentioned by another organizer:

> It was pretty much run by a small group of people. While we tried to extend our philosophy of inclusionary politics we had very limited resources to pool from. You don't necessarily attract the kind of people who want that because they don't share the same vision or they don't have the level of intensity of organizing that you do (Nguyen 1991).

While the organizers might have represented diverse backgrounds, this did not guarantee a varied participant pool. As Aruna pointed out, "The ethnic diversity of the organizers was incredible in terms of representation, but not in issues of voice or visibility" (1992). Representation alone could not combat historical inequities caused by ethnic, class, and generational privilege.

Although many people felt torn by the conflicts expressed in the retreat, other women felt strongly that the differences were too much emphasized and that more stress should have been spent on the similarities. As a participant noted: ". . . when you put that many women together, it's always very difficult to address every need and every concern of every sub-set within a greater set. I would liked to have seen less focus on trying to find the uniqueness of each subset, but more of looking at your common-ality" (Rosales 1991). And there were some women oblivious to the criti-cism; they were in their own world, wrapped up in meeting others and finding lovers. One said, ". . . [t]he criticisms . . . I heard and I didn't find this at all because I was in heaven the whole time" (Urian 1991). These comments underscore that participants represented a range of perspectives and brought many different expectations.

For the most part, however, the women felt sad that there were some who felt invisible and left out, because they themselves had experienced similar feelings in other groups. June Chan's sentiments reflected those in many of the interviews. She remarked: "I understood how the South Asian women felt because I [have] been put in that position just in regular soci-ety" (1991).

Read from another angle, the ability to address conflict at the Santa Cruz retreat could also be taken as an indication of the growing strength of the Asian Pacific lesbian movement. At the Santa Cruz retreat, the com-ments came immediately and with no holding back. This, perhaps, is a sign of the progress made in terms of breaking the internal silences within the Asian Pacific lesbian community. Women were able to speak their minds instead of suppressing their opinions for the sake of community cohesion. In contrast, Willy Wilkinson, a participant in a 1987 West Coast Asian Pacific lesbian retreat in Sonoma, reported that criticism did not emerge about this event until several months later. Wilkinson described conversa-tions with retreat participants in which women felt incapable of voicing their concerns for fear of disrupting the positive atmosphere (1987).

According to June Chan, one of the main advocates for the continu-ation of the Asian Pacific Lesbian Network, the retreat left people with "an impression [of] how dangerous we could be to each other, how empower-ing we could also be; what we could do if we all work together . . . and what we can't do if nobody wants to do it" (1991). For many of the women, the retreat was an eye-opener to the differences among Asian Pacific lesbi-ans, and provided the kind of educational experiences and consciousness-raising needed in order to build trust among Asian Pacific lesbians. As Aruna aptly pointed out:

> In the spirit of the celebration, we should not emphasize similarity and be-come a melting pot. We need to emphasize difference which will lead to fights. That's what struggle is all about. It is like a relationship. If it cannot with-

stand fighting then we really need to look at this. Not just [about] coming together, but can we stay together [?] (1992)

Thus, the 1989 Asian Pacific Lesbian Network retreat in Santa Cruz marked an important moment in the evolution of the Asian Pacific lesbian movement. It was an exciting and exhilarating process which provided a much needed space for Asian Pacific lesbians to articulate their concerns. At the same time, the critique made by underrepresented women at the retreat truly brought out the necessity for Asian Pacific lesbians to be aware of relative power and privilege. It also emphasized that the drive to come together should not override the importance of addressing basic issues of equity within the Asian Pacific Lesbian Network.

The struggle of Asian Pacific lesbians to be recognized in the fullness of their multiple identities, and their attempt to identify the privileges that divide them, marks the growing maturity and changing composition of the Asian Pacific lesbian movement. It will be an ongoing struggle to make the movement inclusive and representative of the Asian Pacific lesbian community. In this regard, the 1989 Asian Pacific Lesbian Network retreat at Santa Cruz can be seen as a significant step in that direction.

Notes

1. This essay is a revised version of a paper presented at the 1992 Annual Meeting of the Association for Asian American Studies in San Jose, California. The author acknowledges the UCLA Institute of American Cultures for providing resources to engage in this research. I would like to thank Dorothy Fujita Rony, whose skillfull editing and sensitive suggestions have contributed to the final version of this study. However, all mistakes herein are my own.
2. The term "Asian Pacific" is used here to denote Asian Americans and Pacific Islanders in the United States. There are some South Asian and Pacific Islander lesbians who do not identify as Asian Pacific lesbians. While understanding the problematic nature of this label, I decided to use the term that the Asian Pacific Lesbian Network named itself.
3. See Hom (1992). The research for this study includes sixteen oral history interviews I conducted with lesbians involved with the Asian Pacific Lesbian Network. Primary documents, such as meeting minutes, correspondence between organizers, grant proposals, brochures, information flyers, and retreat materials provided additional background data. Videos of certain sessions of the retreat also served as data. The sixteen women interviewed for this project ranged in age from their early twenties to early forties. Thirteen of the women were organizers for the retreat. Two headed workshops and the others attended the retreat. Of course, some played dual or triple roles in organizing and facilitating workshops.
4. This woman was deported when officials discovered that the Asian Pacific lesbian retreat was the reason for her coming to the United States.

References

Aruna, V. K. "South Asian Lesbians Stop the Process at APL Retreat." *Phoenix Rising* (August/September/October 1990).

____. Telephone Interview, Silver Springs, Maryland. 20 April 1992.

Chan, June. Interview, New York City. 16 September 1991.

Cho, Milyoung. Interview, Brooklyn. 21 September 1991.

Hom, Alice Y. "Family Matters: A Historical Study of the Asian Pacific Lesbian Network." M.A. thesis, UCLA, 1992.

Islam, Sharmeen. "INS Detains Asian Lesbian En route to Retreat." *Gay Community News*, 19-25 November 1989.

Nguyen, Zoon. Interview, San Francisco. 22 November 1991.

Ordoña, Trinity. Videotape of the opening ceremony of the Asian Pacific Lesbian Retreat, by Annie Moriyasu. Santa Cruz, California, 1-4 September 1989.

Otto, Nancy. Interview, San Francisco. 27 November 1991.

Rosales, Carmen T. Interview, San Francisco. 15 December 1991.

Urian, Tacy. Interview, Oakland. 16 December 1991.

Varney, Joan Ariki. Interview, San Francisco. 22 November 1991.

Wilkinson, Willy. "Of Pride, Identity and Empowerment: Retreat '87 A Weekend to Honor Ourselves." *Coming Up!* July 1987.

____. Written Interview, San Francisco. 5 April 1992.

Wong, Doreena. Interview, San Francisco. 23 November 1991.

Part Four
RACE AND ETHNICITY

The Sites of Race and Ethnicity:
Social Constructions of Consequence

K. Scott Wong

In the struggle to dismantle the racial hierarchies embedded in American society, much has been written in recent years on the social construction of race and ethnicity. When biological and other "scientific" explanations of race fell out of favor in the earlier part of this century, "intrinsic" cultural traits were then called upon to delineate and explain categories of human differences. In the 1960s, as new approaches to social and cultural history emerged, influenced by prevailing trends in anthropology, sociology, and more recently, literary criticism, cultural studies, and critical theory, previously held notions of race and ethnicity have been sufficiently destabilized to the point that it is now common to view categories of race and ethnicity as social constructs of lessening importance. No longer bound solely by color or "cultural values," once conventional understandings of race and ethnicity are now seen to be critically contested, constantly shifting, and freely invented in order to serve a variety of social and personal agendas at any given point of time.

Embracing the idea that race and ethnicity are socially constructed, and thus not fixed categories of difference or similarity, Americans are now said to have the freedom to invent their racial and ethnic selves, choosing when to be racially or ethnically identified and when to be merely "American." In other words, Irish Americans can choose when to be Irish or simply White, Haitians can attempt to distance themselves from other Black

Americans, and Cambodian American students can decide when to be Cambodian, Cambodian American, Asian American, or American. And those Americans of mixed heritage have even more identities from which to choose. Once this freedom to invent our ethnicities is understood and accepted, it is believed by some that racism will decline because it will become evident that our previously held notions of race and ethnicity are false and unfounded. American society will then become "postethnic," where one is not essentialized due to her color or his religion, but it will be acknowledged and appreciated that we all belong to many and simultaneously overlapping affiliations, thus rendering race and ethnicity less important and therefore merely two of many categories of association.

While not refuting the position of viewing race and ethnicity as social constructions, the eleven essays in this section all implicitly or explicitly argue that American conceptions of race and ethnicity have consequences far beyond their formations as social constructs. They also stress that the site of race and ethnicity alone is not sufficient to analyze fully and understand the history of American social and cultural development. Class, gender, sexuality, time, and space all contribute to the shifting formations of our categories of knowledge and how we come to comprehend them.

Manning Marable and Ronald Takaki, the two presenters at the megasession on race, both speak to the enduring power of the concept of race as a site of unequal power relations. Marable emphasizes the danger of a simplistic binary approach to race relations which privileges Black-White interaction, which all too often serves to exclude other groups, such as Asians and Latinos, from the American discourse of race. He also makes a strong plea for us to transcend the strictures of identity politics in order to realize our parallel needs so that all of our communities can achieve the common goals of social equality. Takaki presents a compelling picture of how constructions of race and class have been and continue to be used as ideologies of discipline and punishment in order to maintain prevailing hierarchies of power thereby keeping certain groups disenfranchised in terms of political, social, and cultural capital. Pointing out that Asians have long been used to denigrate or define other racial and ethnic groups, he speaks forcefully of the ever-present power and importance of how concepts of race can be used as means of social control.

Moon-Ho Jung and Wai S. Lee draw historical comparisons between the experiences of Asians and Blacks in America. Jung investigates links between the trans-Atlantic slave trade and how enslaved Africans were treated and perceived in the United States and how Chinese laborers were recruited to work in the Americas and how they fared once here. He argues that the racialization of Blacks had a negative impact on the later racialization of Chinese, thus contributing to a tense relationship between these two groups and an exploitive relationship between these groups and Whites. Lee points out, however, that these historical similarities have been "forgotten" by present-day Korean and African Americans. Seeking to expand the "middleman theory" of ethnic relations, Lee calls attention to the need to supplement economic models with cultural and historical contexts in order to have a clearer understanding of the current racial hostilities and economic inequities between these two communities.

Geraldine Miyazaki Cuddihy and Jonathan Okamura offer two studies which help to locate the site of race in terms of place. Cuddihy explores the development of the ukekibi system (contract sugar cane growing) in Hawaii and its contribution to the growth of the sugar industry there. Long neglected in the historiography of the industry, the presence of the contract growers was indeed instrumental to the social and historical growth of the islands. Okamura maps the modern Filipino diaspora through a transnational mode of analysis which discloses how the compression of space and time affects Filipinos' construction of their ethnicity due to continuities with Philippine culture and their ongoing process of living in the United States.

The next three essays touch on a variety of ways in which race, ethnicity, place, events, and language are integral to the formation of group and individual identities. Scott McFarlane analyzes Joy Kogawa's *Obasan* by unraveling how racialized and gendered language in the novel serves to articulate how the internment of Japanese Canadians is understood in terms which serve to reconstruct the past in a redeemable present. Ruth Gim's research speaks to issues of gender, ethnicity, and levels of acculturation in regard to Asian Americans' attitudes toward mental health services and how these attitudes reflect individual and group ethnic identities and the presence or absence of a core set of common values. Hien Duc Do offers a glimpse into Asian American student culture by presenting a study of Vietnamese American students at the University of California at Santa Barbara, relating their racial, ethnic, and cultural backgrounds to their reasons for choosing certain academic majors and addressing the degree to which their historical and cultural circumstances sets them apart from other members of the university community.

Norma Timbang Kuehl describes the marginalization of Asians and Pacific Islanders (APIs) within the American health-care system largely because providers rarely see APIs as a community at risk for HIV infection. Yet during the last several years, the API population witnessed the largest percent increase among minorities in reported AIDS cases. The stereotype of APIs, points out Kuehl, denies them badly needed resources and culturally-sensitive treatment, and their marginalization is at once both racial and ethnic. With at least 32 distinct ethnicities and over 100 languages and dialects, APIs pose a particular challenge for health-care providers, and underscore the need for equal access.

The final essay by Jesse M. Vázquez brings us full circle. Focusing on the history of Puerto Rican Studies, he outlines the development of Ethnic Studies and how certain current trends in "multiculturalism" can dilute the original goals of Ethnic Studies by flattening out important social differences and inequities in our highly racialized and gendered society. He urges us to stay true to the struggle for the articulation of our voice but to be careful not to allow our distinct voices to be lost in the chorus of "multiculturalism."

The essays that follow in this section, therefore, place the shifting sites of race and ethnicity within social and historical contexts and speak very powerfully to the enduring significance of race in American history and contemporary society. While it is important to recognize that notions of race and ethnicity are indeed socially constructed, it remains imperative to understand how and why these constructions take place, and most vital, the consequences of these social constructs. From exclusion to internment, from Vincent Chin to the Los Angeles uprisings, the centrality of race and racism has been undeniable. The consequences of how race and ethnicity are perceived, constructed, manipulated, and acted upon are revealed in segregation, alienation, poverty, and death. As many of the studies in this volume urge, we must continue to reach across our bounded visions of race, ethnicity, class, gender, and sexuality to construct new and more humane ways of acknowledging and living with each other. There is much work to be done and the road is too long and difficult to negotiate to go it alone.

References

Aguilar-San Juan, Karin, ed. *The State of Asian America: Activism and Resistance in the 1990s.* Boston: South End Press, 1994.

Fields, Barbara. "Ideology and Race in American History." In *Race, Region and Reconstruction,* edited by Morgan Kousser and James McPherson. New York: Oxford University Press, 1982.

Hollinger, David. "Postethnic America." *Contention* 2 (Fall, 1992): 79-96.

Omi, Michael and Howard Winant. *Racial Formation in the United States from the 1960s to the 1980s*. New York: Routledge, 1986.

Smedley, Audrey. *Race in North America: Origin and Evolution of a Worldview*. Boulder: Westview Press, 1993.

Waters, Mary C. *Ethnic Options: Choosing Identities in America*. Berkeley: University of California Press, 1990.

West, Cornel. *Race Matters*. Boston: Beacon Press, 1993.

Beyond Racial Identity Politics: Toward a Liberation Theory for Multicultural Democracy

Manning Marable

Americans are arguably the most "race-conscious" people on earth. Even in South Africa, the masters of apartheid recognized the necessity to distinguish between "coloureds" and "black Africans." Under the bizarre regulations of apartheid, a visiting delegation of Japanese corporate executives, or the diplomatic corps of a client African regime such as Malawi could be classified as "honorary Whites." But in the U.S., "nationality" has been closely linked historically to the categories and hierarchy of national racial identity. Despite the orthodox cultural ideology of the so-called "melting pot," power, privilege, and the ownership of productive resources and property has always been unequally allocated in a social hierarchy stratified by class, gender, and race. Those who benefit directly from these institutional arrangements have historically been defined as "White," overwhelming upper class and male. And it is precisely here within this structure of power and privilege that "national identity" in the context of mass political culture is located. To be an "all-American" is by definition *not* to be an Asian American, Pacific American, American Indian, Latino, Arab American, or African American. Or viewed another way, the hegemonic ideology of "whiteness" is absolutely central in rationalizing and justifying the gross inequalities of race, gender, and class, experienced by millions of Americans relegated to the politically peripheral status of "Others."

As Marxist cultural critic E. San Juan, Jr. has observed, "Whenever the question of the national identity is at stake, boundaries in space and time are drawn .... A decision is made to represent the Others—people of color—as missing, absent, or supplemental." "Whiteness" becomes the very "center" for the dominant criteria for national prestige, decision-making, authority, and intellectual leadership.

Ironically, because of the centrality of "whiteness" within the dominant national identity, Americans generally make few distinctions between "ethnicity" and "race," and the two concepts are usually used interchangeably. Both the oppressors and those who are oppressed are therefore imprisoned by the closed dialectic of race. "Black" and "White" are usually viewed as fixed, permanent, and often antagonistic social categories. Yet, in reality, "race" should be understood not as an entity within the histories of all human societies, or grounded to some inescapable or permanent biological or genetic differences between human beings. "Race" is first and foremost an unequal relationship between social aggregates, characterized by dominant and subordinate forms of social interaction, and reinforced by the intricate patterns of public discourse, power, ownership, and privilege within the economic, social, and political institutions of society.

Race only becomes "real" as a social force when individuals or groups behave toward each other in ways which either reflect or perpetuate the hegemonic ideology of subordination and the patterns of inequality in daily life. These are, in turn, justified and explained by assumed differences in physical and biological characteristics, or in theories of cultural deprivation or intellectual inferiority. Thus, far from being static or fixed, race as an oppressive concept within social relations is fluid and ever-changing. What is an oppressed "racial group" changes over time, geographical space, and historical conjuncture. What is termed "Black," "Hispanic," or "Oriental" by those in power to describe one human being's "racial background" in a particular setting can have little historical or practical meaning within another social formation which is also racially stratified, but in a different manner.

Since so many Americans view the world through the prism of permanent racial categories, it is difficult to convey the idea that radically different ethnic groups may have roughly the identical "racial identity" which may be imposed on them. For example, although native-born African Americans, Trinidadians, Haitians, Nigerians, and Afro-Brazilians would all be termed "Black" on the streets of New York City, they have remarkably little in common in terms of language, culture, ethnic traditions, rituals, and religious affiliations. Yet they are all "Black" racially, in the sense that they will share many of the pitfalls and prejudices built into the institutional arrangements of the established social order for those defined as "Black." Similarly, an even wider spectrum of divergent ethnic groups—

from Japanese Americans, Chinese Americans, Filipino Americans, and Korean Americans to Hawaiians, Pakistanis, Vietnamese, Arabs, and Uzbekis—are described and defined by the dominant society as "Asians," or worse yet, as "Orientals." In the rigid, racially stratified American social order, the specific nationality, ethnicity, and culture of a person of color has traditionally been secondary to an individual's "racial category," a label of inequality which is imposed from without rather than constructed by the group from within. Yet as Michael Omi, Asian American studies professor at U.C. Berkeley has observed, we are also "in a period in which our conception of racial categories is being radically transformed." The waves of recent immigrants create new concepts of what the older ethnic communities have been. The observations and generalizations we imparted "to racial identities" in the past no longer make that much sense.

In the United States, "race" for the oppressed has also come to mean an identity of survival, victimization, and opposition to those racial groups or elites, which exercise power and privilege. What we are looking at here is *not* an *ethnic* identification or culture, but an awareness of shared experience, suffering, and struggles against the barriers of racial division. These collective experiences, survival tales, and grievances form the basis of an historical consciousness, a group's recognition of what it has witnessed and what it can anticipate in the near future. This second distinct sense of racial identity is both imposed on the oppressed and yet represent a reconstructed critical memory of the character of the group's collective ordeals. Both definitions of "race" and "racial identity" give character and substance to the movements for power and influence among people of color.

In the African American experience, the politics of racial identity has been expressed by two great traditions of racial ideology and social protest—integrationism and black nationalism. The integrationist tradition was initiated in the antebellum political activism of the free Negro community of the North, articulated by the great abolitionist orator Frederick Douglass. The black nationalist tradition was a product of the same social classes, but influenced by the pessimism generated by the Compromise of 1850, the Fugitive Slave Act, the Dred Scott decision, and the failure of the slave uprisings and revolts such as Nat Turner's, in ending the tyranny and inhumanity of the slave regime. The integrationist perspective was anchored in a firm belief in American democracy, and in the struggle to outlaw all legal barriers which restricted equal access and opportunities to racial minorities. It was linked to the politics of coalition-building with sympathetic white constituencies, aimed at achieving reforms within the context of the system. The integrationist version of racial politics sought the deracialization of the hierarchies of power within society and the economic system. By contrast, the black nationalist approach to racial politics was profoundly skeptical of America's ability to live up to its democratic ideals. It assumed that "racial categories" were real and fundamentally significant, and that efforts to accumulate power had to be structured along the boundaries of race for centuries to come. The nationalist tradition emphasized the cultural kinship of black Americans to Africa, and emphasized the need to establish all-black owned institutions to provide goods and services to the African American community.

Although the integrationists and nationalists seemed to hold radically divergent points of view, there was a subterranean symmetry between the two ideologies. Both were based on the idea that the essential dilemma or problem confronting black people was the omnipresent reality of race. The integrationists sought power to dismantle the barriers of race, to outlaw legal restrictions on Blacks' access to the institutions of authority and ownership, and to assimilate into the cultural "mainstream" without regard to race. The black nationalists favored a separatist path toward empowerment, believing that even the most liberal-minded Whites could not be trusted to destroy the elaborate network of privileges from which they benefited, called "white supremacy." But along the assimilationist-separatist axis of racial identity politics is the common perception that "race," however it is defined, is the most critical organizing variable within society. Race mattered so much more than other factors or variables, that to a considerable degree, the concept of race was perpetuated by the types of political interventions and tactical assumptions by activists and leaders on both sides of the assimilationist/separatist axis.

Both schools of racial identity espoused what can be termed the politics of "symbolic representation." Both the nationalists and integrationists believed that they were speaking to "white power brokers" on behalf of their "constituents"—black Americans. They believed that the real measure of racial power a group wielded within any society could be calibrated according to the institutions it dominated or the numbers of positions it controlled which influenced others. For the integrationists, it was a relatively simple matter of counting noses. If the number of African Americans in elective offices nationwide increased from 103 in 1964 to over 8,000 in 1993, for example, one could argue that African Americans as a *group* had increased their political power. Any increase in the number of Blacks as mayors, members of federal courts, and on boards of education, was championed as a victory for *all* black people. The black nationalists tended to be far more skeptical about the promise or viability of an electoral route of group empowerment. However, they often shared the same notions of symbolic representation when it came to the construction of social and economic institutions based on private-ownership models. The development of a black-owned shopping plaza, supermarket, or private school was widely interpreted as black social and economic empowerment for the group as a whole.

The problem with "symbolic representation" is that it presumes structures of accountability and allegiance between these blacks who are elevated into powerful positions of authority in the capitalist state with millions of African Americans clinging to the margins of economic and social existence. The unifying discourse of race obscures the growing class stratification within the African American community. According to the Census Bureau, for example, back in 1967 about, eighty-five percent of all African American families earned between $5,000 to $50,000 annually, measured in inflation-adjusted 1990 dollars. Forty-one percent earned between $10,000 to $25,000. In short, the number of extremely poor and destitute families was relatively small. The Census Bureau's statistics on African American households as of 1990 were strikingly different. The size of the black working-class and moderate-income people declined significantly, and the two extremes of poverty and affluence had grown sharply. By 1990, about twelve percent of all black households earned less than $5,000 annually. One-third of all Blacks lived below the federal government's poverty level. Conversely, a strong African American petty bourgeoisie, representing the growth of thousands of white collar professionals, executives, and managers created by affirmative action requirements, had been established.

The median incomes of African American families in which both the wife and husband were employed rose from about $28,700 in 1967 to over $40,000 in 1990, an increase of forty percent. More than fifteen percent of all African American households earned above $50,000 annually, and thousands of black professional families had incomes exceeding $100,000 annually. Many of these newly affluent Blacks have moved far from the problems of the central cities, into the comfortable white enclaves of suburbia. Nevertheless, many of the strongest advocates of racial identity politics since the demise of black power and the black freedom movement come from the most privileged, elitist sectors of the black upper middle class. The dogmatic idea that "race" alone explains virtually everything which occurs within society has a special appeal to some African American suburban elites who have little personal connections with the vast human crisis of ghetto unemployment, black-on-black crime, rampant drugs, gang violence, and deteriorating schools. Moreover, for black entrepreneurs, traditional race categories could be employed as a tool to promote petty capital accumulation, by urging black consumers to "buy black."

Racial identity politics in this context is contradictory and conceptually limited in other critical respects. As noted, it tends to minimize greatly any awareness or analysis of class stratification and concentrations of poverty or affluence among the members of the defined "racial minority group."

Issues of poverty, hunger, unemployment, and homelessness are viewed and interpreted within a narrowly racial context—that is, as a by-product of the large racist contradiction within society as a whole. Conversely, concentrations of wealth or social privilege within sectors of the racial group are projected as "success stories"—see, for example, issue after issue of *Ebony, Black Enterprise*, and *Jet*. In the context of racial identity politics, the idea of "social change" is usually expressed in utilitarian and pragmatic terms, if change is expressed at all. The integrationist generally favors working within the established structures of authority, influencing those in power to dole out new favors or additional privileges to minorities. Their argument is that "democracy" works best when it is truly pluralistic and inclusive, with the viewpoints of all "racial groups" taken into account. But such a strategy rarely if ever gets at the root of the real problem of the persuasiveness of racism—social inequality. It articulates an eclectic, opportunistic approach to change, rather than a comprehensive or systemic critique, informed by a social theory of any kind. In the case of the racial separatists, the general belief that "race" is a relatively permanent social category in all multiethnic societies, and that virtually all Whites are immutably racist, either for genetic, biological, or psychological reasons, compromise, the very concept of meaningful social change. If allies are nonexistent or at best untrustworthy, or if dialogues with progressive Whites must await the construction of broad-based unity among virtually all Blacks, then even tactical alliances with social forces outside the black community become difficult to sustain.

But perhaps the greatest single weakness in the politics of racial identity is that it is rooted implicitly on a competitive model of group empowerment. If the purpose of politics is the realization of a group or constituency's specific, objective interest, then racial identity politics utilizes racial consciousness or the group's collective memory and experiences as the essential framework for interpreting the actions and interests of all other social groups. This approach is not unlike a model of political competition based on a "zero-sum" game such as poker, in which a player can be a "winner" only if one or more other players are "losers." The prism of a group's racial experiences tends to blunt the parallels, continuities, and common interests which might exist between oppressed racial groups, and highlights and emphasizes areas of dissension and antagonism.

The black-nationalist-oriented intelligentsia, tied to elements of the new African American upper middle class by income, social position, and cultural outlook, began to search for ways of expressing itself through the "permanent" prism of race, while rationalizing its relatively privileged class position. One expression of this search for a social theory was found in the writings of Afrocentric theorist Molefi Asante. Born Arthur Lee Smith in 1942, Asante emerged as the founding editor of the *Journal of Black Studies* in 1969. Asante became a leading force in the National Council of Black Studies, the African Heritage Studies Association, and after 1980, chair of the African American Studies Department at Temple University. Asante's basic thesis, the cultural philosophy of "Afrocentrism," began with the insight that people of European descent or cultures have a radically different understanding of the human condition than people of African and/or non-western cultures and societies.

"Human beings tend to recognize three fundamental existential postures one can take with respect to the human condition: feeling, knowing, and acting," Asante observed in 1983. Europeans utilize these concepts separately in order to understand them objectively. Thus "Eurocentrists" tend to understand their subjects "apart from the emotions, attitudes, and cultural definitions of a given context." Scholars with a "Eurocentric" perspective, those who view the entire history of human development through the vantage point and interests of European civilization, are also primarily concerned with a "subject/object duality" which exists in a linear environment. European cultures and people are viewed as the central subjects of history, the creative forces which dominate and transform the world overtime. Asante states that this "Euro-linear" viewpoint helps to explain the construction of institutional racism, apartheid, and imperialism across the nonwhite world.

By contrast, the Afrocentric framework for comprehending society and human development was radically different, according to Asante. Afrocentrism "understands that the interrelationship of knowledge with cosmology, society, religion, medicine, and traditions stands alongside the interactive metaphors of discourse as principle means of achieving a measure of knowledge about experience." Unlike a linear view of the world, the Afrocentric approach is a "circular view" of human interaction which "seeks to interpret and understand." In theoretical terms, this means that the study of African and African American phenomena should be within their original cultural contexts, and not within the paradigmatic frameworks of Eurocentrism. Drawing upon African cultural themes, values, and concepts, Afrocentrism seeks therefore the creation of a harmonious environment in which all divergent cultures could coexist and learn from each other. Rather than seeking the illusion of the melting pot, Asante calls for the construction of "parallel frames of reference" within the context of a multicultural, pluralistic environment. "Universality," Asante warns, "can only be dreamed about when we have slept on truth based on specific cultural experience."

The practical impact of the theory of Afrocentrism was found among black educators. After all, if people of African descent had a radically different cultural heritage, cosmology, and philosophy of being than Whites, it made sense to devise an alternate curriculum which was "Afrocentric." Such an approach to education would be completely comprehensive, Asante insisted, expressing the necessity for "every topic, economics, law, communication, science, religion, history, literature, and sociology to be reviewed through Afrocentric eyes." No African American child should "attend class as they are currently being taught or read books as they are currently being written without raising questions about our capability as a people . . . . All children must be centered in a historical place, or their self-esteem suffers." By 1991, approximately 350 "Afrocentric academies" and private schools were educating more than 50,000 African American students throughout the country. Many large public school districts adopted Afrocentric supplementary and required textbooks, or brought in Afrocentric-oriented educators for curriculum development workshops. Several public school systems, notably in Detroit, Baltimore, and Milwaukee, established entire "Afrocentric schools" for hundreds of school-aged children, transforming all aspects of their learning experience. On college campuses, many black studies programs began to restructure their courses to reflect Asante's Afrocentric philosophy.

There is no doubt that Afrocentrism established a vital and coherent cultural philosophy which appealed to African Americans favorably disposed toward black nationalism. Some Afrocentric scholars in the area of psychology, notably Linda James Myers, formulated some innovative and effective measures for promoting the development of positive self-concepts among African Americans. Asante used his position at Temple to create a scholastic tradition which represented a sharp critique and challenge to Eurocentrism. The difficulty was that this scholarly version of Afrocentrism tended to be far more sophisticated than the more popular version of the philosophy embraced by elements of the dogmatically separatist, cultural nationalist community. One such Afrocentric popularizer was Professor Len Jefferies, once chair of the Black Studies Program at the City College of New York. Jefferies claimed that white Americans were "ice people" due to environmental, psychological, and cultural factors inherent in their evolution in Europe; African Americans by contrast were defined as "sun people," characteristically warm, open, and charitable. At the level of popular history, the vulgar Afrocentrists glorified in an overly simplistic manner the African heritage of black Americans. In their writings, they rarely related the actual complexities of the local cultures, divergences of language, religions, and political institutions, and tended to homogenize the sharply different social structures found within the African diaspora. They pointed with pride to the dynasties of Egypt as the classical foundation of African civilization—without also examining with equal vigor or detail Egypt's slave structure. At times, the racial separatists of vulgar Afrocentrism embraced elements of a black chauvinism and intolerance towards others, and espoused public positions which were blatantly anti-Semitic. Jefferies' public statements attacking Jews and the countercharge that he espoused anti-Semitic viewpoints made it easier for white conservatives to denigrate all African American studies, and to undermine efforts to require multicultural curricula within public schools.

Scholarly Afrocentrism co-existed uneasily with its vulgar, populist variety. When Jefferies was deposed as chair of City College's Black Studies Department in the controversy following his anti-Semitic remarks, Asante wisely stayed outside the debate. Nevertheless, there remained theoretical problems inherent in the more scholarly paradigm. Afrocentric intellectuals gave eloquent lip service to the insights of black scholars such as W. E. B. Du Bois as "pillars" of their own perspective, without also acknowledging that Du Bois's philosophy of culture and history conflicted sharply with their own. Du Bois's major cultural and philosophical observation, expressed nearly a century ago in *The Souls of Black Folk*, claimed that the African American expresses a "double consciousness." The black American was "an American, Negro; two souls, two thoughts, two unreconciled strivings; two warring ideals in one dark body, whose dogged strength alone keeps it from being torn asunder." Africa in effect represents only one-half of the dialectical consciousness of African American people. Blacks are also legitimately Americans, and by our suffering, struggle, and culture we have a destiny within this geographical and political space equal to or stronger than any white American. This realization that the essence of the inner spirit of African American people was reflected in this core duality was fundamentally ignored by the Afrocentrists.

Vulgar Afrocentrists deliberately ignored or obscured the historical reality of social class stratification within the African diaspora. They essentially argued that the interests of all black people—from former Joint Chiefs of Staff Chairman General Colin Powell to conservative Supreme Court Associate Justice Clarence Thomas, to the black unemployed, homeless, and hungry of America's decaying urban ghettoes—were philosophically, culturally, and racially the same. Even the scholarly Afrocentric approach elevated a neo-Kantian idealism above a dialectical idealist analysis, much less speaking to historical materialism except to attack it as such, vulgar Afrocentrism was the perfect social theory for the upwardly mobile black petty bourgeoisie. It gave them a vague sense of ethnic superiority and cultural originality, without requiring the hard, critical study of historical realities. It provided a philosophical blueprint to avoid concrete struggle within the real world, since potential white "allies" certainly were non-existent and all cultural change began from within. It was, in short, only the latest theoretical construct of a politics of racial identity, a worldview designed to discuss the world, but never really to change it.

How do we transcend the theoretical limitations and social contradictions of the politics of racial identity? The challenge begins by constructing new cultural and political "identities," based on the realities of America's changing multicultural, democratic milieu. The task of constructing a tradition of unity between various groups of color in America is a far more complex and contradictory process than any progressive activists or scholars have admitted, precisely because of divergent cultural traditions, languages, and conflicting politics of racial identities—by Latinos, African Americans, Asian Americans, Pacific Island Americans, Arab Americans, American Indians, and others. Highlighting the current dilemma in the 1990s, is the collapsing myth of "brown-black solidarity." Back in the 1960s and early 1970s, with the explosion of the civil rights and black power movements in the African American community, activist formations with similar objectives also emerged among Latinos. The Black Panther Party and the League of Revolutionary Black Workers, for example, found their counterparts among Chicano militants with La Raza Unida Party in Texas, and the Crusade for Justice in Colorado. The Council of La Raza and the Mexican American Legal Defense Fund began to push for civil rights reforms within government and expanding influence for Latinos within the Democratic Party, paralleling the same strategies of Jesse Jackson's Operation PUSH and the NAACP Legal Defense Fund. With the growth of a more class-conscious black and Latino petty bourgeoisie, ironically a social product of affirmative action and civil rights gains, tensions between these two large communities of people of color began to deteriorate. The representatives of the African American middle class consolidated their electoral control of the city councils and mayoral posts of major cities throughout the country. Black entrepreneurship increased, as the black American consumer market reached a gross sales figure of $270 billion by 1991, an amount equal to the gross domestic product of the fourteenth wealthiest nation on earth. The really important "symbolic triumphs of this privileged strata of the African American community were not the dynamic 1984 and 1988 presidential campaigns of Jesse Jackson; they were instead the electoral victory of Democratic "moderate" Doug Wilder as Virginia's governor in 1990, and the anointment of former Jackson lieutenant-turned-moderate Ron Brown as head of the Democratic National Committee. Despite the defeats represented by Reaganism and the absence of affirmative action enforcement, there was a sense that the strategy of "symbolic representation" had cemented this strata's hegemony over the bulk of the black population. Black politicians like Doug Wilder and television celebrity journalists such as black-nationalist-turned-Republican Tony Brown were not interested in pursuing coalitions between Blacks and other people of color. Multiracial, multiclass alliances raised too many questions about the absence of political accountability between middle-class "leaders" and their working-class and low income "followers." Even Jesse Jackson shied away from addressing a black-Latino alliance except in the most superficial terms.

By the late 1980s and early 1990s, however, the long-delayed brown-black dialogue at the national level began crystallizing into tensions around at least four critical issues. First, after the 1990 Census, scores of Congressional districts were reapportioned to have African American or Latino pluralities or majorities, guaranteeing greater minority group representation in Congress. However, in cities and districts where Latinos and Blacks were roughly divided, or especially in those districts which Blacks had controlled in previous years but in which Latinos now were in the majority, disagreements often led to fractious ethnic conflicts. Latinos claimed that they were grossly underrepresented within the political process. African American middle-class leaders argued that "Latinos" actually represented four distinct groups with little to no shared history or common culture: Mexican Americans, concentrated overwhelmingly in the southwestern states; Hispanics from the Caribbean, chiefly Puerto Ricans and Dominicans, most of whom had migrated to New York City and the Northeast since 1945; Cuban Americans, mostly middle- to upper-class exiles of Castro's Cuba, and who voted heavily Republican; and the most recent Spanish-speaking emigrants from Central and South America. Blacks insisted that Cuban Americans definitely were not an "underprivileged minority," and as such did not merit minority set-aside economic programs, affirmative action, and equal opportunity programs. The cultural politics of Afrocentrism made it difficult for many African Americans to recognize any common interest which they might share with Latinos.

Immigration issues are also at the center of recent Latino-black conflicts. Over one-third of the Latino population of more that 24 million in the U.S. consists of undocumented workers. Some middle-class African American leaders have taken the politically conservative viewpoint that undocumented Latino workers deprive poor Blacks jobs within the low wage sectors of the economy. Bilingual education and efforts to impose language and cultural conformity upon all sectors of society such as "English-only" referenda, have also been issues of contention. Finally, the key element which drives these topics of debate is the rapid transformation of America's nonwhite demography. Because of relatively higher birth rates than the general population and substantial immigration, within less than two decades Latinos as a group will outnumber African Americans as the largest minority group in the U.S. Even by 1990, about one out of nine U.S. households spoke a non-English language at home, predominately Spanish .

Black middle-class leaders who were accustomed to advocating the interests of their constituents in simplistic racial terms were increasingly confronted by Latinos who felt alienated from the system and largely ignored and underrepresented by the political process. Thus in May 1991, Latinos took to the streets in Washington, D.C., hurling bottles and rocks and looting over a dozen stores, when local police shot a Salvadorian man whom they claimed had wielded a knife. African American mayor Sharon Pratt Dixon ordered over one thousand police officers to patrol the city's

Latino neighborhoods, and used tear gas to quell the public disturbances. In effect, a black administration in Washington, D.C. used the power of the police and courts to suppress the grievances of Latinos—just as a white administration had done against black protesters during the urban uprisings of 1968.

The tragedy here is that too little is done either by African American or Latino "mainstream" leaders who practice racial identity politics to transcend their parochialism and to redefine their agendas on common ground. Latinos and Blacks alike can agree on an overwhelming list of issues—such as the inclusion of multicultural curricula in public schools, improvements in public health care, job training initiative, the expansion of public transportation, and housing for low to moderate income people; and greater fairness and legal rights within the criminal justice system. Despite the image that Latinos as a group are more "economically privileged" than African Americans, Mexican American families earn only slightly more than black households, and Puerto Rican families earn less than black Americans on average. Economically, Latinos and African Americans both have experienced the greatest declines in real incomes and some of the greatest increases in poverty rates within the U.S. From 1973 to 1990, for example, the incomes for families headed by a parent under 30 years of age declined 28 percent for Latino families and 48 percent for African American families. The poverty rates for young families in these same years rose 44 percent for Latinos and 58 percent for Blacks.

There is also substantial evidence that Latinos continue to experience discrimination in elementary, secondary, and higher education which is in many respects more severe than that experienced by African Americans. Although high school graduation rates for the entire population have steadily improved, the rates for Latinos have declined consistently since the mid-1980s. In 1989, for instance, 76 percent of all African Americans and 82 percent of all Whites who were age 18 to 24 years old had graduated from high school. By contrast, the graduation rate for Latinos in 1989 was 56 percent. By 1992, the high school completion rate for Latino males dropped to its lowest level, 47.8 percent, since such figures were collected by the American Council on Education in 1972. In colleges and universities, the pattern of Latino inequality was the same. In 1991, 34 percent of all Whites and 24 percent of all African Americans age 18 to 24 years were enrolled in college. Latino college enrollment for the same age group was barely 18 percent. As of 1992, approximately 22 percent of the non-Latino adult population in the U.S. possessed at least a four year college degree. College graduation rates for Latino adults were just 10 percent. Thus on a series of public policy issues—access to quality education, economic opportunity, the availability of human services, and civil rights—Latinos and African Americans share a core set of common concerns and long-term interests. What is missing is the dynamic vision and political leadership necessary to build something more permanent than temporary electoral coalitions between these groups.

A parallel situation exists between Asian Americans, Pacific Americans, and the black American community. Two generations ago, the Asian American population was comparatively small, except in states such as California, Washington, and New York. With the end of discriminatory immigration restrictions on Asians in 1965, however, the Asian American population began to soar dramatically, changing the ethnic and racial character of urban America. For example, in the years 1970 to 1990, the Korean population increased from 70,000 to 820,000. Since 1980, about 33,000 Koreans have entered the U.S. each year, a rate of immigration exceeded only by Latinos and Filipinos. According to the 1990 Census, the Asian American and Pacific Islander population in the U.S. exceeds 7.3 million.

Some of the newer Asian immigrants in the 1970s and 1980s were of middle-class origins with backgrounds in entrepreneurship, small manufacturing, and in the white collar professions. Thousands of Asian American small-scale, family-owned businesses began to develop in black and Latino neighborhoods, in many instances taking the place which Jewish merchants had occupied in ghettoes a generation before. It did not take long before Latino and black petty hostilities and grievances against these new ethnic entrepreneurial group began to crystallize into deep racial hatred. When African American rapper Ice Cube expressed his anger against Los Angeles's Korean American business community in the 1991 song "Black Korea," he was also voicing the popular sentiments of many younger Blacks:

> So don't follow me up and down your market, or your little chop-suey ass will be a target of the nationwide boycott. Choose with the people, that's what the boy got. So pay respect to the black fist, or we'll burn down your store, right down to a crisp, and then we'll see you, 'cause you can't turn the ghetto into Black Korea.

Simmering ethnic tensions boiled into open outrage in Los Angeles when a black teenage girl was killed by Korean American merchant Soon-Ja Du. Although convicted of voluntary manslaughter, Du was sentenced to probation and community service only. Similarly in the early 1990s, African Americans launched economic boycotts and political confrontations with Korean American small merchants in New York.

Thus in the aftermath of the blatant miscarriage of justice in Los Angeles last year—the acquittals of four white police officers for the violent beating of Rodney King—the anger and outrage within the African American community was channeled not against the state and the corporations, but small Korean American merchants. Throughout Los Angeles, over 1,500 Korean American owned stores were destroyed, burned, or looted. Following the urban uprising, a fiercely anti-Asian sentiment continued to permeate sections of Los Angeles. In 1992-93, there have been a series of incidents of Asian Americans being harassed or beaten in southern California. After the rail system contract was awarded to a Japanese company, a chauvinistic movement was launched to "buy American." Asian Americans are still popularly projected to other nonwhites as America's successful "model minorities," fostering resentment, misunderstandings, and hostilities among people of color. Yet black leaders have consistently failed to explain to African Americans that Asian Americans as a group do not own the major corporations or banks which control access to capital. Asian Americans as a group do not own massive amounts of real estate, control the courts or city governments, have ownership in the mainstream media, dominate police forces, or set urban policies.

While African Americans, Latinos, and Asian Americans scramble over which group should control the mom-and-pop grocery store in their neighborhood, almost no one questions the racist "redlining" policies of large banks which restrict access to capital to nearly all people of color. Black and Latino working people usually are not told by their race-conscious leaders and middle-class "symbolic representatives" that institutional racism has also frequently targeted Asian Americans throughout U.S. history—from the recruitment and exploitation of Asian laborers, to a series of lynching and violent assaults culminating in the mass incarceration of Japanese Americans during World War II, to the slaying of Vincent Chin in Detroit, and the violence and harassment of other Asian Americans. A central ideological pillar of "whiteness" is the consistent scapegoating of the "oriental menace." As legal scholar Mari Matsuda observes: "There is an unbroken line of poor and working Americans turning their anger and frustration into hatred of Asian Americans. Every time this happens, the real villains—the corporations and politicians who put profits before human needs—are allowed to go about their business free from public scrutiny, and the anger that could go to organizing for positive social change goes instead to Asian-bashing."

What is required is a radical break from the narrow, racebased politics of the past, which characterized the core assumptions about black empowerment since the mid-nineteenth century. We need to recognize that both perspectives of racial identity politics which are frequently juxtaposed, integration/assimilation vs. nationalist/separatism, are actually two different sides of the same ideological and strategic axis. To move into the future will require that we bury the racial barriers of the past, for good. The essential point of departure is the deconstruction of the idea of "whiteness," the ideology of white power, privilege, and elitism which remains heavily embedded within the dominant culture, social institutions, and economic arrangements of the society. But we must do more than to critique the white pillars of race, gender, and class domination. We must rethink and restructure the central social categories of collective struggle by which we conceive and understand our own political reality. We must redefine "blackness" and other traditional racial categories to be more inclusive of contemporary ethnic realities.

To be truly liberating, any social theory must reflect the actual problems of an historical conjuncture with a commitment to rigor and scholastic truth. "Afrocentrism" fails on all counts to provide that clarity of insight into the contemporary African American urban experience. It looks to a romantic, mythical reconstruction of yesterday to find some understanding for the cultural basis of today's racial and class challenges. Yet that critical understanding of reality cannot begin with an examination of the lives of Egyptian pharaohs. It must begin by critiquing the vast structure of power and privilege which characterizes the political economy of post-industrial, capitalist America. According to the Center on Budget and Policy Priorities, during the Reagan-Bush era of the 1980s, the poorest one-fifth of all Americans earned about $7,725 annually, and experienced a decline in before-tax household incomes of 3.8 percent in the decade. The middle fifth of all U.S. households earned about $31,000 annually, with an income gain of 3.1 percent during the 1980s. Yet the top fifth household incomes reached over $105,200 annually by 1990, with before-tax incomes soaring 29.8 percent in the decade. The richest five percent of all American households exceeded $206,000 annually, improving their incomes by 44.9 percent under Reagan and Bush. The wealthiest one percent of all U.S. households reached nearly $550,000 per year, with average before tax incomes increasing by 75.3 percent. In effect, since 1980, the income gap between America's wealthiest one percent and the middle class *nearly doubled.* As the Center on Budget and Policy Priorities relates, the wealthiest one percent of all Americans, roughly 2.5 million people, receive "nearly as much income after taxes as the bottom 40 percent, about 100 million people. While wealthy households are taking a larger share of the national income, the tax burden has been shifted down the income pyramid." A social theory of a reconstructed, multicultural democracy must advance the reorganization and ownership of capital resources, the expansion of production in minority areas, and provide guarantees for social welfare such as a single-payer, national health care system.

The factor of "race" by itself, does not and cannot explain the massive transformation of the structure of capitalism in its post-industrial phase, and the destructive redefinition of "work" itself as we enter the twenty-first century. Increasingly in western Europe and America, the new division of "haves" vs. "have nots" is characterized by a new segmentation of the labor force. The division is between those workers who have maintained basic economic security and benefits—such as full health insurance, term life insurance, pensions, educational stipends or subsidies for the employee's children, paid vacations, and so forth—vs. those marginal workers who are either unemployed, part-time employees, or who labor but have few if any benefits. Since 1982, "temporary employment" or part-time hirings without benefits have increased 250 percent across the U.S., while all employment has grown by less that 20 percent. Today, the largest private employer in the U.S. is Manpower, Inc., the world's largest temporary employment agency, with 560,000 workers. By the year 2000, one-half of all American workers will be classified as part-time employees, or as they are termed within IBM, "the peripherals." The reason for this massive restructuring of labor relations is capital's search for surplus value or profits. In 1993, it is estimated that the total payroll costs in the U.S. of $2.6 billion annually will be reduced $800 million by the utilization of part-time laborers and employees. Increasingly, disproportionately high percentages of Latino and African American workers will be trapped within this second-tiered labor market. Black, Latino, Asian American, and low income white workers all share a stake in fighting for a new social contract relating to work and social benefits: the right to a good job should be as guaranteed as the human right to vote; the right of free quality health care should be as secure as the freedom of speech. The radical changes within the domestic economy require that black leadership reach out to other oppressed sectors of the society, creating a common program for economic and social justice. Vulgar Afrocentrism looks inward; the new black liberation of the twenty-first century must look outward, embracing those people of color and oppressed people of divergence ethnic backgrounds who share our democratic vision.

The multicultural democratic critique must consider the changing demographic, cultural, and class realities of modern, post-industrial America. By the year 2000, one-third of the total U.S. population will consist of people of color. Within seventy years, roughly one half of America's entire population will be Latino, American Indian, Asian American, Pacific American, Arab American, and African American. The ability to create a framework for multicultural democracy intergroup dialogue and interaction within and between the most progressive leaders, grassroots activists, intellectuals, and working people of these communities will determine the future of American society itself. Our ability to transcend racial chauvinism and inter-ethnic hatred and the old definitions of "race," to recognize the class commonalties and joint social justice interests of all groups in the restructuring of this nation's economy and social order, will be the key in the construction of a nonracist democracy, transcending ancient walls of white violence, corporate power, and class privilege. By dismantling the narrow politics of racial identity and selective self-interest, by going beyond "Black" and "White," we may construct new values, new institutions, and new visions of an America beyond traditional racial categories and racial oppression.

References

Apple, R.W ., Jr. "In Clashes, A Hispanic Agenda Enters." *New York Times*, 9 May 1991.

Asante, Molefi. *The Afrocentric Idea.* Philadelphia: Temple University Press, 1987.

_____. "The Ideological Significance of Afrocentricity in Intercultural Communication." *Journal of Black Studies* 14 (September 1983): 3-19.

_____. "Systematic Nationalism: A Legitimate Strategy for National Selfhood." *Journal of Black Studies* 9 (September 1978): 115-28.

_____. "Transracial Communication and the Changing Image of Black Americans." *Journal of Black Studies* 4 (September 1979): 69-80.

Barringer, Felicity. "Rich-Poor Gulf Widens among Blacks." *New York Times*, 25 September 1992.

"Capital Unrest Reminds Latins of Their Past." *New York Times*, 8 May 1991.

Coughlin, Ellen K. "Sociologists Examine the Complexities of Racial and Ethnic Identity in America." *Chronicle of Higher Education*, 24 March 1993.

DePalma, Anthony. "College Still Remains an Elusive Goal for Minority Students." *New York Times,* 18 January 1993.

Du Bois, W. E.B. *The Souls of Black Folk: Essays and Sketches*. Chicago: A.C. McClurg, 1903.

Hamamoto, Darrell Y. "Black-Korean Conflict in Los Angeles." *Z Magazine*, July/August 1992.

Hutchinson, Earl Ofari. "Black-Latino clashes shatter solidarity myth." *Guardian*, 25 September 1991.

Kurashige, Scott. "How We Got to This Point: An Asian Pacific Perspective on the Los Angeles Rebellion." *Forward Motion* 3 (July 1992): 5-12.

Magner, Denise K. "Hispanics Remain 'Grossly Underrepresented' on Campuses, Report Says." *Chronicle of Higher Education*, 25 January 1991.

Matsuda, Mari. "Are Asian Americans a Racial Bourgeoisie?" *Katipunan* 1 (September 1990): 12.

Omi, Michael. "Shifting the Blame: Racial Ideology and Politics in the Post-Civil Rights Era." *Critical Sociology* 18 (Fall 1992).

San Juan, E., Jr. "Racism, Ideology, Resistance." *Forward Motion* 3 (September 1991): 35-42.

Sklar, Holly. "The Truly Greedy." *Z Magazine*, June 1991.

Takaki, Ronald. *Strangers from a Different Shore*. Boston: Little, Brown, 1989.

Race as a Site of Discipline and Punish

Ronald Takaki

The theme of this megasession is "race as a site." But how do we define "race"? All of us agree that race is a social construction, and in terms of the United States, the 1992 Los Angeles explosion offered a crucial lesson: race can no longer be viewed in binary terms of Whites and Blacks. Asian Americans have to be included as well. Furthermore, the study of race needs to be comparative in approach: we must learn about one another in order for Americans to get along in a racially diverse society. Such a multiracial perspective will also help us reach toward a view of the big picture and understand developments related to the various racial groups within a broader and more comprehensive context.

But why choose race as a site, in view of William Julius Wilson's contention of "the declining significance of race"? Class, he argues, has become more important than race as a factor determining the life chances of Blacks. "It is clearly evident . . . that many talented and educated Blacks are now entering positions of prestige and influence at a rate comparable to or, in some situations, exceeding that of Whites with equivalent qualifications. It is equally clear that the Black underclass is in a hopeless state of economic stagnation, falling further and further behind the rest of society" (1978:1-2).

Could it be, however, that race is actually inclining rather than declining in significance as American society approaches the twenty-first century and the time when Whites will become a minority of the total population? What exactly is the significance of race?

Moreover, of what is race a site? This question has already been addressed by my two distinguished fellow panelists—Martin Bernal and Manning Marable.

For Bernal, author of *Black Athena,* race is a site of the contested scholarship over the intellectual construction of Western civilization: how "Western" is "Western" civilization? During the nineteenth century, this debate revolved around two models—the "Ancient" and the "Aryan." The first acknowledged the influences of Egyptian and African civilizations on Greek civilization as well as the crisscrossing of these different cultures. The second denied such sharing and insisted on the purity of Western civilization. During this period of history, the "Aryan" triumphed over the "Ancient" model. For European "Romantics and racists" of that time, Bernal notes, "it was simply intolerable for Greece, which was seen not merely as the epitome of Europe but also as its pure childhood, to have been the result of the mixture of native Europeans and colonizing Africans and Semites. Therefore the Ancient Model had to be overthrown and replaced by something more acceptable" (1991:1-2, 27, 32, 52, 53, 241-42).

For Marable, race is a site of how capitalism underdeveloped black America and how capitalism developed by exploiting and degrading African Americans. "The most striking fact about American economic history and politics," he observes, "is the brutal and systemic underdevelopment of Black people. . . . Capitalist development has occurred not in spite of the exclusion of Blacks, but because of the brutal exploitation of Blacks as workers and consumers. Blacks have never been equal partners in the American Social Contract, because the system exists not to develop, but to underdevelop Black people" (1983:1-2).

If we bring together the views of both Bernal and Marable, we will see how they not only complement one another, but how they also expand and analytically enrich each other.

Bernal documents how Blacks were degraded ideologically during the era of Western imperialism. This helps to explain how Blacks were subjected to labor exploitation—how they were "underdeveloped." Marable, in turn, highlights the economic context—how the overthrow of the "Ancient" model and the ascendancy of the "Aryan" model were instrumental in the development of Western capitalism.

In my essay, I would like to pursue this juxtaposition of Bernal and Marable by examining, from a comparative perspective, race as a site where intellectual and material forces dynamically interacted in relationship to what I have described as the "iron cages," especially the "republican iron cage" of individualism and the "corporate iron cage" of modern bureaucratic capitalism (Takaki 1979).

Let me begin by telling you about a debate on affirmative action that Nathan Glazer and I had at the University of Wisconsin several years ago. After we each presented our papers, we engaged in a direct exchange of views and arguments. As I recall, Glazer contended that ethnic groups in

American society were assimilating, but progressing at different rates. To illustrate his thesis, he suggested that we think of this pattern as one of concentric circles: the innermost circle was occupied by the middle-class mainstream (presumably White and Protestant), the second circle by the white "ethnic" groups like Italians and Jews, and the third circle by groups of color like African Americans and Asian Americans. Glazer noted that the groups in the second circle had assimilated and entered the core circle through education and individualism, and that Asian Americans had followed this same path to success. What made the Asian American example significant was evident: victims of racial discrimination, they had advanced themselves economically without reliance on government interventionist policies. If Asian Americans were able to make it on their own, Glazer reasoned, African Americans should also be able to do it without affirmative action. Here was a reaffirmation of the republican ideology of our country's founding fathers with its emphasis on the "republican" values of self-reliance, thrift, hard work, and individualism.

In his argument, however, Glazer exaggerated Asian American "success" and therefore helped to create a new myth. Economic comparisons between Asian Americans and Whites fail to recognize the regional location of the Asian American population. Concentrated in California, Hawaii, and New York, Asian Americans reside mostly in states with higher incomes but also higher costs of living than the national average: 59 percent of all Asian Americans were living in these three states in 1980, compared to only 19 percent of the general population. In addition, comparisons between Asian Americans and Whites have usually relied on family incomes, but this is very misleading, for Asian American families have more persons working per family than white families (Takaki 1984, 1985).

Actually, in terms of personal incomes, Asian Americans have not reached equality. In 1980 the mean personal income for white men in California was $23,400. While Japanese men earned a comparable income, they did so only by acquiring more education (17.7 years compared to 16.8 years for White men, 25-44 years old) and by working more hours (2,160 hours compared to 2,120 hours for white men in the same age category). In reality, then, Japanese men are still behind white men. Income inequalities for other Asian men are even more evident: Korean men earned only $19,200 or 82 percent of the income of white men, Chinese men only $15,900 or 68 percent, and Filipino men only $14,500 or 62 percent. In New York the mean personal income for white men was $21,600, compared to only $18,900 or 88 percent for Korean men, $16,500 or 76 percent for Filipino men, and only $11,200 or 52 percent for Chinese men. In the San Francisco Bay Area, Chinese immigrant men earned only 72 percent of white men, Filipino immigrant men 68 percent, Korean immigrant men 69 percent, and Vietnamese immigrant men 52 percent. The incomes of Asian American men were close to and sometimes even below those of black men (68 percent) and Mexican American men (71 percent) (Cabezas and Kawaguchi 1988:143, 154; Cabezas 1986:6, 8, 9; Cabezas, Shinagawa, Kawaguchi 1986:9-10).

But we make a mistake to think that Glazer's comparison between the two groups is really just about statistics. What we have in his analysis is, in effect, the representation of Asian Americans as a "model minority." For Glazer, Asian Americans serve as an example for African Americans. His deeper purpose is to demonstrate that a racial minority can make it into the American mainstream through individual initiative and industry without government intervention.

Actually, the view of Asian Americans as a model for other groups is not a recent concept.

During the 1850s, for example, sugar planters in Hawaii consciously pitted Chinese against Hawaiian workers. Praising the Chinese for their efficiency and using them to set the work pace for the Hawaiians, planters noted gleefully how the Chinese worked hard and how the immigrant laborers called the Hawaiians, "wahine! wahine!" ("women, women"), when the native laborers did not keep up with them.

Chinese laborers were used in a similar way by planters in the South after the abolition of slavery. A year after the end of the Civil War, a planter declared: "We can drive the niggers out and import coolies that will work better at less expense, and relieve us from the cursed nigger impudence." The plan was to turn from Black to Chinese labor. "Emancipation has spoiled the Negro and carried him away from the fields of agriculture," the editor of the *Vicksburg Times* in Mississippi complained in 1869. "Our prosperity depends entirely upon the recovery of lost ground, and we therefore say let the Coolies come." That same year, the Southern planters' convention in Memphis announced that it was "desirable and necessary to look to the teeming population of Asia for assistance in the cultivation of our soil and the development of our industrial interests." In his address to the convention, labor contractor Cornelius Koopmanshoop announced that his company had imported 30,000 Chinese laborers into California and offered to make them available in the South (Caldwell 1971; Steinberg 1981:184; Loewen 1971:22; Commons 1910-11:81).

Planters soon saw that the Chinese could be employed as models for black workers: hardworking and frugal, the Chinese would be the "educators" of the former slaves. During the 1870s, Louisiana and Mississippi planters imported several hundred Chinese laborers and pitted them against black workers. They praised the foreign workers for outproducing Blacks and for "regulating" the "detestable system of black labor." A Southern governor frankly explained: "Undoubtedly the underlying motive for this effort to bring in Chinese laborers was to punish the Negro for having abandoned the control of his old master, and to regulate the conditions of his employment and the scale of wages to be paid him." An editor in Kentucky spoke even more bluntly when he predicted that the introduction of Chinese labor would change the "tune" from "'forty acres and a mule'" to "'work nigger or starve'" (Todd 1870:284-85; Cohen 1984:109; Loewen 1971:23; Barth 1964:189).

Meanwhile, above the Mason-Dixon line, Chinese laborers were being used to discipline Irish workers. In 1870, shoe manufacturer Calvin Sampson brought seventy-five Chinese workers from San Francisco to North Adams, Massachusetts, to break a strike of Irish workers. Sampson's experiment caught the attention of other capitalists as well as the national news media. Within three months after their arrival in North Adams, the Chinese workers were producing more shoes than the same number of white workers had been making before the strike. The success of Sampson's strategy was celebrated in the press. "The Chinese, and this especially annoys the Crispins," the editor of *The Nation* wrote, "show the usual quickness of their race in learning the process of their new business, and already do creditable hand and machine work" (23 June 1870, p. 397).

The Chinese were held up as a model for Irish laborers. Writing for *Scribner's Monthly*, William Shanks compared the Chinese to the Irish workers. The Chinese "labored regularly and constantly, losing no blue Mondays on account of Sunday's dissipation nor wasting hours on idle holidays," he reported. "The quality of the work was found to be fully equal to that of the Crispins." Through the use of Chinese labor, Sampson had widened his profit margin: the weekly saving in labor costs was $840, or $40,000 a year. These figures inspired Shanks to calculate: "There are 115 establishments in the State, employing 5,415 men . . . capable of producing 7,942 cases of shoes per week. Under the Chinese system of Mr. Sampson, a saving of $69,594 per week, or say $3,500,000 a year, would be effected, thus revolutionizing the trade" (Shanks 1871:495-96).

Commenting on the significance of Sampson's experiment of substituting Chinese for Irish laborers, Shanks concluded: "If for no other purpose than the breaking up of the incipient steps toward labor combinations and 'Trade Unions' . . . the advent of Chinese labor should be hailed with warm welcome." The "heathen Chinee," he concluded, could be the "final solution" to the labor problem in America (Norton 1871:70).

Here we have the use of the Chinese to discipline Hawaiians, African Americans, and Irish immigrants as laborers.

But what do we find when we turn from the past to the present, to the 1980s and 1990s? Here I think we have a similar, but also different situation.

Of course, Glazer would not approve of the practices of nineteenth century employers of Chinese immigrant laborers. But like them, Glazer is also urging African Americans to emulate Asian Americans.

But Glazer is not alone. There is a robust and growing group of intellectuals and pundits who are also celebrating Asian American "success" while condemning African American "failure."

One of them is Charles Murray, author of *Losing Ground*. Published in 1984, this widely read attack on welfare was hailed as the bible for Ronald Reagan's social policies. Why, Murray asks, did the situation of Blacks deteriorate during the late sixties and the seventies—a time of expanded government social programs and an increasingly interventionist state? Murray's answer is clear: they became worse off because of the government's social policies. Expenditures for social welfare "quadrupled" between 1968-80 as welfare rolls mushroomed and as an increasing number of Blacks became dependent on government handouts. The very programs designed to alleviate poverty instead contributed to the formation of a dependent and growing welfare class. Thus the government itself had corrupted these people by offering them incentives not to live by the republican virtues of hard work and self-sufficiency (1984:227).

Significantly, in his study of the increasing welfare dependency among Blacks, Murray admiringly notes that Asian Americans have gained ground: as a group, they have become "conspicuously above the national norms on measures of income and educational achievement." According to Murray, they did it on their own, through self-reliance and individualism—principles that this society has always held dear. Murray's praise for Asian American success is a jeremiad—a call for a rededication to the republican virtues of hard work, thrift, and industry: after all—the war on poverty, civil rights legislation, affirmative action—none of them was really necessary. Asian Americans are represented as proof of the American dream (1984:55).

Here we have Murray's articulation of "white popular wisdom." This perspective is grounded in the traditional republican belief that men and women should be defined as individuals and be responsible for themselves. They should be judged according to their individual merits or lack of them.[1]

The celebrators of Asian American "success" also include black intellectuals. In *Ethnic America,* Thomas Sowell congratulates the Chinese and Japanese for their triumph over racial discrimination through hard work and individual industry. "Some of the most remarkable advances in the face of adversity," he claims, "were made by groups that deliberately avoided politics—notably the Chinese and Japanese." For Sowell, Chinese laundrymen and Japanese gardeners are paragons of the model minority. "What made these humble occupations avenues to affluence was the effort, thrift, dependability, and foresight that built businesses out of 'menial' tasks and turned sweat into capital." On the other hand, Sowell castigates Blacks for their dependency on government and condemns militant Blacks for erroneously thinking that political agitation is the path to equality (1981:274-83).

Like Sowell, Shelby Steele scolds his fellow Blacks for blaming racism for their plight. In The *Content of Our Character,* he argues that Blacks should pursue the middle-class values and attitudes of "individual initiative," responsibility, and "delayed gratification." They should try to be like Asian Americans. "It is rarely wise to compare blacks to other minority groups," Steele writes, "but in this context it may be helpful." Asian Americans have "certainly endured racial discrimination and hostility. Yet, as a group, they have by most measures thrived in America. One of the things this indicates is that, today, race is not the determining variable it once was." The difference between black failure and Asian American success, Steele argues, reflects the fact that "Asians came to this country with values well suited to the challenges and opportunities of freedom" (1990:68-69).

Thus, the values of America's middle class originated not only in England with its Protestant Ethic but also in Asia with its work ethic. This point has also been advanced by an Asian American intellectual—Francis Fukuyama. His stunningly brilliant study, *The End of History and the Last Man,* is more than a bold declaration that history has come to an end with the triumph of liberal democratic capitalism over communism. At the same time, Fukuyama is aware of the problem of proclaiming victory when our society continues to be plagued with the reality of racial inequality. "Even

American democracy," he acknowledges, "has not been particularly successful in solving its most persistent ethnic problem, that of American blacks." But, Fukuyama argues, the problem of the black underclass arises from culture: young inner-city Blacks lack the middle-class cultural values they need to take advantage of the opportunities provided by American capitalism. Moreover, "precisely those social policies undertaken to help the black underclass have hurt them by undercutting the family and increasing their dependence on the state." Despite the rise of affirmative action programs giving preference to Blacks, "a certain sector of the American black population not only failed to advance economically, but actually lost ground." Like Murray, Fukuyama blames the interventionist programs of the government. What then is the solution? "The work ethic," Fukuyama points out, "remains very strong in Japan" (1992:xiii, 118, 291-92, 230).

Like the planters in Hawaii, shoe manufacturer Sampson in New England, and the planters in the South, Glazer, Murray, Sowell, Steel, and Fukuyama are making comparisons between different racial groups. While these nineteenth-century employers were using Chinese laborers to discipline Black and Irish workers directly in the workplace, these contemporary scholarly celebrators of Asian American and Japanese "success" have shifted the location of control to the cultural terrain.

The importance of ideology as a site of discipline is underscored by Michel Foucault. In his provocative study *Discipline and Punish: The Birth of the Prison*, Foucault points out that during the late eighteenth century, European society turned from the use of direct and cruel punishment of criminals to the enlightened techniques of social rehabilitation and control. People had to be taught how to behave and what to think; schools and prisons had to become the sites of such education. The most powerful example of this new method of discipline and punish is the modern prison with its panopticon—a guard-observation tower located in the center of a circle of cells. This arrangement is designed to make prisoners feel they are constantly under surveillance, or the watchful "gaze" of the guard. The panopticon resembles a "circular cage," and the prison cells are "like so many cages, so many small theatres, in which each actor is alone, perfectly individualized and constantly visible" (1979:200).

For Foucault, however, the panopticon is more than a striking illustration of the new penitentiary practices: it is also a graphic metaphor of modern society's emphasis on ideology as a mechanism of social control— what he describes as the installation of representations in "the soft fibres of the brain." Through selected representations, or images, information, knowledge, pictures, and simulations of the world, men and women can be disciplined and taught to behave. In society, the "art of punishing" rests on "a whole technology of representation." The content of the representation "normalizes" the behavior and thought of individuals. Unlike the public tortures of criminals in the past, this mechanism of ideology is hidden. "Disciplinary power . . . is exercised through its invisibility." The "gaze" of social control is "alert everywhere" (1979:103, 104, 187, 195).

But what is the purpose of the modern social panopticon? Foucault relates it to the development of capitalism: "The growth of a capitalist economy gave rise to the specific modality of disciplinary power, whose general formulas, techniques of submitting forces and bodies, in short, 'political economy,' could be operated in the most diverse political regimes, apparatuses or institutions." This ideology condemning idleness and promoting thrift as well as industry seeks to make "machine-men"—efficient and obedient workers (1979:221, 242).

As it turns out, Foucault is not studying the "birth of the prison" but rather the emergence of ideology as a new technology of social control. In fact, the title of his book in French is *Surveiller et Punir*. The translator explains in a note that the verb "*surveiller*" has no adequate English equivalent. The word "observe" is too neutral to describe a system of watching in order to discipline.[2] While Foucault's analysis completely overlooks race, it invites us to relate his insight to the views of both Bernal and Marable. What Bernal regards as representations of race, whether they be of ancient Africa, African Americans, or Chinese immigrants, conceals a larger ideology that serves to discipline and punish laborers within the economic framework of what Marable calls the development of capitalism.

But the perspectives of both Bernal and Marable need to be applied to contemporary interaction between ideological and economic developments. The last three decades have witnessed radical economic transformations and the growth of a black underclass—what William Julius Wilson describes as "the truly disadvantaged." At the core of this new group has been the dramatic rise of black families headed by single women: between 1960 and 1980, the percentage of such families doubled, reaching 40 percent of all black families. This development can be measured in terms of black welfare enrollment. While Blacks composed only 12 percent of the American population in 1980, they constituted 43 percent of all welfare families (1987).

Why has there been this growth of the black underclass? Murray blames the welfare system, but his analysis is both misleading and mistaken. Welfare mainly provided the necessary support for families in desperate need because of economic changes .

One of them is the suburbanization of production. The movement of plants and offices to the suburbs has isolated inner city Blacks in terms of employment: in 1980, 71 percent lived in central cities whereas 66 percent of Whites resided in suburbs. Illustrating this dynamic interaction of economic relocation, unemployment, and welfare, Chicago lost 229,000 jobs and enrolled 290,000 new welfare recipients in the 1960s, while its suburbs gained 500,000 jobs. Trapped in inner cities, many unemployed Blacks were unable to find new employment as easily as white workers living in suburbs where the economy continued to expand.

Meanwhile, Blacks also suffered from the devastating effects of the "deindustrialization of America." The corporate "iron cage" operates in a globalized economy and is no longer dependent on domestic labor. Tens of millions of American workers have lost their jobs due to the relocation of production in low-wage countries like South Korea and Mexico. In the ranks of this new army of displaced workers has been a disproportionately large number of Blacks. According to a study of plant closures in Illinois during the late 1970s, Blacks constituted only 14 percent of the state's work force, but they totaled 20 percent of the laid-off laborers. The decline of employment in manufacturing industries such as automobile and steel production has had a particularly severe impact on black workers. A 1986 study by the Congressional Office of Technology Assessment reported that 11.5 million workers lost jobs because of plant shutdowns or relocations between 1979 and 1984, and that 60 percent of them found new jobs in that period. But of the displaced black workers, only 42 percent were able to find new employment. "The decline in blue-collar employment hit black men especially hard," sociologist Andrew Hacker reported. "Blacks have been severely hurt by deindustrialization," Wilson explained, "because of their heavy concentration in the automobile, rubber, steel, and other smokestack industries" (Reid 1982:7; Illinois Advisory Committee 1981:8, 32-34; Bluestone and Harrison 1982:270; Hacker 1992:101; Wilson 1987:72-92).[3]

But what made these economic changes especially damaging to Blacks was also racism in the form of "American apartheid." In their important study of residential racial discrimination, Douglas Massey and Nancy Denton argue that housing segregation has contributed significantly to the making of the black underclass. "For the past twenty years," Massey and Denton write, "this fundamental fact [of segregation] has been swept under the rug by policymakers, scholars, and theorists of the urban underclass. Segregation is the missing link in prior attempts to understand the plight of the urban poor." They disagree with Wilson: "Although rates of black poverty were driven up by the economic dislocations Wilson identifies, it was segregation that confined the increased deprivation to a small number of densely settled, tightly packed, and geographically isolated areas." The existence of this desperately poor and alienated group of Blacks in the inner cities has generated images of menacing Blacks and fears among many middle-class Whites, which, in turn has driven the latter to the suburbs for security and made them even more determined to erect walls of residential segregation. Here we have a modern example of what Gunnar Myrdal called the "vicious cycle" (Massey and Denton 1993:3, 8; Myrdal 1962).

The economic hollowing out of inner cities and "American apartheid" have created a new racial crisis: the issue is no longer whether inner city Blacks are employable or can become employable, but whether they are even needed in the American economy of the late twentieth century. Many of them are conscious of their grim employment prospects, and their despair has given rise to what Cornel West has described as the "nihilism that increasingly pervades Black communities" (1993:14).

In this brave new world of economically devastated inner cities, what is the function of the ideology of Foucault's discipline and punish? Ideology here is defined essentially in terms of Antonio Gramsci's view of cultural hegemony, "an order in which a certain way of life and thought is dominant, in which one concept of reality is diffused throughout society in all its institutional and private manifestations, informing with its spirit all taste, morality, customs, religious and political principles, and all social relations." In other words, as ideology, the panopticon is something pervasive in society, an unseen force directing "the soft fibres of the brain" (Williams 1960:587).

The domination of hegemonic culture has never been complete, for counter ideas and interests have always challenged it. But in its striving for cultural control, ideology relies on representations—images designed to provide instruction to society. Intellectuals have inordinate power to create representations, and in the construction of images, they become complicit in the manufacture and operation of ideology. This complicity may indeed be unwitting, but its very unintentionality marks the very powerfulness of ideology.

In their creating of representations of Asian American "success," Glazer and pundits like him are probably not deliberately seeking to discipline and punish African Americans who have "failed." But they are perplexed and worried about the existence of this discontented class of unemployed Blacks. For them, the purpose of ideology concealed in their representations of Asian Americans is not so much to create docile Black workers as to instruct them on how to become obedient members of society. A primarily social rather than economic function of ideology has emerged in a post-industrial capitalistic America, marking profound difference between the past and the present. Earlier, Blacks were valuable as laborers in the agricultural South and the industrial North; today, however, many of them have been rendered economically superfluous. They face the depressing prospect of permanent unemployment. How then are they to be instructed in social behavior? One way is to encourage them to emulate Asian Americans. Thus, the standard of acceptable social manners leading to Asian American "success" telegraphs a message: Blacks should not depend on welfare and should not riot or resort to stealing and robbing.

But behind this "soft" strategy of moral suasion by Asian American example is a "hard" strategy. Glazer, Sowell, Steele, and Fukuyama would probably be reluctant to support the harsh techniques of social control advocated by Murray. Indeed, they would likely recoil from them as draconian and mean-spirited. But they and many others like them share some, perhaps much of Murray's rage and perplexity. What should be done to address the problem of the existence of the black underclass? Murray aggressively urges the restoration of individualism, the entire "scrapping" of social welfare programs, and the forcing of poor people into the labor market. His is a Hobbesian solution. Murray emphasizes punishment for individuals lacking republican virtues: "Do not study, and we will throw you out; commit crimes, and we will put you in jail; do not work, and we will make sure that your existence is so uncomfortable that any job will be preferable to it" (1984:177).

In a sense, here is the cold and stern "gaze" of a racial panopticon, watching the "success" of Asian Americans and also placing discontented African Americans under surveillance. But this very way of viewing the world obstructs understanding of the problem of racial inequality and precludes the possibility of addressing it constructively. While pitting Asian Americans and African Americans against each other, this perspective reaffirms the republican values of individualism that shroud the denial of equal opportunity to racial minorities and that also protect the very cultural and economic structures perpetuating class and racial hierarchy. A philosopher once said that the task before us is not only to comprehend the world but also to transform it. The ideological construction of race as a site of discipline and punish prevents the pursuit of this challenge.

Notes

1. See e.g., Schmeisser (1988); Wilson (1987); Tilly (1986); Kuttner (1983); Ehrenreich (1986); Wicher (1988); Wycliff (1987); and Murray (1984). "Middle-class" income is defined as between 75 percent and 125 percent of median household income.
2. From translator's note to Foucault (1979).
3. According to the *New York Times*, 7 February 1986, quoting a report from the Congressional Office of Technology Assessment, this statistic is for black men who had held their previous jobs for at least three years.

References

Barth, Gunther. *Bitter Strength: A History of the Chinese in the United States, 1850-1870.* Cambridge:Harvard University Press, 1964.

Bernal, Martin. *Black Athena: The Afroasiatic Roots of Classical Civilization.* New Brunswick: Rutgers University Press, 1991.

Bluestone, Barry and Bennett Harrison. *The Deindustrialization of America: Plant Closings, Community Abandonment, and the Dismantling of Basic Industry.* New York:Basic Books, 1982.

Cabezas, Amado. "The Asian American Today as an Economic Success Model: Some Myths and Realities." Paper presented at Break the Silence: A Conference on Anti-Asian Violence, 10 May 1986, University of California, Berkeley.

____. and Gary Kawaguchi. "Empirical Evidence for Continuing Asian American Income Inequality: The Human Capital Model and Labor Market Segmentation." In *Reflections on Shattered Windows: Promises and Prospects for Asian American Studies,* edited by Gary Y. Okihiro, Shirley Hune, Arthur Hansen, and John Liu. Pullman: Washington State University Press, 1988.

____. Larry Hajime Shinagawa, and Gary Kawaguchi. "A Study of Income Differentials among Asian Americans, Blacks, and Whites in the SMSAs of San Francisco-Oakland-San Jose and Los Angeles-Long Beach in 1980." Paper presented at the All-UC Invitational Conference on the Comparative Study of Race, Ethnicity, Gender, and Class, 30-31 May 1986, University of California, Santa Cruz.

Caldwell, Dan. "The Negroization of the Chinese Stereotype in California." *Southern California Quarterly* 53 (June 1971).

Cohen, Lucy M. *Chinese in the Post-Civil War South: A People without a History.* Baton Rouge:Louisiana State University Press, 1984.

Commons, John R. et al., eds. *A Documentary History of American Industrial Society.* Cleveland:A. H. Clark Company, 1910-11.

Ehrenreich, Barbara. "Is the Middle Class Doomed?" *The New York Times Magazine,* 7 September 1986.

Foucault, Michel. *Discipline and Punish: The Birth of the Prison.* New York:Pantheon Books, 1979.

Fukuyama, Francis. *The End of History and the Last Man.* New York:Free Press, 1992.

Hacker, Andrew. *Two Nations: Black and White, Separate, Hostile, Unequal.* New York:Scribner's, 1992.

Illinois Advisory Committee to the United States Commission on Civil Rights. *Shutdown: Economic Dislocation and Equal Opportunity.* Washington, D.C.:U.S. Commission on Civil Rights, 1981.

Kuttner, Bob. "The Declining Middle." *The Atlantic Monthly,* July 1983.

Loewen, James W. *The Mississippi Chinese: Between Black and White.* Cambridge:Harvard University Press, 1971.

Marable, Manning. *How Capitalism Underdeveloped Black America: Problems in Race, Political Economy and Society.* Boston:South End Press, 1983.

Massey, Douglas S. and Nancy A. Denton. *American Apartheid: Segregation and the Making of the Underclass .* Cambridge:Harvard University Press, 1993.

Murray, Charles. *Losing Ground: American Social Policy, 1950-1980.* New York:Basic Books, 1984.

Myrdal, Gunnar. *An American Dilemma: The Negro Problem and Modern Democracy.* New York:Harper & Row, 1962.

Norton, Frank. "Our Labor System and the Chinese." *Scribner's Monthly,* May 1871.

Reid, John. "Black America in the 1980s." *Population Bulletin* 37:4 (December 1982).

Schmeisser, Peter. "Is America in Decline?" *The New York Times Magazine,* 17 April 1988.

Shanks, William. "Chinese Skilled Labor." *Scribner's Monthly,* September 1871.

Sowell, Thomas. *Ethnic America: A History.* New York:Basic Books, 1981.

Steele, Shelby. *The Content of Our Character.* New York:St. Martin's Press, 1990.

Steinberg, Stephen. *The Ethnic Myth: Race, Ethnicity, and Class in America.* New York:Atheneum, 1981.

Takaki, Ronald. "Comparisons between Blacks and Asian Americans Unfair" *Seattle Post-Intelligencer,* 21 March 1985.

_____. "Have Asian Americans Made It?" *San Francisco Examiner,* 10 January 1984.

_____. *Iron Cages: Race and Culture in 19th Century America.* New York:Knopf, 1979.

Tilly, Chris. "U-Turn on Equality: The Puzzle of Middle Class Decline." *Dollars & Sense,* May 1986.

Todd, John. *The Sunset Land.* Boston, 1870.

West, Cornel. *Race Matters.* Boston:Beacon Press, 1993.

Wicker, Tom. "Let 'Em Eat Swiss Cheese." *The New York Times,* 2 September 1988.

Williams, Gwynn. "The Concept of 'Egemonia' in the Thought of Antonio Gramsci: Some Notes on Interpretation." *Journal of the History of Ideas* 21 (1960).

Wilson, William Julius. *The Declining Significance of Race: Blacks and Changing American Institutions.* Chicago:University of Chicago Press, 1978.

_____. *The Truly Disadvantaged: The Inner City, the Underclass, and Public Policy.* Chicago:University of Chicago Press, 1987.

The Influence of "Black Peril" on "Yellow Peril" in Nineteenth-Century America

Moon-Ho Jung

Large numbers of Asian immigrants began arriving in the United States in the mid-nineteenth century;[1] by 1880 there were 105,465 Chinese, 75,132 of whom resided in California (Sandmeyer 1973:17). Many scholars have argued that these immigrants, like their European counterparts, left China in search of better economic opportunities and that their struggles in the U.S. resembled those faced by all immigrants. As historian Roger Daniels writes:

> Differences between the Asian and the European immigrants were of degree rather than of kind. . . . Like other immigrants, Chinese "greenhorns" learned "the ropes" with varying effectiveness. . . . It is true that Chinese immigrants wore their "Chinese-ness" on their skins, but millions of European immigrants carried their "German-ness," or their "Italian-ness" or their "Polish-ness" at the tips of their tongues for the rest of their lives (1988:20).

Such propositions diminish the integral role that racism played in the exploitation of Chinese labor. Although Daniels acknowledges the presence of racial prejudice in the anti-Chinese movement, he fails to observe the connection between structural racism—and its intimacy with capitalism—and Chinese migration.

The first large group of nonwhite labor transported to the "New World" arrived from Africa long before the Chinese migration of the nineteenth century. Through trans-Atlantic slavery, racism emerged as the predominant ideology among Whites in Europe and the Americas (Edmondson 1976). Deemed inherently "inferior," Africans were forced to work jobs that "superior" white men rejected. When another group of nonwhite laborers arrived in California from China, European Americans perceived and treated them in a similar manner. Although this study focuses on the similarities between the exploitation of African slaves and Chinese laborers, it does not attempt to equate the two systems. Rather, I argue that the importation and treatment of the Chinese evolved from trans-Atlantic slavery and that white Americans' fears of the Chinese (commonly referred to as the "yellow peril") developed, in part, from their fears of Africans and African Americans.

Some scholars, especially those of the Marxian tradition, argue that capitalistic development produced racism to justify trans-Atlantic slavery; others emphasize that European notions of African "inferiority" existed long before slavery. Both sides of this debate, however, recognize the intimate relation between racism and capitalism. As political scientist Locksley Edmondson states: "it goes without saying . . . that the rise of capitalism was integrally associated with the rise of racial exploitation on a worldwide scale" (1976:17). Africans and Chinese were two such groups that were exploited "on a world-wide scale."

It is estimated that Europeans and European Americans transported at least nine million Africans to the "New World" through the trans-Atlantic slave trade (Curtin 1969:268).[2] Historian Margaret Washington demonstrates in her study of South Carolina's Sea Island region that white planters played the most important role in trans-Atlantic slavery by creating the demand and, to a great extent, determining when and which African ethnic groups were to be imported. For instance, she points out that white Carolinians preferred and received Africans from the Senegambia region for their expertise in rice cultivation in the mid-eighteenth century (Creel 1988:29-37). Moreover, planters of the "New World" were not alone in establishing and controlling the slave trade. As historian Philip D. Curtin notes, although "the European metropolis imported very few slaves for its own use . . . it controlled the shipping and created the economic policies that governed both the 'plantations' and the maritime leg of the trade" (1969:xv).

Fellow Africans also acted as middlemen by helping to capture and control slaves in Africa and the Americas. Powerful ethnic groups within Africa established trade ties with Europeans and provided them with slaves (Harding 1981:8-9; Creel 1988:38-44; Gueye 1979). Middlemen in the United States also helped to support the slave system dominated by upper-class Whites. Slave drivers and other selected slaves, particularly domestic servants, often identified their interests with those of the white planters.

Perhaps more importantly, the slaveocracy fostered such divisions to weaken solidarity among the slaves and to inhibit slave uprisings (Aptheker 1963:61-64).

The European and European American shipping industry also gained much from the slave trade, catering to the demands of the slaveholders (Inikori 1979:56-66; Williams 1961:51-84). During the Middle Passage, Africans committed suicide (believing they would return to Africa in the afterlife), rebelled collectively against white crews, and attempted to regain their freedom by any means necessary (Harding 1981:10-23). Approximately 345,000 African slaves were imported to the United States until 1808, the year that the federal government officially prohibited participation in the slave trade. This, however, did not impede the importation of at least 54,000 more Africans until the Civil War. Meanwhile, the mortality rate on ships throughout the trans-Atlantic slave trade was somewhere between 13 and 33 percent. Curtin explains that the actual mortality rate was much higher since: "For every slave landed alive, other people died in warfare, along the bush paths leading to the coast, awaiting shipment . . . Once in the New World, still others died on entering a new disease environment" (1969:72-75, 275-76).

On land, Africans endured further inhumane confinement. Olaudah Equiano wrote in his narrative that after being "all pent up together like so many sheep in a fold," he and other captured Africans were finally released from the traders when "on a signal given, such as the beat of a drum, the buyers rush[ed] at once into the yard where the slaves are confined, and make choice of that parcel they like best" (1987:37). Africans' struggles continued under slavery in the United States and elsewhere in the Americas. The brutality of the U.S. system that used physical coercion, legal codes, and paramilitary methods has been amply demonstrated by numerous historians.[3] In the same manner, Europeans and South Americans instituted a system of transporting Chinese labor to South America and the Caribbean, called the "coolie trade," that used similar techniques.[4]

The historical connection between trans-Atlantic slavery and Asian labor migration is probably more apparent in these regions than in North America. The abolition of the trans-Atlantic slave trade during the nineteenth century created a mass shortage of labor in plantations across the Caribbean and South America. Historian Hugh Tinker has argued convincingly that this shortage led white planters to import Asian Indian "coolies" under "a new system of slavery, incorporating many of the repressive features of the old system, which induced in the Indians many of the

responses of their African brothers in bondage" (1974:19). Similarly, plantation owners, mainly from Cuba and Peru, demanded shipments of cheap labor
from southern China. The Chinese coolie trade also attracted British West
Indian authorities who imported 14,120 Chinese indentured laborers during a
concentrated period between 1859 and 1866 (Look Lai 1993:42).

Chinese middlemen also helped to establish and perpetuate this trade
that lasted from about 1847 to 1874. Although the Chinese government
prohibited all emigration until 1860 and banned coerced emigration afterwards, Europeans and the middlemen developed and maintained the illegal coolie trade. Principal brokers, who dealt mainly with Whites, and
subordinate brokers, who were responsible for procuring potential coolies,
supplied Europeans with Chinese laborers. To meet the quotas established
by white agents, these brokers often resorted to kidnapping and deception.
Either physically coerced or deceived with hyperboles of wealth and comfort, hundreds of thousands of Chinese coolies were driven into "barracoons"
where "they immediately lost their freedom and were completely cut off
from the outside world" (Yen 1985:57-59). From these barracoons, the
coolies traveled across the Pacific under conditions similar to those of the
Middle Passage. Like their African counterparts, Chinese coolies also
struggled to regain their freedom. Robert Irick states: "there were few voyages, if any, in which some of the Chinese did not go to any extreme to
escape from these floating hells. Many took the passive route of suicide;
others jumped overboard, either in port or at sea; still others set fire to the
ships, or organized mutinies" (1982:211). Physical brutality was common
both in the barracoons and on the voyages that had mortality rates as high
as 33 percent (Yen 1985:62).

For those who survived, their struggles continued as they were sold to
white planters in markets like the one Equiano described. Long hours and
immensely low wages often kept these laborers in debt bondage for the
duration of their contracts, most of which were set for eight years. Yen
Ching-hwang, however, notes that white plantation owners often had no
intention of complying with these contracts, a conviction that led to life-
time bondage. Moreover, Chinese coolies encountered merciless physical
punishment, ranging from "confinement, chained feet, flogging, [to] cutting fingers, ears and limbs" (Yen 1985:66-71). More than 224,000 Chinese coolies were driven into this system of unofficial slavery in the latter
half of the nineteenth century (Irick 1982:8).[5]

The coercive coolie trade and the voluntary credit-ticket system, which
facilitated the migration of the majority of Chinese laborers to California

in the nineteenth century, were not always clearly distinguishable (Schwendinger 1988:19-62; Arensmeyer 1979:21-38; Cohen 1984:41-44). "All arrangements were subject to abuse," notes Robert J. Schwendinger, "and as emigration grew, observers tended to distinguish 'free' emigrants from 'coolie' emigrants, believing the ability to pay for the voyage was a measure of qualitative difference between the two" (1988:20). For instance, the American vessel *Robert Browne,* although officially bound for San Francisco, was probably involved in the coolie trade when the Chinese passengers revolted against the officers and the crew in 1852.[6] Western ships that carried Chinese coolies to South America and voluntary laborers to the U.S. were concentrated in southern China, an area that was undergoing tremendous turmoil in the nineteenth century. Western imperialism, increased competition with foreign products, the T'ai-p'ing Rebellion, internal warfare, the commercialization of agriculture, and natural disasters displaced many residents from their homes and farms. Despite the numerous factors involved, June Mei argues that "the strand of imperialism runs like a thread through virtually everything that affected emigration" (1984:244).[7] She, however, adds that political, social, and economic dislocations, whether caused or exacerbated by Western incursion, alone do not explain why or how Chinese migrated in large numbers to California.

Chinese middlemen played a significant role in the implementation and maintenance of the credit-ticket system. Historian Gunther Barth has declared (and probably overstated) that the system "camouflaged a debt bondage that turned indentured emigrants into slaves of their countrymen who ruled through influences unfamiliar to outside observers" (1964:51). Although his analysis attributes the strife between Whites and the Chinese to the "filth of Chinatown" and the Chinese "sojourner" outlook—that is, the Chinese were at fault for the rise of anti-Chinese sentiments—it does point out the importance of these middlemen (Barth 1964:1-8, 129-56). Under the credit-ticket system, Chinese laborers borrowed money from the middlemen to pay for their trans-Pacific voyages. In return, these laborers were often forced to work under the direction of these middlemen until their debts and interests were paid off. Low wages and ever-increasing debts, however, drove many Chinese laborers to prolonged debt bondage. The U.S. shipping industry also fueled the system through advertisements and agents who often overexaggerated the chances of quick wealth (Mei 1984:238). As the demand for Chinese migration rose in the 1850s, the shipping industry transported up to 840 Chinese a day to San Francisco from Hong Kong. On these ships, Chinese laborers were kept below deck—"one of the surest ways to avoid fights between the Chinese and the crew"—and when rebellions against inhuman conditions arose among the Chinese, the crews did not hesitate to use physical force (Barth 1964:67-71). In general, however, Chinese labor migration to California did not involve physical coercion as under the slave and coolie trades.

In contrast to the Chinese emigrants' aspirations to become rich quickly through the gold rush, the owners of California mining companies, railroad companies and agricultural lands needed their cheap labor to develop America's West and to compete in the international market. Some of these U.S. companies, Mei states, "played an active part in publicizing the need for laborers, recruiting them, and even financing their journeys" (1984:242). Edna Bonacich and Lucie Cheng categorize these owners as "dependent" capitalists, since "they were forced to operate within the constraints of outside investments and a market whose price structure they could not control . . ." (1984:8). Unlike more industrialized capitalists who could cut costs through technological investments or price increases, these dependent capitalists relied on cheap labor to keep the costs of production low. Like Southern plantation owners who depended mainly on the agricultural and textile markets of Great Britain and consequently demanded African slaves, the dependent capitalists of California (which entered the union as a "free" state in the Compromise of 1850) needed Chinese laborers to work for wages below those offered to Whites. And as in trans-Atlantic slavery, white capitalists instigated and maintained the demand for transportation of nonwhite labor.

In sum, African slaves, Asian coolies, and Chinese laborers arrived in the Americas within the global capitalist system that demanded cheap, nonwhite labor in the "New World." Although the conditions under which the three groups arrived and lived certainly differed, I would argue that these differences were of degree rather than of kind.

Edna Bonacich (1984:176) attributes the development of the anti-Chinese movement during the nineteenth century mainly to the large number of anti-capitalists, or independent small producers and white laborers, in California who felt threatened by the cheap labor force. She argues that they formed popular political alliances against dependent capitalists who generally favored the importation of Chinese labor. The "yellow peril" ideology, however, encompassed more than simply a labor threat; white America felt "endangered" in other ways. Moreover, European Americans did not formulate this ideology spontaneously as the number of Chinese laborers increased in California. Rather, they applied the negative African images they had conjured up throughout slavery to the Chinese and consequently perceived that the Chinese, like Africans, were "threats" to their moral and social order. In the same manner, white workers began to feel threatened economically by Chinese laborers as they had by black slaves and free laborers.

Historian Stuart Creighton Miller argues that the negative American images of the Chinese preceded their arrival in the U.S., images promulgated initially by early American traders, missionaries, and diplomats in China. For example, one missionary commented that the Chinese "inmost soul, their very conscience, seems to be seared dead—so insensible that they are as regards a future life, like beasts that perish" (1969:71).[8] As Chinese workers arrived in the U.S. in the mid-nineteenth century, according to Miller, the earlier stereotypes incorporated "newer critical themes . . . the fear of slavery, the emphasis on racial difference, and the menace of loathsome, contagious disease" (1969:146). These themes had also been applied to the negative images of Blacks.

In his *Iron Cages,* historian Ronald Takaki contends: "What whites did to one racial group had direct consequences for others" (1979:xiv).[9] This may have been epitomized by the popular images that Whites conferred on the Chinese. European Americans, from the nation's founding, have characterized Blacks (and American Indians) as "savages" who could not control their "barbaric" nature. Thus, according to Takaki, Whites had to control Blacks' "barbarism" to preserve the new republican order for themselves, which emphasized self-autonomy (1979:10-13). This image helped to justify the myriad anti-miscegenation laws against Black-White marriages in the U.S. The white media conjured up similar images for another group of "heathens," claiming, for example, that "the 'innumerable hells' burrowed beneath every Chinese settlement held captive white girls for 'crimes that cannot be named'" (Miller 1969:198). Such perceptions led to the passage of an anti-miscegenation law in California to include "negro, mulatto, or Mongolian" (Takaki 1989:102). At the same time, the image that many European Americans associated, at least publicly, with black slaves was the "Sambo" stereotype. The typical slave was characterized as "docile but irresponsible, loyal but lazy, humble but chronically given to lying and stealing" (Caldwell 1971:126). Although Dan Caldwell points out that the Chinese stereotype was "Negroized" to incorporate such qualities, he neglects to mention that the Chinese had a positive character absent in the African image. The Chinese were considered more "intelligent" than the "ignorant and brutish" Blacks; this, in turn, justified the usage of Chinese labor in machine-operated factories (Takaki 1979:219). Nevertheless, the Chinese were still considered "inferior" in comparison to Whites.

Hinton Rowan Helper's observations of the South and California may provide the clearest example of the convergence of the African and Chinese characterizations. Two years before the publication of his more famous work *The Impending Crisis of the South*—which historian George M. Fredrickson describes as perhaps "the most important single book, in terms of its political impact, that has ever been published in the United States" (1988:28)—Helper wrote *The Land of Gold* in 1855. Unable to find employment in New York City, this native North Carolinian had migrated to California with hopes of becoming rich quickly. His failure in gold mining drove him to write *The Land of Gold,* a book designed "to determine the true value of this modern El Dorado" (1855:13). Describing the Chinese as "semi-barbarians," Helper called for the end of Chinese immigration because:

> No inferior race of men can exist in these United States without becoming subordinate to the will of the Anglo-Americans, or foregoing many of the necessaries and comforts of life. They must either be our equals or our dependents. It is so with the negroes in the South; it is so with the Irish in the North; it was so with the Indians in New England; and it will be so with the Chinese in California (1855:96).

In *The Impending Crisis of the South,* originally published in 1857, he argued for the abolition and resettlement of Blacks since slavery held back non-slaveholding Whites (1963). Thus, Helper believed that nonwhites of Asia and Africa should be excluded and removed from white America.

The California Supreme Court confirmed and sanctioned this popular perception of nonwhites in *People v. Hall* (1854). In this landmark decision against the Chinese, the court ruled that "the word Indian, Negro, Black, and white are generic terms designating races. That therefore Chinese and all other people not white are included in the prohibition from being witnesses" (Caldwell 1971:128). Thus, the California legal system viewed all nonwhites as "inferior" beings that were incapable of being witnesses either for or against Whites. These negative characterizations also strengthened arguments that black and Chinese workers constituted economic "threats" to white American prosperity.

As mentioned earlier, Bonacich concludes that a political alliance existed between white laborers and small producers, who believed that the Chinese labor force undermined their economic security. They argued that they could and should not have to compete with the Chinese labor force that was willing to work for meager wages. Furthermore, they perceived that millions of Chinese were ready to migrate to the U.S. to take over more jobs unless they were curtailed through an anti-immigration policy. This type of threat from a cheap nonwhite labor force did not originate with the Chinese, for Blacks were deemed as such by white laborers before and after the Civil War. By the early nineteenth century, the eastern United States was largely divided into two economic regions, North and South (Inikori 1979:58-66). Southern planters relied on black slaves to work their agricultural fields whereas the North relied mostly on "skilled" white labor in their more developed industries. These Northern capitalists were non-dependent capitalists who could cut costs either through price increases or investments in technology, as Bonacich states. The South, on the other hand, was comprised of agricultural capitalists who were controlled by markets outside their region. Thus, the two regions developed two different forms of the "black peril" concept. Northern white workers felt threatened by the presence of a potentially large, cheap labor force represented by Blacks in the North and South. Southern slaveholders, on the other hand, felt threatened by black slave revolts that sought to overthrow their economic system.

In parts of the South, black slaves significantly outnumbered Whites, a fact that the slaveholders anxiously recognized (Aptheker 1963:114; Takaki 1979:129). Contrary to the "Sambo" stereotype, as historian Herbert Aptheker has argued, "discontent and rebelliousness were not only exceedingly common, but, indeed, characteristic of American Negro slaves" (1963:374).[10] For instance, the Stono Rebellion alerted South Carolinians of potential mass revolts in 1739. Despite the passage of repressive laws in 1740, collective revolts, conspiracies, and personal defiance continued. Gabriel Prosser and his brother were prosecuted for attempting to plan an uprising in 1802. The Vesey Conspiracy of 1822 drove Whites to great alarm as Denmark Vesey and his cohorts reportedly established an immense black network throughout the Charleston area (Creel 1988:114-31, 150-66). And the Nat Turner rebellion in 1831 in southern Virginia was perceived by Whites as direct proof of the "black peril." Furthermore, personal rebellions such as running away, arson, and sabotage persisted throughout the slavery era. Vincent Harding notes: "Even when there were no open confrontations, white men and women dreamed of them, expected them, feared them, sometimes expanded actual events to epic proportions" (1981:33). This, of course, does not mean that confrontations did not exist. It simply means that the threat of a mass overthrow (i.e. the "black peril") was engrained in the minds of Southern Whites (Aptheker 1963:18-52). In short, black slaves constantly demanded their freedom, a demand that threatened the economic order of the pre-Civil War South.

The dependent capitalists in California, however, instituted a system of exploitation that differed from trans-Atlantic slavery. As Takaki states:

> American capitalists would "avail" themselves of this "unlimited" supply of "cheap" Chinese labor to build their railroads and operate their factories; then, after they had completed their service, the Chinese migrant workers would return individually to the "homes" and the "land they loved," while others would come to replace them. The employers of Chinese labor did not want these workers to remain in the country and to become "thick" . . . in American society (1979:236).

These capitalists had planned a system in which they could control the laborers perhaps more effectively than in the South. Denied citizenship rights, Chinese laborers would not have access to American institutions; moreover, their sojourning status, a condition encouraged under migrant labor, would minimize the possibility of mass revolts or trade unions.

As under slavery, however, the exploited did not react as the dependent capitalists had expected or desired. Thus, the dependent capitalists' version of the "yellow peril" surfaced: contrary to their plans, the Chinese protested and demanded equal rights. For instance, the Chinese began to fight within the American legal system against discriminatory acts as early as 1852 when Chinese sought to recover stolen gold and owed money in the courts. Historian Sucheng Chan estimates that more than 100 legal cases involving Chinese were heard by the various state and territorial supreme courts of America's West between 1854 and 1882 (1991:90-91). And although many Chinese laborers espoused the sojourner outlook, they established permanent settlements and organizations from the very beginning.

Perhaps the most salient form of Chinese resistance to the dependent capitalists' system was the struggle for equal economic opportunities. For instance, 2,000 Chinese workers struck in 1867 against the Central Pacific Railroad company for higher wages, 8-10 hour work-days, prohibition of corporal punishment, and the right to leave their jobs whenever they desired. The strike lasted only a week since Central Pacific managers cut off their supply of provisions (Chan 1991:81-82; Takaki 1989:86). Such repressive measures, however, did not suppress further strikes against California's dependent capitalists, confirming Chan's observation that "despite the fact that the Chinese have been widely depicted as docile, there is considerable evidence to show that when their sense of justice was violated, they rose up in revolt" (1991:81). These revolts against an unjust economic system were the "perils" that these dependent capitalists had desired to avoid. Thus, the 1882 Chinese Exclusion Act may have been supported by white anti-capitalists but the law also served the needs of the dependent capitalists. Since the law prohibited only the Chinese from immigration, an "unlimited" amount of cheap labor was still available in other Asian countries. Furthermore, these capitalists could exploit and control these new workers more effectively than they did the Chinese, who had developed their own settlements and organizations.

The North, in general, did not involve a system of labor exploitation based on race, at least in comparison to the South; this, however, did not diminish the significance of race in the political economy of the region. After the American Revolution, according to historian David R. Roediger, Northern white workers "creatively pursued the vision of a republic of small producers" in which they would gain political and economic independence, even as their dependence on wage labor rose dramatically between 1800 and 1860 (1991:43). He argues that Blacks—free and enslaved—represented a counterpoint against which white workers reassured themselves of relative freedom and independence. Henceforth, Northern white workers began "to concentrate its fire downward on to the dependent and Black than upward against the rich and powerful" (1991:60).

Denied entrance into industries reserved for the white labor force, as historian Leon F. Litwack discusses in *North of Slavery,* Northern Blacks were relegated to the least paying, menial jobs. Furthermore, Northern employers used Blacks as strikebreakers against white labor organizations from which Blacks were excluded (Litwack 1961:153-86). This created the other facet of the "black peril": white laborers viewed free and enslaved African Americans as sources of economic insecurity. In other words, white workers argued that millions of Blacks could potentially displace them in the job market since they worked and were willing to work for lower wages. "The white man cannot labor upon equal terms with the negro," argued a group of white Connecticut residents in 1834. "Those who have just emerged from a state of barbarism or slavery have few artificial wants. Regardless of the decencies of life, and improvident of the future, the black can afford his services at a lower price than the white man" (Litwack 1961:161). They implored the state legislature to pass a bill to restrict the immigration of Blacks; indeed, almost all of the Northern states at least considered adopting such measures before the Civil War.[11]

Small producers and white laborers in California reacted against the Chinese in a similar fashion.[12] These fears were partly founded on white employers' using Chinese laborers as strikebreakers, as Northern capitalists had used Blacks (Takaki 1979:239-40). This practice was not limited to California as white employers began using the Chinese as strikebreakers as far east as North Adams, Massachusetts. Furthermore, white employers also attempted to pit black and Chinese workers against one another. For instance, during Radical Reconstruction when Blacks threatened white domination with their voting rights, Chinese laborers were transported to the South to replace Blacks (Loewen 1988:21-26; Cohen 1984:22-101; Chan 1991:82-83). In the same manner, during the Chinese strike against the Central Pacific Railroad company, the management inquired about the feasibility of replacing the striking Chinese workers with 10,000 Blacks (Takaki 1979:231).

The anti-immigration campaigns against Blacks and Chinese were often accompanied by violent expulsion attacks across the North and the West (Litwack 1961:72-74; Chan 1991:48-51). The exclusion movement against the Chinese, however, differed from those against Blacks in that the "black peril" emanated from a potential labor force already within the United States while the "yellow peril" stemmed from a potential labor force outside (i.e. China) and within the U.S. Nonetheless, white exclusionists recognized the vital connection between the two "perils." The *San Francisco Alta* editor commented in 1853: "Every reason that exists against the toleration of free blacks in Illinois may be argued against that of the Chinese here" (Takaki 1979:217). This viewpoint was furthered by President Rutherford B. Hayes who wrote in 1879: "the present Chinese labor invasion . . . is pernicious and should be discouraged. Our experience in dealing with the weaker races—the Negroes and Indians, for example,—is not encouraging. . . . I would consider with favor any suitable measures to discourage the Chinese from coming to our shores" (Miller 1969: 190). In other words, European Americans should not allow another group of non-whites to "invade" the U.S. since they would create "problems" for American society as a whole.

The end of the trans-Atlantic slave trade instigated European Americans to seek cheap labor outside western Africa. Although the Chinese labor migration to California did not involve as much physical coercion as the slave or coolie trades, its organized system of importation and debt bondage resembled them in many ways. In the same manner, Whites' fears of the Chinese were shaped significantly by their fears of Blacks. Popular images that Whites reserved for Blacks were applied to the Chinese, presenting both groups as "threats" to the social and moral order of white America. Furthermore, Southern and Californian dependent capitalists relied on their respective cheap labor forces to compete in international markets. But when black slaves and Chinese laborers rebelled against their systems, they were viewed as threats (or perils) to economic stability. Moreover, white laborers across the U.S. viewed both the Chinese and Blacks as sources of economic insecurity. As stated earlier, this analysis does not seek to equate Chinese labor migration with African slavery. But the evidence shows clearly that the exploitation and exclusion of Chinese laborers were integrally associated with the exploitation and alienation of another group of nonwhites, Africans and African Americans.

Notes

1. This paper developed out of a Cornell history seminar on the "yellow peril" in the spring of 1991, taught by Gary Y. Okihiro. I thank him for his generous guidance and encouragement.
2. For a discussion on what other historians have estimated, see Curtin (1969:3-13).
3. For early works that overturned U. B. Phillips's (1966) romantic interpretation of slavery, see Aptheker (1963), Franklin (1947:184-212), and Stampp (1956:141-91).
4. For a discussion on the origins of the term "coolie," see Irick (1982:2-6).
5. This figure includes only those sent to Cuba and Peru.
6. For a discussion of the *Robert Browne* revolt and the ensuing diplomatic conflict between U.S. and Chinese officials, see Schwendinger (1988: 29-44) and Irick (1982:32-43).
7. See also Chan (1991:3-8).
8. For an analysis of such characterizations of Africans, see Harris (1972).
9. See also Saxton (1971:1, 19-45, 104-09).
10. Aptheker's pioneering study (1963) documented 250 slave revolts and plots within the present borders of the United States.
11. Many states adopted such measures: Illinois (1848), Indiana (1851), and Oregon (1857) included such provisions in their state constitutions (Litwack 1961:66-74).
12. For a comprehensive analysis of white labor's role in the anti-Chinese exclusion movement, see Saxton (1971).

References

Aptheker, Herbert. *American Negro Slave Revolts.* New York: International Publishers, 1963.
Arensmeyer, Elliott C. "British Merchant Enterprise and the Chinese Coolie Labour Trade: 1850-1874." Ph.D. diss., University of Hawaii, 1979.

Barth, Gunther. *Bitter Strength: A History of the Chinese in the United States, 1850-1870.* Cambridge: Harvard University Press, 1964.

Bonacich, Edna. "Asian Labor in the Development of California and Hawaii." In *Labor Immigration under Capitalism: Asian Workers in the United States before World War II,* edited by Lucie Cheng and Edna Bonacich. Berkeley: University of California Press, 1984.

Bonacich, Edna and Lucie Cheng. "Introduction: A Theoretical Orientation to International Labor Migration." In *Labor Immigration under Capitalism: Asian Workers in the United States before World War II,* edited by Lucie Cheng and Edna Bonacich. Berkeley: University of California Press, 1984.

Caldwell, Dan. "The Negroization of the Chinese Stereotype in California." *Southern California Quarterly* 53 (June 1971): 123-31.

Chan, Sucheng. *Asian Americans: An Interpretive History.* Boston: Twayne Publishers, 1991.

Cohen, Lucy M. *Chinese in the Post-Civil War South: A People without a History.* Baton Rouge: Louisiana State University Press, 1984.

Creel, Margaret Washington. *"A Peculiar People": Slave Religion and Community-Culture among the Gullahs .* New York: New York University Press, 1988.

Curtin, Philip D. *The Atlantic Slave Trade: A Census.* Madison: University of Wisconsin Press, 1969.

Daniels, Roger. *Asian America: Chinese and Japanese in the United States since 1850.* Seattle: University of Washington Press, 1988.

Edmondson, Locksley. "Trans-Atlantic Slavery and the Internationalization of Race." *Caribbean Quarterly* 22 (June-September 1976):5-25.

Equiano, Olaudah. *The Interesting Narrative of the Life of Olaudah Equiano, or Gustavus Vassa, the African.* Reprinted in *The Classic Slave Narratives,* edited by Henry Louis Gates, Jr. New York: New American Library, 1987.

Franklin, John Hope. *From Slavery to Freedom: A History of American Negroes.* New York: Alfred A. Knopf, 1947.

Fredrickson, George M. *The Arrogance of Race: Historical Perspectives on Slavery, Racism, and Social Inequality.* Middletown: Wesleyan University Press, 1988.

Gueye, Mbaye. "The Slave Trade within the African Continent." In *The African Slave Trade from the Fifteenth to the Nineteenth Century.* Paris: UNESCO, 1979.

Harding, Vincent. *There Is a River: The Black Struggle for Freedom in America.* New York: Vintage Books, 1981.

Harris, Joseph E. *Africans and Their History.* New York: New American Library, 1972.

Helper, Hinton Rowan. *The Impending Crisis of the South: How to Meet It.* New York: Collier Books, 1963.

_____. *The Land of Gold: Reality Versus Fiction.* Baltimore: Henry Taylor, 1855.

Inikori, Joseph E. "The Slave Trade and the Atlantic Economies, 1451-1870." In *The African Slave Trade from the Fifteenth to the Nineteenth Century.* Paris:UNESCO, 1979.

Irick, Robert L. *Ch'ing Policy toward the Coolie Trade, 1847-1878.* Taipei: Chinese Materials Center, 1982.

Litwack, Leon F. *North of Slavery: The Negro in the Free States, 1790-1860.* Chicago: University of Chicago Press, 1961.

Loewen, James W. *The Mississippi Chinese: Between Black and White.* Prospect Heights: Waveland Press, 1988.

Look Lai, Walton. *Indentured Labor, Caribbean Sugar: Chinese and Indian Migrants to the British West Indies, 1838-1918.* Baltimore: Johns Hopkins University Press, 1993.

Mei, June. "Socioeconomic Origins of Emigration: Guangdong to California, 1850 to 1882." In *Labor Immigration under Capitalism: Asian Workers in the United States before World War II,* edited by Lucie Cheng and Edna Bonacich. Berkeley: University of California Press, 1984.

Miller, Stuart Creighton. *The Unwelcome Immigrant: The American Image of the Chinese, 1785-1882.* Berkeley: University of California Press, 1969.

Phillips, U. B. *American Negro Slavery: A Survey of the Supply, Employment and Control of Negro Labor as Determined by the Plantation Regime.* Baton Rouge: Louisiana State University Press, 1966.

Roediger, David R. *The Wages of Whiteness: Race and the Making of the American Working Class.* London: Verso, 1991.

Sandmeyer, Elmer Clarence. *The Anti-Chinese Movement in California.* Urbana: University of Illinois Press, 1973.

Saxton, Alexander. *The Indispensable Enemy: Labor and the Anti-Chinese Movement in California.* Berkeley: University of California Press, 1971.

Schwendinger, Robert J. *Ocean of Bitter Dreams: Maritime Relations between China and the United States, 1850-1915.* Tucson: Westernlore Press, 1988.

Stampp, Kenneth M. *The Peculiar Institution: Slavery in the Ante-Bellum South.* New York: Alfred A. Knopf, 1956.

Takaki, Ronald T. *Iron Cages: Race and Culture in Nineteenth-Century America.* New York: Alfred A. Knopf, 1979.

_____. *Strangers from a Different Shore: A History of Asian Americans.* Boston: Little, Brown, 1989.

Tinker, Hugh. *A New System of Slavery: The Export of Indian Labour Overseas, 1830-1920.* London: Oxford University Press, 1974.

Williams, Eric. *Capitalism and Slavery.* New York: Russell & Russell, 1961.

Yen, Ching-hwang. *Coolies and Mandarins: China's Protection of Overseas Chinese during the Late Ch'ing Period (1851-1911).* Singapore: Singapore University Press, 1985.

The "Middleman" Theory of Culture: An Analysis of Korean and African American Relations

Wai Suen Lee

On March 16, 1991 in Los Angeles, Soon Ja Du, a Korean American storeowner shot to death Latasha Harlins, a fifteen-year-old African American apparently over a dispute concerning a $1.79 bottle of orange juice.[1] The store closed due to threats of firebombing (Mydans 1991; Hutchinson 1991:554). In January 1990, African American residents of Flatbush in New York City staged a boycott of several months of the Red Apple grocery alleging that its owner Bong Jae Jang had harassed and beaten Ghiselaine Felissaint, a Haitian woman, over $3 worth of plantains and limes (Pooley 1990:39). Such are the incidents from a long list of other Korean and African American conflicts that have occurred in recent years, ever since Korean American small businesses (groceries, wig shops, liquor stores, gas stations, and "convenience" places) have proliferated in the predominantly black inner-cities (Banks 1985; Noel 1981). For both academic and socio-political reasons, we should account for the nature and cause of these dynamics between the Korean entrepreneur and black clientele. The theoretical framework for my study is the hypothesis of the "middleman minority."[2]

Previous "middlemen" studies on Korean American entrepreneurs have concentrated primarily on explaining or describing why these "subjects" choose particular trades, and why they are "successful" and over-represented in these businesses. The literature has dealt only superficially with an analysis of the interactions (or lack thereof) and with the tensions (and sometimes violent conflicts) between the Korean American "middlemen" and their African American customers. "Host hostility" is taken as a given (rather than as a phenomenon to be explained), thus leaving little room for discussion. What has been studied takes an inadequate structuralist ("status gap" or "niche") approach which may account for Korean business entry, growth, and development in the largely black-populated central cities, but it still sheds little light on the period after consequential conflicts. Structuralist or "contextual" theories[3] may explain why immigrant groups in general congregate toward small businesses (or even why they establish them in poverty-stricken areas), but they do not demonstrate why Koreans, more than any other foreign-born peoples, have "taken it to heart." In other words, why have not other immigrant groups of the post-1965 "new wave" (such as other East Asians, Southeast Asians, Filipinos, Asian Indians, Russians, Eastern Europeans, and Latin and Central Americans) opened up stores in U.S. metropolitan areas at comparable rates? (Light 1980:33-34).

For all Asian American immigrant men, South Koreans far surpass others in the proportion of workers who are self-employed, 24.6 percent, followed by Chinese, 16.2 percent, Asian Indians, 11.1 percent, Japanese, 10 percent, and Filipinos, 6.3 percent. The insufficiency of contextual theories (like the "disadvantage" theories)[4] is even more revealing if we consider other East Asian immigrants, like those from Hong Kong and Taiwan who face discriminatory circumstances similar to Koreans, but engage in dissimilar occupational practices and do not incite black antagonism. Additionally, structuralist theories cannot explain why black response to the Korean "middlemen" has especially been intense when compared, say, to that of Mississippi Delta Blacks toward their Chinese counterparts, as James Loewen shows in his sociological study on race relations, *The Mississippi Chinese* (1988). According to Loewen, Chinese intermarriage with Blacks led to the latter viewing the former "mostly in a friendly light" (1988:64).

Compared to their response to Koreans, black reaction to other ethnic "middlemen" storekeepers like Jews, Italians, and recently, Asian Indians seem relatively mild. According to Hutchinson,

> The big difference [from Koreans] . . . is that other immigrants were Europeans determined to shed their old-country languages and customs in the American melting pot. When they opened businesses in black neighborhoods, they acted like friendly uncles. They knew their customers on a first-name basis, they willingly extended small loans and credit, they employed local youth to do menial chores. Their stores often served as meeting places where the locals exchanged news or gossip. This approach appealed to blacks, most of whom had come from the rural South and who were accustomed to intimacy and informality in their personal relationships (1991:554).

Structuralist accounts of the "middleman" beg the question about the specificity of present-day black anti-Koreanism and Korean anti-Africanism and deny the fact that this particular ethnic strife has reached an altogether different and higher plane.

Do "cultural" theories of the "middleman minority" add to an understanding of African and Korean American relations? Bonacich (and Modell 1980; 1988) acknowledges the plausibility of cultural theories, yet neglects to give them comprehensive treatment. Light (1972, 1980) utilizes a cultural theory of the "rotating credit associations"; however, his account based on studies of pre-World War II Chinese and Japanese are inapplicable to the contemporary situation of Koreans. I will consider both the "orthodox" and "reactive" approaches to cultural theory (Light 1980:34), without degenerating into a purely "orthodox," "phenomenological," or "ethnomethodological" argument. In other words, I do not reject the contextual approach to the "middleman" hypothesis, but merely add to it, thereby engendering a more complete analysis of African and Korean American relations that integrates both structuralist and cultural concepts and transcends the arbitrarily imposed distinction between structure and agency.

The "cultural" theory of entrepreneurship serves a dual purpose in that aspects of Korean and Korean American cultures lend themselves to "middlemen" occupational structures and explain the resulting conflicts that arise from those structures. Not only are cultural concepts compatible with contextual ones, but the former elucidates the latter (the opposite is less true) as the two "feed off" each other. Hence, I suggest that certain uniquely "Korean" cultural factors have somewhat, though implicitly, created the ethnic tensions in and of themselves; that is, the ethnic conflict between Korean American entrepreneurs and their African American clientele is mostly a "clash of cultures." Thus, Bonacich's (1973:589) rejection of the hypothesis that "host hostility" is never self-generated by the "middleman minority" is premature. In taking this stance, I am not laying blame on the "middlemen" for their plight, but merely noting that their suffering occurs in some ways, in spite of them, because their culture or perceived cultural attributes seem to contradict those of their antagonists.

In contrast to the black inner-city poor, many Korean Americans are highly educated and "bourgeois" (Kim 1981:38; Hamill 1990:80). Kim (1988:xii) remarks that Korean immigrants brought with them modern "ethnic class resources," consisting of "advanced education, economic motivation or 'success ideology,' and money." These "resources" are attainable for them in Korea, an ethnically and culturally homogeneous state, because

in the absence of class-bound or organization-bound norms or bonds, individual initiative largely determined economic success even in traditional

[Korean Yi] society. In traditional Korea the seeds of a social character with an elective affinity for survival in modern mass society were already sown. That is to say, if modern industrial society favors individuals who strive for rapid social mobility, Koreans have already prepared themselves historically and culturally. Largely due to the cultural and social legacy of centralism, Koreans are prepared to accept and emulate any new social and economic system once they view it as offering economic opportunities and as being powerful and ascendant (Kim 1981:295).

Coming from an ethnically homogeneous nation with a relatively fluid class structure of which they were near the top, many of the Korean American "middlemen" can hardly conceive of the notion of permanent and persistent racial or class discrimination, although it is a reality for their African American clientele. The legacy of slavery and the battles for civil rights that have long been the history of African Americans are virtually unknown or irrelevant to the Korean immigrant entrepreneur. Many Korean Americans do not understand why some African Americans cannot just quit "complaining" about so-called unfair advantages that Korean small entrepreneurs have, and instead start their own businesses. Man Ho Park, a Korean storekeeper expressed these shared sentiments: "I don't understand this kind of problem. So much anger. So much time doing nothing. Why not work? Why not use time for, for . . . improve life?" (Hamill 1990:80).

Korean Americans, due mostly to their somewhat opportune time and place of entry (into a racially dichotomized United States), have never been discriminated against in the manner that the Delta Chinese have been in that they have never been classified as "Black" (or "anti-White"); they have thereby avoided the consequences of that "ascriptive" status. In fact, Min rejects the hypothesis that in Atlanta, "the majority of the [Korean American entrepreneurial] respondents started businesses because of host discrimination in the job market" (1984:342-43). Like Bonacich's (1973:591) classic "middleman minority," Korean American entrepreneurs are, more so than other non-White ethnics, "charged with being clannish, alien, and unassimilable. They are seen as holding themselves aloof, believing they are superior to those around them ('a chosen people') and insisting on remaining different." Kay Lee, a Korean American admitted: "We're monolithic and not very giving. We don't know and we are not interested in [the African American's] language, music or culture. But we have learned [through the boycotts] that we have to mingle more with others" (Awanohara 1991:38). In fact, many Korean American entrepreneurs have realized this need to reach out to the black community, if only for "rational" economic reasons. They acknowledge that a bad reputation in the African

American community translates into bad business. In response to black "host hostility," the Korean American business community have banded together in ethnic solidarity, in hopes of improving their "public relations" (Kim 1981:259; Light and Bonacich 1988:319, 320, 591; Banks 1985).

Korean American prejudices have led to unpleasant, though seemingly "justified" allegations by African Americans that "Koreans—*all Koreans!*—were rude to blacks, suspecting them of shoplifting, acting curt with them, refusing to touch their hands when making change." An African American demonstrator on Church Avenue in Brooklyn commented: "Fuckin' people don't know how to *treat* people" (Hamill 1990:78). Perhaps, a great deal of the time, the rudeness and contempt displayed is not imagined, but very real. It is indeed a vicious cycle in the sense that some Korean Americans despise and disregard their black clientele, and then that attitude is "magnified by the frustration many blacks feel at their lack of power in their own neighborhoods ("Cracked Mosaic" 1990:764). Many African Americans think that "they are once again being denied their place in the ethnic queue by newcomers who are leaping over them" (Hutchinson 1991:20).

Their grievances are further exacerbated as they think that the few economic resources that their community have are being slowly drained by the "parasitic" Korean American entrepreneurs who frequently do not contribute to neighborhood affairs and live elsewhere in predominantly white suburbs. Chung Lee, a Korean inner-city entrepreneur, comments: "Koreans look at (store ownership) as an investment, a way to make a living. Their goal is to spend a few years there, make a little money, then buy a store in a better environment. They don't look at it as a lifelong investment and that's a source of the problem" (Banks 1985). This sort of "sojourning" mindset "encourages thrift and hard work for the purpose of amassing capital as quickly as possible and promotes the retention of ethnic solidarity" (Bonacich and Modell 1980:30). Korean "sojourning" intentions, thus, coupled with subsequent "sojourning" actions have exacted the fury of the black community who can rightly believe having been "exploited." The Korean middleman's economic power appears to cause "devastation to host members, who believe their [community] is being 'taken over' by an alien [sic] group" (Bonacich 1973:592).

Still, Light and Bonacich (1988:323, 456n) suggest that these African American apprehensions are somewhat unfounded because the purely economic conflict of interest that the Korean American entrepreneurs present is negligible. This appears to corroborate Bonacich's (1973:592) thesis that, although there is a "rational component" on the part of the host society toward the "middleman minority," usually "the extremity of the host reaction reveals a strong irrational force at work." In other words, the Korean "middleman" has become a "scapegoat" for African American problems. Light and Bonacich also assert that "it is generally true that the sanctions exceeded any economic misbehavior for which Koreans were responsible. In this sense, the 'middleman' theory does not offer a wholly successful explanation of why Koreans experienced so much sanctioning" (1988:323-25).

Light and Bonacich's application of the "middleman" hypothesis is insufficient because it is a structuralist and reductionist account of the nature of Korean and black relations, that fails to account for *qualitative* factors and does not transcend the basic assumptions that undergird their "rational actor" theories. The primacy of *culture* is necessary when considering *class*. "Class" is not merely an economic category based on "objective" numerical analysis, but also consists of cultural notions of shared aspirations, beliefs, ideologies, and the like among those who comprise a class. Korean "middlemen" are not simply a "class-in-itself," but also a "class-for-itself." That understanding explains why it is so difficult for Koreans and Blacks to resolve their differences, because those contrasts stem not only from ethnic, but deeply imbued *(culturally*-constructed) class differences as well. Bonacich implicitly notes the likelihood of such an interrelated and complex web of conflicts:

> A [culturally-based] class interpretation of entrepreneurship is also possible. Insofar as the bourgeoisie also turns over to its children the entrepreneurial values, motivations, and skills requisite to reproducing the private economy. This is a cultural transmission. In this sense entrepreneurship is an essential part of the class culture of a bourgeoisie. Naturally, a class effect is compatible with an ethnic effect (1988:280).

Korean American entrepreneurs are endowed with what sociologists call "cultural capital." Korean entrepreneurs see the reproduction of this "cultural capital" especially in the education of their children who, with fewer social and cultural (e.g. language) barriers, can aspire to even higher levels of mobility than they themselves would ever find in small businesses (Kim 1981:302, 303). So when these same elder Koreans hear of high academic achievements by their own or other people's children (often through circulation in the church social organizations, alumni associations, and ethnic media), they slowly but surely begin *seeing* themselves as a "model minority." In contrast, as they observe in the communities where they set up shop the activities of a disproportionate number of black high school dropouts and unemployed youth, they are led to an extremely poor evaluation of all black people in general, "stereotyping backwards" as Loewen (1988) would say. Korean Americans have inferred uninhibitedly negative values for African Americans based on their perception of the latter's behavior and seeming inability to cultivate adequate sources of "cultural capital." In that way, through their stress on "cultural capital," Korean "middlemen" have further exacerbated tensions with their black clientele. In other words, not only have many Koreans bought the "model minority" myth, but also the "culture of poverty" thesis.

An understanding of why Korean Americans have so easily believed in an African American "culture of poverty" helps to explain why their conflict with the black community is so intense. Korean culture is somewhat "incompatible" or "incommensurable" or, more significantly, *perceived* by Koreans to be so, with that of the host society, especially the black community. Because most Korean "middlemen" see their "culture" or cultural "attributes" to be superior to that of their African American hosts, within the *context* of the black inner-city, they render and implicate black "culture" to be inferior. Of course, that view of African American "culture" is flawed in that they impute what are essentially structural causes of black social problems to be those which are "internal" and "natural." Nonetheless, that Korean American perception leads me to argue that both cultural and contextual approaches are critical to a proper understanding of Korean-black conflicts.

The sources of this Korean worldview are linked inextricably with their time and place of entry into the United States. The large majority of Korean American immigrants arrived in the major metropolitan centers such as Los Angeles, New York, and Chicago at the same time that black poverty was greatly worsening. Wilson documented the drastically increasing rates of social dislocation and concentration of the African American poor in the central city, resulting in the emergence of a new urban "underclass" (1987:26-29). Black family dissolution and welfare dependency especially, characteristic of that underclass, were seen by the Korean business class as inherent components of black "culture." This Korean misconstrual seemed *self-evident* especially because family stability and economic independence are key features of the cultural "consciousness" of Koreans.

The reasons why Korean Americans find such social "pathologies," as described by Wilson (1987:26-29), so difficult to deal with may lie in the historical and cultural traditions or predispositions with which they have been conditioned. Despite the fact that a substantial number of Korean Americans consider themselves Protestant (especially Presbyterian) (Kim 1981:298-303), Confucianism still plays a dominant role in guiding the ethical conduct and beliefs of Koreans and Korean Americans in contemporary life. Confucianism rests on the fundamental ethical principle of "shame" that results from "improper social behavior" (Kim 1981:299). This idea of "shame" and "saving face" is why Korean American inner-city entrepreneurs find it morally repugnant that some of their African American customers are on Aid to Families with Dependent Children (AFDC) or pay their grocery bills with food stamps. According to Hamill (1990:80): "talk to Koreans, and they tell you they would rather starve than be on welfare; that would be a loss of face." Similarly in a 1974 address to the New York State Advisory Committee to the United States Commission on Civil Rights, a Korean community leader boasted:

> Koreans do not make demands on the American system. We don't draw welfare checks or unemployment benefits. As recent immigrants, there are not even very many of us who draw Social Security benefits. We don't want public housing or bilingual education or special social services. We don't want a free ride anywhere, anytime. Today, most Americans have grown up in a climate of affluence, and many people seem to feel that America owes them a living. We Koreans believe it is we who are indebted to America (Kim 1981: 301).

This Korean Confucianist adherence to social conformity and conservatism and this conception of "face" or "honor" also explains the Korean repulsion against Black family dissolution and single, female-headed households. In a survey of 560 Korean Americans in New York, 86 percent of them were married and living with their spouses (Hamill 1990:80). For Korean Americans, "loyalties and obligations to the family supersede all others, and furthermore, an individual is still defined and evaluated as a part of the family. One's success is construed as a success for the family; one's failure is counted as a family failure. Koreans scold their own family members by saying that 'you are a shame to our family,' or 'you are a cause of disgrace to our family'" (Kim 1981:302). So, for example, when Korean American storekeepers see African American women customers who are either husbandless or have children out of wedlock, they not only see them as "disgraces" to their families, but also as "disgraces" to society. Almost normatively-bound to pass negative moral judgments on most, if not all blacks, Korean Americans who make such imputations of values only further perpetuate the prejudices and cultural struggles already existent between themselves and their African American neighbors.

In conclusion, it is difficult for me to imagine that these *cultural* conflicts between the two groups will truly decline in the near future. However, they must if there will be an end to Korean anti-African Americanism and black anti-Koreanism. Bonacich's proposal for an ending resolution is inadequate, if not unrealistic. She urges Korean immigrant entrepreneurs to break free of the manipulated status as legitimating capitalist "propaganda tools" (1987:462), to transcend that which limits "their vision to that of capitalism," and to cease striving for "their individual and group competition within it" (Light and Bonacich 1988:435). Underlying this plea is the structuralist argument again. Bonacich sees the Korean-black problem as deriving from such, and so reasons that the only answer is a total overthrow and rejection of the economic structures of American society. However attractive (or not) this may sound, it is just not feasible.

This is mostly because not many Koreans are ready to relinquish their (perceived) status as "model minorities"; in fact, many Korean American business owners do not even see themselves as a "minority," in the connoted sense of the word. As I have mentioned, the referential framework of Korean American self-definition lies strictly within the family or community itself, not so much the "outside world." In light of this, some Korean "middlemen" do not necessarily see themselves as in the "middle," what Light and Bonacich (1988) consider "petit bourgeois." Instead, many Korean American entrepreneurs believe that if not they themselves, then their children will eventually realize the "American dream," at the top of the socio-economic hierarchy. Unlike some pre-World War II Asian migrants, Korean immigrants are less of a "sojourning" people, and a number of them have indeed planned to settle, in hopes of a long and prosperous life in the United States (Light and Bonacich 1988:294-97). In fact, many left South Korea in the first place because of their displeasure with its undesirable economic, political, and military circumstances, seeing no future there for either themselves or their families (Kim 1981:33). They do not really think of their migration as a "wrenching, disruptive experience" (Light and Bonacich 1988:430, 435) nor do they see themselves as "victims of world capitalism." So we find the structurally-based resolutions to Korean-black antagonisms to be wanting, because for the most part, Korean American "middlemen" are happy with the way the "structures" are.

Instead, we must look to culturally-based solutions, to bridge what are essentially cultural "gaps" between African and Korean Americans. Of course, these will not easily come about, but they are possible and can be enacted. Acceptance of cultural pluralism on the part of both parties is key.

Blacks and Korean Americans must learn to appreciate their cultural differences as well as their similarities. Because many Koreans and Blacks share in common the Christian faith, churches in both communities have sought spiritual, social, and cultural alliances. This kind of goodwill has led Reverend H. P. Rachal, president of the Black Ecumenical Fellowship in Los Angeles, to comment that the "impression that Koreans didn't like blacks" is sometimes unfounded and misleading, and may be altogether false, if only Korean and African Americans can get the opportunity to know each other a little better (Dart 1985).

Notes

1. I wrote this paper in February 1992, a few months before the Los Angeles reaction to the Rodney King trial took place. As such, it describes many of the events leading up to, but not during the infamous "riots." However, I think the explanatory power of the theory used here, with respect to Korean and African American relations, applies equally to events before and after the "riots." Unfortunately, in retrospect, I am afraid the theory may have applied too well.
2. Despite the obvious sexism and obsolescence of this terminology, especially because a majority of Korean American "middlemen" firms today are owned jointly by husband-and-wife teams, what Light (1980:47-52) calls "mom-and-pop establishments" I will use in this paper only for convenience.
3. Contextual theories see middleman minorities "as creatures of the societies in which they are found. They are concentrated in marginal trading activities, not because of any inherent group inclination or talent in this direction, but because the surrounding society makes them assume these positions" (Bonacich and Modell 1980:24).
4. Disadvantage theories "claim that foreigners pile up in small business self-employment because they are disadvantaged in the general labor market by poor English, inferior educational credentials, unemployment, discrimination, and so on. Labor market disadvantages encourage foreigners to turn to business in greater proportion than do the native born" (Light 1980:33).

References

Awanohara, Susumu. "All in the Family." *Far Eastern Economic Review* 14 (March 1991): 36-38.

Banks, Sandy. "Korean Merchants, Black Customers—Tensions Grow." *Los Angeles Times,* 15 April 1985.

Bonacich, Edna. "Making It in America: A Social Evaluation of the Ethics of Immigrant Entrepreneurship." *Sociological Perspectives* 30 (October 1987): 446-66.

____. "The Social Costs of Immigrant Entrepreneurship." *Amerasia Journal* 14 (1988): 119-28.

____. "A Theory of Middleman Minorities." *American Sociological Review* 38 (1973): 583-94.

Bonacich, Edna and John Modell. *The Economic Basis of Ethnic Solidarity: Small Business in the Japanese American Community.* Berkeley: University of California Press, 1980.

"Cracked Mosaic." *The Nation,* 4 June 1990.

Dart, John. "Korean Immigrants, Blacks Use Churches as Bridge to Ease Tensions." *Los Angeles Times,* 9 November 1985.

Hamill, Pete. "The New Race Hustle: Why the Legion of the Invincibly Stupid Is Picking on Asians." *Esquire,* September 1990.

Hutchinson, Earl Ofari. "Blacks and Koreans: Fighting the Wrong Enemy." *The Nation,* 4 November 1991.

Kim, Illsoo. "Editorial Forum: A New Theoretical Perspective on Asian Enterprises." *Amerasia Journal* 14 (1988): xi-xiv.

_____. *New Urban Immigrants: The Korean Community in New York.* Princeton: Princeton University Press, 1981.

Light, Ivan. "Asian Enterprise in America: Chinese, Japanese, and Koreans in Small Business." In *Self-Help in Urban America,* edited by Scott Cummings. Port Washington: Kennikat Press, 1980.

_____. *Ethnic Enterprise in America: Business and Welfare among Chinese, Japanese, and Blacks.* Berkeley: University of California Press, 1972.

Light, Ivan and Edna Bonacich. *Immigrant Entrepreneurs: Koreans in Los Angeles, 1965-1982.* Berkeley: University of California Press, 1988.

Loewen, James W. *The Mississippi Chinese: Between Black and White.* Prospect Heights: Waveland Press, 1988.

Min, Pyong Gap. "From White-Collar Occupations to Small Business: Korean Immigrants' Occupational Adjustment." *Sociological Quarterly* 25 (Summer 1984):333-52.

Mydans, Seth. "Shooting Puts Focus on Korean-Black Frictions in Los Angeles." *New York Times,* 6 October 1991.

Noel, Peter. "Koreans Vie for Harlem Dollars." *New York Amsterdam News,* 4 July 1981.

Pooley, Eric. "The Koreans: Caught in the Furor." *New York,* 28 May 1990.

Wilson, William Julius. *The Truly Disadvantaged: The Inner City, the Underclass, and Public Policy.* Chicago: University of Chicago Press, 1987.

Japanese Independent Sugar Planters: A Study of the *Ukekibi* System in Hawaii

Geraldine Miyazaki Cuddihy

To date, no one has fully examined the Japanese contract sugar growers, an unrecognized but "vital unit" of the Hawaiian sugar plantations in the existing literature about the Japanese immigration experience. Today, a mere dozen sugar planters remain in the Hilo coast area from a high of 900 reported in 1938. In 1994, when the last sugar processing company along the Hilo coast shuts down, this will mark an end to contract sugar growers.

This ethnographic inquiry examines the *ukekibi* system or contract sugar growing in Hawaii and its effects on the Japanese independent sugar planters and their families. The purposes of this research are to describe and to analyze the interactions of the Japanese independent sugar planters and the processes in the *ukekibi* system from a socio-cultural perspective.

For about a century now, the *ukekibi* system has survived. Previous research contends that the *ukekibi* system was developed prior to 1895 to increase labor productivity (Odo and Sinoto 1985:56). Recently, I, a third-generation female independent sugar planter, in a participant-observer role, investigated the *ukekibi* system through archival documents and oral interviews, and discovered that there were other contributing variables which accounted for the *ukekibi* system's long existence. The boundaries of this research confine it to Japanese independent sugar planters along the Hilo coast of Hawaii.

This study begins with a discussion of the economic advantages of the *ukekibi* system for the plantations and also reviews aspects of the unfair contract agreements to the planters. This research also examines the contract sugar grower's life and why and how sugar growing became a way of life, involving and affecting the entire family.

The *ukekibi* system was based on a capitalist system to benefit the plantations. Kotani reported that the plantations realized quickly that the sharecropping system could indeed provide an "enhanced profit" for them and that "tenant growers received payment for only one-seventh of the total value of their crop from sugar companies" in the early 1900s (1985:32). From its early inception, the plantations benefited at the expense of the Japanese growers so they could turn a profit. That was the primary purpose of the system. Sugar cane cultivation was labor intensive. By shifting the labor required for sugar cultivation on the Japanese sugar planters, the plantations were able to reduce their cost of labor. This was advantageous to the plantations. For example, Honomu Sugar Company reported that cultivating contracts resulted in half of the regular expenses for planting at $1.70 per ton of cane. The plantations also understood that by having a greater number of sugar planters and increasing the production of sugar, their per unit cost of producing sugar and the fixed cost of operating a plantation could be significantly reduced, especially if these expenses were paid by the sugar planters. Excessive overhead charges were applied to sugar planters' accounts as the following analysis of a Puna Sugar directive entitled *Charges Against Outside Planters' Cane* will illustrate.

In addition to the regular charges for harvesting, railroad and flume repairs were added on and charged to the sugar planters. Office expenses were deemed chargeable against planters' cane proceeds too. The planters also paid for the plantation's Hawaiian Sugar Planters' Association (HSPA) dues. One-fourth to one-third of various management positions were charged to planters, so were timekeepers' and scaling workers' salaries. One-half of the auditing expense and one-third of the legal expense were billed to planters. Planters also paid for sanitation, fuel, hospital, and medical expenses; these benefits were not free as previously believed.

The plantations also had to contend with the problem of having many different landowners. By 1937, sugar cane was being grown on approximately 250,000 acres of land, and B. H. Wells, then secretary-treasurer of the HSPA, testified that ownership of sugar cane lands was as follows: 53 percent owned by plantation, 34 percent leased from over 600 private lessors, and 13 percent were government lands leased from the Territory of Hawaii (Bolles 1938:13). How did the plantations achieve this high land ownership? It appears through the exploitation of the *ukekibi* system, unpaid advances could result in a delinquency of accumulated debts which in turn could further result in foreclosure of mortgages. Noticeable interest was demonstrated by plantations in the issue of land tenure. Through their correspondences, their time-consuming intent of acquiring land ownership was recorded, including homestead lands near or around the plantation area and by keeping track of records of heirs and researching land documents. Plantations secured an acknowledgement of debt in writing in the advance agreement.

With the homesteaders, the agreement was notarized and approved by the governor and recorded. A letter dated August 24, 1915 to R. A. Hutchison, manager of Laupahoehoe Sugar read, ". . . we stated that we thought not only should we have a written agreement covering an advance, but that it should be recorded . . . we thought it advisable to secure some sort of an acknowledgement of debt in writing . . . we should enter into a formal agreement with the homesteader, such agreement to be properly acknowledged before a Notary Public, submitted to the Governor for his approval, and then recorded." Theo. H. Davies had also informed Joshua D. Tucker, commissioner of public lands, on July 21, 1915 that the twelfth clause in the Kihalani Homesteaders Contract stated: " All advances of cash for merchandise shall be charged against the Homesteader and the Company may deduct the amount of such charges together with interest thereon at the rate of eight per cent (8%) per annum from any and all payments coming under the agreement." In addition, in order to secure advances, the homesteader had to agree to: "sell, assign and convey unto the said company all of the present crops and all crops hereafter, during the term hereof, to be planted upon the whole or any part of the said land." If the homesteader failed to comply with the terms of the contract or repay the advances, the company was entitled to take full possession of the growing crop on the land and "sell the same as provided by Law for the foreclosure of mortgages."

But, an undesirable feature of one of the contracts to the planters was the price paid for their cane. The planter had no control over the crop purchase agreements and was at the mercy of the plantations. One attorney complained that "it has always been a matter of the plantation deciding what it is willing to pay and the planters taking it or getting out." When there was a drop in sugar price as the one that occured in 1915, Theo. H. Davies advised Hutchison on September 23, 1915 to make arrangements with individual planters for the purchase of cane for the 1916 crop based on the price of sugar. The planters could not control unstable sugar prices. If a planter lost money from a harvest, his debit balance was carried forward to the next crop, expecting to eventually work off the balance. In fact, once a planter incurred a debt, he was forced to continue raising sugar cane until the debt was paid off. Many planters/homesteaders actually lost money after final accounting despite the planters' "labor, expense and risk" (Bolles 1938:351, 367-70). Few of the homesteaders even received enough for their cane to break even and pay their expenses. The difference between the prices paid to the planters for their cane by the plantation as compared to the prices at which the sugar was sold was too great.

The one-sided intentions of the contracts were in the plantations' best interests. The different contracts written up by the plantations were monitored and continually revised. After 1900, the plantations paid workers for short- and long-term contracts. Under the terms of the short-term contract, workers were paid according to the amount of work accomplished or at piecework rates (Takaki 1983:84). These workers were paid a specified amount for completing an assigned unit of work, such as cutting cane or loading cane on a "per ton" basis or planting and weeding on a "per row" basis. Considerable time was spent reviewing field operations which in turn affected the short term contracts. Plantations were instructed to keep up-to-date daily field costs which were written up on a daily labor and animal distribution record, a part of the general and field accounts. The cost of transportation was itemized into various phases of cane transportation. Based on the information from the previous day's turnout, short term contracts could be prepared by the plantations. But, the responsibility of harvesting remained with the plantation and not the planters. The plantation or mill agreed to provide flume transportation of the cane to the mill at a set price. For each ton of cane delivered to the mill by the planter, the mill paid a specified price per ton of cane delivered. But, harvesting costs were high.

In 1938, John Ramsay, manager of Honomu Sugar commented that the adherent planters were made up largely of Japanese (Bolles 1938:329). It was not difficult to locate the earlier contract sugar planters to participate in the *ukekibi* system because selective recruitment had been conducted by Robert W. Irwin. The instructions to Irwin by the Hawaiian government were that he "recruit workers from the countryside who had previous experience in farming." Moriyama stated that these emigrants were people who could not succeed in Japan and had to travel overseas in order to survive. Ninety-six percent of the government sponsored emigrants between 1885-1894 came from four prefectures: Hiroshima, Yamaguchi, Kumamoto, and Fukuoka. Between 1868 and 1929, some 231,206 Japanese emigrated to Hawaii. Approximately 124,000 Japanese workers were sent to fifty sugar plantations in Hawaii (Moriyama 1982:xvii-xix, 13-16, 43).

Farming was a way of life for these Japanese workers. In fact, they were so adroit at farming that Katharine Coman would report in 1903 that the sharecropper's yields (from sugar crop harvested) were greater than the plantations' (Kotani 1985:37-38). And, in many cases, proportionately more acreage of sugar was cultivated by contractors than by the plantation's own workforce such as in the case of Wailea Milling Company where as much as sixty percent of the sugar cultivated was by individual planters, and forty percent by Wailea Milling (Bolles 1938:317). Hakalau Sugar Company, Olaa Sugar, and Laupahoehoe Sugar also reported that fifty percent of their acreages harvested were small growers'. On the Hamakaua Coast, Paauhau Plantation obtained twenty-five percent of its sugar cane from lands owned by independent planters. Sugar planters certainly contributed a major share of the sugar grown on these plantations.

Yet interestingly, as far back as 1895, Walter Maxwell of the HSPA had identified "on upland or *mauka* lands, lower temperature but greater falls of rain." This meant that "the upper fields of sugar cane grow more slowly, experience more weed problems . . . and have other higher elevation growth problems. The lower fields of sugar cane usually mature earlier and tend to be drier at harvest—thus experiencing few field work delays" (Holderness et al. 1979:6-7). In the early 1900s, plantations had already recognized the economic advantage of lower slope production. However, many of the sugar growers' lands leased from the plantations were marginal lands such as *mauka* lands. Despite these odds, the sugar planters were knowledgeable farmers and raised good sugar cane. Sugar planters also introduced innovative techniques in sugar cultivation. For example, they planted entire stalks of cane instead of just the top cane as seeds. And by changing their direction when covering the seed or by stepping backward instead of walking forward and covering the seed with the hoe, they discovered that the covered seed was simultaneously being stepped on to get the air out. And, many of the plantations' cultivation supervisors were sugar planters. In the case of Wailea Milling Company, Satoru Kurisu, an *issei* sugar planter, became its revered assistant manager. Arata Kansako was able to purchase the Honomu plantation manager's house in 1947. And in at least two cases, Hilo Coast Processing Company and Wailea Milling Company, sugar planters became part owners of sugar companies.

Japanese participation in the *ukekibi* system was based primarily on economic reasons. Plantation wages were also simply insufficient to raise a family of seven or eight. Planters cultivated sugar cane on about fifteen acres of land to obtain the advances that plantations provided in order to survive. The advances gave the planters "borrowing power." Kazuki Okura, a former independent sugar grower, explained, "They cannot make a living with the wages, so they had to raise cane during their spare time to support the family. When they had cane land, they can charge grocery credit."

In 1938, at Olaa, the advance was $20 per month for men and $10 a month for women. Additional advances were given when a case required it. Advances were usually charged off against the gross proceeds after the crop was sold. Honomu had no set advance and depended on the discretion of management. But, Honomu included a limiting clause at no more than $100 per acre up to the time of maturity with an amount set aside for fertilizer, animal hire, and labor. What was left could be advanced to the grower himself. Yet, a grower testified in 1938 that even with the advances made to cultivation contractors, this was barely enough to support his family of five before the period when cane is harvested (Bolles 1938:374, 351-53, 367-70).

The planters viewed themselves as partners with the plantations. "We are like partners with the plantation, as there is no crop except cane that we can grow on our lands, and if the plantation should stop, we would be in a very bad position," explained Koji Iwasaki (Bolles 1938:359). The planters required the mules, the plows, technology such as the processing of the field cane, and advances in the form of money to purchase food for the family and to survive the two years before harvesting, and in some cases, even the land to grow the cane on from the plantations.

Life was difficult for the sugar planters. The early sugar planters lived alone instead of in camps. Their houses were constructed in a portion of the cane fields near a water source. Some of the planters had to clear forest lands. This was called *yama hiraki* (to clear the forest). Since the mules could not pull out the tree stumps, the patient planters burned them with kerosene. Some slept in the fields in a shack made with the branches of trees. Finally, when the lands were plowable, their contracts were not renewed. They were forced to move on and clear more forest lands.

Some of the men endured a ten or, in some cases, a twenty-year separation from their families in Japan. Without relatives, the sugar planters depended on their neighbors to help them in the cane fields. The sugar planters had to work hard to raise good cane. After working at the plantation, they worked four to six hours longer in their cane fields. As long as they could see, some with lanterns on moonlit nights *hoehanaed* (weed with a hoe) or *moi moied* (to bury the grass in the soil) the *honohono* grass or *hole holed* (strip the leaves) the cane. Many of the sugar growers' lands leased from the plantations were marginal lands, *mauka* (upper) or *pali* (hollow land which made harvesting the sugar crop difficult) lands. But, despite these odds, they were still capable of producing good sugar cane.

When their wives and children arrived, sugar cultivation involved the entire family. There was no division of labor in the fields between the sugar planters and their womenfolk. Women did what men did: cutting cane, planting cane, poisoning, and fertilizing. Mothers even took their children with them into the fields and constructed ingenious shading for them. For example, a *sasho* (shading) was made by overlapping the cut fronds of the *hapu* (fern) or using an umbrella attached to a cane stalk so the umbrella could not damage the baby's eyes or with a piece of cloth. Babies were also put in *kago* (baskets) or carried *opa* (piggy back) fashion on their mothers' back or on a material used as a matting. Sugar planters' children under the age of fourteen were exempted from the child labor laws. Growing up in a sugar planter's family introduced the children first to an anticipatory role of the sugar planter which eventually led some of them to a participatory role.

Becoming a sugar planter was also tied to deep Japanese cultural values such as helping the family or following the father. Shigeru Kansako, president of United Cane Planters, felt that sugar growing "was handed to him," as sons were expected to follow in their fathers' footsteps. In the case of Tatsuo Miyazaki, his father, Tatsuhei Miyazaki, was visiting Japan when the war broke out and was unable to return to Hawaii. So Tatsuo took over his father's cane fields from 1941. He remained a planter for fifty-one years until his death in 1992. "I got stuck. I had no choice," Tatsuo had said.

A sugar planter's daughter explained, "Once, my grandfather thought it was their duty to survive. My father and brothers helped each other. My father borrowed money from *tanomoshi*. Because grandfather couldn't buy land since he was an alien, Father bought homestead land, and together, they raised cane. No other choice."

In addition, sugar planters also enjoyed the pride and distinction of being a sugar planter, and the independence of working without the constant supervision of a *luna*. And all sugar planters depended on the *kakoze* (sixteen dollars compliance payment, a subsidy under the sugar quota system) or waited for the spike year when their sugar earnings would erase their accumulated debts. But, if the small grower had a debt, he had to continue raising sugar cane until he paid that debt off.

In summary, there were a variety of reasons for the sugar growers' participation in the *ukekibi* system. Some were economic reasons such as for the advances or borrowing power, waiting for the spike year, the *kakoze*, and the inability to quit sugar cultivation until the sugar debt was paid off. Cultural factors were also cited as well as independence and pride of being a planter.

For about a century, Japanese sugar planters tenaciously cultivated sugar cane and kept sugar viable along the Hilo coast in Hawaii. These sugar planters assumed more than an ancillary role in the development of the sugar industry in Hawaii; they occupied a major role. Under the *ukekibi* system, the plantations exploited the sugar growers. The contracts were written up by the plantations in their interests and benefit. Early Japanese contract sugar planters paid for everything, including the operating costs of the plantations.

Life was arduous for the early contract sugar planters. Far from their homeland without relatives, they endured long separations from their families. They were given marginal lands to raise their cane. Some even cleared forest lands. Contract cane planters lived alone, not in camps, in isolated areas near a water source. Despite the great challenges confronting them, the sugar planters were still able to cultivate productive sugar cane, even on marginal lands with the assistance of their wives, children, and neighboring cane planters. Early sugar planters' yields exceeded those of the plantations. Sugar growing encumbered the entire family. They were competent farmers and introduced innovative techniques in sugar cultivation which were adopted by the plantations.

This research challenges our existing paradigms about the development of the sugar industry. The plantations have been credited with building up the sugar industry, and this concept needs to be revised. Contract sugar growers played a major role in building the sugar industry. They contributed not only to the economic development of the sugar industry, but to the overall social and historical development of Hawaii.

References

Bolles, Elizabeth D., *Stenographic Report of Hearing: In The Matter Of Fair And Reasonable Wage Rates For Persons Employed In The Production, Cultivation, Or Harvesting Of Sugarcane During The Calendar Year 1938 On Farms With Respect To Which Applications For Payment Under The Act Are Made, And, Fair and Reasonable Prices For The 1938 Crop of Sugarcane To Be Paid, Under Either Purchase Or Toll Agreements, By Processors Who As Producers Apply For Payment Under The Said Act, And Terms And Conditions Of Contract Between Producers And Processors Of Sugarcane Pursuant To Sections 301 (b) and (d) and Section 511 Of The Sugar Act of 1937 (Public Number 414, 75th Congress).* At Lihue, on the Island of Kauai, on April 8, 1938; At Honolulu, on the Island of Oahu, on April 11, 1938; At Wailuku, on the Island of Maui, on April 14, 1938; At Hilo, on the Island of Hawaii, on April 18, 1938. United States Department of Agriculture Agricultural Adjustment Administration.

Charges Against Outside Planters' Cane. Puna Sugar Company Files.

Coman, Katharine. *The History of Contract Labor in the Hawaiian Islands.* New York: Arno Press, 1978.

Davies, Theo. H. to R. A. Hutchison, Manager of Laupahoehoe Sugar, 24 August 1915 and 23 September 1915. HSPA Archives, Aiea, Oahu.

Davies, Theo. H. to Joshua D. Tucker, Commissioner of Public Lands, 21 July 1915. HSPA Archives, Aiea, Oahu.

Hakalau Plantation Co. Annual Reports 1935-47.

Holderness, James S. et al. *Economic Viability of Independent Sugarcane Farms on Hilo Coast: Final Report of Part 1 of Two Part Study to the Tenth Legislature, 1980 Regular Session in Response to House Concurrent Resolution No. 99 Ninth Legislature 1978 Regular Session Requesting a Study of Independent Sugar Growers.* Honolulu: State Department of Agriculture, 1979.

Horner, A., Territorial Sugar Expert, to John Waterhouse, HSPA President, 9 December 1919. HSPA Archives, Aiea, Oahu.

Kotani, Roland. *The Japanese in Hawaii: A Century of Struggle.* Honolulu: Hawaii Hochi, 1985.

Maxwell, Walter. *Report of Work of the Experiment Station of the Hawaiian Sugar Planters' Association. Report for the Year 1895.* Honolulu, 1905.

Moriyama, Alan Takeo. *Imingaisha: Japanese Emigration Companies and Hawaii, 1894-1908.* Honolulu: University of Hawaii Press, 1985.

Odo, Franklin and Sinoto, Kazuko. *A Pictorial History of the Japanese in Hawaii 1885-1924.* Honolulu: Bernice Pauahi Bishop Museum Press, 1985.

Takaki, Ronald. *Pau Hana: Plantation Life and Labor in Hawaii, 1835-1920.* Honolulu: University of Hawaii Press, 1983.

The Filipino American Diaspora: Sites of Space, Time, and Ethnicity

Jonathan Y. Okamura

Filipinos can be found in over 130 countries and territories throughout the world including both developed and developing countries (Tyner 1992:11). Taking into consideration the substantial number of undocumented Filipinos living and/or working abroad, a necessarily very rough estimate of the Filipino population residing overseas either permanently or temporarily would be between four and five million. The largest overseas Filipino community is in the United States with a population of 1.4 million, a figure which does not include thousands of undocumented Filipinos. Including the latter, Filipino Americans may represent as much as one-fourth to one-third of the population of the ever increasing number of overseas Filipinos.

In this study, I apply a diaspora perspective to both the Filipino American population and the ongoing process of immigration of Filipinos to the United States that has resulted in the emergence and continued development of that population. This perspective can be contrasted with other sociological approaches that focus on Filipino Americans as a bounded social and cultural grouping, defined either locally or nationally, insofar as it places the Filipino American community in a global transnational context that includes the Philippines and other overseas Filipino communities. A diaspora approach is consistent with recent emphases in studies of international migration on "transnationalism" or the social "processes by which immigrants build social fields that link together their country of origin and their country of settlement" (Schiller et al. 1992:1). These transnational relations, in which primarily immigrant Filipinos are involved, are necessary for a full understanding of the cultural and social dynamics of the Filipino American community. As Clifford (1992:3) has noted, "diaspora cultures are ways of conceiving community, citizenship, and identity as simultaneously here and elsewhere." A diaspora approach to the Filipino American community also emphasizes its pivotal place in the larger global context of the international Filipino diaspora and the multitude of widely dispersed overseas Filipino communities (Okamura 1992).

From another perspective, I would like to distinguish Filipino Americans, whether as a diaspora community or as an ethnic minority, from other Asian American groups to call attention to their politically and economically disadvantaged status in American society. Despite the long history of immigration and settlement of Filipinos in the United States, which dates back to the late eighteenth century, and their emergence as the second largest Asian American group, they remain a marginalized population at the political and economic edges of American society. This peripheral status is evident in observations of Filipino Americans that "not much is known about them" (Cabezas et al. 1986-87:1) or that they are the "forgotten Asian Americans" (Cordova 1983).

The Filipino American diaspora can be viewed in terms of sites of space, time, and ethnicity. Following Foucault (1986:23), sites can be defined by sets of "relations of proximity between points or elements." This very broad conception minimally implies social boundaries and structure. However, with regard to the Filipino American diaspora, these boundaries must be understood as relatively open and shifting rather than being well-defined and rigid because of the transnational relations of the Filipino American community and its internal cultural and social diversity in terms of ethnolinguistic, generational, class, extent of acculturation, and other differences. For conceptual purposes, I place the Filipino American diaspora at the center of its various sites, that is, I view the diaspora in terms of its relations in space, time, and ethnicity.

The notion of space as a site of the Filipino American diaspora refers to the relations between the latter and the Philippine homeland and also to the relations between the Filipino American and other diaspora communities such as those in Canada, Japan, Australia, Europe, Southeast Asia, Micronesia, and the Middle East. These relations can include kinship, economic, political, religious, organizational, and other social ties. More specifically, they are evident in diverse sociocultural transfers from the Filipino American diaspora to the Philippines such as monetary remittances, *balikbayan* (return to nation) visits, consumer goods sent in "*balikbayan* boxes," and charitable contributions from hometown and other locality associations. Spatial relations also include sociocultural transfers from the

Philippines to the diaspora community in the United States such as television programs, film videotapes, music cassettes, and popular magazines.

Time as a site of the Filipino American diaspora encompasses its passage through the various historical and contemporary periods of the development of the Filipino American community. These time periods and the relations among them can be construed in different ways. A commonly used approach, particularly in terms of immigration sequences, is to speak of the pre-World War II, the post-World War II to 1965, and the post-1965 periods. I will focus on the latter period which resulted from the liberalization of United States immigration laws in 1965. The beginning of this immigration phase immediately precedes the emergence of the "condition of postmodernity" in the early 1970s (Harvey 1989).

Ethnicity as a site of the Filipino American diaspora consists of the relations of Filipinos with other ethnic groups in American society, including other Asian American groups. These essentially unequal relations have structured and continue to structure the subordinate social status of Filipino Americans within the larger society. Inequalities of power and status thus are incorporated in this site. Ethnicity as a site also would include expressions and manifestations of Filipino American culture and ethnic identity: language and values maintenance, religious rituals, residential and commercial areas, radio and television programs, and voluntary associations.

The sites of space, time, and ethnicity certainly do not exhaust the cultural, political, and economic dimensions and manifestations of the Filipino American diaspora. Other significant sites would include class, gender, and power, and the latter is certainly a relevant dimension in all sites since power is an aspect of all social relations. However, I focus on time, space, and ethnicity in order to emphasize especially the relation between the sites of time and space. The last twenty years have been distinguished by what has been called "time-space compression" in the organization of capitalism (i.e., from Fordist to flexible modes of capital accumulation) that is related to, if not has resulted in, profound changes in how we experience time and space (Harvey 1989). I seek to show that time-space compression, in particular what has been referred to as the "annihilation of space through time" (Harvey 1989:293), is quite evident in the post-1965 phase of the Filipino American diaspora and distinguishes this phase from previous historical periods of Filipino immigration to and settlement in the United States. Clifford (1992:1-2) has noted the significance of the dimensions of space, time, and ethnicity specifically in relation to diasporas which he conceives as "spatio-temporal paradigms of interculture" to emphasize their historical processes of intercultural crossing at regional, national, and global levels. He maintains that diasporas "follow and express distinct maps/histories" and can be viewed as particular representations in space and time (Clifford 1992:10).

The concept of diaspora tends to be defined either somewhat loosely or rather specifically. An example of the former type of definition is the following: "ethnic minority groups of migrant origins residing and acting in host countries but maintaining strong sentimental and material links with their countries of origin—their homelands" (Sheffer 1986:3). The recent publication, *Diaspora: A Journal of Transnational Studies*, also takes a broad approach to its subject matter

> to indicate our belief that the term that once described Jewish, Greek, and Armenian dispersion now shares meanings with a larger semantic domain that includes words like immigrant, expatriate, refugee, guest worker, exile community, overseas community, ethnic community. This is the vocabulary of transnationalism . . . (Tololyan 1991:4-5).

More specific definitions of the concept of diaspora emphasize the relation of such "expatriate minority communities" to their original homeland whence they have been dispersed (Safran 1991:83). According to these definitions, which are based on the classic Jewish diaspora as the ideal type, the members of these communities consider, through a collective myth or memory, their ancestral homeland as their "true" home and as where they or their descendants would or should eventually return when conditions are appropriate. They believe that they should collectively be committed to the maintenance or reestablishment of their homeland and to its well being and thus continue to relate to the homeland in one way or another (Safran 1991:84). According to this more restricted definition of diaspora, many long settled and assimilated ethnic groups in the United States, such as Irish, Italians, and Poles, would not be considered diaspora communities because they no longer maintain a "myth of return" to their respective homelands.

By the above criteria, the Filipino American community also would not appear to represent a diaspora since American-born Filipinos probably have little desire to reside permanently in the Philippines. Somewhat surprisingly, a sample survey of Filipinos who were issued immigrant visas to the United States in 1986 reported that a substantial percentage (36.2%) expressed their expectation that they eventually would return permanently to the Philippines, even though almost three-fourths (74.3%) of them indicated that they planned to become U.S. citizens (Carino et al. 1990:78-79). However, the survey was conducted before the respondents had arrived in the United States which very likely influenced their responses concerning returning to the Philippines on a permanent basis.

Regarding space as a site, spatial relations between the Filipino American diaspora and the Philippine homeland can take various economic and cultural forms. Perhaps the most significant economic manifestation of these relations is the remittance flows to relatives and friends in the Philippines. In 1991 remittances sent by Filipino Americans through the Philippine banking system totaled $1.16 billion. This amount represents almost 80 percent of the $1.5 billion in official foreign exchange remittances of Filipinos living abroad for that year (POEA nd). Remittances from Filipino Americans have increased tremendously in recent years, more than tripling in three years from $324 million in 1988. The official remittance figures cited above, especially the annual total amount, are gross underestimates of the actual amount of remittances sent by Filipinos in the United States and other countries since money also is remitted through unofficial channels such as returning relatives and friends. The total amount of remittances sent each year has been estimated as at least twice and even up to three times the official figures (Abella 1989:10).

As examples of time-space compression evident in spatial relations, remittances can be transferred directly to the bank accounts of recipients in the Philippines through U.S. branch offices of Philippine-based banks. One such bank recently inaugurated an on-line remittance service based on "real time" processing from Hong Kong to the Philippines that enables the relatives of overseas Filipinos to withdraw funds from automatic teller machines at virtually the same time that remittances are being deposited. Money and *balikbayan* boxes containing various consumer goods also can be sent literally "door to door" to the Philippines in a few days by delivery services that cater to the Filipino American community. These various economic transfers represent a transnational redistribution of wealth and highly desired cultural products from the Filipino American diaspora to the Philippine homeland and are part of the increasing globalization of consumer culture (Featherstone 1991). In addition, they contribute to the presentation of images and appearances of an immigrant's socioeconomic success in American society without him or her having to return in person for a *balikbayan* visit to the Philippines, which is the most direct, but also much more expensive, means for such economic and cultural transfers.

Cultural transfers also extend from the Philippines to the Filipino American diaspora. They are evident in Philippine daily newspapers, popular weekly magazines, and television news and entertainment programs that make their appearance in Filipino American communities very shortly after their publication or broadcast in Manila. In Honolulu, it is possible to purchase a Manila newspaper on the same date of its publication in the Philippines due to the eighteen hour time difference but also because of the numerous daily flights that connect the two cities. A wide variety of consumer items imported from the Philippines, such as music cassettes, film videos, and processed foodstuffs, also are available for sale in Filipino American communities.

Communication linkages are a representation of spatial relations between the Filipino American diaspora and the Philippine homeland. In this regard, several American long distance telephone companies have advertising campaigns targeted directly to Filipino Americans which include 800 numbers for "Pilipino" speakers to call to apply for service. One such newspaper advertisement is based on certain Filipino cultural themes ("Count on us for the most **personalized** [emphasis added] service, beginning with Filipino customer representatives") and employs appealing phrases in Tagalog such as *Ikaliligaya ng pamilya* ("For the happiness of the family"), and *Mula sa bayang sinilangan tungo sa bagong bansa't tahanan* ("From the place where you were born to the new home country"). The advertisement features a picture of what appears to be a three-generation Filipino family comprised of grandmother, father, and two children, perhaps implying that the absent mother, possibly a nurse employed on a contractual basis, is working in the United States. This marketing specifically to the Filipino American community is remarkable for a population that otherwise receives little national media attention. It also represents a commodification of the diaspora experience and culture beyond the use of Filipino immigrant labor. I might add that direct dial, long-distance telephone service was initiated this year from Manila to the United States thus compressing time and space from the homeland to the diaspora.

Space as a site also can be conceived of in terms of the geographic distribution of the Filipino American diaspora. According to 1990 U.S. Census data, the 1,406,770 Filipino Americans remain concentrated in the West where resides 70.5 percent of their population (Barringer et al. 1993:111). Much smaller proportions of the Filipino American population are in the South (11.3 percent), Northeast (10.2 percent), and Midwest

(8.1 percent). These percentages are roughly comparable to those for the distribution of Filipino Americans in 1980.

Filipino Americans can be found in every state; however, a majority of their population is in California (52.0 percent) where they are the largest Asian American group (Barringer et al. 1993:112). In California, metropolitan areas with substantial Filipino populations (greater than 100,000) include San Francisco-Oakland and Los Angeles-Long Beach. Los Angeles is one of the fastest growing manufacturing centers in the world, a development based on a burgeoning Third World labor pool, including Filipino immigrants, in a First World global city (Shapiro 1992:100). With the largest Filipino community in the United States, Los Angeles may be viewed as a center of the Filipino American diaspora, even though it lies literally on the edge of the continental United States.

The site of time for the Filipino American diaspora indicates the significance of the current phase of post-1965 immigration. Filipinos obviously have migrated previously to other places in the world, even before they were known as Filipinos and before there was a political entity called the Philippines. But in the past twenty-five years, they are migrating farther, faster, to many more places, and in much greater numbers than ever before.

The dramatic growth in the Filipino American population during the past two decades has been made possible by the 1965 Immigration Act which provided for the reunification of families and for the entry of skilled workers needed in the United States. As a result of ongoing immigration from the Philippines, the Filipino American population has increased from 337,000 in 1970 to 775,000 in 1980 and to 1.4 million in 1990 (Barringer et al. 1993:4). In the first five years after the 1965 immigration law was enacted, more than 7,300 Filipino doctors, surgeons, engineers, and scientists were admitted as professionally skilled workers needed in the United States. However, since the 1970s the great majority of Filipino immigrants have arrived under the family reunification provisions. About one million Filipinos have immigrated to the United States since the 1965 Act was passed, and the trend has been toward increasing numbers. To put these figures in comparative historical perspective, between 1909 and 1946, about 127,000 Filipinos went to Hawai'i as plantation labor recruits, and almost one-half of them returned home (Okamura 1983:73). With immigration limited by a 100 person quota established when the Philippines attained independence in 1946, from that year to 1965 only 34,000 Filipinos entered the United States.

During the decade of the 1980s, some 474,000 Filipinos settled in the United States (Gardner 1992:69), and almost 64,000 arrived in 1991 *(Honolulu Star-Bulletin* 1992). The Philippines currently represents the second largest annual source of immigrants to the United States after Mexico (949,000 in 1991) with Vietnam third (55,000) *(Honolulu Star-Bulletin* 1992). The extent of Philippine immigration is such that an estimated 71.5 percent of the Filipino American population in 1990 was foreign born, a significant increase from the 65.3 percent for those born abroad in 1980 (Ong and Hee 1993:21). With an estimated backlog of 600,000 visa applications pending review at the U.S. embassy in Manila, it is very likely that Filipinos will continue to immigrate at their relatively high level. Accordingly, the Filipino American population is projected to increase to 2.1 million in the year 2000, when they will emerge as the largest Asian American group, and to 3.4 million in 2020 (Bouvier and Agresta 1987:292 as cited in Barringer et al. 1993:50).

The question arises why such great numbers of Filipinos are immigrating to the United States. In a recent lecture on "Sites of Crossing: Borders and Diasporas in Late 20th Century Expressive Culture," James Clifford (1992:11) posed that question in more specific terms: "Why Philipinos [sic] have been coming to California, not Spain (where an earlier generation, Jose Rizal and the other *illustrados* [sic], went to articulate Philipino [sic] nationalism)?" He noted that "'Third World' border and diaspora cultures follow and symbolize determined colonial and neocolonial routes" and that the latter "have always been laid down by economic contacts, by old and new, usually unequal political relations" (Clifford 1992:11). Such a view is consistent with the totalizing "core-periphery" paradigm that would account for international labor migration flows from Third World developing to First World developed countries essentially in terms of dependent relations of economic and political inequality between those nation-states.

As evident from the above, there is a general assumption that the primary reason that Filipino and other Third World immigrants come to the United States pertains to economic factors: having a higher standard of living, a higher income, or a better job. However, Filipino immigrants may have a different understanding of their migration intentions and behavior. Surveys and other research conducted with Filipino immigrants have indicated that they report joining family members as their primary reason for immigrating to the United States (Carino et al. 1990:57; Lasman et al. 1975; Okamura 1983). A representative sample survey of 2,077 adult

Filipinos who were issued immigrant visas to the United States in 1986 (from hereon referred to as the 1986 immigrant survey) found that the reason most frequently given for immigrating was family affiliation (41.8 percent), followed by "work/livelihood/income" (28.7 percent), and "other affiliation" (20.2 percent) (Carino et al. 1990:57). Thus, a considerable majority (62.0 percent) of Filipinos immigrate to the United States primarily for affiliative rather than economic reasons, although the latter also may be of significance to them.

I am not arguing that widespread conditions of poverty, unemployment, and underemployment in the Philippines, and its dependent status in the global capitalist economy are of minimal relevance in the analysis of Filipino immigration to the United States. I only wish to indicate that, from their perspective, immigrants' explanations of their migration behavior, when they are asked, are not necessarily in accordance with macrolevel structural theories that essentially provide an explanation for the overall direction and magnitude of international population movements. However, these theories do not provide a sufficient understanding of the internal structure of the immigration process, particularly the relevance of kinship, hometown, and other affiliation ties in transnational migration.

Besides influencing their decision to immigrate, the presence of family members also is the determining factor in terms of where newly arrived immigrants intend to settle in the United States. The 1986 immigrant survey found that an overwhelming majority of them (92.4 percent) reported the presence of relatives as the main reason for selecting their intended destination in the United States (Carino et al. 1990:63). Economic factors (6.2 percent), including the availability of jobs and "spouse's work is there," and even the presence of other Filipinos (0.1 percent) are of much less importance in immigrants' decisions concerning where to settle (Carino et al. 1990:63). Thus, a majority of the survey respondents indicated that their intended destination would be California (50.6 percent) where, as noted above, resides a majority of the Filipino American population. The other states reported as primary destinations, Hawai'i (10.6 percent), Illinois (4.4 percent), New York (3.8 percent), and New Jersey (3.1 percent), are those with the largest Filipino American populations in that order (Carino et al. 1990:62). Kinship ties also are very significant among Filipino immigrants to Hawai'i and can determine the particular city or town on the various islands where immigrants initially settle (Okamura 1984:34). These underlying family and kinship relations are very likely contributing to the increasing concentration of Filipino immigrants in the western states and in particular cities and towns within those states, despite regional or local economic conditions.

As a site of the Filipino American diaspora, ethnicity comprises the relations between Filipino Americans and other ethnic groups. These are highly unequal and structured relations that historically have maintained the subordinate status of Filipinos in American society since their arrival as agricultural labor recruits in the early 1900s. Ethnicity is essentially a site of political and economic exclusion for Filipino Americans, as well as other ethnic minorities, to maintain them in their marginalized position in American society.

The contradiction in the subordinate socioeconomic status of Filipino Americans has become increasingly more apparent with the arrival of professionally trained and college educated immigrants during the post-1965 immigration phase. The 1986 immigrant survey found that they had a relatively high median level of educational attainment (12.1 years) with substantial percentages of attendance in or graduation from college (46.7 percent), from graduate school (10.0 percent) and from high school (27.0 percent) (Carino et al. 1990:28). The post-1965 immigrants have contributed substantially to the relatively high rank of Filipino Americans on various socioeconomic indicators compared to other ethnic groups and the total American population. In 1980, Filipino Americans had a higher mean number of years of education completed (13.6 years) than Whites (12.3), Japanese Americans (13.3), and Chinese Americans (13.1) (Barringer et al. 1990:31), and the 1990 U.S. Census data, when available, may very likely indicate the same. Filipino American women have possibly the highest percentage of college graduates among females of all ethnic groups (25 years and older), and the percentage of university educated Filipino American men far exceeds the national median for males (Bureau of the Census 1988:6).

Despite such educational qualifications, Filipino Americans appear to receive less economic returns in terms of income and occupational status for their educational attainment level compared to other ethnic groups which is very likely the result of discriminatory employment practices (Barringer et al. 1990:31, 40; Cabezas et al. 1986-87:13). This unequal treatment especially affects professionally trained and college educated immigrants who encounter occupational downgrading from their previous positions in the Philippines. The 1986 survey of Filipino immigrants reported that while substantial percentages of employed men (20.1 percent) and women (34.2 percent) held professional or technical positions in the year before immigrating, these proportions had declined dramatically after two years in the United States for both employed men (9.0 percent) and women (15.3 percent) (E-W Population Institute 1990:12-14). Occupational downgrading also is evident in the increased number of the 1986 immigrants in blue collar work. While relatively low percentages of male (5.7 percent) and female (9.0 percent) immigrants held service or recreational jobs prior to immigrating, these figures had increased tremendously two years later for both men (33.3 percent) and women (24.3 percent).

It is not surprising then that the most frequently mentioned problem reported by the 1986 Filipino immigrants after two years in the United States was finding a suitable job (43.1 percent) (E-W Population Institute 1990:16). The cumulative result of employment discrimination and occupational downgrading, which also are serious problems for American-born Filipinos, is that Filipino Americans are distinguished by "low income and occupational status, poor occupational mobility, and minimal economic and political empowerment" (Cabezas et al. 1986-87:2), a description which unfortunately also would have applied to them prior to World War II.

Ethnicity as a site of the Filipino American diaspora also includes the expression and maintenance of their culture and ethnic identity. Particularly in Hawai'i but also in some cities in California, such cultural manifestations are evident in Filipino American residential and commercial districts. The houses in these neighborhoods are decorated with various Spanish style embellishments such as wrought iron fences and railings, balustrades, red tile roofs, and heavy doors made of Philippine narra hardwood with ornately carved designs. The yards of these homes are distinguished by various edible plants and trees, especially the *marunggay* or horseradish tree. Filipino American communities also are notable for the variety of Filipino-owned small business establishments such as video rental shops featuring the latest Philippine films, grocery stores selling imported Philippine food products, restaurants, bakeries, travel, real estate and insurance agencies, and money and *balikbayan* box delivery shops. The number and variety of these commercial establishments in terms of the goods and services they offer have proliferated in the past twenty years with the arrival of the post-1965 immigrants. As manifestations of Filipino American identity and culture, these homes and small businesses symbolize and situate the ethnic boundaries of Filipino American communities within the larger context of multiethnic cities or towns.

Other cultural and social expressions of Filipino American identity are evident in the continued use of Philippine languages, the maintenance of family and kinship norms and values, the conduct of Catholic rituals following Philippine custom, and the establishment of locality and other voluntary associations (Okamura 1991). While having obvious continuities with Philippine culture, Filipino American identity is based on historical and ongoing processes in the United States and therefore changes and evolves over time.

Ethnicity as a site of the Filipino American diaspora also can be viewed in terms of the relations of Filipinos with other Asian American groups. Within the Asian American community and particularly within Asian American studies as an academic discipline, a decentering is necessary to focus greater attention and action on the specific concerns and issues of relevance to Filipino Americans such as equality of access to economic and political power. This decentering can take the form of more equitable sharing of power, representation, support, and other resources among Asian American groups; otherwise the structures of domination in the larger society are replicated and reinforced within the Asian American community. In similar terms, a call has been made for "shifting the paradigm" of the Asian American community from its focus primarily on Chinese and Japanese Americans to include other Asian American groups such as Filipino, Asian Indian, and Vietnamese Americans (Hune 1993:7).

Emphasis on the "heterogeneity, hybridity and multiplicity" among Asian Americans has been advocated (Lowe 1991), but it is not sufficient merely to recognize and acknowledge group differences however they might be defined: culture, ethnic identity, language, national origin, class, generation, or history. The crucial differences are those of power and status and, in those terms, Filipino Americans are very much a marginalized rather than a model minority in American society. Power and status differences within the Asian American community need not only to be acknowledged but also acted upon through, as I stated above, power sharing. I am not arguing against maintaining and presenting a united and collaborative front in political and personal relations with the dominant society. But within the Asian American community, the diversity of identities and inequalities of status needs to be addressed beyond simply noting their existence.

The sites of space, time, and ethnicity also can be applied to other Asian American diasporas such as the Chinese, Korean, Vietnamese, and Asian Indian. Time-space compression and articulation of culture and ethnic identity are similarly evident in the post-1965 immigration phase of these various diasporas. Nonetheless, these general commonalities should not lead to minimizing the significant cultural, political, and economic differences among Asian American groups. As expressions of distinct "maps/ histories" and ethnic identities, each of the various Asian American diasporas is a unique representation of the sites of space, time, and ethnicity.

References

Abella, M. "Policies and Practices to Promote Migrants' Remittances." *Philippine Labor Review*, 13 (1989):1-17.

Barringer, H. R., R. W. Gardner and M. J. Levin. *Asians and Pacific Islanders in the United States*. New York: Russell Sage Foundation, 1993.

Barringer, H. R. , D. T. Takeuchi and P. Xenos. "Education, Occupational Prestige, and Income of Asian Americans." *Sociology of Education* 63 (1990):27-43.

Bouvier, L. F. and A. J. Agresta. "The Future Asian Population of the United States." In *Pacific Bridges.*, edited by J. T. Fawcett and B. V. Carino. Staten Island: Center for Migration Studies, 1987.

Bureau of the Census. *We, the Asian and Pacific Islander Americans*. Washington, D.C.: U.S. Department of Commerce, 1988.

Cabezas, A., L. H. Shinagawa and G. Kawaguchi. "New Inquiries into the Socioeconomic Status of Pilipino Americans in California." *Amerasia Journal* 13 (1986-87):1-21.

Carino, B. V., J. T. Fawcett, R. W. Gardner and F. Arnold. *The New Filipino Immigrants to the United States: Increasing Diversity and Change*. Papers of the East-West Population Institute, no. 115 (1990).

Clifford, J. "Sites of Crossing: Borders and Diasporas in Late 20th Century Expressive Culture." The Seeger Lecture, Society for Ethnomusicology, Seattle. Condensed version appears in *Cultural Currents* 1 (January 1992).

Cordova, F. *Filipinos: Forgotten Asian Americans*. Seattle: Demonstration Project for Asian Americans, 1983.

East-West Population Institute. *Recent Filipino Immigration to the United States: A Profile*. Population Institute, East-West Center, 1990.

Featherstone, M. *Consumer Culture and Postmodernism*. London: Sage Publications, 1991.

Foucault, M. "Of Other Spaces." *Diacritics* (Spring 1986):22-27.

Garner, R. W. "Asian Immigration: The View from the United States." *Asian and Pacific Migration Journal* 1 (1992):64-99.

Harvey, D. *The Condition of Postmodernity*. London: Basil Blackwell, 1989.

Honolulu Star-Bulletin , 15 June 1992.

Hune, S. "An Overview of Asian Pacific American Futures: Shifting Paradigms." In *The State of Asian Pacific America: Policy Issues to the Year 2020*. Los Angeles: LEAP Asian Pacific American Public Policy Institute and UCLA Asian American Studies Center, 1993.

Lasman, L., O. J. Buluran, J. Nolan and L. O'Neil. "A Study of Attitudes of Filipino Immigrants about Hawai'i." M.A. thesis, University of Hawai'i, 1971.

Lowe, L. "Heterogeneity, Hybridity, Multiplicity: Marking Asian American Differences." *Diaspora* 1(1991):24-44.

Okamura, J. Y. "Immigrant Filipino Ethnicity in Honolulu, Hawai'i." Ph.D. diss., University of London, 1983.

____. "Kinship and Community: Filipino Immigrants in Honolulu." *Dialogue* 20 (1984):27-43.

____. "Beyond Adaptationism: Immigrant Filipino Ethnicity in Hawai'i." *Social Process in Hawai'i* 33 (1991):56-72.

_____. "The International Filipino Diaspora: Diversity and Dispersal." Paper presented at Fourth International Philippine Studies Conference, Australian National University, 1-3 July 1992.

Ong, P. and S. J. Hee. "The Growth of the Asian Pacific Population: Twenty Million in 2020." In *The State of Asian Pacific America: Policy Issues to the Year 2020.* Los Angeles: LEAP Asian Pacific American Public Policy Institute and UCLA Asian American Studies Center, 1993.

Philippine Overseas Employment Administration. *Overseas Employment Statistical Compendium (1982-1991).* POEA, n.d.

Safran, W. "Diasporas in Modern Societies: Myths of Homeland and Return." *Diaspora* 1 (1991):83-99.

Shapiro, M. J. *Reading the Postmodern Polity: Political Theory as Textual Practice,* Minneapolis: University of Minnesota Press, 1992.

Sheffer, G. "A New Field of Study: Modern Diasporas in International Politics." In *Modern Diasporas in International Politics*, edited by G. Sheffer. Beckenham, Kent: Croom Helm, 1986.

Shiller, N. G., L. Basch and C. Blanc-Szanton. "Transnationalism: A New Analytic Framework for Understanding Migration." In *Towards a Transnational Perspective on Migration: Race, Class, Ethnicity and Nationalism Reconsidered,* edited by N. G. Shiller, L. Basch and C. Blanc-Szanton. Annals of the New York Academy of Sciences, 1992.

Tololyan, K. "The Nation-State and Its Others: In Lieu of a Preface." *Diaspora* 1 (1991):3-7.

Covering *Obasan* and the Narrative of Internment

Scott McFarlane

The internment of Japanese Canadians is arguably the most documented instance of ethnic civil rights abuse in Canadian history.[1] The internment has certainly become a yardstick for racism in Canada. For example, in 1986 Ann Sunahara told Nikkei at a human rights workshop that

> Japanese Canadians are unique in Canada, not only because of what you went through, not only because of the unique characteristics which enabled you to survive it and come back so strong, but also because you can keep Canadians aware of how perilous their rights are in times of emergency, and you can initiate processes which may make it possible to protect the weakest in those times, protections which do not presently exist (1989:29).

In this sense, the Canadian context varies greatly from the internment of Japanese Americans whose narrative is woven into the dense histories of African Americans and other racially defined ethnic groups. In comparison, the Japanese Canadian internment and redress movement is a precedent for other Canadian ethnic groups which are only recently gaining media attention in their struggles for redress and acknowledgments of the Canadian government's racist legislation in the past.[2]

Sunahara has pointed out that the internment is unusually well documented because the papers of Ian Alistair Mackenzie, the infamous Member of Parliament for Vancouver Centre, miraculously arrived in the national archives intact and not on the other end of the shredding machine (1989:33-34). This archival material was initially presented in the work of Sunahara but a general knowledge of the internment has been made available to the public by a plethora of histories such as those by Sunahara, Ken Adachi, Roy Ito, Tom Berger, Maryka Omatsu, the Japanese Canadian Centennial Project, Roy Miki and Cassandra Kobayashi, and the numerous articles by Audrey Kobayashi.[3] Canadian awareness of the internment was also

orchestrated by the National Association of Japanese Canadians who stra-
tegically established the highly successful National Coalition for Japanese
Canadian Redress. The National Coalition was made up of public figures
and supporters from all backgrounds channeling educational information
into the media. Since the success of the redress movement, Canadian awareness of the internment has been furthered by various documentary films,
including those by Ruby Truly, Linda Ohama, Michael Fukashima, and
Mark de Valk. Private accounts of the internment, such as those in Keibo
Oiwa's *Stone Voices* and the letters of Muriel Kitagawa, have been published. The internment has also been the subject of poetry, most notably
the work of Roy Miki and Dorothy Livesay. But no single text concerning
the internment has had a greater impact on the Canadian imaginary than
Joy Kogawa's *Obasan*. Published in 1981, *Obasan* was awarded the Canadian Authors' Association Book of the Year and the *Books in Canada* first
novel award. Kogawa's work is now one of the most well-known Canadian
novels and the subject of numerous critical articles written in North America
and Europe. It is taught in most Canadian literature courses and throughout the social sciences. As well, *Obasan* played a significant role in the
redress movement as evidenced by its being quoted by both Ed Broadbent
and Gerry Weiner during the announcement of the settlement with the
government. Thus *Obasan* has played, and continues to play, a significant
role in the way in which the internment is understood.

With this outpouring of documentation, and there is a large quantity
of material I have not mentioned, why is it that many Japanese Canadians
feel silenced and subsequently the need to testify concerning their experience of the internment? Why is it that so many *sansei* and *yonsei* feel
shrouded in silence, detached from the experience of their parents and
unable to articulate the impact of the internment on their lives? Is the
answer to these questions simply that individuals must learn to come to
terms, literally to come to language, with their own histories and that this
outpouring of documentation is evidence of an increasingly healthy community? Perhaps. But this argument suggests that there is an objective, real
internment to be known by each individual and reflected in the particularity of each narrative. Linguistic theorists since Sausaurre have given reasons to be wary of both the mimetic capabilities of language and a
historiography based on hermeneutic assumptions.

In fact, the intense accounting, recounting, and documentation suggests that the internment cannot be said to exist outside of language. That
is to say, what 'really happened' happens as an effect of language. This is

why the redress movement was so concerned with control of the media and the language used to reconceive the events of the war. Furthermore, if the internment is an effect of language then it should be understood as a process to be continually negotiated. This would suggest that the uprooting, internment, and dispersal of Japanese Canadians were the results of representational struggles that are ongoing. In fact, the political struggle for redress is currently ongoing.[4] Finally, if the internment is a process of language then it is important to ask how it is being circulated in discourse. Thus, this study will explore the discursive formation of the internment and Japanese Canadians in the specific context of Kogawa's influential novel, *Obasan*.

Throughout the novel Japanese Canadians are compared to yellow chicks. This is the central metaphor of an elaborate representational scheme which initiates a series of conflations within universal discourses. The yellow chick metaphor is partially articulated while Naomi is in the hospital after almost drowning. She recounts:

> Obasan has also brought me a thin book with a picture of animals in it called Little Tales for Little Folk. There is an oversized baby chick called "Chicken Little" standing on the front cover.
>
> What is this thing about chickens? When they are babies, they are yellow. Yellow like daffodils. Like Goldilocks' yellow hair. Like the yellow Easter Chicks I lost somewhere. Yellow like the yellow pawns in the Yellow Peril game.
>
> The Yellow Peril is a Somerville Game, Made in Canada. It was given to Stephen at Christmas. On the red and blue box cover is a picture of soldiers with bayonets and fists raised high looking out over a sea full of burning ships and a sky full of planes. A game about war (152).

The association of the Japanese with the chicks is made explicit with the comparison to the "yellow peril" (sic). This association is extended to Japanese Canadians as the "Yellow Peril" game is "Made in Canada." However, the association of the Japanese Canadian chicks with the vulnerability of babies makes the reference to the yellow peril (sic) ironic. In *Obasan* it is the Japanese Canadians who are at peril. For example, the reference to yellow chicks alludes to the incident earlier in the novel when Naomi placed a dozen chicks in a cage with a white hen who subsequently killed many of them. Instead of the nurturing response that Naomi naively expected from the hen, a violent "pecking order" is established paralleling the Japanese Canadian internment. In other words, instead of providing a nurturing environment, the Canadian government destroyed what is depicted in the novel as a child-like, trusting, Japanese Canadian community. This is a community repeatedly described as lacking any agency, as naive pawns in the Canadian government's "Yellow Peril" game. Naomi states, "We are the Issei and the Nisei and the Sansei, the Japanese Canadians. We disappear in the future undemanding as dew" (112).

The destruction of the community takes place in both a material and spiritual sense. The reference to Goldilock's hair reminds the reader of the violence being done to Naomi by the aggressive combing of the nurse while the children's tale emphasizes the child-like experience of the pain received from one who should be a nurturing figure. The violent combing foreshadows all the violent hair imagery in the recounting of the bombing of Nagasaki. The bombing is also foregrounded by the reference to "Chicken Little" who thought the sky was falling and the cover of the "Yellow Peril" game which depicts "a sky full of planes." Just as the chicks are attacked by the bombing beak of the hen, the hens have to be wary of the circling King Bird; the Japanese Canadians are uprooted and scattered by orders-in-council, which are described as sailing like "giant hawk(s) across a chicken yard" (188), and the Japanese are bombed by the Americans. A vicious pecking order is established in "a game about war" in which the lowly yellow chicks are the most vulnerable to violence.

The historical reasons for the war and the internment are never fully explored in the novel. Naomi argues "Time has solved few mysteries. War and rumors of wars, racial hatreds and fears are with us still" (78). Instead, it is suggested that the ironic yellow peril is the result of a lack of Christian love. The fact that the "Yellow Peril" game is a Christmas gift suggests that a symbol of mediation and transcendent community has been insidiously translated into a symbol of human violence and destruction. The Easter chicks that Naomi was saving to welcome home her mother are symbolic of faith and the rebirth of community and have, like her mother, been "lost somewhere." What is missing then, is *yasashi kokoro*, the tender heart or nurturing spirit which characterizes Naomi's mother (46). In its place, like the violent nurse, the Canadian government nurtures codes of violence as represented by the torture and killing of the chicken by the Slocan schoolboys.

Violence is also represented in the figure of Aunt Emily who is described as a "word warrior." Naomi writes,

> All of Aunt Emily's words, all her papers, the telegrams and petitions, are like scratchings in the barnyard, the evidence of much activity, scaly claws hard at work. But what good they do, I do not know—those little black typewritten words—rain words, cloud droppings. They do not touch us where we are planted here in Alberta, our roots clawing the sudden prairie air (189).

The comparison of Aunt Emily's well intended words to black rain make it clear that, lacking in the tenderness and sympathy needed to touch the heart, her language is a destructive force threatening the community. Uncle describes her work as both un-Japanese and unbecoming of a woman (40, 36). "Like that there can be no marriage," he tells her. There can be no understanding of *Kodomo no tame*—[enduring silence], "for the sake of the children"—the policy adopted by he and his wife in an effort to shelter the young from racism and the harsh reality of their historical context.

This policy too, is described as well-intended but ultimately destructive because it fails to communicate love to the naive child—Naomi. By the end of the novel, however, Naomi learns that to attend both the sound of Obasan's stony silence and Aunt Emily's linguistic rage demands a pathos capable of bearing witness to the loving intentions of both. The two aunts, like the two red tabs of the folder holding the letter from her grandmother, are united by the red, loving string of transcendent empathy which conflates words and silence, presence and absence, and testifies to the presence of an absent nurturing mother's love— *yasashi kokoro*.

Learning to attend to this love, to conflate differences, is part of Naomi's maturing process. Naomi states:

> I am thinking that for a child there is no presence without flesh but perhaps it is because I am no longer a child I can know your presence though you are not here. The letters tonight are skeletons. Bones only. But the earth still stirs with dormant blooms, love flows through the roots of the trees by our graves (243).

Naomi's maturity is signaled by the development of her ability to become a better reader—by her ability to transcend the silences and gaps in the fractured text of her family and community with *yasashi kokoro,* itself conflated with a Christian love that would make the word flesh.

The reader too, is confronted with a fractured text. The temporally fractured narrative, which constantly shifts from one genre to another, is surrounded by a proem, plus a comment regarding the historical reality of the text and an official government document. The novel's form then, resembles Aunt Emily's loose bundle. Thus the anonymous reader, like Naomi, is asked to penetrate and transcend this fictional account with a reading capable of attending to the essential spirit of Japanese Canadians. Within this structure, "Japanese" and "Canadian" have become conflated in the pathos of universal love.

So how does the internment enter discourse through Kogawa's representation of Japanese Canadians as yellow chicks? I will argue that the internment enters discourse by means of a symbolic order which alienates the Japanese Canadian from Japanese Canadian culture.

The split of the Japanese Canadian subject is evident in the Penguin edition cover of *Obasan*, released in 1983. The photo is racist as it depicts a Japanese Canadian within stereotypical assumptions of what a Japanese woman is like. The young girl is separated from the viewer by the train's window which is framed by pieces of steel held together by large rivets. Her looking away depicts her as an object lacking the power to do the same to the viewer. We see this lack of power functioning in the novel's rhetorical strategy so dependent on pathos. This rhetorical strategy is problematic and limited because it mistakenly argues that Japanese Canadians are subjects when we imagine ourselves as objects. Agency in this strategy is therefore only apparent. I will expand on this shortly. For now, it is important to note that this use of pathos inscribes the victimization of Japanese Canadians as their value.

That the girl in the photo is depicted as vulnerable is suggested by the fact that she is young, alone, and clutching a doll. In this way the photo suggests to the viewer that the novel will fulfill cultural assumptions regarding oriental [sic] women who are often portrayed as child-like, quiet, passive, and in need of protection. In the novel, this Orientalist representation is extended to the whole community. For example, when Old Man Gower comes over to discuss keeping possession of the Nakanes' furniture during the internment, Naomi sees her father as a feminine figure. She says,

> He [Gower] seems more powerful than Father, larger and more at home even though this is our house. He sounds as if he is trying to comfort my father, but there is a falseness in the tone (69).

Without the presence of pathos—the nurturing *yasashi kokoro*—gender roles deemed natural by patriarchal discourse are confused and replaced with falsehood and victimization. For example, the artful father and his son, Stephen, who are able to compose harmonies on their "flutes," are rendered silent during the internment.

Even the aggressive "mighty mouse," Aunt Emily, is rendered helpless as many of her letters to the government go unanswered and her knowledge reaches Naomi only well after the internment. In this way Aunt Emily greatly varies from Muriel Kitagawa, the historical person on whom her character is based. Kitagawa continued to be published in the Japanese Canadian English newspaper, the *New Canadian*, regularly until 1952.

Aunt Emily's writing functions primarily in the private sector as a *passive* record of past events rather than as an *active* narrative of opposition to the internment. In a sense, Aunt Emily is a "domesticated" version of Kitagawa.

The photo on the front cover also represents the novel's description of Naomi's transportation to the internment camp by train and hence it alludes to the Japanese Canadian internment itself. The train, however, frames the girl within an institutional discourse in which it is an icon of the development of Canada. The girl is thus framed by a narrative which displaces her story within a national *bildungsroman*. This displacement allows for the suggestion that both Naomi and Canada have grown from their internment.

For example, the Penguin front cover describes *Obasan* as "A moving novel of a time and suffering we have tried to forget." Who is the "we" in this statement? "We" seems to refer to an imagined community made up of those possessing an homogenous "Canadian memory." The Canadian memory, it is suggested, has struggled with its past; nostalgia is no longer an option. *Obasan* and the internment of Japanese Canadians serve as a reminder of this fact. Furthermore, the comment suggests that the novel has filled in gaps in this imagined Canadian memory. Whoever the "we" are, they are made more complete, or perhaps "redeemed," by the novel. Finally, the imagined Canadian community that has profited from *Obasan* does not include Japanese Canadians who have not forgotten about the internment.

Is *Obasan* a novel about *Canadian* growth and maturity? In the novel, Japanese Canadians and the internment are doubly displaced. First, understanding *Obasan* as a national *bildungsroman* establishes the perspective of a redeemed present and alleviates the immediacy of guilt felt by anyone who feels responsible for the internment by suggesting the girl and nation will come of age by the end of the novel. Her suffering is displaced as a distant thing that has been overcome. As a vulnerable yellow chick in the redeemed present, however, Naomi, and by extension Japanese Canadians, are signs of a violated past and violable future. Her subjectivity in the present has been displaced.

Second, it has been argued that Naomi is no longer a child when she develops the pathos required for hermeneutic cultural reading and that the development of this skill must assume the object status of her community as a means to pathos. Naomi, a Japanese Canadian reader, places herself in a pecking order of readers who learn to read Japanese Canadian culture not in a way that erases it, but rather, forces it to stand as a sign for a violated *Canadian culture and past.* Sympathetic Japanese Canadian and Canadian readers are conflated in the cultural act of "good" reading. Furthermore, to characterize Naomi's experience in terms of a *bildungsroman* is politically meaningless because it ultimately requires that "Canadian readers" ignore the cultural codes that make possible the articulation of her experience. In the novel, Naomi is unable to articulate these codes and therefore the racist discourse of internment remains displaced within an appeal for transcendental Christian love. Subsequently, *Obasan* has been judged by a pre-established value system which recognizes its own codes of pathos as a means of self perpetuation. Within the narrative of baby yellow chicks, Japanese Canadian cultural production has come to signify a violated and violable *Canadian* spirituality and culture in need of constant surveillance and maintenance by a patriarchal government whose redemption is signified by the re-establishing of its codes. The interests of the homogenous "we" have been extended to include Japanese Canadians at the latter's expense.

The cost of inclusion is evident in the national *bildungsroman* in which "Japanese Canadian" has come to signify an identity category of a developing Canada. Because Japanese Canadian "exteriority" has come to signify a vulnerable Canadian spirituality, or interiority, Japanese Canadian cultural production is not visible in the context of this "progressive" Canadian cultural identity. For Japanese Canadians then, Canadian cultural identity continually signifies their own *alieNation.* The double displacement producing this alieNation offers an explanation for the continued sense of *sansei* and *yonsei* silence and cultural detachment. This alieNation is the precedent that *Obasan's* narrative establishes for other ethnic groups and sadly, it enacts a policy of cultural dispersal.

It is my hope that this study has begun to develop a language of internment in that it draws attention to the need to develop narratives which do not inscribe Japanese Canadians as already interned and already internable. As well, I hope that this study has shown internment to be a language in itself whose grammar can be located in, for example, the inadvertent racist cultural presuppositions of the Penguin cover of *Obasan* and the novel itself. These presuppositions encode Japanese Canadian bodies within what can ultimately be described as romantic discourse which sees us as feminized, innocent, naive children in need of pedagogical, patriarchal mastery in order to protect an already fallen yet redeemable nation.

To see the internment as a linguistic process is to acknowledge our agency and ability to change racist discourses. I would like to conclude with an historical example of both the magnitude and the nature of the challenge I see facing us today—a challenge made more important by our position in the Canadian context.

With respect to the study of Japanese Canadian writing, the key to an oppositional language and the establishment of a Japanese Canadian politics of cultural difference is the development of methodologies of reading/writing that encounter the paradox of Japanese Canadian "success." The paradox of Japanese Canadian success is characterized by our community's contribution to human rights exemplified by the redress agreement and the subversive ways in which that "success" has been re-inscribed by institutional "readers" in the Canadian Ministry of Multiculturalism and critics in general who celebrate *Obasan* in ways which doubly displace Japanese Canadians from Japanese Canadian cultural production.

The functioning of this paradox and its urgency is evident in the National Association of Japanese Canadian's (NAJC) demand for a negotiated redress settlement. Implicit in this demand was the acknowledgment of agency, of the ability of Japanese Canadians to participate in important decision-making processes. It also afforded the negotiators a chance to set their own terms of dialogue; to not be only responsive, and to explore their own cultural encoding of the event. The demand for a negotiated settlement also challenged and disrupted the discourse or the "child-like, vulnerable Japanese Canadian." However, it was not until Art Miki had been elected president of the NAJC in 1984 and united the redress movement; until an all-party Special Committee on Participation of Visible Minorities in Canadian Society released a brief entitled, "Equality Now!" supporting the redress movement in principle; until the Price Waterhouse report, "The Economic Losses of Japanese Canadians After 1941," was released in 1986 revealing losses totaling over $443 million dollars; until the NAJC developed techniques to control the media; until three ministers of multiculturalism tried to impose unilateral decisions regarding the settlement; until Japanese Americans received a redress settlement on 4 August 1988; until the pressures on the government to fulfill election promises mounted with the upcoming election that, finally, the eleventh hour decision was made to negotiate with Japanese Canadians. On 22 September 1988 a settlement was reached. The negotiating process took seventeen hours (Miki and Kobayashyi 1991:64-139). Shortly after the signing of the agreement, *Obasan,* a narrative of the internment written largely from the perspective of a child, was invoked to sing the settlement's praises.

Notes

1. I would like to thank Richard Cavell, Kirsten McAllister and especially Roy Miki for their suggestions and comments regarding this paper. I would also like to acknowledge the assistance of the Social Sciences and Humanities Research Council of Canada.
2. Recently Italian, Ukranian, Chinese, and Sikh Canadians denounced the Mulroney Government's offer of an "eleventh hour" apology without financial compensation for past treatment. See Platiel (1993).
3. See, for example, Sunahara (1981); Adachi (1987); Ito (1984); Berger (1986); Omatsu (1992); Japanese Canadian Centennial Project (1978); Kitagawa (1985); Miki and Kobayashi (1991); and the many articles and press releases concerning the internment and Japanese Canadian history.
4. Five years after the signing of the redress agreement, the National Association of Japanese Canadians (NAJC) is still seeking redress for both Canadians of Japanese ancestry entrapped and stranded in Japan and prohibited from returning to Canada in the period between 1941 and 1949 and also Canadians of Japanese ancestry born in exile as a direct consequence of their parents' deportation from Canada. In recent meetings with the Ministry of Multiculturalism the NAJC was told that these outstanding claims were excluded from redress as their suffering was not the result of the War Measures Act. The Ministry acknowledged that the policies of the government were racist, but argued it was a time of war (National Association of Japanese Canadians 1993). The ministry's argument clearly contradicts the intent of the agreement seeking to redress injustices inflicted on the Japanese Canadian community. The agreement acknowledges, "In retrospect, government policies of disenfranchisement, detention, confiscation and sale of private and community property, expulsion, deportation and restriction of movement, which continued after the war, were influenced by discriminatory attitudes" (Miki and Kobayashi 1991:138).

References

Adachi, Ken. *The Enemy That Never Was.* Toronto: McClelland and Stewart, 1987.

Berger, Tom. *Reflections on Redress.* Vancouver: Vancouver JCCA Redress Committee, 1986.

Ito, Roy. *We Went to War: The Story of Japanese Canadians Who Served during the First and Second World Wars.* Stittsville, Ontario: Canada's Wings, 1984.

Japanese Canadian Centennial Project. *A Dream of Riches: The Japanese Canadians. 1877-1977.* Vancouver: JCCP, 1978.

Kitagawa, Muriel. *This Is My Own: Letters to Wes and other Writings on Japanese Canadians 1941-1949,* edited by Roy Miki. Vancouver: Talonbooks. 1985.

Miki, Roy and Cassandra Kobayashi. *Justice in Our Time: The Japanese Canadian Redress Settlement.* Vancouver: Talonbooks, 1991.

National Association of Japanese Canadians. "An Agreement Unfulfilled, A Promise Not Kept." Paper submitted to the Greater Vancouver Japanese Canadian Citizens Association by Randy Enomoto, 13 September 1993.

Omatsu, Maryka. *Bittersweet Passage: Redress and the Japanese Canadian Experience.* Toronto: Between the Lines, 1992.

Platiel, Rudy. "Ethnic Groups Denounce Offer of Apology for Past Treatment." *Globe and Mail,* 29 May 1993.

Sunahara, Ann. "Illusory Protection: The Enemy Within." In *Spirit of Redress: Japanese Canadians in Conference,* edited by Cassandra Kobayashi, Roy Miki. Vancouver: JC Publications, 1989.

____. *The Politics of Racism: The Uprooting of Japanese Canadians during the Second World War.* Toronto: Lorimer, 1981.

The Sites of Race and Ethnicity in Psychological Research on Asian Americans

Ruth H. Chung Gim

Introduction

In psychological research on Asian Americans, race has been preferred over ethnicity. The notion of an Asian American is generally predicated on an identity that is transcendent of specific ethnicity.

A collective identity has many important functions. It reminds us of our shared history of oppression as people of Asian ancestry in America. It also fills a practical demographic need in describing a certain population of people who share a degree of commonality in the context of America. In turn, these factors facilitate coalition-building and greater political empowerment.

Despite these laudable aspects, the use of a collective term is not without hazards. It is deceptive in its simplicity and belies a sense of homogeneity that in reality does not exist. It serves to perpetuate the popular misconception that Asian Americans are all alike. This myth has been reified in the academic arena where Asian Americans and other people of color are perceived simplistically and treated as unidimensional beings with race as the only, or primary, dimension of salience. Until recently, most of the available research on Asian Americans and other minority groups seldom took into account other dimensions of diversity such as ethnicity, acculturation, gender, and class. According to an examination of cross-cultural counseling literature in the *Journal of Counseling Psychology* between 1976 and 1986, only thirty percent of the published articles included within-group variables in their design as an independent variable, all of which were published after 1980 (Ponterotto 1988). Furthermore, early studies on Asian Americans were conducted on Chinese and Japanese Americans then generalized to the entire Asian American population, or worse, there was no thought given to generalization because of the perception that Chinese and Japanese Americans constituted the entirety of the Asian American population.

While a racially-based, pan-ethnic identity as Asian Americans is needed and useful, the meaningfulness of a collective identity is questionable from psychological and phenomenological perspectives. The majority of Asian Americans are first generation. Psychological literature on cultural identity and acculturation indicates that the first generation have a closer affinity to the culture of origin than mainstream American culture, and prefer to use ethnic-specific self-designation such as Vietnamese or Filipino (with or without the "American" attachment) than the term Asian American.[1] Given this, it is necessary to ask "is it still possible to speak of a single Asian American identity?" (Liu 1988) Is there enough commonality among the various Asian American ethnic groups to support a collective identity that is psychologically meaningful? Is there empirical evidence of the dimensions where there are sufficient similarities to merit the use of a collective designation in describing the population? In raising these questions the purpose is not to essentialize what an Asian American is but rather to define the contexts in which the ethnic-specific approach is indicated, and where a failure to do so constitutes an oversimplification and generalization.

A brief review of the findings of a series of studies conducted by the author on ethnic group differences in various aspects of mental health will provide the context for the current study.

The first in the series of studies (Atkinson and Gim 1989) examined the relationship between the dimensions of gender, ethnicity, and level of acculturation to attitudes toward seeking psychological help.[2] Studies have established that Asian Americans underutilize mental health services. The stigma of having psychological problems, the ensuing loss of face for the individual and the family unit, and traditional beliefs about the nature and origin of psychological illnesses engender negative attitudes toward seeking professional psychological help among Asian Americans.[3] A survey was administered by mail to a randomly selected group of Chinese, Japanese, and Korean American college students to test for differences among ethnic, gender, and acculturation levels in attitudes toward counseling. Highly significant differences were observed for acculturation level but differences in ethnic and gender groups were statistically insignificant.[4] Thus, while acculturation level was clearly related, there was no significant difference among Chinese, Japanese, and Korean Americans in attitudes toward seeking psychological help.[5]

A subsequent study (Gim, Atkinson, and Whiteley 1990) explored the relationship of ethnicity, gender, and acculturation level to the type and severity of problems that Asian American students experience, and their willingness to see a counselor for these problems. A survey, which contained a comprehensive list of commonly known problems of college students was distributed by mail to all Asian American undergraduates at a major public university in California. Consistent with the previous study, a highly significant acculturation effect was observed, but unlike the previous study, there was a significant effect for ethnicity as well.[6] The acculturation effect was explained by higher mean severity ratings given by low-acculturated students than high-acculturated students. The effect of ethnicity was accounted for by differences in severity of problems indicated by the five major ethnic groups: Chinese, Filipino, Japanese, Korean, and Southeast Asian Americans. Southeast Asians consistently gave the highest severity ratings across all problems except for conflict with parents, even when controlling for acculturation. Conversely, Japanese Americans consistently gave the lowest ratings, except for health problems, across all groups. Thus, in both type and severity of problems experienced, there were significant differences depending on the level of acculturation and ethnicity. However, this study yielded mixed results regarding significance of ethnicity because in the second part of the study on willingness to seek help for the problems, ethnicity was once again non-significant.[7]

The third study (Atkinson, Whiteley, and Gim 1990) examined the relationship of gender, ethnicity, and acculturation level to actual preferences for help-providers. On a mailout survey, Asian American students were asked to rank their preferences from a list of potential help-providers ranging from immediate and extended family members to community members and helping professionals. Analysis of the data did not reveal significant differences in preferences for help-providers among the ethnic groups.[8]

In observing the pattern of results from these three studies, an inconsistent picture emerges for the significance of ethnicity. In only one of the three studies a significant difference among the major Asian American ethnic groups was observed. The two studies in which no ethnic group differences were found were on attitudes and preferences that are more culturally-based than problem areas, which are more vulnerable to socioeconomic factors and immigration pattens. The lack of consistently significant ethnic group differences support the notion of a collective identity.[9]

However, since the results of the three studies cannot conclusively address the issue, further research was indicated. In the previous studies, the dependent variables were psychological phenomenon that are oblique manifestations of culture. A more direct examination of a core aspect of culture, such as values, would provide more compelling indication as to whether there is sufficient commonality among the Asian American groups to warrant a collective treatment, or whether an ethnic-specific approach must be taken. Thus, the purpose of this study was to test for significant differences in values among the major Asian American ethnic groups. A lack of significant differences would provide additional evidence in support of a core set of values that can be broadly defined as Asian American whereas significant differences would suggest that it is important to make ethnic group distinctions when talking about a certain set of values.

Methods

A survey containing demographic questions and a measure of values was mailed to randomly selected Asian American undergraduate students at a major public university in California. Of the 285 Asian American respondents, 84 were Chinese, 62 were Southeast Asian, 47 were Korean, 33 were Japanese, 24 were Filipinos, with the remaining 15 combined in an "Other Asian" category. Twenty of the respondents did not indicate their ethnic origin and were therefore excluded from analysis.

The Values Scale, a cross-culturally validated instrument was used to measure values (Neville and Super 1986).[10] This instrument was developed by an international consortium of psychologists with the goal of measuring intrinsic and extrinsic values that are not measured by existing instruments. It is oriented toward, but not limited to, measuring values related to vocational choice.

The 106-item instrument yields nine factored value dimensions for the college population which are: need for (1) authority; (2) expression of creativity; (3) prestige; (4) material rewards; (5) utilization of ability; (6) social interaction; (7) physical activity; (8) diversity in the work environment; and (9) autonomy.

Findings and Discussion

Multivariate analysis of variance (MANOVA) was used to test for statistical significance of differences among the six ethnic groups for the nine value dimensions. The MANOVA revealed an overall significance in terms of value differences among the ethnic groups.[11] Subsequent univariate analysis for each of the nine value dimensions revealed significant ethnic group differences in four of them: need for authority, creativity, prestige, and autonomy. *Post hoc* comparisons which were conducted to determine the exact nature of ethnic group differences for these four values revealed a fairly clear pattern. In each of the four values, Filipino responses were significantly different from all of the other groups. In three of the four values, Chinese and Japanese American responses were significantly different from those of the other groups.

Not only did Filipino responses differ significantly from all other groups combined, they also indicated the highest need for authority, expression of creativity, prestige, and autonomous lifestyle, whereas Japanese Americans consistently indicated the lowest need for these values, with the exception of creativity. Chinese Americans, although having neither the highest nor the lowest mean scores (except for creativity) were still significantly different from the other ethnic groups on the authority and creativity value dimensions. The mean scores by Korean Americans, Southeast Asians, and the combined Other Asians did not differ significantly from the other groups in any of the values. Their means, which were fairly close to each other, generally fell between the Filipino and Japanese American extreme mean scores.

Table 1

Tables of Mean Ratings of Values by Ethnicity

	Authority	Creativity	Prestige	Autonomy
Filipino Americans	16.33**	17.58**	17.04*	36.00***
Korean Americans	15.41	16.50	15.76	33.00
Other Asian Americans	14.53	16.27	15.53	33.53
Southeast Asian Americans	14.31	15.89	15.63	33.16
Chinese Americans	13.81**	15.12*	15.89	31.69*
Japanese Americans	13.45*	15.30	13.79***	30.91**

*p<.05   **p<.01   ***p<.001

It is interesting to note that of the four value dimensions which were significant, two of the values, need for authority and prestige, are consistent with Asian cultures while the other two values, need for expression of creativity and autonomy, are associated with mainstream American culture. If the differences in values were a function of acculturation level, then more recent groups such as Southeast Asian and Korean Americans should have the highest mean scores on authority and prestige values whereas Chinese and Japanese Americans should have the highest scores on creativity and autonomy values.[12] The fact that Filipinos scored highest on all four of the value dimensions suggests that acculturation cannot account for the ethnic group differences in values. Additional analyses were conducted to obtain empirical evidence of this view. The MANOVA analysis was repeated, but this time acculturation level was held constant.[13] The result was nearly identical to that of the initial one.[14] Thus, ethnic group differences in values is independent of acculturation level.

Conclusion

The results of this study indicate that it is necessary to make ethnic group distinctions in some value dimensions. Filipino and Japanese Americans are most different from the other Asian ethnic groups. These groups also serve as extreme endpoints on authority, prestige, and autonomy value dimensions.

This study contributes to the discussion of a pan-Asian identity based on a common culture as reflected by values, by empirically delineating the value dimensions which are held in common versus those that are different among groups. The fact that significant ethnic group differences were observed in some of the value dimensions but not in others precludes a clear statement in support of race over ethnicity or ethnicity over race. On one hand, it is possible to say that Asian Americans believe in the importance of material rewards, utilization of ability, social interaction, physical activity, and work environment to a similar degree, but on the other hand, Filipino and Japanese Americans differ significantly on the value dimensions of authority, prestige, creativity, and autonomy.

Additional research is needed to further specify both the commonalities as well as differences, not only with regard to value dimensions but also in other salient manifestations of culture. Until the parameters of a common cultural base are clearly defined, it is necessary to include dimensions of within-group diversity such as ethnicity, gender, class, and acculturation level in social science research on Asian Americans. Consistent inclusion of these factors can lead to a body of literature which can be used to formulate a theory of ethnicity and, eventually, how it interacts with the other sites of gender, class, and acculturation level.

Notes

1. Cultural identity and acculturation process for first generation is moderated by age at time of migration and heterogeneity of the residential community. Those who came at a very young age and/or grew up in a primarily White, middle class, suburban environment tend to acculturate rapidly and may approximate the second generation.
2. Due to practical constraints, socioeconomic class was not included in these studies.
3. For example, see Sue and Morishima (1982). Use of term "Asian American" hereafter is for demographic purposes in describing a population and does not necessarily imply a sense of collective identity.
4. A 3 (ethnicity) x 2 (gender) x 2 (acculturation level) MANOVA with four subscales of the ATTSPH (Attitudes Toward Seeking Professional Psychological Help) was conducted using SYSTAT statistical analysis package. Wilks Lambda value: $F(8, 1084) = 3.476$, $p<.001$.
5. For a more detailed description of the methodology and results, refer to the actual studies. Findings related to acculturation and gender are not discussed in this article as to not detract from the primary focus on ethnicity.
6. A 2 (sex) x 2 (acculturation level) x 5 (ethnicity) x (8 factored problem areas) repeated measures analysis of variance was conducted using SAS statistical analysis package. Acculturation was significant at $p<.001$ and ethnicity at $p<.01$.
7. For willingness to see a counselor, repeated measures analysis of variance (ANCOVA) revealed significance at $p<.05$ level for both gender and acculturation but not for ethnicity.
8. A 2 (sex) x 2 (acculturation) x 5 (ethnicity) MANOVA was computed for the help provider ratings. This resulted in a significant main effect for sex ($p<.001$), near-significance for acculturation ($p<.057$), and non-significance for ethnicity ($p<.10$).
9. Although lack of significant ethnic group differences suggests a commonality based on race, it cannot be taken as proof of racial commonality because, according to the assumptions of hypothesis testing, the null hypothesis cannot be proven; it can only be disproved.
10. Two measures of internal reliability are provided by Neville and Super (1986). The alpha coefficients for high school, university and adult samples range from .60 to .86. Test-retest (over a 2 to 4 week period) correlations which are available only for the university populations range from .52 to .82. Also, careful validation procedures were used in various phases of development of this instrument. Three teams of specialists from different countries wrote the items. Cross-cultural generalizability was attained by teams from at least two different cultures working on the same values.
11. Wilks' Lambda = .778, $F(45, 1116) = 1.435$, $p<.033$.
12. In the three previous studies (Atkinson and Gim 1989; Gim, Atkinson, and Whiteley 1990; Atkinson, Whiteley, and Gim 1990), Japanese Americans were consistently the most acculturated whereas Southeast Asians were least acculturated.
13. The MANOVA was conducted for those only in the high acculturation level group. The same could not be done for the low acculturation group because of small sample size ($n = 32$) and unequal distribution across the ethnic groups.

14. Wilks Lambda = .760, $F(45, 1009)$ = 1.418, p<.038. The one small variation was in the subsequent univariate analyses. Significant ethnic group differences were observed for three of the four values: authority, creativity, and autonomy. Prestige only approached statistical significance (p=.059).

References

Atkinson, Donald R. and Ruth H. Chung Gim. "Asian American cultural identity and attitudes mental health services." *Journal of Counseling Psychology.* 36 (1989):209-12.

Atkinson, Donald R., Scott Whiteley, and Ruth H. Chung Gim. "Asian American acculturation and preferences for help providers." *Journal of College Student Development.* 31 (1990):155-61.

Gim, Ruth H. Chung, Donald R. Atkinson, and Scott Whiteley. "Asian American acculturation, severity of problems, and willingness to see a counselor." *Journal of Counseling Psychology.* 37 (1990):281-85.

Liu, John M. "The Relationship of Migration Research to Asian American Studies: Unity and Diversity within the Curriculum." In *Reflections on Shattered Windows: Promises and Prospects for Asian American Studies,* edited by Gary Y. Okihiro, Shirley Hune, Arthur A. Hansen, and John M. Liu. Pullman: Washington State University Press, 1988.

Neville, Dorothy and Donald Super. *Manual: Values Scale.* Palo Alto: Consulting Psychologists Press, 1986.

Ponterotto, Joseph G. "Racial/ethnic minority research in the *Journal of Counseling Psychology*: A content analysis and methodological critique." *Journal of Counseling Psychology.* 35 (1988):410-18.

The New Outsiders: Vietnamese American Students in Higher Education

Hien Duc Do

Although much has been written about Vietnamese refugees, previous research has primarily focused on the processes of social adaptation and economic adjustment (Chan 1988). On the other hand, research on Asian American and academic achievement has concentrated primarily on their success, and whether or not they perform better in school than European Americans and other groups, but not on how the students have used their cultural knowledge and ethnicity to adapt to an institution of higher learning. This study examines the college experiences of a new group of refugees in the United States through the study of Vietnamese undergraduate students at the University of California, Santa Barbara (UCSB).

In addition to learning their roles as university students, Vietnamese students have to negotiate their roles as refugees, and their role as a member of a minority group in a predominantly European American institution. Moreover, unlike their fellow students, who are generally responsible only for themselves, these students are responsible for more than simply themselves, at least financially. In many instances, they are also responsible for the welfare of their families as well. In general, then, as newcomers to the university, Vietnamese students may be expected to operate outside of the mainstream student cultures, but they come to the campus strongly oriented toward educational success.

Table 1 provides a summary of the class distribution and year of arrival in the United States of Vietnamese students attending the UCSB.[1] The table illustrates a fairly even distribution, both in terms of their class standing as well as their year of arrival. There are a few students who for academic, personal, or financial reasons are fifth year seniors.

Table 1

Vietnamese Students Class Distribution by Year of Arrival

Class	1975-79	1980-89	Born in U.S.
Freshman	11.9%	11.9%	0%
Sophomore	10.1%	10.1%	0%
Junior	11.0%	15.6%	1.0%
Senior	6.4%	9.2.%	0%
Fifth Year Senior	5.5%	6.4%	1.0%

(N = 109)

Thirty-five percent of Vietnamese students reported engineering or computer science as their major as compared to only eight percent of all students attending UCSB.[2] Men tend to choose engineering as a major more than women by a ratio of 4:1. Although this finding may be surprising at first, it should not be. First, engineering has classically been a male-dominated field. What is surprising however is that the ratio of women is larger for Vietnamese 4:1 as opposed to 8:1 for the overall student body. That is, since there is a general understanding that there is a longstanding Vietnamese cultural expectation, as well as a general societal expectation, that the sons will be more responsible for providing the necessary financial assistance to the family, there would be more pressure for them to pursue those majors which offer immediate monetary rewards upon graduation.

In contrast, although women were traditionally encouraged to attend college to obtain a bachelors degree and perhaps additional knowledge, they were not necessarily expected to financially support the family in Viet Nam. However, perhaps due to the financial pressure and the language barrier, women in the United States are expected to provide economic assistance to the family. Seventy-five percent of those who major in engineering and computer science are students who arrived in the United States during the second period. Again, this fact should not be surprising since engineering and computer science are those majors that require the least amount of English proficiency as well as those majors which are perceived to offer immediate employment after graduation.

Biological sciences is the second most frequently reported major at 19 percent as compared to 12.9 percent for the overall student body. The fact that the two most frequently reported majors are engineering or computer science and biological sciences seem to reflect a certain degree of expectation from the parents. Given the social status of doctors in Viet Nam as well as in the United States, we would expect the parents to encourage their children to choose a major that would lead to a profession in the medical field. It was not uncommon during the interviews for the students to report that their parents expected their children to attend college in order to become professionals.

Business economics was the next most popular major at fifteen percent. This statistic is comparable to the overall statistic reported by all students at 16.5 percent. Social sciences as their choice of major was next; twelve percent chose psychology, political science, and law and society. That choice is lower than the 19.1 percent reported for all students. Vietnamese students reporting arts and humanities as their major was similar to the overall students at 9 percent and 7.9 percent respectively. Finally, 10 percent of the students were "undeclared."

The main goal mentioned by Vietnamese students for attending college was for pre-professional training. The issue was explored further in the personal interviews. With very few exceptions, the students' reasons for majoring in engineering were pragmatic. The following reasons were those most frequently cited: (1) students will be able to find jobs immediately following graduation; (2) parents are pressuring students to choose a "practical" field, and expect them to financially assist and support their families after graduation; and (3) in general, engineering and physical science majors do not require as much English proficiency as other humanities and social sciences disciplines.

This last concern was especially important and prevalent among those who came to the United States after 1980. Many students expressed personal frustrations and anguish at not being able to achieve their career goals simply because they are not fluent in English, saying that they would rather be poets, writers, social scientists, lawyers, or psychologists, but had to settle for engineering, computer science, or the physical sciences to earn the elusive college degree and perhaps achieve financial security. Both recent and earlier immigrants cite lack of English proficiency as an important determinant in choosing a major.

In addition to choosing majors that are practical, all students, regardless of their length of stay in the United States expressed the need and often pressure to help their families financially after graduation. Students who arrived after 1980 were constantly reminded of their obligations to their families, many of whom are still living in Viet Nam. Since their families sacrificed a great deal to send many of them to the United States to avoid the draft, or to offer them the opportunities for a better life, they feel deeply obligated. There is a sense of urgency for them to think of their educational experience in terms of short, concrete, and practical goals. They were at the university to obtain a degree that will help them fulfill their obligations to their families.

Although Vietnamese students' choice of major and career goals appear similar to the choices of other students, their motivation for choosing those majors are quite different. Unlike students who chose professional careers as a way to insure their personal material success in the future as in the case of the "me generation" of the 1970s and early 1980s (Levine 1980; Horowitz 1987), Vietnamese students are choosing these professions as a result of their felt moral obligations to their families who have struggled, suffered, and sacrificed a great deal to help them in their education.

Put differently, there is a profound tension between traditional values and beliefs from the old culture and the new environment in which the students find themselves. On one hand, there is the longstanding cultural belief that the scholar should be accorded the highest social position in Vietnamese society. On the other hand, as a result of being uprooted, displaced, and becoming refugees in the United States, combined with the pressure from their family, students have likely chosen those fields to offer some immediate financial security upon graduation. As a result of these conflicting pressures, the students have abandoned or deferred the pursuit of scholarship in order to fulfill their obligations to their families. At least at this stage of their development, the welfare of the family seems to outweigh the desire for advanced education. What remains to be seen in the future is whether the students will be satisfied with their choice of careers, or whether they will return to graduate school to pursue and follow the path of the serious scholar.

Sixty-three percent of all students reported as having speaking fluency in Vietnamese. Since it is generally easier to retain speaking fluency in languages and more difficult to retain writing and reading skills, I would expect that the students' literacy would decrease as indicated in the data in Table 2.

Table 2

Vietnamese Students' Language Fluency

	Speak	Read	Write
Fluent	63.3%	38.5%	34.9%
Somewhat	31.2%	30.3%	31.2%
None	5.5%	31.2%	33.9%
Total	100%	100%	100%

(N = 109)

Generally, there are two variables which differentiate those who identify themselves as Vietnamese Americans and those who identify themselves only as Vietnamese: the period during which the student arrived to
the United States; and the student's age upon arrival. Despite differences
between those who view themselves as Vietnamese Americans and those
who view themselves as Vietnamese, identifying with, or at least acknowledging, their culture seems to be a significant practice for both groups.
Asked to explain further their strong identity with their culture, a student
explained:

> I guess it's our ancestors. So from them, you become who you are. That's
> what culture is about right? If everyone came from the same ancestors, we
> would all be the same . . . . That's how you get your identity. I guess that's one
> thing that makes people different in this world is where you came from.[3]

The interviews show that Vietnamese students view critically those
who deny, or do not acknowledge their cultural heritage, especially fellow
Vietnamese students. Such criticism is prevalent even among those who
understand and acknowledge society's pressure to assimilate to avoid discrimination. Students still find it difficult to accept anyone's denial of her/
his culture. For them, denying one's culture, is like "a slap in the face to
your parents, grandparents and ancestors." One should "be proud of where
we come from. It's our identity, at least, it's a part of us that shouldn't be
denied."

The theoretical framework for this section is guided by the typology
of student subcultures of Clark and Trow (1966) and Tinto (1975) on
dropout behavior. According to Tinto, the college social subsystem is composed of peer group and faculty interactions. The greater the contacts with
both groups as well as the more meaningful the contacts, the better the
student's level of social integration. Finally, this paper follows the modification of Tinto's framework as suggested by Loo and Rolison (1986). They
suggest that peer group interactions can be conceptualized in terms of the
fit of the student with both the overall student community and with her or
his particular student subculture. Put differently, Loo and Rolison argue
that minority students may feel alienated from the larger campus community but well integrated into their own ethnic subculture and therefore
integrated into the life of the institution.

Because of the lack of diversity of UCSB's student body,[4] in addition
to learning their roles as university students, Vietnamese students are constantly reminded of their physical, cultural, and economic differences.
Moreover, as a result of their understanding of race relations in America,

the students are also aware of their status as a minority group in a predominantly Euro-American institution. In short, Vietnamese students view themselves both culturally and racially as a minority group at the university.

A variety of actors can deter students from participating in the larger collegiate life, such as whether or not they view themselves as belonging to the university. In general, many Vietnamese students do not see the university as their own. Statements such as, "I don't feel like it's my school" or "when I go somewhere, I think it's my school but when I come back, it feels like it's their school" surfaced frequently during the interviews.

Although images of spelling bee champions, high school valedictorians, and Westinghouse Science competition winners *(Newsweek* 1982; *Newsweek* 1984; *U.S. News and World Report* 1984; *Time* 1985; *New York Times Magazine* 1986) are typical media portrayals of Vietnamese American students, some of the students interviewed reported academic difficulties. Those reports will likely confirm official university studies, however, the administration refuses to release those records to protect the students' privacy rights. Throughout my interviews, students reported having academic difficulties in completing their assignments, maintaining their grade point average, and staying in their chosen major. These difficulties seem to be exacerbated by having to adjust to the "model minority" stereotype as well as living up to their parents' expectations. They expressed frustrations and anger over these images, placing unnecessary pressure on them by society and their parents. In stark contrast to those media images, Keiko Inoue, director of UCSB's Asian Pacific American Educational Opportunity Program reported that each quarter, "about one-third of our students, many of whom are Vietnamese, found themselves on academic probation."[5]

According to Tinto, a student's relationship to a faculty member also determines her or his level of social integration into the university. The greater the degree of interaction with the faculty, the greater the students' feeling of acceptance and of belonging. Vietnamese students reported very little interaction with faculty. In general, the students felt intimidated by the faculty either because of their status, or because they perceived faculty to not have time for students. None of the students reported feeling comfortable talking to the faculty at a social level. Statements such as "I only talk to the teaching assistants" or "I don't talk to them [faculty] because I don't know what to talk about" reflected their sentiment.

In addition to feeling intimidated by the faculty, some students felt as if they were evaluated differently because of their ethnicity. The following statement is a student's recollection of her experience:

> I love to write so I take a lot of English classes. They [teaching assistants and professors] immediately look at my paper and give me a B- because they assumed I had tutor help. I had to prove to them that I didn't get any tutor help before they raise my grade. They don't look at my worth, just what they want to see. It happened to me twice at this school.

Students also reported being the objects of prejudice, or differential treatment by their peers in the classrooms: "It's not just that you don't fit in but you notice a lot of things. It's the look they gave . . . . They don't really show any prejudice but it's there. For example, in my class, they passed around a paper to do independent group study, you feel like they don't want to pass it on to you."

Although none of the students reported direct discrimination, and only one-third reported that racism was a significant problem, there was an uneasy feeling about the ways in which they were received and treated by different members of the university. There was a hesitancy or a sense of self-doubt in their acknowledgment that they were treated differently because of language or ethnicity. They wonder if they are overly sensitive to their social reception on campus.

As a result of their perceptions of the faculty and teaching assistants, as well as their believed alienation from the larger campus, Vietnamese students have developed study groups with other Vietnamese students in order to address and alleviate some of the academic difficulties. It was not uncommon for students of all majors, but especially engineering, computer science, and physical science students to enroll in courses with friends and to choose each other as laboratory partners. In those ways, they consciously avoid situations that force them to interact with non-Vietnamese students.

Students' views were not limited to the classrooms, but extended to the social environment of the general campus. A student pointedly observed:

> I think that if I go to one of those fraternities, I would not be accepted because of my race, because of the way I look is different . . . . I intentionally avoid those places . . . . I actually went to a few of them with some friends. They wouldn't say anything directly to us that would show they were prejudice—but personally, we felt different, we didn't feel like we belonged there.

In sum, although Vietnamese American students choose majors that are similar to the overall student body, their reasons for their choice differ from their non-Vietnamese peers. Vietnamese students select their majors by parental pressure, English language proficiency, and their status as recent refugees in the United States. Furthermore, students have minimal interaction with faculty and feel alienated from other students. Finally, they are acutely aware of being perceived and treated as members of a minority group by other students as well as the faculty.

Notes

1. The data for this paper is from a survey sent out to all Vietnamese American students at UCSB, and from in-depth interviews of 25 Vietnamese students.
2. The data for the overall UCSB student major was obtained from a report from "University of California, Santa Barbara Fall 1990 Freshman Class ACE Results." Office of Budget and Planning. January 1991.
3. All of my interviews with Vietnamese students occurred in 1990. Out of respect for the privacy of the students involved, I do not use their names here.
4. The overall student body at UCSB is 71.4 percent White, 11.3 percent Asian/Pacific Islander, 10.8 percent Hispanic, 3.3 percent African American, 1.2 percent American Indian, 0.4 percent East Indian/Pakistani, and 1.5 percent other. From 1990-1991 UCSB Campus Student Profile. Office of Budget and Planning.
5. Field interview, Fall 1989. University of California, Santa Barbara.

References

Chan, Sucheng. "Asian Americans: A Selected Bibliography of Writings Published since the 1960s." In *Reflections on Shattered Windows: Promises and Prospects for Asian American Studies,* edited by Gary Y. Okihiro, Shirley Hune, Arthur A. Hansen, John M. Liu. Pullman: Washington State University Press, 1988.

Clark, B., and M. Trow. "The Organizational Context." In *College Peer Groups,* edited by T. M. Newcomb and E. K. Wilson. Chicago: Aldine, 1966.

Horowitz, Helen Lefkowitz. *Campus Life: Undergraduate Cultures from the End of the Eighteenth Century to the Present.* New York: Knopf, 1987.

Levine, Arthur. *When Dreams and Heroes Died: A Portrait of Today's College Students.* San Francisco: Jossey-Bass, 1980.

Loo, Chalsa and Garry Rolison. "Alienation of Ethnic Minority Students at a Predominantly White University." *Journal of Higher Education* 57 (1986): 58-77.

Newsweek. "Asian Americans: A 'Model Minority.'" 6 December 1982.

Newsweek. " A Formula For Success." 23 April 1984.

New York Times Magazine. "Why Asians Succeed Here." 30 November 1986.

Time. "To American with Skills." 8 July 1985.

Tinto, V. "Dropout from Higher Education: A Theoretical Synthesis of Recent Research." *Review of Education Research* 45 (1975):89-125.

Communities at Risk:
Asian Pacific Islanders and AIDS

Norma Timbang Kuehl

Between 1981 and 1987, gay and bisexual men were the first to be devastated by the AIDS epidemic, and AIDS acquired by having sex with homosexual or bisexual men was the leading form of transmission of this deadly disease. But now, due to advances in HIV/AIDS education and awareness programs in the gay community, this trend generally seems to be reaching a plateau (Holmes 1993). Closer examination of the statistics, however, reveals that people of color remain increasingly susceptible to the AIDS virus. The numbers of reported AIDS cases continues to rise in the African American and Latino communities, particularly among gay males and males who use intravenous drugs. And for the Asian Pacific Islander (API) community, long considered to be a low-risk group, AIDS surveillance reports from regions with large API populations reveal startling growth in the number of reported AIDS cases. According to the National Commission on AIDS, current national data on APIs show that the spread of the AIDS disease bears a strong resemblance to early trends in the Latino and African American communities. In fact, HIV/AIDS is expected to strike APIs at similarly alarming rates (Chang 1993b).

AIDS activists in API communities across the country are drawing attention to the specific needs of APIs in relation to the AIDS virus. In doing so, they have had to contend with the health care providers' lack of general knowledge regarding the API population (Chang 1993a).

Why have APIs become marginalized in discussions about AIDS? One problem in assessing the spread of AIDS among APIs is that they are a generally underserved population in terms of social services and health care. Lack of access is often a result of socioeconomic status, discrimination, language barriers, and cultural issues (Chang 1993b). The "model minority" myth, which portrays APIs as wealthy, assimilated, academic overachievers, masks the reality that many face (Fran-Stromberg 1991). In examining the status of subpopulations, we find that most live in poverty and are underrepresented in colleges and universities around the country (Fran-Stromberg 1991). Changing demographics have also increased the numbers of APIs in need of public assistance for shelter, food, and health care. Post-1965 immigrants are sometimes isolated by language and cultural barriers, and include refugees from the wars in Southeast Asia and Chinese refugees seeking political asylum in the United States. These newer members of the API community are frequently traumatized by war and political repression (Lin-Fu 1988).

Another reason for the lack of attention to Asian Pacific Islander AIDS patients is the relatively small numbers of those cases, and the community's consequent status as a low-risk group for the transmission of AIDS. In June 1993, only 2,036 Asian Pacific Islander AIDS cases were reported out of a national total of 315,390 (Chang 1993b), thus comprising only 0.006 of the population of people with AIDS. Although the number of HIV-infected APIs alone merits attention, further analysis of these statistics discloses even more urgency. Reported AIDS cases among APIs in San Francisco have increased almost fifteen times between 1985 and 1992, more than doubling for each intake year, from 22 cases in 1985 to 326 cases in 1992 (Woo et al. 1988). Washington state statistics follow a similar pattern, with numbers increasing more than sixteen times during the same period, from three cases in 1985 to fifty cases in 1992 (Tyree 1993).

A further problem in addressing the needs of APIs and AIDS is that national HIV/AIDS surveillance methods currently do not provide enough data to define disease trends within API communities. Even in major cities like Chicago and Boston, surveillance reports list APIs under the category "other." Most health care providers know very little about the heterogeneity of the API community and may not be familiar with cultural aspects that would prevent them from providing appropriate care. Despite the tendency to classify APIs as a single homogenous group, in fact, 29 distinct ethnicities have been identified within that population with over 100 languages and dialects (Chang 1993b). Given these parameters, it is difficult for health care professionals to decipher an API's specific ethnicity, especially if the subpopulation is one of the lesser known groups.[1]

To begin assessing the incidence of AIDS among APIs, we must rely on selected data from areas which identify API groups during their intake procedures. In this study, I draw data from materials organized by San

Francisco and Washington state, which provide better records because of their large, diverse API populations. Although the data can only yield tentative results because they are incomplete, they help us to consider issues relevant to APIs.

Analysis of the data helps us to compare APIs with the general population. In San Francisco, for example, a 1988 report showed that among APIs, 7 percent obtained transmission by transfusion, as compared to 1 percent in the non-API population, and 4 percent of APIs received transmission by sexual contact with homosexual and bisexual intravenous drug users, versus 12 percent among non-APIs (Woo et al. 1988).

San Francisco's data, which has been separated by ethnic group reveals that risk factors vary among different groups. For example, San Francisco's surveillance report for March 1993 shows that in the API community HIV transmission by intravenous drug use is highest among the Southeast Asians at 8.7 percent (n=23), as compared to 0.0 percent in the Japanese community (n=47). In the category of homosexual or bisexual transmission the greatest percentage reported was 7.4 percent (n=27) in the Pacific Islander community, as compared to 6.4 percent (n=47) in the Japanese community, 4.8 percent (n=124) in the Filipino community, and 9.9 percent in the Chinese (n=89), Southeast Asian (n=23), and Korean (n=4) communities. The highest percentage of transmission by transfusion in the San Francisco API communities was found in the Chinese, 11.2 percent (n=89), as compared to 3.7 percent (n=27) in the Pacific Islander community, and the lowest rate of 0.0 percent (n=4) in the Korean community. The only API subpopulation to report transmission by contact with lesbian or bisexual intravenous drug users was the Pacific Islander group at 3.7 percent (n=27) (SFDPH 1993).

Unfortunately, the information at hand is still very limited. The reported numbers within the heterosexual transmission, female, and pediatric categories, and among smaller subpopulations such as Korean and "other," are not substantial enough for us to make any comparisons of percentages in the routes of transmission among other API ethnic groups. Nor is it likely that we can calculate incidence rates, which would give us a more reasonable picture of the impact of the disease. Until a larger sample can be evaluated or the number of reported cases increases, data regarding heterosexual, pediatric, and smaller subpopulations of APIs will be meaningless.

By analyzing the risk factors for different samples by ethnicity, we can also begin to identify culture-bound issues that may affect particular groups.

As illustration, a recent report in the *Philippine News* indicates that Filipinos have the highest number of reported cases of AIDS in San Francisco, a trend consistent since 1981. In addition, approximately one-half of the HIV infected Filipinos in San Francisco are foreign-born (Rose 1993). Data from Washington state similarly indicates that almost half (23 out of 50) of the reported cases of the API population through 1992 are foreign-born. Of those cases, 47.83 percent were Filipino (Tyree 1993). (Unfortunately, Washington does not record the ethnic identities of reported cases in the American-born APIs.) This information suggests that comparative studies of Filipino AIDS cases in both the United Sates and Philippines might yield crucial information about the transmission of the disease, as well as culture-bound attitudes towards AIDS. For example, because Filipinos both in the U.S. and the Philippines are not generally considered to be at high risk for intravenous drug use, this information may have some implication for the design of culturally appropriate outreach and treatment programs.

Analyzing this data further suggests a myriad of other questions. Why are reported cases so prevalent in the Filipino community as compared to the other API subpopulations? Why is transfusion the most likely mode of HIV transmission among the Chinese community? Are there more risk factors associated with generational status, such as being an immigrant versus being American-born? What are the language and other cultural barriers that occur when caring for Asian Pacific Islander PLWAs? How are providers and service agencies meeting the needs of Asian Pacific Islander PLWAs?

Although those questions will require further research outside the scope of this study, it is clear that one important step for rectifying the invisibility of APIs is more appropriate methods of surveillance. Since the HIV/AIDS Asian Pacific Islander reported cases are low as per current surveillance methods (especially because APIs are often listed as "other" or not delineated by ethnicity), it will be useful to revise current data collection efforts. Intake and reporting procedures at local health departments, clinics, advocacy agencies, and other organizations servicing PLWAs could provide more comprehensive data by delineating subpopulations of APIs with the highest incidence of HIV/AIDS. Because this kind of additional effort requires extensive funding, perhaps a more viable approach is to obtain larger samples by focusing expanded data collection efforts on areas with large API populations. As recently suggested by Yu and Liu (1992), useful data on the health of APIs might best be obtained by surveying the top ten states, where 79 percent of the APIs resided in 1990, or the top fifteen metropolitan areas which have had the most rapid increase in APIs in recent years. We would then be better able to draw more reliable conclusions about disease frequency, routes of transmission, and the impact of AIDS in each subpopulation. In addition, outreach and education services could be concentrated towards those APIs who have demonstrated increased risk for HIV/AIDS.

Public policy and health care reform represent another area of concern for AIDS activists working within the API community. As a measure of this lack of attention to APIs, no national surveys and only minimal health-related research have been accomplished in regards to HIV/AIDS knowledge, attitudes, beliefs, and behaviors of APIs as a separate population. Those active in advocating HIV/AIDS prevention efforts and equal access to programs for Asian Pacific Islander PLWAs are currently promoting extensive coalition-building and information exchange. In addition, outreach and education services could be concentrated towards those APIs who have demonstrated increased risk for HIV/AIDS. Enhancing the visibility of API communities will facilitate funding and other forms of political and economic support, ultimately enabling more access to health care (Manzon 1993; Fung 1993; Parrish 1993; Chang 1993a).

In conclusion, one of the primary barriers to health care for HIV/AIDS is the misperception that APIs are not at high risk for the disease. Yet, as mentioned before, current national epidemiological data in the API community shows a similar trend to early patterns of disease frequency among other people of color. It is of vital importance that funding agencies and health care providers begin to recognize that APIs are extremely diverse and in need of funding for culturally-appropriate HIV/AIDS related services. Only then can the needs of different API ethnic groups be accurately and effectively addressed. The general inattention of the scientific academy and health care professionals to the varied health care needs of the API communities demonstrates, once again, that APIs lack equal access to health care systems.

Note

1. Although no studies have been done that would help us fully discuss the reliability of reported AIDS surveillance information on APIs, anecdotal information from activists with PLWA (People Living With AIDS) advocacy groups indicate problems with the accuracy of information obtained at intake. For instance, case workers and interviewers have been known to report Filipinos as Hispanics because many Filipinos

have Spanish surnames. Filipinos will sometimes self-report as "Pacific Islander" and those of "mixed blood" or "mestizos," will sometimes self-report or be reported as "White." Because of language barriers and cultural differences, health professionals might also misclassify APIs or fail to obtain an translateable response. In other instances, even though ethnic membership might be obtained at intake, most forms limit categories of APIs thus making it difficult for interviewers to accurately categorize a client. For example, the term "Southeast Asian" could include refugees from Vietnam or Cambodia, or recent immigrants from Thailand and the Philippines, depending on the interviewer's perspective and how s/he has been trained to make assessments at intake. A client might also represent more than one ethnic background or national origin.

References

Chang, Rafael. Asian Pacific AIDS Coalition of San Francisco. Personal communication, May 1993a.

____, ed. *U.S. National Asian and Pacific Islander HIV/AIDS Agenda.* San Francisco, 1993b.

Frank-Stromberg, Marilyn. "Changing Demographics in the United States: Implications for Health Professionals." *Cancer* 67 (1991):1773-78.

Fung, Chris. Asian Pacific AIDS Coalition of Seattle. Personal communication, May 1993.

Holmes, King K. "The Changing Epidemiology of HIV Transmission." In *AIDS Problems and Prospects*, edited by Lawrence Corey. New York: Hospital Practice, 1993.

Lin-Fu, Jane S. "Population Characteristics and Health Care Needs of Asian Pacific Americans." *Public Health Reports* 103 (January-February 1988):19-21.

Manzon, John. Asian Pacific Islander HIV/AIDS Coalition of New York. Personal communication, May 1993.

Parrish, Rick. Asian Pacific AIDS Intervention of Los Angeles. Personal communication, May 1993.

Rose, N. "AIDS and the Filipino Community." *Philippine News,* 31 March 1993.

San Francisco Department of Public Health, AIDS Office. *AIDS Surveillance Report.* March 1993.

Tyree, P. Timothy. State of Washington Department of Health, Office of HIV/AIDS Epidemiology and Evaluation. Personal written communication, 6 May 1993.

Woo, Joan M., George W. Rutherford, Susan F. Payne, J. Lowell Barnhart, and George F. Lemp. "The Epidemiology of AIDS in Asian and Pacific Islander Populations in San Francisco." *AIDS* 2 (1988): 473-75.

Yu, Elena S. H. and William T. Liu. "U.S. National Health Data on Asian Americans and Pacific Islanders: A Research Agenda for the 1990s." *American Journal of Public Health* 82 (1992): 1645-52.

Ethnic Studies and the New Mullticulturalism: The Founding Principles of Puerto Rican Studies Revisited

Jesse M. Vázquez

Because of the tumultuous history of Ethnic Studies in the academy, we have very little choice, but to look upon the current efforts at "multiculturalizing" the curriculum with some skepticism and a degree of suspicion.[1] It is difficult for many to believe that a university system that has been so inhospitable to ethnic studies programs, as well as to women's studies, is now ready to transform its curricular base into one which is truly multicultural.

This chapter examines how one movement, which essentially grew out of the dramatic protests and confrontations of the late 1960s and early 70s, compares with another curricular reform movement, which is emerging in a radically different political and social context. This comparison will focus on the underlying pedagogical and academic principles of each. In order to begin to better understand the differences between these two curricular reform movements, I will review some of the founding principles and underlying assumptions of Puerto Rican studies and draw some comparisons between general ethnic studies scholarship and curriculum and the "new" multiculturalism which is sweeping our nation's universities.

However, before I do this, allow me to touch upon some underlying assumptions usually shared by ethnic studies practitioners. *First*, most ethnic studies proponents strongly maintain that there are critical linkages that exist between race, ethnicity, gender, and our socioeconomic and sociocultural systems. One of the underlying assumptions that is central to the thinking and critical analysis of many ethnic studies scholars is the belief that the struggle over cultural pluralism *does not simply begin and end* with an examination of race, ethnicity, and gender as isolated extensions of culture. *Second*, radical curricular reformists suggest that any institutional proposal calling for a multicultural initiative will necessitate a re-examination of the entire structure. This radical approach goes well beyond the simple "celebration" of differences and an appreciation of our cultural similarities; it essentially challenges the status quo and its traditional relationships; and in its more radical form, ethnic studies seeks to effect social and structural change well beyond the boundaries of the institution (Sleeter and Grant 1987). Therefore, proposed changes calling for a radical restructuring of the curriculum would necessitate much more than simple add-ons to the reading lists of a particular traditional course syllabus.

These are not the "ethnocentric" or "particularistic" narrow demands that Diane Ravitch and others would have us believe (Ravitch 1990). It would seem that traditionalist academicians would much rather see race, culture, ethnicity, and gender treated as *sui generis* phenomena, without any social and structural linkages that would extend beyond these specific domains of study.

What follows is a brief overview of some of the founding principles, methods, and objectives that we found to be common in the formation of Puerto Rican studies, and I might add, other ethnic and women's studies programs of the late 1960s and early 70s.[2] While this comparative analysis uses portions of a retrospective essay on the history of Puerto Rican studies in the university, it is clear that these issues are also commonly shared by other ethnic studies and women's studies programs.[3] Keep in mind that I simply want to see how the ideas currently being proposed for the development of a broad-based, university-wide multicultural curriculum stand up against these earlier ethnic studies principles.

Consider the following ideas as they might contrast with the current multicultural thrust in higher education. Nieves et al. said the following:

> Puerto Rican Studies, (therefore) was an organizational form through which we challenged the university and created a separate space in which to test and develop our own educational agenda. The commitment of Puerto Rican faculty and students to examine facts or principles in order to act on our condition as a people, formed the essence of our intellectual work in the university. Like Black Studies and Chicano Studies, and Women's Studies, Puerto Rican Studies began with a purpose and content which went beyond intellectualism. The era of social upheaval, community conflict, and demands for institutional change, gave these ethnic programs a stamp and character of social practice and theory building different from most other university programs. So here we were proposing a new academic structure and approach which was indeed very different from the ones which were a part of the traditional

university. Our efforts involved, in particular, a critique of the way in which social science theory and methods had served to legitimize our colonial history. Hence a basic set of principles was almost uniformly established in all colleges (1987:5).

We called for a "*separate space in which to test and develop our agenda.*" We also were committed to an examination of "*facts or principles in order to act on our condition as a people.*" And, these programs had a "*stamp and character of social practice and theory building different from most other university programs.*" And most interesting, this statement concludes with an idea that seems to pre-date the fashionable deconstructionist and postmodernist critics by about twenty years: these efforts called for a "*critique of the way in which social science theory and methods had served to legitimize our colonial history.*" This broad societal analysis slowly began to give shape to a particular set of pedagogical principles for Puerto Rican studies, and as indicated, other ethnic and women's studies programs.

The conditions in many of our communities have gotten much worse, particularly for that segment of our population which finds itself trapped in poverty and on the margins of the working poor. However, in many of our discussions about multiculturalism, we hear very little, if anything, about the devastating socioeconomic realities that continue to plague our communities, and how they might be addressed in the academy. In most instances, the multicultural initiatives which we see developing seem to be very far removed from these issues, and tend to position the question of culture in a place in the curriculum that is *not* openly or directly connected to questions of economic and social development. In contrast, ethnic studies aggressively incorporated these issues and concerns into its curriculum, and continues to see these as an integral part of the work of the ethnic studies scholar. It seems, therefore, that in some quarters, the multicultural debate in the academy has effectively re-directed or de-railed the discourse from a broader cultural, socioeconomic, gender, and racial debate to a purely "culturalist" preoccupation.[4]

Allow me to quickly review some of the *founding principles* of Puerto Rican studies, and comment on each of these points as they may relate to the current interest in multiculturalism.

(1) A very important principle, which I believe might have been compromised along the way, is the idea of academic *autonomy*—"the demand for separate departments or programs wherein Puerto Ricans would have decision-making power over content of curriculum, hiring of faculty, and direction of policy" (Nieves et al. 1987:6).

It is this very issue of autonomy and control in the university that makes me wonder how, and if we can operationalize the notion of a multicultural curriculum, and at the same time guarantee authentic curricular diversity. The on-going presence of distinct autonomous ethnic studies programs and departments will at least secure a place in the curriculum where specific ethnic communities will continue to receive careful and focused attention. Departments of ethnic studies—either specific ethnic studies or combined departments consisting of distinct ethnic-specific sequences— offer the greatest guarantee of autonomy and academic stability. Programs or other non-departmental academic entities, however, drawing as they do from a variety of departments, lack departmental privileges and perogatives and often are structurally situated on the academic margins of the institution. Multiculturalism, as devised in some places, tends to be so all-inclusive that an analysis of specific subordinated and continually oppressed groups in the society are lost under a very broad conceptual and curricular umbrella. So broad in fact that it does not allow for an integrated curricular vision.

(2) The second is the overriding issue of *methodology*. Initially in Puerto Rican and other ethnic studies programs there was "a rejection of traditional approaches to learning, a defining of new sources of knowledge stemming from within our own Puerto Rican experience, and an experimentation with collective methods of doing intellectual work." bell hooks recently described this as the "authority of experience" (1990:29).

What Puerto Rican studies and other ethnic studies scholars were saying, and continue to say, is that we must be allowed to experiment with new methodologies in order to better understand the experience and effectively share that experience with others (Hernandez 1980). But to the traditionalists, these experimental or non-conventional methodologies (collective work in the community, oral histories, ethnographic and qualitative studies) may not be sufficient for promotion and tenure.

The methodologies that prevailed in the 1950s and 60s were those that looked for and focused on failures, deficits, and pathologies of racial/ ethnic minorities, and generally resulted in very negative and frequently inaccurate and distorted portrayals of those racial and ethnic communities under study. The one example that stands out for Puerto Ricans is Oscar Lewis's ethnographic work, *La Vida* (1965).[5]

(3) The issue of *theoretical framework*. Puerto Rican studies encouraged "a discarding of apologist and colonizing ideologies, and the design of theoretical constructs within which to produce fresh analyses about the Puerto Rican condition" (Nieves et al. 1987:6). While we cannot dismiss

out of hand and label all of the research that preceded the beginnings of ethnic studies as apologist or colonialist, or racist for that matter, we know that studies by a new generation of scholars from the 1960s to the 90s have started to look at a broader range of interconnected issues from very different perspectives.[6]

Puerto Rican studies scholars and creative artists tend to be very different in their approach, and their theoretical concerns and ways of looking at society will not necessarily be the same concerns of earlier generations of social scientists and humanities researchers. Their approach, by and large, is interdisciplinary, drawing from a variety of theoretical frameworks and sources. These are responsible scholars and artists, doing serious work, who are keenly interested in understanding the reality of the experience of Puerto Ricans, Latinos, and other racial/ethnic communities in the United States.[7] Of course, a critical part of the Puerto Rican analysis lies in our ability to understand the relationship and impact of United States policies and practices on Puerto Rico and on the Puerto Ricans in the U.S.

So, when we consider whether or not it is likely that a general university curriculum can be enriched by infusing it with a multicultural strand, it is somewhat difficult for many of my ethnic studies colleagues to imagine how traditional scholars, focused and schooled in other kinds of research questions, can be expected to replicate the unique skills, interests, and knowledge of ethnic studies practitioners and to be able to do it in a generic multicultural way.

(4) The idea of nurturing and maintaining a *community base*. There was "an insistence on applying new knowledge and the intellectual capacities and other university resources to struggles and issues in the community, not as intellectual elites but as university-based intellectual workers" (Nieves et al. 1987:6).

Puerto Rican and other ethnic studies programs encouraged direct links to a community engaged in struggle. If you look at the traditional academic departments in a university, you will find that the links to communities—if there are any—are designed primarily to facilitate data collection and very little else beyond that. Charles Valentine in *Culture and Poverty* (1968) is highly critical of the artificial *disconnections* that exist between the observer and the observed. These disconnections have been promoted and practiced as *essential* for the maintenance of so-called scientific objectivity by most social scientists.

What is interesting about the need for a community connection is that in some form, most Puerto Rican studies scholars asked their initial research questions about community and how the gathering of more re-fined data and information could be applied to the *needs* of that particular community. Their research, in essence, was guided by the belief that this new knowledge might at some point create or promote social and political change for the betterment and transformation of that community. Not all, but a good deal of research was guided by this belief. Now, more than ever, university workers need to revitalize those linkages to communities that continue to find themselves in great social and economic chaos and distress.

This link to the community in many ways shaped the curriculum, and gave it a grounding that one does not usually find in traditional aca-demic departments. My criticism is that this link may have been weakened in recent years, and that we have to do more in ethnic studies to restore that part of the curriculum.

The connection to the community gave ethnic studies programs a very different perspective on what issues we believed should occupy a high priority on our research and teaching agenda. Again, I have not seen the idea of developing such a *community base* as something that is part of the overall university effort to multiculturalize the curriculum.

(5) The issue of *pedagogy* as it relates to the development of ethnic studies programs. Working with predominantly Puerto Rican, other Latinos, African American, Asian American, and Native American students forces one to come to terms with a number of teaching-learning issues, such as:

(a) The quality and nature of the *material* selected for one's courses. Sometimes the limitations force us to be very creative in our selection of materials. The matter of limited printings of some publications, and the reluctance of some publishers to re-issue documents or older texts make our work that much more challenging.

(b) How one is compelled to experiment with different *methods* and *strategies* in teaching.

(c) How the work requires that we answer very critical questions about the nature of *our own ethnic and racial identity and commitments*. As an instructor, it is almost impossible to talk about race, ethnicity, and gender in American society, without having your own experiences and viewpoints—both intellectual and personal—challenged.

(d) What the basic differences are between teaching classes made up of students from predominantly one ethnic group versus teaching classes that are ethnically and racially heterogeneous. What are the dynamics of each, and what are the implications and pedagogical challenges of each of these student-teacher interactions?

In other words, it would seem that we have learned a great deal about what it is that we think we *ought* to be doing in ethnic studies from the very students we teach. Addressing those dynamics is something that keeps us current and involved. How does one teach about race and ethnic relations to students— ethnic minority or not—who never dared question the assumptions that were passed down to them by their parents, teachers, and the media?[8]

Similarly, what are the dynamics that are set in motion when ethnic racial minorities are the ones who are teaching students about issues which affect them directly? Perhaps those who have been involved in this process might be able to explore these issues in a more systematic way, and share these experiences with those colleagues who are now interested in incorporating these teaching/learning concerns into the mainstream curriculum. Ethnic studies practitioners have much to share in the arena of pedagogy.

This very abbreviated comparative overview between ethnic studies and the new multiculturalism would suggest that the push for greater multicultural content in our curriculum may be moving us farther away from some of the original principles, goals, and purposes of the ethnic studies mandate. As universities struggle with the multicultural debate, we see a persistence of old familiar ideological conflicts played out in the new curriculum wars. The politics of the new pedagogical debate raging over the new multiculturalism once again reveals the old distrust for ethnic studies and its proponents (Vázquez 1991).

What we must be aware of, however, is that there are new players who have recently joined in the discourse. It is no longer a dialogue between the proponents of ethnic studies on one side, and the traditionalists on the other. We now see the emergence of a sector of the university which, heretofore, was not aligned with ethnic studies, but which is now beginning to use its language as well as the language of the oppressed, and the strategies of the socially and culturally marginalized.

An example of this can be seen in two recent *Chronicle of Higher Education* articles on men's studies where the issues of race or ethnicity are never mentioned in their discussions about masculinity and patriarchy—a rather strange lacuna (Heller 1993). They talk about masculinity and culture without considering how these intersect with race, ethnicity, and social class. In addition, if you consider the work of many scholars of popular culture, or the much acclaimed work of white scholars writing about "Otherness" in American society, or the theoretical "cutting edge" studies of the deconstructionists and postmodernists, with some exceptions, we can safely conclude that very few are listening to the concerns voiced by ethnic studies scholars about race, racism, and ethnicity in American society. bell hooks wonders where all of these abstract and competing theoretical discussions about Otherness are taking us. She writes:

> Yes! everyone seems to be clamoring for "difference," only too few seem to want any difference that is about changing policy or that supports active engagement and struggle (another no-no word; recently a member of the new radical chic announced to me her sense that "struggle" is a tired term, and she's just not into it). Too often, it seems, the point is to promote the *appearance* of difference within intellectual discourse, a "celebration" that fails to ask who is sponsoring the party and who is extending the invitations. For who is controlling the new discourse? Who is getting hired to teach it, and where? Who is getting paid to write about it (1990:54).

In places where faculty members continue to nurture competing and conflicting basic assumptions about the role of race, culture, and gender in research, learning, and teaching processes, the likelihood of finding a common ground for curricular reform will be greatly diminished. Too many academic traditionalists still believe that ethnic studies scholarship is slightly off the mark, if not off the mark entirely. They attack the extremists in the field by engaging in laments over the lost values of America, and suggest that ethnic studies constitute a potential threat to the fundamental democratic values of this society (Schlesinger 1990; Ravitch 1990a, 1990b). Perhaps to them, Latino, African American, Native American, and Asian American scholars continue to represent the "unruly" subjective chaotic fringe of the academic establishment. hooks thinks that it is "time to look closely at how and why work by white scholars about nonwhite people receives more attention and acclaim than similar work produced by nonwhite scholars (while at the same time, the latter's work is devalued—for being too angry—even as it's appropriated)" (1990:55).

Seen in this light, the rush to create a multicultural base in the university, especially by those who mightily opposed the presence of ethnic studies, takes on a rather curious shade of insincerity (Jones 1990). Arguments against ethnic studies scholarship steer away from what has been accomplished in the field (Gates 1990). It would seem that the detractors of ethnic studies either are not aware of, or simply choose to ignore the breadth and range of scholarship in this field:

> Critics like Diane Ravitch, Arthur Schlesinger, Dinesh D'Souza and others never mention the abundance of social science and humanities studies that are, perhaps for the very first time, with different theoretical frameworks, exploring how class, ethnicity, race and gender interact with other societal and cultural variables to produce distinct educational, health, political, psychological and linguistic patterns. The critics rarely mention the fact that

ethnic studies scholars are engaged in wide ranging research such as, sociolinguistic analysis, migration and immigration studies, second language acquisition research, the exploration of ethnic voting patterns, the epidemiological studies that might bring to light health problems limited to certain ethnic communities, labor market studies that look carefully at employment and underemployment pattens among distinct ethnic communities, the psychological research that examines the stress related to relocation and immigration, the studies that examine the oral and written traditions of particular ethnic communities, and so on (Vázquez 1992).

These kinds of scholarly pursuits, with few exceptions, do not make the pages of the *New York Times* or the *Wall Street Journal*, because they sound too much like scholarship and activism in pursuit of uncovering new connections.

Given the history of the struggle to establish ethnic studies in higher education, one's belief that a truly multicultural curriculum can actually take hold in the university must remain less than sanguine. If we add to this, the suspicion by many that the current rush to "multiculturalize" the curriculum is just the latest assault on ethnic studies and nothing more then a new window-dressing, then, our watchfulness and moderated response may be well justified—the jury is still out.

Despite the expressed commitment of many institutions to diversify their curriculum, survivors of the original canon wars of the 1960s and 70s remain suspicious of the avowed enthusiasm for multiculturalism. Will institutions that claim that cultural diversity must transcend the so-called parochial boundaries of ethnic studies, gradually shift their commitment back to the traditional departments? (DePalma 1991a, 1991b). Many others fear that traditionalists will soon re-define multiculturalism in ways that may culminate in the destruction of some ethnic studies programs (Magner 1991). Students, faculty, and community members are pressing the university administration to grant departmental status to the long neglected Chicano studies at UCLA (*Chronicle of Higher Education*, 19 May 1993). Apparently, the administration's preference is to continue to pepper the departments with courses in Chicano studies—their version of multicultural education—instead of supporting a fully autonomous department. The weakness of programs not given the privileges and control that comes with departmental status is evident in the institutional marginality of many ethnic studies programs throughout the United States.

Given the curricular direction now being taken by many universities, is there a role that ethnic studies practitioners can play as institutions struggle with this new mandate? Is it possible to imagine that the ethnic studies principles discussed herein, could, in some ways, help shape and direct the new multicultural curriculum? Should we even bother to participate in a process that could, in places, effectively threaten the very autonomy and survival of our programs? To a great extent, the answers to these questions depend on the unique political landscapes of each campus.

Of course, one of the central themes that should be part of curriculum reform is the idea that in order for education to be truly democratic it must first be anti-racist, anti-sexist, and anti-homophobic. Unfortunately, racist, sexist, and homophobic beliefs and practices too often continue to hide behind the facade of cultural pluralism. If in our zeal to give equal time to *all* forms of cultural expression, we simply gloss over these fundamental and persistent inequities, then, as educators, we would fail to address one of the most critical problems in our universities and indeed in our society.

Finally, I would say that critical shifts have indeed taken place in the American university. There is a noticeable presence, where there was none, and there is clear hope for continuing the struggle for positive and more inclusive change in the university curriculum (Painter 1990).[9]

As we move into the 1990s, many campuses will mark the beginning of the third decade of the existence of *intentional ethnic studies programs* in the American university. Despite our continuing struggle, and despite the litany of naysayers and apocalyptic visionaries who forecast a threat to the very core of the republic, like Arthur Schlesinger, Jr. (1992), we can now begin to see change in the face of the university curriculum.

Though I conclude on an optimistic note, I would urge all of us to remain vigilant.

Notes

1. The earliest version of this chapter was first presented as part of a panel discussion on "The Multicultural Debate and the Puerto Rican Community," which was sponsored by the Puerto Rican Research Exchange and the Institute for Puerto Rican Policy, Inc., New York. A later version was presented at the annual conference of the National Association for Ethnic Studies, University of Utah, Salt Lake City, March 1993. The manuscript, as presented at the 1993 conference of the Association for Asian American Studies (AAAS) was published in *IMPART: Journal of Open Mind* 1 (Fall 1993). This chapter is a slightly revised version of that AAAS presentation, and has been re-titled. On behalf of my fellow panelists and the Puerto Rican Studies Association, I would like to thank Gary Okihiro, and his AAAS colleagues, for inviting us to join the program at Cornell University.
2. A portion of this analysis is taken from Nieves et al. (1987).

3. This common base of principles can also be gleaned from all of the articles found in a special issue of *Explorations in Ethnic Studies* 11 (January 1988). What is most significant about this issue is that the contributors—representing a number of different ethnic and women's studies programs and departments—address some of the same underlying principles set forth in this paper. C. E. Irby, L. H. Jones, R. L. Perry and S. M. Pauly, J. M. Vázquez, and Otis Scott each take a close look at the historical beginnings, contemporary challenges, and future prospects for ethnic studies in the twenty-first century. In all of these essays, the reader can see the common pedagogical threads and theoretical underpinning that gave shape and substance to ethnic studies and women's studies programs.

4. See the following essays and critiques on Puerto Rican and ethnic studies by Vázquez (1992, 1988a, 1988b, 1989).

5. Lewis's work created quite a stir. Contributing to the "culture of poverty" thinking, *La Vida* was picked up by non-academicians and read for its prurient content and its sensationalist portrayal of those Puerto Ricans caught below the poverty line. Today's jargon and analysis would have placed them in the *underclass*. Most readers skipped over the hundred odd pages of scholarly introduction describing his ethnographic methodology, and his theoretical and cross-cultural speculations about the "culture of poverty." Parenthetically, this book, which was essentially an anthropological monograph, was high on the best seller list like Bloom's (1987). That fact makes for an interesting literary phenomenon.

6. For a critique of the social science method and its application to Puerto Rican studies, I recommend Hernandez (1980) and Bonilla (1987). See also Rodriguez (1990).

7. Rodriguez (1990) looks at the future of Puerto Rican studies around the emergence of several areas of scholarly inquiry which seem to be consistently addressed in the literature: (1) the history of Puerto Rico; (2) the migration of Puerto Ricans to the mainland; (3) the Puerto Rican racial experience in the U.S.; and (4) the assimilation or minoritization of Puerto Ricans in the U.S. To get an additional but different perspective on the breadth and diversity of this newly emerging scholarship, see Vázquez (1992).

8. Tatum (1992) explores the many complexities of teaching about race in the college classroom.

9. Painter (1990) acknowledges this critical shift and presence when she reminds us of the historical process we have all been engaged in for more than twenty years. She says: "I am a black woman with a memory of what things were like before the advent of affirmative action, feminist theories, African-American studies, and diversified faculties and student bodies. I recall the time when virtually no people of color or white women taught at the great research universities, many of whose undergraduate student bodies were exclusively male . . . . I wish that those who take potshots at what they see as a new 'political correctness' would give a thought to what American universities used to be like. Then, perhaps, they would hesitate before assailing the attempt to forge a pedagogy appropriate for newly diversified student bodies and faculties."

References

Bloom, Alan. *The Closing of the American Mind.* New York:Simon &Schuster, 1987.

Bonilla, Frank. "Puerto Rican Studies and the Interdisciplinary Approach." In *Towards a Renaissance of Puerto Rican Studies: Ethnic and Area Studies in the University,* edited by M. Sanchez and A. Stevens-Arroyo. Highland Lakes: Social Science Monographs, 1987.

DePalma, Anthony. "Hard-Won Acceptance Spawns New Conflicts around Ethnic Studies." *New York Times,* 2 January 1991a.

_____. "Upgraded Status Urged for Chicano Studies." *New York Times,* 10 February 1991b.

Gates, Henry Louis Jr. "Academe Must Give Black-Studies Programs Their Due." *Chronicle of Higher Education,* 20 September 1990.

Heller, Scott. "Disconcerted by the 'Iron John' Movement, Many Scholars Call It Simplistic." *Chronicle of Higher Education,* 3 February 1993a.

_____. "Scholars Debunk the Marlboro Man: Examining Stereotypes of Masculinity." *Chronicle of Higher Education,* 3 February 1993b.

Hernandez, Jose. "Social Science and the Puerto Rican Community." In *The Puerto Rican Struggle: Essays on Survival in the U.S.,* edited by C. E. Rodriguez, V. Sanchez, and J. O. Alers. New York: Puerto Rican Research Migration Consortium, 1980.

hooks, bell. *Yearning: Race, Gender, and Cultural Politics.* Boston: South End Press, 1990.

Jones, Bruce Anthony. "Multicultural Education, Racism and Reason for Caution." *Black Issues in Higher Education,* 22 November 1990.

Lewis, Oscar. *La Vida: A Puerto Rican Family in the Culture of Poverty - San Juan and New York.* New York: Vantage Books, 1965.

Magner, Denise K. "Push for Diversity in Traditional Departments Raises Questions about the Future of Ethnic Studies." *Chronicle of Higher Education,* 1 May 1991.

Nieves, Josephine, Maria Canino, Camille Rodriguez, Sherry Gorelick, Hildamar Ortiz, and J. M. Vázquez. "Puerto Rican Studies: Roots and Challenges." In *Towards a Renaissance of Puerto Rican Studies: Ethnic and Area Studies in the University,* edited by M. Sanchez and A. Stevens-Arroyo. Highlands Lakes: Social Science Monographs, 1987.

Painter, Nell Irvin. "Who's to Say What's Acceptable." *New York Times,* 9 December 1990.

Ravitch, Diane. "Diversity and Democracy: Multicultural Education in America." *American Educator* 14 (Spring 1990a).

_____. "Multiculturalism Yes, Pariticularism No." *Chronicle of Higher Education,* 24 October 1990b.

Rodriguez, Clara E. "Puerto Rican Studies." *American Quarterly* 42 (1990):437-55.

Schlesinger, Arthur Jr. *The Disuniting of America: Reflections on a Multicultural Society.* New York: W. W. Norton, 1992.

_____. "When Ethnic Studies Are Un-American." *Wall Street Journal,* 23 April 1990.

Sleeter, C. E. and C.A. Grant. "An Analysis of Multicultural Education in the United States." *Harvard Educational Review* 57 (1987):421-44.

Tatum, Beverly. "Talking about Race, Learning about Racism: The Application of Racial Identity Development Theory in the Classroom." *Harvard Educational Review* 62 (1992): 1-24.

Valentine, Charles A. *Culture and Poverty: Critique and Counter Proposals.* Chicago: University of Chicago Press, 1968.

Vázquez, Jesse M. "The Co-opting of Ethnic Studies in the American University: A Critical View." *Explorations in Ethnic Studies* 11 (January 1988a): 23-36.

_____. "Embattled Scholars in the Academy: A Shared Odyssey." *Callaloo* 15 (1992):1039-51.

_____. "Ethnic Studies Programs Are in Danger of Being Lost in the Current Rush to 'Universalize' the College Curriculum: Point of View" *Chronicle of Higher Education.,* 16 November 1988b.

_____. "The Public Debate of Multiculturalism: Language and Ideology." *California Sociologist* 14 (Winter/Summer 1991): 11-32.

_____. "Puerto Rican Studies in the 1990s: Taking the Next Turn in the Road." *Centro Bulletin: Bulletin of the Center for Puerto Rican Studies* 11 (1989): 8-19.

Notes on Contributors

Marilyn Alquizola is a lecturer at University of Colorado, Boulder, and a doctoral candidate in Ethnic Studies at the University of California, Berkeley.

Edna Bonacich is a professor of sociology and Ethnic Studies at the University of California, Riverside.

Kandice Chuh is a doctoral student in English at the University of Washington, Seattle.

Geraldine Miyazaki Cuddihy is a member of the board of directors of Hilo Coast Processing Co., treasurer for United Care Planters Cooperative, and an English teacher.

Hien Duc Do is an assistant professor in the Social Science Department at San Jose State University.

Marilyn Elkins is an associate professor of English at California State University, Los Angeles.

Ruth H. Chung Gim is an assistant professor of psychology at the University of Southern California.

Alice Y. Hom is a doctoral student in history/American Studies at Claremont Graduate School.

Moon-Ho Jung is a doctoral student in history at Cornell University.

Elaine H. Kim is a professor of Ethnic Studies at the University of California, Berkeley.

Hyun Sook Kim is an assistant professor in the Sociology/Anthropology Department at Wheaton College.

Karen K. Kosasa is a doctoral student in Visual and Cultural Studies at the University of Rochester.

Norma Timbang Kuehl is a graduate student in public health at the University of Washington.

Peter Kwong is professor of Urban Affairs and Planning and director of the Asian American Studies Program at Hunter College, City University of New York.

Wai Suen Lee is an undergraduate student in philosophy and sociology at Stanford University.

Patricia Nelson Limerick is a professor of history at the University of Colorado, Boulder.

Mary Ting Yi Lui is a doctoral student in history at Cornell University.

Colleen Lye is a doctoral student in English at Columbia University.

Martin F. Manalansan IV is a doctoral student in anthropology at the University of Rochester.

Dolores de Manuel is an assistant professor in the English and World Literature Department at Manhattan College.

Manning Marable is a professor of Afro-American Studies at Columbia University.

Scott McFarlane is a doctoral student in English at Simon Fraser University, British Columbia.

Roy Miki is a professor of English at Simon Fraser University, Burnaby, British Columbia and is the editor of *West Coast Line*.

Jeff Nunokawa is an assistant professor of English at Princeton University.

Mona Oikawa is a doctoral student in Sociology in Education at the Ontario Institute for Studies in Education, Toronto.

Jonathan Y. Okamura is a researcher in the Office of Student Equity, Excellence and Diversity at the University of Hawai'i, Manoa.

Gary Y. Okihiro is a professor of history and director of the Asian American Studies Program at Cornell University.

Keith Hiroshi Osajima is an assistant professor of education and director of Race and Ethnic Studies at the University of Redlands.

Eric Estuar Reyes is a graduate student in American Civilization at Brown University.

Dorothy Fujita Rony is an assistant professor of Asian American Studies at the University of California, Irvine.

Vicki L. Ruiz is a professor of history at Arizona State University.

Patricia A. Sakurai is a doctoral student in English at the State University of New York, Stony Brook.

Dana Y. Takagi is an associate professor of sociology at the University of California, Santa Cruz.

Ronald Takaki is a professor of Ethnic Studies at the University of California, Berkeley.

John Kuo Wei Tchen is an associate professor of urban studies and director of the Asian/American Center at Queens College, City University of New York.

Jennifer Ting is a doctoral student in American Civilization at Brown University.

Jesse M. Vázquez is a professor of education and community programs and director of the Puerto Rican Studies Program at Queens College, City University of New York.

William Sakamoto White is a doctoral student in sociology at Georgia State University, and senior planner in socio-economic analysis for the Atlanta Regional Commission.

K. Scott Wong is an assistant professor of history at Williams College.

Sau-ling Cynthia Wong is an associate professor of Ethnic Studies at the University of California, Berkeley.